# SOCIOLOGICAL STUDIES OF CHILDREN AND YOUTH

# SOCIOLOGICAL STUDIES OF CHILDREN AND YOUTH

Series Editor: David A. Kinney (from 1999)

Series Editors: David A. Kinney and Katherine Brown Rosier (from 2004)

Volume 1: 1986 Patricia A. Adler and Peter Adler, Editors; Nancy Mandell, Associate Editor

Volume 2: 1987 Patricia A. Adler and Peter Adler, Editors; Nancy Mandell, Associate Editor

Volume 3: 1990 Patricia A. Adler and Peter Adler, Editors; Nancy Mandell, Guest Editor; Spencer Cahill, Associate Editor

Volume 4: 1991 Patricia A. Adler and Peter Adler, Editors; Spencer Cahill, Guest Editor

Volume 5: 1993 Patricia A. Adler and Peter Adler, Series Editors

Volume 6: 1994 Nancy Mandell, Editor; Elaine Porter, Geoffrey Tesson, and John Lewko, Volume Editors

Volume 7: 1995 Nancy Mandell, Editor; Anne-Marie Ambert, Volume Editor

Volume 8: 2001 David A. Kinney, Series Editor

Volume 9: 2003 David A. Kinney, Series Editor; Katherine Brown Rosier, Guest Editor

Volume 10: 2005 David A. Kinney and Katherine Brown Rosier, Series Editors; Loretta E. Bass, Guest Editor

SOCIOLOGICAL STUDIES OF CHILDREN AND YOUTH
VOLUME 11

# SOCIOLOGICAL STUDIES OF CHILDREN AND YOUTH

EDITED BY

## DAVID A. KINNEY

and

## KATHERINE BROWN ROSIER
*Central Michigan University, Michigan, USA*

ELSEVIER
JAI

Amsterdam – Boston – Heidelberg – London – New York – Oxford
Paris – San Diego – San Francisco – Singapore – Sydney – Tokyo

| | | | |
|---|---|---|---|
| ELSEVIER B.V. | ELSEVIER Inc. | ELSEVIER Ltd | ELSEVIER Ltd |
| Radarweg 29 | 525 B Street, Suite 1900 | The Boulevard, Langford | 84 Theobalds Road |
| P.O. Box 211 | San Diego | Lane, Kidlington | London |
| 1000 AE Amsterdam, | CA 92101-4495 | Oxford OX5 1GB | WC1X 8RR |
| The Netherlands | USA | UK | UK |

© 2005 Elsevier Ltd. All rights reserved.

This work is protected under copyright by Elsevier Ltd, and the following terms and conditions apply to its use:

Photocopying
Single photocopies of single chapters may be made for personal use as allowed by national copyright laws. Permission of the Publisher and payment of a fee is required for all other photocopying, including multiple or systematic copying, copying for advertising or promotional purposes, resale, and all forms of document delivery. Special rates are available for educational institutions that wish to make photocopies for non-profit educational classroom use.

Permissions may be sought directly from Elsevier's Rights Department in Oxford, UK: phone (+44) 1865 843830, fax (+44) 1865 853333, e-mail: permissions@elsevier.com. Requests may also be completed on-line via the Elsevier homepage (http://www.elsevier.com/locate/permissions).

In the USA, users may clear permissions and make payments through the Copyright Clearance Center, Inc., 222 Rosewood Drive, Danvers, MA 01923, USA; phone: (+1) (978) 7508400, fax: (+1) (978) 7504744, and in the UK through the Copyright Licensing Agency Rapid Clearance Service (CLARCS), 90 Tottenham Court Road, London W1P 0LP, UK; phone: (+44) 20 7631 5555; fax: (+44) 20 7631 5500. Other countries may have a local reprographic rights agency for payments.

Derivative Works
Tables of contents may be reproduced for internal circulation, but permission of the Publisher is required for external resale or distribution of such material. Permission of the Publisher is required for all other derivative works, including compilations and translations.

Electronic Storage or Usage
Permission of the Publisher is required to store or use electronically any material contained in this work, including any chapter or part of a chapter.

Except as outlined above, no part of this work may be reproduced, stored in a retrieval system or transmitted in any form or by any means, electronic, mechanical, photocopying, recording or otherwise, without prior written permission of the Publisher.

Address permissions requests to: Elsevier's Rights Department, at the fax and e-mail addresses noted above.

Notice
No responsibility is assumed by the Publisher for any injury and/or damage to persons or property as a matter of products liability, negligence or otherwise, or from any use or operation of any methods, products, instructions or ideas contained in the material herein. Because of rapid advances in the medical sciences, in particular, independent verification of diagnoses and drug dosages should be made.

First edition 2005

British Library Cataloguing in Publication Data
A catalogue record is available from the British Library.

ISBN-10: 0-7623-1256-4
ISBN-13: 978-0-7623-1256-6
ISSN: 1537-4661 (Series)

∞ The paper used in this publication meets the requirements of ANSI/NISO Z39.48-1992 (Permanence of Paper). Printed in The Netherlands.

Working together to grow
libraries in developing countries

www.elsevier.com | www.bookaid.org | www.sabre.org

ELSEVIER   BOOK AID International   Sabre Foundation

*Dedicated to the Children and Youth of Iraq,
and to the Children of Fallen American Soldiers in the Iraq War*

# CONTENTS

EDITORIAL BOARD ix

INTRODUCTION TO VOLUME 11: HISTORICAL AND
CONTEMPORARY PRESSURES ON CHILDREN'S
FREEDOM
*Katherine Brown Rosier and David A. Kinney* 1

## PART I: EMPIRICAL STUDIES

ADOLESCENT RESIDENTIAL MOBILITY AND
PREMATURE LIFE-COURSE TRANSITIONS: THE
ROLE OF PEER NETWORKS
*Scott J. South, Amy Lutz and Eric P. Baumer* 23

BUILDING DEMOCRACY, PROMOTING
TOLERANCE: ADOLESCENT RESPONSIVENESS TO
SOCIAL MOVEMENT MESSAGES
*Greg Scott and Julie E. Artis* 53

THE MESSY NATURE OF DISCIPLINE AND ZERO
TOLERANCE POLICIES: NEGOTIATING SAFE
SCHOOL ENVIRONMENTS AMONG
INCONSISTENCIES, STRUCTURAL CONSTRAINTS
AND THE COMPLEX LIVES OF YOUTH
*Linda M. Waldron* 81

ATHLETICISM AND FEMININITY ON A HIGH
SCHOOL BASKETBALL TEAM: AN INTERPRETIVE
APPROACH
*Janet Enke* 115

## WHO ARE THE EXPERTS? MEDICALIZATION IN TEEN MAGAZINE ADVICE COLUMNS
*Janice McCabe*     *153*

## THE INTERSECTION OF PRIVATE AND PUBLIC EXPERIENCE AMONG FAMILIES ADOPTING ROMANIAN CHILDREN
*Roberta Goldberg*     *193*

## PART II: INNOVATIONS IN THEORY AND RESEARCH METHODS

## CHILDREN'S AGENCY AND CINEMA'S NEW FAIRY TALE
*Ingrid E. Castro*     *215*

## CHILDREN AS SOCIAL MOVEMENT PARTICIPANTS
*Diane M. Rodgers*     *239*

## 'YEAH, ME TOO!': ADOLESCENT TALK BUILDING IN GROUP INTERVIEWS
*Laura Fingerson*     *261*

## ABOUT THE AUTHORS     *289*

# EDITORIAL BOARD

Patricia A. Adler
*University of Colorado*

Peter Adler
*University of Denver*

Spencer Cahill
*University of South Florida*

William A. Corsaro
*Indiana University*

Donna Eder
*Indiana University*

Gary Alan Fine
*Northwestern University*

Sandra L. Hofferth
*University of Maryland*

Jens Qvortrup
*Norwegian University of Science and Technology*

Barbara Schneider
*University of Chicago*

Alford A. Young, Jr.
*University of Michigan*

# INTRODUCTION TO VOLUME 11: HISTORICAL AND CONTEMPORARY PRESSURES ON CHILDREN'S FREEDOM

Katherine Brown Rosier and David A. Kinney

Rosier's father, a child of the 1930s and 1940s, recently told a story about neighborhood play in his youth. His parents enjoyed attending a Saturday night movie in a nearby town, and he often accompanied them. By the time he was seven, however, he remembers his parents cruising the neighborhood until they found him at play, and then offering him an option: "Do you want to come with us to the movies, or do you want the dime?" If he chose the dime, which he often did, they left him to play with his friends for the evening, while they attended the movie five miles down the road.[1]

Thirty years later, our (Rosier's and Kinney's) own 1960s childhoods were more constrained, and we both routinely endured babysitters until we were 9 or 10. But we were nonetheless often free to spend long afternoons and evenings on bicycles, with few restrictions on where we could go. We spent countless hours exploring and inhabiting our surrounding environments: Rosier in the wild and natural places within a few miles radius of her Northern Michigan home; Kinney enjoying both college town and its rural edge. "Be home before dinner," or "be home by dark" was often the only directive heard when we would announce that "I'm going out to play!"

---

Sociological Studies of Children and Youth
Sociological Studies of Children and Youth, Volume 11, 1–20
Copyright © 2005 by Elsevier Ltd.
All rights of reproduction in any form reserved
ISSN: 1537-4661/doi:10.1016/S1537-4661(05)11001-0

The decline in children's freedom is increasingly noted in both scholarly and popular literature. For example, in his recent contribution to *Newsweek's* long-running "My Turn" column, reader Robb Moretti describes a baby-boomer childhood fraught with danger and fun! Free to roam San Francisco neighborhoods on bikes and go-carts (actually sleds on wheels), Moretti facetiously decries the lack of bike helmets, crossing guards, seat belts, and parental supervision of his childhood, and wonders "how my friends and I survived childhood at all?" "But," he more sincerely continues, "I believe we experienced the kind of freedom that children who came after us have not." And, Moretti concludes, "we were the last generation ... to have fun" (Moretti, 2002; also see Albom, 2002).

Today, growing evidence demonstrates that typical middle-class American children do indeed experience a childhood much different from Moretti's, our own, and our parents'. Spontaneous, child-directed play in neighborhoods has dramatically declined, while adult organized and supervised activities have increased (Adler & Adler, 1994, 1998; Corsaro, 2005; Dunn, Kinney, & Hofferth, 2003; Hofferth & Sandberg, 2001; Lareau, 2003). In their on-going research on the "time crunch" experienced by many middle-class children and their families, Kinney and his colleagues (Kinney, Hofferth, & Dunn, 2001) have documented the type of schedules kept by many young people in a small, relatively affluent city in the Midwest. The "typical Wednesday" described by "Annette" (a 10-year-old, 4th grader) was not unusual:

> 7:00 a.m.: Wake-up time, chores, eat breakfast, get dressed.
>
> 8:00 a.m.: Get on bus for school – 8:45 arrive at school.
>
> 8:50 a.m.: School starts. Social studies, science, recess, lunch, art, math, literature circles, band (plays clarinet).
>
> 3:36 p.m.: End of school day. Take bus home.
>
> 4:00 p.m.: Arrive home. Work on homework and eat dinner. Mother drives her to sister's basketball practice.
>
> 5:30 p.m.: "Assistant coached" younger sister's basketball practice.
>
> 6:45 p.m.: Annette has basketball practice and scrimmage, then stayed for older sister's basketball practice.
>
> 8:45 p.m.: Dad drives his daughters home.
>
> 9:00 p.m.: Arrive home, have snack.
>
> 9:30 p.m.: Bedtime.

Annette clearly had little or *no* time during the week for play with friends absent adult monitoring. The daily schedules kept by the young people Kinney, Dunn, and Hofferth studied were nearly as chocked-full on weekends as they were during the school week, but did permit a few hours for some interaction with neighborhood friends. Specifically, many children interviewed lamented the fact that they had little time to see and play with their friends outside of school, because they were so involved in structured after-school activities on weekdays and weekends. Along these lines one father angrily stated that: "I certainly do not think [my children] get enough playtime [with friends] at home." All parents interviewed noted that they personally know and observe many families who appear to over-schedule or overwhelm their children with too many activities. One mother (Hofferth, Kinney & Dunn, 2005) summed up this relatively common situation in the following way:

> I know some people ... the parents really push the kids to get involved in not just school activities, but two or three other extracurricular activities at a real young age. And the kids end up being very burned out, and then don't want to do anything. And [the parents say] 'I've invested all this time and energy and money into dance lessons over the last four years and you will continue on.' And then who is actually doing it? Is it the parents living through the child, or is it because the kids want to learn a skill?

The list of activities children and youth are involved in these days at younger and younger ages is extensive and includes soccer, ballet, karate, ice hockey, band, dance, theater, scouts, softball, baseball, basketball, football, wrestling, cheerleading, pom-poms, gymnastics, art, jump rope, religious education, etc.[2]

These findings reflect national trends uncovered by the *Child Development Supplement from the National Panel of Income Dynamics* (Hofferth, 1998). Between 1981 and 1997, young people aged 8–12 experienced a significant decline in their "free time" (i.e., time spent on activities other than personal care, eating, sleeping, and school), and a significant increase in the amount of time in structured activities outside of school. For example, this age group experienced a 27% increase in participation in organized sports (Hofferth & Sandberg, 2001). Lareau's recent work illustrates, however, that these changes are not experienced evenly across income groups; middle-class children are much more heavily involved in structured, adult-supervised activities than are the children of working-class and poor parents (Lareau, 2003). This should be kept in mind when observing changing patterns of activity for the population as a whole, which – because of the difference by social class – tend to *underestimate* time spent in structured activities for youth in more affluent families.

Change in how children spend their time has been quite dramatic over the last 20–25 years, but in truth this change continues a historical trend traceable back to 150 years or more. The historical picture looks something like this: with industrialization and the extensive changes in family structure and function that accompanied the economic revolution, dramatic changes in the nature of childhood also took place. As children's labor became less necessary and less acceptable, mothers' productive labor did as well. With both middle-class mothers and children "freed" from most manual labor at essentially the same historical moment, large numbers of both age groups had considerably more time on their hands. This was perhaps especially true for mothers, whose separation from productive economic activity was also accompanied by a rapid decline in fertility. A new focus on domesticity and emotional well-being increasingly dominated middle-class women's lives, and their children were increasingly monitored and controlled; "domesticated," if you will (for discussion of these historical trends, see, e.g., Corsaro, 2005; Hareven, 1982; Stacey, 1990).

At first consideration, it might seem that as late nineteenth- and early twentieth-century American children were freed of their economic obligations, they should have experienced a general *increase* in their overall freedom. Corsaro (2005) argues that previous to the dramatic rearrangement of work and family life, children had indeed been required to put in long hours of productive labor, and in this regard, they were hardly free. Once their labors were completed, however, their time was for the most part their own, and they were largely left to their own devices to pursue creative, entertaining, and autonomous activities, in collaboration with their peers. With the idea of "adolescence" just beginning to take shape (Hall, 1904), individuals in what we now consider "middle childhood" – approximately aged 7–10 – were viewed as much more competent and responsible than is currently the case. These perceptions changed, however, in the context of industrialization and the cult of domesticity that it inspired.

As sociologists well know, industrialization inspired remarkably rapid transformation of everyday life. But in addition and as was true for the family more generally, childhood continued its evolution throughout the twentieth century – its duration ever increasing, its freedoms ever on the decline. As discussed above, throughout the 1980s, 1990s, and now into the new century, children's loss of freedom to independently navigate their environments has again escalated. This escalation has been propelled in part by middle-class fear of sinister events; most notably, stranger kidnappings and school shootings. Wide news coverage of high profile cases heightened parents' anxiety and their perception of real risk to their own children.

Beginning most notably with the 1981 kidnap/murder of Adam Walsh (whose father, John Walsh, is co-founder of the National Center for Missing & Exploited Children and now host of FOX television's popular "America's Most Wanted: America Fights Back"), Americans followed the heartbreaking kidnap/murder of Polly Klaas (1993), and the kidnapping and successful recovery of Elizabeth Smart (2002–2003), among others. Several multiple homicides at largely white suburban high schools in the mid- and late 1990s also served to heighten parents' fears of unpredictable school shootings. Following several earlier, highly publicized school shootings, students Eric Harris and Dylan Klebold's execution of 10 classmates and a teacher at Columbine High School in 1999 was especially dramatic. Extensive media coverage throughout the long hours of the siege at Columbine and for months following contributed mightily to growing general anxiety about school safety. Little known and rarely noted are the facts that children and youth remain *much* safer at school than they are in either their communities or their family homes; that child abductions are rare and declining; and that deaths at school have declined markedly since the early 1990s (see Best, 2002; Donohue, Schiraldi, & Ziedenberg, 1998; National Public Radio, 2002).

Joel Best argues that the "monster hype" associated with these kidnap and school shooting cases has contributed to a gross exaggeration of threat to typical American children and adolescents (Best, 2002; also see Best, 1993). Similarly, Corsaro (2005) describes a "bogey-man syndrome" that afflicts middle-class American parents, whereby fear of sinister rare events dominates parents concerns, while attention to very real and common threats to children – such as poverty, inner-city violence, domestic violence, and sexual exploitation by known family members and other acquaintances – is lacking (also see Donohue, Schiraldi, & Ziedenberg, 1998). Reflecting this fear of children's random victimization, "don't talk to strangers" has become a required mantra of adequate contemporary American parenting, and numerous entrepreneurs have seized the opportunity to exploit this fear for profit (e.g., producing videos that teach children how to spot and resist pedophiles' attempts to inspire trust, teaching children self-defense tactics, selling identification kits to parents who are fearful of their children's sudden disappearance, and even the production of "leashes" for young children).

On-going changes in family structure, and in neighborhood ecology, have also likely contributed to increasing constraints on children's and adolescents' freedom. The decline in fertility rates, the increasing prevalence of single-parent families, and the increased labor-force participation of both married and single mothers (Corsaro, 2005) mean that if children and adolescents are home during daytime hours, they are much more likely to be home alone than was true in the past. Neighborhoods are less cohesive and often seem abandoned on weekdays; few adults are available to keep a watchful eye on the street and on other people's children. In this context, parents are logically more anxious about kids being home alone, and this anxiety is ignited by the sinister events that are so hyped by the media. The rare events, and the routine circumstances of many families, combine to increase both parental fear about their children's safety, and restrictions of children's activities.

Certainly, some parents (ourselves included!) may resist this pressure toward fear and anxiety, and attempt to teach children to be cautious, yet informed about the rarity of sinister events on the one hand, and adventurous and self-reliant on the other. This becomes an increasingly difficult stance to take in the face of public campaigns to warn and protect children from omnipresent dangers. Conjuring "milk-carton" images of missing children, photography companies, in cooperation with the National Center for Missing and Exploited Children, distributed "safe kids" cards to children they photographed for school pictures in Fall 2004. Rosier discovered that her son's image and school, along with personal identification numbers, had been entered in a national database, without her knowledge or consent. Glen brought home (two copies of) the card displayed below. Note that the "image is accessible through December 2005." We can only assume that we should expect annual up-dates, unless we decide to forego the traditional yearly photos.[3]

This *feels* like a real escalation of the fear campaign concerning children's safety in their routine environments, reminding parents of their obligation to be ever wary of sinister threats to their children. It also parallels the political rhetoric produced by the Bush administration since 9/11 about the threat of terrorism to individual (adult) Americans. Indeed, the *threat of terrorism to children's (emotional and physical) well-being* is now being officially touted as an important consideration for responsible American parents. Following close on the heels of Bush's re-election in November 2004, a new public information television campaign began to chide parents that "there's no reason *not* to have a plan in case of a terrorist attack" (see press release, Office of the Press Secretary (November 22, 2004)). Wide-eyed, vulnerable children inquire: "How long should I wait for you?" "What if the phones don't work?" "Should I go to Grandma's?" "Can you tell me?" If television viewers follow the commercials' invitation to visit the web-site http://www.ready.gov, the U.S. Department of Homeland Security there offers advice for creating a "family plan" in case of disaster, as well as information and advice for dealing with biological, nuclear, chemical, and radiation threats. A "Ready Kids" portion of the website was briefly operational in Spring 2005, but is apparently undergoing revision, and is "Coming [back] Soon" (June 2005).

Just as many American adults have grudgingly accepted revision of their basic freedoms in hopes of protecting the nation from further terrorist attack (especially through *The Patriot Act* and the powers granted to the Department of Homeland Security), many American parents seem to find growing restrictions on the freedom of adolescents a reasonable price to pay for increased security. While the possibility of stranger abduction preoccupies many parents of pre-school and elementary-school-aged children, the possibility that their teens will fall victim of school violence – and the fear of more general "negative peer pressure" to engage in criminal activity – are more likely to haunt parents of adolescents. And while parents must rely primarily on their own restrictions and vigilance to protect their young children, many parents of teens seem willing to give much of that role over to the schools and law enforcement.

Since Columbine in 1999, and the 9/11 attack, schools across the nation have spent millions of dollars on security technology (e.g., cameras, weapons detectors, armed guards, etc.) to create "safe" schools (see Waldron, this volume, for an analysis of students' and school personnel's negotiation of safe schools). Schools require students to participate in practice drills to address potential school shootings or terrorist threats. Moreover, students in the United States are being subjected to increasing numbers of random searches of their persons and lockers by police and narcotic detection dogs (Best, 2002). Most recently, some schools have begun to use a new product called "'Drug Wipe' that identifies as little as one billionth of a gram of drugs left on lockers, vending machines or anything else a student touches" (Bates, 2004, p. 89). Some schools administer random breathalyzer tests at their dances.

Outside of school, students' lives are coming under increasing surveillance as technology companies aggressively advertise sophisticated devices and products to parents designed to monitor their children's everyday behaviors. For instance, parents can now purchase small boxes to install on the family car that monitor their teenage drivers' speed and location. The Internet is awash in websites hawking home drug test kits to parents. Adults can now easily purchase test kits that analyze their children's hair, urine, and saliva for the presence of such drugs as marijuana, heroin, cocaine, amphetamines, methamphetamine, valium, Ecstasy, and nicotine. These sites have quickly become popular; for example, one site, Mrs. Test (http://www.mrstest.com/drugs) was visited over 11 million times in span of 15 months from June 2003 to October 2004. Computer programs that track students' Internet and library usage are readily available to parents and school officials. Cell phone companies increasingly market "family packages" so that all children are equipped with a phone and are theoretically in touch with their parents regarding their current activities and location. Overall, recent events in society that increase fear in the minds of parents and school administrators have sparked a remarkable growth in technology designed to keep an eye (and ear) on children and youth.

Kidnappings, school shootings, "peer pressure," and now – terrorist attacks! These cultivated concerns now routinely and often severely constrain the freedoms of American children and youth. At issue here is not only the experiences and opportunities of individual children, of course, but the very nature of American childhood itself. Just how thoroughly changed childhood and adolescence will emerge from this era of fear and anxiety remains to be seen, but it seems clear that the freedoms enjoyed by past generations of American children will not soon, if ever, be restored.

In our highly age/race/SES segregated society,[4] contact with others unlike themselves is rare for many children and youth, especially for those who are white and middle-class. This, in and of itself, should be of great concern. In our present social climate, we add to this lack of contact with others the deliberate cultivation of a basic lack of *trust* of those outside our children's routine social circles. Concluding this discussion, now, we posit that the growing fundamental distrust of others – and of "The (pedophile/teen predator/terrorist) Other" – may well be the most serious implication of the patterns of children's declining freedoms that we have observed, and discussed above. Consider here the war on terror that currently occupies the nation.

Undoubtably, the post-9/11 transformation of life in the U.S. conjures images of an Orwellian society; the "Bush/Cheney in 1984" bumper-stickers that emerged during the 2004 election season suggested that for at least some segment of the population, the parallels are clear. Drawing these parallels in a stinging and sobering indictment of the current administration and the military–industrial complex, Tiryakian writes:

> ...[T]he war on terrorism depends on keeping our own population terrorized by the threat of another 9/11, a threat that must be periodically reinforced by a fancy, color-coded threat advisory system, reinforced by highly elaborate security precautions at some entry points, severe visa restrictions, and extensive new means of surveillance. Americans must be made to feel, on the one hand, grateful for the security that the system provides against terrorists and, on the other, insecure from head-to-toe airport security checks. We are now urged to report to Homeland Security (which might as well be called the Ministry of Insecurity) any person who engages in suspicious behavior or arouses suspicion. Our "doublethink" makes it easy to mask the curtailment of civil liberties under the guise of the 'Patriot Act...' (2005, p. 24).

This state of affairs (thankfully) arouses considerable anger and alarm among those like Tiryakian who hold those civil liberties dear and who question the current administration's motives as well as their tactics. And (again, thankfully), a robust critique routinely graces the opinion pages of national and small-town newspapers alike. Curtailment of liberties, increased surveillance, and demonization of The Other are hard sells to many American adults, and their protests are comforting, and reaffirming of what have been basic American values (for example, freedoms of speech and assembly; freedom from unreasonable search and seizure, and other basic privacy rights). But the public discourse has not yet begun to consider what, if any, role the dramatic changes in American childhood may play in this critical social drama. And so we here urge social analysts and commentators to begin to question how the changing nature of contemporary American childhood, and the rhetoric of fear that supports it, may influence future resistance to the suspension of basic liberties. It seems plausible that such fundamental revisions of American life might become less remarkable, and less resisted, in the not-so-distant future, for those whose childhoods were marked by growing fear, distrust, surveillance, and general constraint. In large part, this underlying concern prompted the writing of this chapter.

At the same time, however, we wonder how American children and youth interpret the climate of fear that increasingly dictates their activities. While we see evidence all around that *parents* and other adults are fearful and anxious, we wonder: are children? How *do* children and youth make sense of the fearful rhetoric that permeates the culture, and negotiate shared understandings of "terror," adult surveillance, and their own elusive freedom? To what extent do they feel threatened by sinister possibilities, or comforted by the stepped-up efforts to keep them safe? Are children and – especially – adolescents developing and valuing strategies that undermine or demean new restrictions? Or are adult fears incorporated largely unchanged into the peer cultures and practices of American youth? (How) have the civic values and priorities of young Americans changed?

Those of us with expertise in the Sociology of Children and Youth are uniquely prepared and positioned to ask and answer these questions, and to raise collective consciousness of these critical issues. To the extent that this research is currently underway, we applaud these efforts. But we are not aware of published work that goes beyond a focus on 'helping parents handle children's fears about terrorism.' C. Wright Mills (2000[1959], p. 191) makes clear our *obligation*, as social scientists, in such matters: if we hope to cultivate (or protect) liberating, democratic publics, we must "deliberately present controversial theories and facts," "actively encourage controversy," and challenge the propaganda that stands as "official definition of reality." Never have his directives seemed so apropos. And so just as Tiryakian (2005) suggests we all re-read Orwell's *1984*, we advise a refresher in *The Sociological Imagination*.

## INTRODUCTION TO THE CHAPTERS IN VOLUME 11

This volume of *Sociological Studies of Children and Youth* showcases the timely and important work of active, early career sociologists, who are helping to define the direction of the sub-field. Their work shares basic premises and concerns, and these underlie and provide cohesion to this diverse collection of chapters. Children and youth are active agents in their own "socialization," producing meaning and action collaboratively with their peers, and they struggle for agency and control in various social contexts – these are the themes that, both explicitly and implicitly, shape essentially all of the contributions. The underlying concern of our own introduction above, and of many of the chapters, is that the current processes and practices may stifle children's creativity and undermine their potential to collaboratively construct innovative solutions to societal problems.

The volume is organized in two parts. Six chapters make up the "Empirical Studies" of Part I. We begin with two (primarily) quantitative analyses, the first examining residential mobility, peer networks, and life-course transitions, the second a look at adolescents' participation in a particular social movement. These are followed by two ethnographic studies – here the foci are "Zero Tolerance" school discipline policies, and female athletes' construction of femininity. A comparative content analysis of teen magazine advice columns, and a qualitative study of construction of "adoptive family" identities round out Part I.

In the first chapter of Part I, "Adolescent Residential Mobility and Premature Life-Course Transitions: The Role of Peer Networks," Scott South, Amy Lutz, and Eric Baumer use survey data to examine the relationship between residential mobility and problematic adolescent behaviors. The authors use data from three waves of the National Survey of Children to delineate the extent to which several mediating factors account for the impact of residential mobility on the risk of dropping out of school and the early initiation of sexual intercourse. Specifically, South and his associates use logistic regression models to explicate how the nature of general adjustment problems, and adolescents' relations with peers, parents, and schools can mediate the effect of residential mobility on school dropout and initiation of intercourse. The authors note that frequent moves during childhood can place significant stress on young people's relations with peers and parents and negatively impact youth's academic performance. Residential mobility also can negatively influence adolescents' levels of self-efficacy and increase depression. Subsequently, this stress is believed to be associated with problem behaviors.

Overall, the longitudinal data analysis conducted by South and his associates indicates that mobile youth are significantly more likely to report having friends who become involved in sexual behavior at relatively young ages and who are at risk of dropping out of school. These findings support related research that documents the critical role that peers play in structuring problem behaviors among adolescents. Other theoretically relevant variables (e.g., parent–child and child–school relationships) were found to play only a small role in transmitting the effects of residential mobility to school dropout and early sexual activity. The authors discuss how peer networks potentially become the critical mediators of the residential mobility and problematic behavior relationship among adolescents and call for future research that provides a more comprehensive and long-term examination of effects of childhood residential mobility on adolescent and adult behavior. While this chapter increases our understanding of how peers can negatively impact mobile youth's behaviors, the next chapter examines how youth can shape their peers' actions in a positive direction by reducing racism.

"Building Democracy, Promoting Tolerance: Adolescent Responsiveness to Social Movement Messages" is the first of two chapters in this volume that considers children's and adolescents' participation in social movements (see Rodgers' theoretical chapter in Part II). Here, Julie Artis and Greg Scott draw upon existing theories of social movements and creatively weave and test a novel explanation of youth's active involvement in a contemporary movement. The chapter reports on the authors' evaluation of a program designed to lessen hostility and increase tolerance among youth attending high schools in Chicago and the surrounding suburbs. The program includes an innovative intervention, centered on exposing the messages conveyed by popular "white power" music that attempts to mobilize white adolescents who are leaders in their school to work with their less knowledgeable and less tolerant peers in an effort to organize more youth against racism.

Artis and Scott collected survey data from 325 program participants and conducted 28 follow-up telephone interviews with youth, who participated in the intervention program. Analyses of the survey data indicate that female students and students who have at least one college-educated parent report higher levels of tolerance of racial difference and higher levels of adult support at school (i.e., support in terms of perceiving that adults care what happens to them, offer advice about problems, and help with projects). Hostility was found to be inversely related to adult support; especially for males. In addition, the survey data show that males exhibit a significantly stronger inverse relationship between hostility and tolerance than females, while white students report a stronger negative relationship between hostility and tolerance than non-white students. The telephone interview data indicate that the program is effective by inspiring many of the target students to "spread the word" about the hate messages in white power music with numerous peers, school adults, and parents. In sum, Artis and Scott show how connections with adults can actually foster activist activity among youth and not constrain it as some social movement theorists argue. The authors close with important policy recommendations and suggestions for future research in this area.

Artis and Scott have demonstrated how youth with proper resources and supports can make a positive difference in their worlds. In Chapter 4, Linda Waldron argues that while many youth have insights into the critical issue of safe schools, their knowledge and creativity is not often tapped by school personnel, therefore precluding a truly violence-free school environment. Specifically, she addresses the timely issue of how safety is maintained and negotiated between students and adult staff at two suburban high schools in her chapter entitled: "The Messy Nature of Discipline and Zero Tolerance Policies: Negotiating Safe School Environments among Inconsistencies, Structural Constraints and the Complex Lives of Youth." The author aptly discusses how the increasing emphasis on safety at contemporary schools has grown out of the particular historical context in the United States that emphasizes discipline, efficiency, and order in public educational institutions. Waldron was motivated by the recent tragic and highly publicized cases of school shootings and the attendant concerns over school violence, to examine adolescents' everyday experiences with increasing levels of surveillance and zero tolerance policies. Using qualitative, ethnographic methods, she examined security, students, and staff at two suburban schools; one primarily white and middle-class and one with mostly African-American students from diverse social class families.

Waldron draws on her extensive interviews with students and school staff to vividly illustrate the vast inconsistencies between school safety policy as written and how that policy is actually enacted on a day-to-day basis. She shows how students from disadvantaged social backgrounds receive harsher treatment than more privileged students for similar behaviors, and how students creatively find ways to defy authority and avoid detection for participation in "deviant" and "illegal" behaviors on school grounds. Waldron concludes with a number of interesting and important suggestions for school policy that culminate in her insightful call for an effective integration of adolescents' perspectives and propositions in the development of violence prevention strategies to promote a violence-free culture throughout schools. This concern dovetails nicely with our call for research on how children and youth experience declining freedom. Waldron's chapter includes evidence of some adolescents' active attempts to produce peer interactions that allow them to deal with adults' attempts to control their everyday behaviors in the school setting. Similarly, the next chapter shows how youth actively and creatively respond to cultural currents, proximate peers, and adult authority figures by developing a unique, and complex peer culture within the context of high school female athletic teams.

Janet Enke spent three academic school years observing and interviewing female athletes at a Midwestern high school and found that these youth developed a peer culture that allowed them to creatively deal with their concern with femininity within the context of sports. In her well-crafted chapter, "Athleticism and Femininity on a High School Basketball Team: An Interpretive Approach," she focuses on the everyday routines among the basketball players to document the development of peer culture over the course of a season. Enke immersed herself into the setting; attending practices, games, special team events, and even riding with the team to away games. During bus trips with the team and in the locker room, she observed and tape-recorded naturally occurring conversations among teammates. She also conducted semi-structured interviews with all the varsity basketball players. Her methodology section includes important information regarding reflexivity and how she developed high levels of rapport and trust with the basketball players and coaches.

Enke also expertly provides a theoretical and historical context within which to interpret her ethnographic data and attendant recurrent themes. The themes are illustrated with rich data that make readers feel as though they are right there with Enke in the field, watching and listening as these young women build friendships within the athletic arena that is permeated with competition within and between teams. The author documents daily social interactions and cultural routines (e.g., teasing, gossip) that show how these youth collectively produced their own unique peer culture with emotional dynamics that signal salient concerns. Enke concludes by discussing her findings in relation to previous writings on sport, femininity, and sexuality, and shows how a systematic ethnography can significantly increase our understanding of the nature and extent of the productive and reproductive aspects of adolescents' peer culture in specific contexts.

Chapter 6 continues the focus on adolescent girls. Here, in "Who are the Experts? Medicalization in Teen Magazine Advice Columns," Janice McCabe presents a comparative content analysis of the advice offered to girls in two "mainstream" teen magazines (*Seventeen* and *YM*) and two "alternative" magazines (*New Moon* and *Teen Voices*). She examines the questions and answers published in the magazines' monthly advice columns, focusing on the ways that, and the extent to which, girls' problems and issues are medicalized by the columnists.

This chapter offers a sophisticated interpretive framework, clear discussion of the author's innovative methods, and insightful analyses and conclusions. In her analysis, McCabe attends especially to the mainstream versus alternative advice columns' recognition of girls' own agency and competence. Perhaps predictably, advice provided by *Seventeen* and *YM* is considerably more likely to encourage girls to seek the expert council of medical and other adult professionals, while *New Moon* and *Teen Voices* columnists – who, importantly, are teenaged girls themselves – are more likely to stress the normality of girls' experiences and concerns, their ability to competently manage their own lives and bodies, and the value of discussing their questions and problems with other girls and with family members. In these and other ways, the mainstream magazines privilege the authority of adult experts and encourage girls to do the same, while the alternative magazines acknowledge and encourage the girls' own competence and self-efficacy. The alternative magazine columns were also more likely to place girls' concerns in larger social context, thus providing a critique of the social processes through which girls' experiences are problematized or normalized, as the case may be.

The seventh is Roberta Goldberg's "The Intersection of Private and Public Experience among Families Adopting Romanian Children." Herein, Goldberg offers an alternative to the private, individualistic, and clinical approaches that dominate the study of adoptive families. She concentrates instead on the processes through which adoptive families define and present themselves, both privately, and in various public contexts. Drawing on intensive qualitative interviews with adoptive mothers, completed shortly after adoption and again 6 years later, Goldberg explicates three distinct stages in adoptive families' development. These stages are characterized by increasing comfort with the adoptive family identity, and the diminishment of overt public performance or acknowledgment of the families' adoptive status. Throughout the Initiation, Stabilization, and Integration stages, family members collaborate to produce complex private and public definitions of themselves that reflect a balance of both the "normalcy" of their situations, and the often negative public perceptions of adoption. These negative public perceptions are heightened by the "crisis" in social context within which the adoption of these young Romanian children took place.

Goldberg portrays decisions to reveal and openly discuss adoption as among the most difficult that adoptive parents make. Her data focus on the perceptions, practices, and negotiations of mothers, and she provides the theoretical frame for future research on children's decisions concerning construction of their own public identities, independent of their parents. The "adopted" identity – like the "adoptive family" status examined in this chapter – offers rich possibilities for examination of processes through which children construct and present themselves to others in various social contexts.

Three chapters (8–10) constitute Part II of this volume, "Innovations in Theory and Research Methods." The first chapter in Part II is Ingrid Castro's "Children's Agency and Cinema's New Fairy Tale." In it, Castro offers an innovative and refreshing analysis of two films that explore children's struggle for agency and control over their (really messed up!) lives. *Manny and Lo* and *Lawn Dogs*, are both R-rated films that are somewhat bizarre, and often violent and disturbing. Castro examines them in terms of their classic fairy tale elements and structure. Most importantly here, she highlights the young female heroines' abuse at the hands of wicked adults, and their subsequent willful acts of defiance and power. Castro also notes the films' shared themes of stark hierarchy/stratification, the linkage of children with the natural and the out-of-doors, and the capabilities and shortcomings of families. The familial theme present in both films is an updated classic fairytale device; young girl abused or neglected by an evil parent figure, finds comfort and assistance from an unlikely source (who becomes the new family in-practice) in her quest for independence and relief from her predicament.

Castro's own prose seems to capture the character and plot development of the medium it analyzes. We can picture the characters as they confront the classic struggle for autonomy, and the search for meaning in a chaotic and often cruel world. The films also compliment and exemplify current interpretive theoretical frameworks, and Castro deftly draws these uncanny parallels as well. This is such a *fun* chapter to read; while also scholarly and sophisticated, it inspires the whimsy and creativity of readers as well as offers an insightful analysis of cinematic themes.

In Chapter 9, "Children as Social Movement Participants," Diane M. Rodgers employs existing literature and first-person accounts to develop and exemplify a typology of children's participation in social movements. Children are symbolic participants, participants by default (this includes children whose parents 'brought them along' both for convenience, and for deliberate political socialization), and active participants. An eclectic collection of fascinating examples illustrates these different forms of children's social movement participation: examples from the Pro-Life, Civil Rights, and Hate movements; examples from Communist Party and unionizing activities in the US; and examples from international children's movements including Bhima Sangha, a working children's union in India, and the Columbian Children's Peace Movement. These colorful historical and contemporary examples are a real strength of this theoretical contribution to the volume.

While a good deal has been written about the symbolic participation of children in social movements, much less sociological attention has been devoted to the other types. Rodgers' work addresses this gap in the research literature. She notes that the extant literature's strong emphasis on adults' use of children as symbols reflects the dominant view of children as primarily passive rather than active participants in social life. She concludes the chapter with a call for future social movement research that is informed by both the growing body of literature on children's culture, and by the theoretical typology developed in this current work.

In the final chapter of the volume, "'Yeah, Me Too!': Adolescent Talk Building in Group Interviews," Laura Fingerson insightfully illustrates how group interviewing of youth allows researchers to obtain rich and detailed data when investigating sensitive issues such as sexuality issues and family problems. Specifically, she uses qualitative data from her group interviews with high school age girls and boys on the sensitive topic of menstruation to show how youth simultaneously accomplish their talk sociolinguistically and develop deeper understandings of issues important to them. Fingerson aptly draws on symbolic interactionism and the interpretive approach to socialization to inform her group-interviewing method, and investigate how youth actively construct and interpret menstruation within their peer cultures.

Fingerson finds that the girls were quite comfortable discussing menstruation in group interviews and that the boys, while not as comfortable as the girls, shared their social experiences related to menstruation during their group interviews. Fingerson worked with a male research assistant, who conducted the group interviews with the boys. In addition to the group interviews, Fingerson and her male associate conducted individual interviews with the girls and boys, respectively to better understand their individual histories, families, and understandings of menstruation. Overall, the group interviews show how the girls and boys accomplish talk in a group setting, develop a shared perspective on the issue, and how the girls engage in telling stories in a supportive fashion. Specifically, the girls learn that while they experience different physiological symptoms, their own experiences are "normal," and affirm an important experience that they share. Moreover, the group interviews capture stories among the girls that are empowering, helping to build a community of young women who often share personal strategies for dealing with menstruation. Fingerson closes by discussing how group interviews capture teen talk that occurs in natural peer group settings, and how this talk strongly shapes gender identities.

In closing, we thank all the authors for their creative contributions. We believe that their work provides many important insights into the core concerns and everyday lives of children and youth. We would also like to thank members of the *Sociological Studies of Children and Youth* Editorial Board who generously gave time to review manuscripts for this volume: Peter Adler, Spencer Cahill, Donna Eder, and Barbara Schneider. In addition, several colleagues provided critical and constructive reviews of several chapters. Along these lines we extend thanks to Loretta Bass, Sampson Blair, Molly George, Dave MacLeod, and Suzanne Staggenborg. Two students offered skillful assistance, and their efforts are much appreciated. Michelle Wilson, our undergraduate assistant editor, read and offered helpful and thoughtful comments on nearly every chapter in the volume; Thank you, Michelle. And thanks also to Daniel Sturgeon, who helped in final editing of references for all chapters. An earlier version of this introductory chapter was presented at 2004 Annual Meeting of the Michigan Sociological Association in Mount Pleasant, Michigan, and we thank attendees for their comments and questions. Our thanks go also to our colleagues Mary S. Senter and Nancy J. Herman-Kinney for their thoughtful comments on the manuscript, and to Rosier's Sociology of Childhood students, who offered their thoughts and comments as well. Finally, both of us would like to acknowledge the support of family members who were particularly patient while we reviewed, edited, and finalized this volume. Katherine thanks her children, Mary and Glen, for their joyful collaboration in family life – and also thanks Glen for his permission to reproduce his likeness in this chapter. David thanks his wife Nancy for her compassion and understanding, and his rambunctious and precocious son Matthew Michael for helping his parents see the world through his eyes and teaching them to appreciate the specialness of all the little things in life. We respectfully dedicate this volume to the children and youth of Iraq, and to the children of fallen American soldiers from the Iraq War.

# NOTES

1. In earlier presentations of this piece, audiences have questioned the validity of Rosier's father's recall – specifically, they have reasonably wondered if he was not, perhaps, older than seven? However, as is true for many people, a particular dramatic event (e.g., a family move, or the serious illness or death of a parent) occurred during the summer he turned 8 years old, after which things were never again the same. Such events help to increase the confidence we can have in the dating of childhood memories; in Rosier's father's case, there is simply no doubt that he was left to fend for himself, while his parents attended a movie prior to the summer he turned eight.

2. While many, especially middle-class, families are struggling to meet the time pressure and transportation demands associated with their children being involved in multiple activities at the same time, Kinney found some families in one community scaling back on the numbers of activities the parents allowed their children to participate in at any one given time (Hofferth et al., 2005).

3. Several months later, Glen's weekly papers included a "Family Preparedness Guide," distributed courtesy of the Michigan State Police. As is true for the various federal sources of emergency information, the guide advises families on how to prepare for severe weather, technological hazards (e.g., toxic spills), and terrorist attacks.

4. Persistently high levels of residential and educational segregation in the United States, by race and by social class, are well documented and show little, if any, improvement (see e.g., Massey & Denton, 1993; Orfield, Bachmeier, James, & Eitle, 1997; Reardon & Yun, 2001). Children's and adolescents' friendship groups tend also to be highly segregated along racial and especially along social class lines, within their already relatively homogenous schools, neighborhoods, and organized activities. "Popular" groups are composed largely of kids from middle-class and more affluent families, who have few positive interactions with those of more modest means (Adler & Adler, 1998; Eder, Evans, & Parker, 1997). In addition, geographic and social mobility in American society has contributed to a high level of age-segregation, with contact between the elderly and youth being especially rare (Corsaro, 2005).

# REFERENCES

Adler, P. A., & Adler, P. (1994). Social reproduction and the corporate other: The institutionalization of after-school activities. *Sociological Quarterly, 35*, 309–328.

Adler, P. A., & Adler, P. (1998). *Peer power: Preadolescent culture and identity*. New Brunswick, NJ: Rutgers University Press.

Albom, M. (2002). A girl dies, and we worry for all kids. *Detroit Free Press*. Accessed online at www.freep.com/sports/albom/mitch21_20020721.htm.

Bates, E. (2004). National affairs update: Schools spy on potheads. *Rolling Stone, 956*(September 2), 89.

Best, J. (1993). *Threatened children: Rhetoric and concern about child-victims*. Chicago: University of Chicago Press.

Best, J. (2002). Monster hype: How a few isolated tragedies – and their supposed causes – were turned into a national epidemic. *Education Next, Summer 2002*, 51–55 Retrieved September 8, 2004, from http://www.educationnext.org/20022/index.html.

Corsaro, W. A. (2005 [1997]). *The sociology of childhood*. Thousand Oaks, CA: Pine Forge Press.

Donohue, E., Schiraldi, V., & Ziedenberg, J. (1998). School house hype: School shootings and the real risks kids face in America. Retrieved from Center on Juvenile and Criminal Justice, http://www.cjcj.org/pubs/shooting/shootings.html on April 23, 1999.

Dunn, J. S., Kinney, D. A., & Hofferth, S. L. (2003). Parental ideologies and children's after school activities. *American Behavioral Scientist, 46*(10), 1359–1386.

Eder, D., Evans, C. C., & Parker, S. (1997). *School talk: Gender and adolescent culture*. New Brunswick, NJ: Rutgers University Press.

Hall, G. S. (1904). *Adolescence*. New York: Appleton.

Hareven, T. K. (1982). American families in transition: Historical perspectives on change. In: F. Walsh (Ed.), *Normal Family Processes* (pp. 446–466). New York: The Guilford Press.

Hofferth, S. L. (1998). Healthy environments, healthy children: Children in families. *Child Development Supplement of the Panel Study of Income Dynamics.* Ann Arbor, MI: Institute for Social Research, University of Michigan.

Hofferth, S. L., Kinney, D. A., & Dunn, J. S. (2005). *The hurried child: Myth or reality.* Working Paper. Department of Family Studies, University of Maryland, College Park.

Hofferth, S., & Sandberg, J. L. (2001). Changes in American children's time, 1981–1997. In: S. Hofferth & T. Owens (Eds), *Children at the Millennium: Where did we come from, where are we going?* (pp. 193–229). New York: Elsevier Science.

Kinney, D. A., Hofferth, S. L., & Dunn, J. S. (2001). Family strategies for managing the time crunch. Paper presented at the Dutiful occasions: Working families, everyday lives Conference sponsored by the Alfred P. Sloan Center for the ethnography of everyday life at the University of Michigan, Ann Arbor, MI.

Lareau, A. (2003). *Unequal childhoods: Class, race, and family life.* Berkeley: University of California Press.

Massey, D. S., & Denton, N. A. (1993). *American apartheid: Segregation and the making of the underclass.* Cambridge, MA: Harvard University Press.

Mills, C. W. (2000 [1959]). *The sociological imagination* (40th anniversary ed.). New York: Oxford University Press.

Moretti, R. (2002). The last generation to live on the edge. *Newsweek, CXL*(6), 14.

National Public Radio. (2002). Parents taking steps to increase children's safety amid recent news reports of abductions. *Morning Edition,* hosted by Renee Montagne (August 21).

Office of the Press Secretary. (2004). Department of Homeland Security. Homeland Security and The Ad Council launch new ready campaign public service advertisements (November 22).

Orfield, G., Bachmeier, M., James, D. R., & Eitle, T. (1997). Deepening segregation in American public schools. *Equity and Excellence in Education, 30*(2), 5–24.

Reardon, S. F., & Yun, J. T. (2001). Suburban racial change and suburban school segregation, 1987–95. *Sociology of Education, 74*(2), 79–101.

Stacey, J. (1990). *Brave new families: Stories of domestic upheaval in late twentieth century America.* New York: Basic Books.

Tiryakian, E. A. (2005). From the welfare state to the warfare state. *Contexts: Understanding People in their Social Worlds, 4*(2), 23–24.

U.S. Department of Homeland Security. Retrieved March 8, and June 2, 2005, http://www.ready.gov.

# PART I:
# EMPIRICAL STUDIES

# ADOLESCENT RESIDENTIAL MOBILITY AND PREMATURE LIFE-COURSE TRANSITIONS: THE ROLE OF PEER NETWORKS

Scott J. South, Amy Lutz and Eric P. Baumer

## INTRODUCTION

Adolescence has traditionally been considered a time of substantial turmoil in the life course, as youth struggle with establishing self-images, finding appropriate and supportive peer groups, and begin their psychological, emotional, and, in some cases, physical separation from their parents. Among the many factors that have been thought to exacerbate adolescent adjustment during this often-difficult period are residential mobility and the school changes that frequently accompany these geographic relocations. Numerous recent studies have found statistically significant and substantively important effects of residential mobility and school changes on problematic adolescent behaviors. Although the observed strength of the association varies across studies and outcomes, recent investigations have reported significant effects of residential mobility and/or school changes on poor academic performance (Ingersoll, Scamman, & Eckerling, 1989; Kerbow, 1996; Pribesh & Downey, 1999), school dropout and low educational attainment (Astone & McLanahan, 1994; Entwisle, Alexander, &

Olson, 1997; Hagan, MacMillan, & Wheaton, 1996; Haveman, Wolfe, & Spaulding, 1991; McLanahan & Sandefur, 1994; Rumberger, 1995; Swanson & Schneider, 1999; Teachman, Paasch, & Carver, 1996), drug and alcohol abuse (Hoffman & Johnson, 1998), risky sexual activity, including early sexual initiation and numerous sex partners (Baumer & South, 2001; Stack, 1994), premarital childbearing (South & Baumer, 2000; Sucoff & Upchurch, 1998), and other behavioral problems (Tucker, Marx, & Long, 1998; Wood, Halfon, Scarlata, Newacheck, & Nessim, 1993).

However, in many – perhaps most – of these studies, residential mobility is treated predominantly as a control variable, and thus its effects on adolescent development have been under-theorized, and important empirical issues relevant to these associations have gone unexplored. Even when the consequences of residential mobility are the explicit focus of investigation, few studies have attempted to identify the *mechanisms* through which residential mobility and school changes lead to disadvantaged adolescent outcomes (Fenzel, 1989). Although several observers attribute the deleterious consequences of residential mobility to a reduction in children's social capital (Coleman, 1988, 1990), few studies have attempted to clearly delineate the types and sources of social capital that presumably account for this effect. Moreover, residential mobility among children and adolescents has been linked to other attitudes and conditions, including relations with parents (Pittman & Bowen, 1994) and schools (Entwisle et al., 1997), social stress (Raviv, Keinan, Abazon, & Raviv, 1990), poor self-concept (Hendershott, 1989), and social isolation (Myers, 1999; Vernberg, 1990) that might help to explain its effects on problematic behaviors. Little attention has been given to the possible role of peer networks in mediating the effects of mobility on adolescent behaviors, despite the acknowledged salience of such networks in shaping adolescent behavior (Adler & Adler, 1998).

Using the longitudinal National Survey of Children (NSC), the purpose of this paper is to examine the impact of frequent adolescent residential mobility on two key events in the adolescent life course – the initiation of sexual activity and dropping out of high school. Both early sexual initiation and premature exit from schooling have important ramifications for later life. Early sexual initiation, for example, increases the risk period for premarital childbearing and, in turn, places young parents and their children at a heightened risk of social and economic disadvantage (National Research Council, 1987). The failure to complete high school severely compromises later employment and occupational opportunities (Jencks et al., 1972). We give particular attention to factors that might account for any observed impact of repeated residential mobility on these life-course events.

# THEORY

Current theorizing on the effects of residential mobility on adolescent behavior invokes four broad categories of explanatory factors: relations with parents, relations with schools, relations with peers, and general adjustment problems. Admittedly, the specific mechanisms subsumed by these general categories do not always fall neatly into distinct and mutually exclusive theoretical camps; rather, they often overlap and, indeed, frequently complement one another. Yet, these mechanisms encompass the most frequently cited reasons for the detrimental impact of adolescent residential mobility on potentially problematic behaviors, and thus warrant empirical examination.

### *Relations with Parents*

One possible reason residential mobility increases adolescents' risk of early intercourse and dropping out of school is that frequent relocations impair adolescents' relationships with their parents. The stresses incurred by frequent moves may strain parent–child relations and reduce the amount of support and social control parents provide for their children (Raviv et al., 1990; Stack, 1994). Some observers argue that strong parental attachment effectively cushions the otherwise disruptive impact of mobility (Pittman & Bowen, 1994). Because geographic relocations place adolescents in peer groups and neighborhood environments unfamiliar to their parents, residential mobility also makes it difficult for parents and other adults to monitor and supervise children's behavior, thereby increasing adolescent problem behavior (Sampson, 1997). Frequent mobility is thought to weaken the bonds between adolescents, their friends, and their parents – a key dimension of children's social capital (Coleman, 1988). Indeed, Coleman (1988) goes so far as to use residential mobility as an indicator of children's access to social capital, on the assumption that "the social relations that constitute social capital are broken at each move" (p. S113). In particular, the fission and subsequent reconstitution of adolescent peer groups upon moving means that parents of mobile adolescents are unlikely to know their children's friends. In turn, the removal of parents from adolescents' social networks may eliminate an important constraint on youth behavior (Coleman, 1990; Portes, 1998).[1] Prior studies have not attempted to determine the degree to which differences between mobile and non-mobile children in parental relationships and parental monitoring can account for the effect of residential mobility on adolescent behaviors such as early intercourse or dropping out of school.

## *Relations with Schools*

Frequent residential mobility might also increase the risk of early sexual activity and dropping out of school because it negatively impacts adolescents' educational aspirations and school attachment. Residential mobility has been shown to reduce adolescent's academic performance (Entwisle et al., 1997; Pribesh & Downey, 1999), increase their behavioral problems (Swanson & Schneider, 1999), and generally detract from children's school lives (Tucker et al., 1998). One likely consequence of these unfavorable educational experiences is that, compared to their residentially stable counterparts, mobile adolescents will have lower educational aspirations and be less committed to and satisfied with their schools. In turn, youth with low educational aspirations and low levels of school attachment are apt to perceive few opportunity costs to engaging in early sexual activity – thus risking early and likely non-marital parenthood. Students' relationship to their schools might be particularly important for explaining the effect of residential mobility on school dropout, given that low educational aspirations and weak school attachment lead to higher dropout rates and other diminished educational outcomes (Rumberger & Lawson, 1998). Yet, while residential mobility has been linked to educational aspirations and performance, and these latter variables are known to be associated with adolescent problem behavior, no study has yet attempted to determine the degree to which behavioral differences between mobile and non-mobile children can be attributed to differences in their relationship with their schools.

## *Relations with Peers*

Alternatively, residential mobility may exacerbate problematic adolescent behavior because it disrupts their relationships with peers. Two dynamics might operate here. First, because moving so often severs social ties, frequent relocation is likely to reduce the number and quality of close friendships enjoyed by adolescents (Vernberg, 1990). Developmental psychologists generally find that, compared with their residentially stable counterparts, mobile youth report having fewer close friends and less personal intimacy with the friends they do have (Humke & Schaefer 1995; Vernberg, Abwender, Ewell, & Beery, 1992). In addition, as relatively new arrivals to their communities and schools, mobile adolescents are probably less likely to be selected or identified as close friends by their classmates (i.e., mobile youth are less popular) and are less likely to be the center of peer social networks.

Second, mobility might be related to the *composition* of adolescents' peer networks. Recent in-movers are perhaps more likely than long-term residents to find themselves near the nadir of the school status hierarchy, where deviant and otherwise problematic behavior is apt to be more common, accepted, and encouraged. In turn, exposure to peers whose values are conducive to early sexual intercourse and weak academic performance promotes these very behaviors. These peer groups might influence adolescent behavior directly via imitation processes, or indirectly through the inculcation and internalization of norms and attitudes favorable to sexual activity and hostile to educational success. Students' relationship with their peers might be especially important for explaining the impact of residential mobility on sexual initiation, since sexual partners are likely to be chosen from members of peer social networks.

## General Adjustment Problems

Two other potential mechanisms linking residential mobility to problematic adolescent behaviors reflect general adjustment problems. First, and perhaps partly as a result of deteriorating relations with parents, peers, and schools, residential mobility has been characterized as a stressful life event for adolescents (Raviv et al., 1990), and one that threatens their self-concept and self-esteem (Hendershott, 1989). The general strains of moving, including the need to adjust to new schools and find new peer networks, in concert with a reduction in social support available to adolescents (Raviv et al., 1990), increases adolescents' psychosocial stress. Hendershott (1989), for example, in a sample of sixth through eighth graders, finds significant (although variable) negative effects of residential mobility on children's sense of mastery over the environment, self-esteem, self-denigration, and depression. Hence, the general strains of moving, including the need to adjust to new schools and find new and supportive peer networks, appears to increase adolescents' psychosocial stress along several dimensions. In turn, such stress is likely to create behavioral problems.

Second, social disorganization theory posits that the unstable community environments generated by frequent residential mobility increase adolescents' propensity to engage in delinquent behaviors, and such associations have been observed at both the individual and the community level (Elliott et al., 1996; Sampson & Groves, 1989). Bereft of the traditional controls exercised by families, neighborhood actors, and other community institutions, residentially mobile youth are relieved of the constraints that otherwise induce conformity, and are thus free to engage in deviant and delinquent behaviors. In turn, higher rates of delinquency are likely associated with other non-normative acts, such as engaging in risky sexual behavior or dropping out of school. But whether differences between mobile and non-mobile youth in either psychosocial stress or delinquent behaviors can account for the impact of residential mobility on other adolescent problem behaviors is a question that has not yet been addressed in the extant research literature.

## DATA AND METHODS

Data for this analysis come from the NSC. The NSC is a three-wave, nationally representative survey of US children aged 7–11 when first interviewed in 1976 (Zill, Furstenberg, Peterson, & Moore, 1990). Black children were oversampled, and constitute about one-quarter of the initial sample. A subset of these children was reinterviewed in 1981 (when they were at ages 12–16) and again in 1987 (at ages 18–22). The NSC includes sampling weights that allow the results to be generalized to the population. Despite non-trivial attrition rates over the three waves, the observed timing of key events in the adolescent life course –including sexual initiation and dropping out of school –in the NSC is quite similar to that observed in other datasets (Moore & Glei, 1995).[2] The sample used in our analysis includes the 1,105 young women and men who participated in all three waves of interviews and who provided valid information on the dependent variables. To our knowledge, the NSC is the only longitudinal dataset that provides information on the cumulative number of adolescents' residential moves, measures of the hypothesized mediating variables, and relevant measures of adolescent sexual and educational behaviors. Table A1 provides brief descriptions and summary statistics for all of the variables used in our analysis, along with interview wave(s) from which these measures were constructed (see the appendix).

*Dependent Variables*

Much of the research examining the impact of frequent residential mobility on youth behavior focuses on two pivotal events in the adolescent life course: the initiation of sexual activity and dropping out of school. We measure the *initiation of sexual activity* with a binary variable, derived from questions asked at the wave 3 interview, indicating whether respondents first had voluntary sexual intercourse at age 16 or younger. *High school dropout* is a binary variable, also derived from the wave 3 interview, indicating whether respondents ever dropped out of high school for more than 1 month. Thirty-eight percent of the respondents reported having had first intercourse by age 16, and 14% reported having dropped out of school.

### Independent Variable

The primary independent variable is a count of the *number of residential moves* made prior to the wave 3 interview. At the first interview in 1976, the parents of the NSC respondents were asked to report the number of residential moves made by the family in the 5 years preceding the interview; in waves 2 and 3, the NSC respondents themselves were asked the number of moves made since the preceding interview. We sum the number of moves reported at all three interviews. The NSC respondents moved an average of 3.8 times between 1971 and 1987.[3]

### Mediating Variables

Three of the variables that potentially mediate the effect of residential mobility on sexual initiation and school dropout involve adolescents' relations with their parents. *Parental control* of adolescents is a standardized scale derived from five questions in the wave 2 interview, asking respondents how much it is like their mother and their father to want to know the child's whereabouts and activities (the three response categories are "not at all like my mother (father)," "somewhat like my mother (father)," and "very much like my mother (father),"); and whether the family has rules regarding keeping parents informed about the child's whereabouts, doing homework, and dating and going to parties (the latter three variables scored "no" or "yes"). The summated scale of these items (after converting the items to standard scores) is arrayed such that high values indicate higher levels of parental control over the child's behavior ($\alpha = 0.60$).[4] The child's *attachment to parents* is measured by a scale comprised of seven items asked of the child at the wave 2 interview. We use the questions asked about the respondent's mother, but substitute the analogous questions asked about the father when information about the mother is missing. The seven items ask the respondents how often they argue with their parent and do enjoyable things with their parent (the four response categories for these two items range from "never" to "often"); whether the parent spends enough time with the child (a dichotomous variable); how much affection the parent gives the child (the four response categories range from "doesn't want affection" to "all the affection you want"); how close the child feels to the parent (response categories range from "not very close" to "extremely close"); how much the child wants to be the kind of person the parent is (the four responses range from "not at all" to "a lot"); and how much it is like the parent to love and be interested in the child (the three responses range from "very much like my mother (father)" to "not at all like my mother (father)"). Higher scores on this scale indicate greater attachment to parents. This scale has moderate internal reliability ($\alpha = 0.68$). The degree of connectivity between parents and their children's social network, considered by some to be an important element of children's social capital (Coleman, 1988), is tapped by a single wave 2 questionnaire item asking the parent *how many of the child's friends the parent knows* by sight and by first and last name. The five possible response categories range from "none of them" to "all of them."

Two of the potentially mediating variables tap respondents' relations with educational institutions. Respondents' *attachment to school* is measured by a three-item scale comprised of questions in the wave 2 interview asking how respondents feel about going to school (the four response categories range from "hate school" to "love school"); how interested respondents are in their schoolwork (the three response categories are "hardly ever," "just some of the time," and "most of the time"); and their degree of satisfaction with their schoolwork (the three response categories are "not too satisfied," "somewhat satisfied," and "very satisfied"). The school-attachment scale is created by summing the standard scores for these variables; high values indicate greater attachment to school. This scale has moderate internal reliability ($\alpha = 0.58$). Respondents' *educational aspirations* are measured by a single item in the wave 2 interview asking respondents: "Looking ahead, what would you like to do about school?" The five response categories are "quit school as soon as possible," "finish high school," "get some college or other training," "finish college," and "take further training after college."

Respondents' relations with peers are captured by several variables. *Number of friends* is a simple count of the respondents close friends reported at the wave 2 interview. *Loneliness* is measured by a single wave 2 item asking respondents: "Do you feel lonely and wish you had more friends?" The four response categories range from "never" to "often." *Peers' sexual behavior* is measured by a standardized scale comprised of three items: (1) the respondent's report of the number of the respondent's friends who had become parents by age 16 (the five response categories range from "all" to "none"); (2) the number of the respondent's friends who had had sex by age 16 (the five response categories range from "all" to "none"); and (3) a dichotomous variable indicating whether the respondent's friends encouraged the respondent to have sex during the teen years ($\alpha = 0.43$). Somewhat analogously, *peers' educational performance* is a standardized scale comprised of three items. Respondents were asked, "When you were about 16, how many of your friends planned to go to college"; "got really good grades – A's and B's"; and "had dropped out of school?" For each of the three items, the five possible responses ranged "none of them" to "all of them" ($\alpha = 0.58$). The indexes of peers' sexual behavior and peers' educational performance are arrayed such that high values indicate less frequent sexual activity and higher educational performance among respondents' friends. The scale of peers' sexual behavior is used as an intervening variable in the analysis of sexual initiation, while the scale of peers' educational performance is used as an intervening variable in the analysis of school dropout.

Finally, two of the potentially mediating variables tap adolescent adjustment problems. *Stress* is a scale comprised of two items asked at the wave 2 interview; how often respondents report feeling "nervous, tense, or on edge" and how often they report feeling "unhappy, sad, or depressed." The four response categories range from "hardly ever" to "very often." The correlation between these two items is 0.39. The index of *delinquent behavior* is an eight-item scale comprised of questions asked at the wave 2 interview. The respondents were asked to report the frequency of the following behaviors during the year preceding the wave 2 interview: "hurt someone badly enough to need bandages or a doctor"; "taken something from a store without paying for it"; "damaged school property on purpose"; "gotten drunk"; and "skipped a day of school without permission." The four possible response categories range from "never" to "more than twice." In three separate questions, respondents were also asked whether they had used alcohol, marijuana, and other drugs during the 2 weeks preceding the wave 2 interview. The possible responses were "no" or "yes." Higher scores on this index indicate a greater frequency of delinquent behavior and drug use ($\alpha = 0.71$).

## Control Variables

Adolescent residential mobility is likely to be related to characteristics of their families that might also influence youth sexual and educational behavior. Accordingly, the ensuing regression models include several characteristics of the NSC respondents and their families that might be related to residential mobility, the hypothesized mediating factors, or the outcome variables.

Indicators of the socioeconomic status of the respondent's family include *family income* (measured with an 8-point scale ranging from less than $5,000 to $50,000 or more), completed *years of schooling* of the more highly educated parent, and a dummy variable for whether the family *owns its home*. *Race* and *sex* differences in the outcome variables are captured by dummy variables for African-American respondents (*Black*) and for male respondents (*Male*), respectively.

*Family disruption* is measured here by a dummy variable, scored 0 for respondents who, at the wave 2 interview, resided with both biological parents, and 1 for respondents with other family compositions. *Number of siblings* refers to the total number of respondents' sisters and brothers living in the household as of the wave 2 interview. *Class standing* is measured by a single wave 2 item asking respondents about their overall academic performance; the five response categories are: (1) near the bottom of the class; (2) below the middle; (3) in the middle; (4) above the middle; and (5) one of the best students in the class.

Although missing data on the explanatory variables are relatively uncommon (over 95% of the cases have no missing data and no single variable is missing for more than 2% of the 1,105 observations), we prefer to maintain the maximum possible sample size. Accordingly, missing values on the continuous independent variables are replaced with the valid mean, and missing values on the categorical independent variables are replaced with the valid mode. Following the suggestions of Cohen and Cohen (1983), we then tally, for each respondent, the number of variables for which missing values were imputed and include this count (called *number of imputations*) as a control variable in the regression models.

## RESULTS

Table 1 presents the correlation matrix for all variables used in the analysis. Several correlations are worth highlighting. First, at the bivariate level, the number of residential moves is positively and significantly correlated with the probability of both engaging in early sexual intercourse ($r = 0.10$) and dropping out of school ($r = 0.20$). Second, most of the correlations between number of residential moves and the hypothesized intervening variables,

**Table 1.** Correlation Matrix: National Survey of Children ($N = 1,105$).

| Variables | X1 | X2 | X3 | X4 | X5 | X6 | X7 | X8 | X9 | X10 | X11 | X12 | X13 | X14 | X15 | X16 | X17 | X18 | X19 | X20 | X21 | X22 | X23 |
|---|---|---|---|---|---|---|---|---|---|---|---|---|---|---|---|---|---|---|---|---|---|---|---|
| X1 First intercourse < age 16 | 1.00 | | | | | | | | | | | | | | | | | | | | | | |
| X2 High school dropout | 0.24 | 1.00 | | | | | | | | | | | | | | | | | | | | | |
| X3 Number of residential moves | 0.10 | 0.20 | 1.00 | | | | | | | | | | | | | | | | | | | | |
| X4 Family income | −0.17 | −0.15 | −0.05 | 1.00 | | | | | | | | | | | | | | | | | | | |
| X5 Parental education | −0.20 | −0.21 | −0.02 | 0.56 | 1.00 | | | | | | | | | | | | | | | | | | |
| X6 Home ownership | −0.14 | −0.17 | −0.20 | 0.42 | 0.26 | 1.00 | | | | | | | | | | | | | | | | | |
| X7 Black | 0.14 | 0.06 | −0.04 | −0.41 | −0.28 | −0.28 | 1.00 | | | | | | | | | | | | | | | | |
| X8 Male | 0.11 | 0.02 | −0.07 | 0.04 | 0.02 | −0.01 | 0.00 | 1.00 | | | | | | | | | | | | | | | |
| X9 Family disruption | 0.12 | 0.14 | 0.10 | −0.54 | −0.32 | −0.41 | 0.35 | 0.00 | 1.00 | | | | | | | | | | | | | | |
| X10 Number of siblings | 0.06 | 0.03 | 0.00 | −0.09 | −0.09 | 0.04 | 0.20 | −0.01 | −0.07 | 1.00 | | | | | | | | | | | | | |
| X11 Class standing | −0.10 | −0.17 | −0.04 | 0.11 | 0.19 | 0.01 | −0.04 | −0.03 | −0.05 | −0.02 | 1.00 | | | | | | | | | | | | |
| X12 Number of imputations | −0.03 | 0.04 | 0.00 | −0.02 | −0.04 | −0.04 | −0.03 | 0.07 | −0.04 | 0.01 | −0.04 | 1.00 | | | | | | | | | | | |
| X13 Parental control | 0.03 | −0.02 | −0.06 | 0.05 | 0.05 | 0.03 | −0.03 | −0.04 | −0.02 | 0.00 | 0.02 | 0.01 | 1.00 | | | | | | | | | | |
| X14 Parental attachment | −0.09 | −0.05 | −0.11 | 0.03 | 0.02 | 0.04 | 0.04 | 0.05 | −0.03 | 0.00 | 0.14 | −0.05 | 0.19 | 1.00 | | | | | | | | | |
| X15 Parent knows child's friends | −0.08 | −0.05 | −0.06 | 0.25 | 0.22 | 0.16 | −0.28 | −0.09 | −0.17 | −0.04 | 0.10 | −0.01 | 0.06 | 0.09 | 1.00 | | | | | | | | |
| X16 School attachment | −0.10 | −0.17 | −0.05 | −0.07 | 0.03 | 0.01 | 0.07 | −0.10 | 0.01 | 0.07 | 0.38 | 0.01 | 0.08 | 0.23 | 0.04 | 1.00 | | | | | | | |
| X17 Educational aspirations | −0.09 | −0.20 | 0.00 | 0.17 | 0.32 | 0.07 | 0.00 | −0.03 | −0.04 | −0.04 | 0.29 | −0.08 | 0.09 | 0.12 | 0.07 | 0.33 | 1.00 | | | | | | |
| X18 Number of friends | 0.07 | 0.04 | 0.01 | −0.04 | −0.10 | −0.01 | −0.01 | 0.07 | 0.04 | 0.05 | −0.03 | 0.00 | 0.00 | 0.02 | −0.10 | −0.02 | −0.01 | 1.00 | | | | | |
| X19 Loneliness | −0.02 | 0.08 | 0.09 | −0.05 | −0.01 | −0.01 | −0.05 | −0.04 | 0.02 | 0.05 | −0.03 | 0.00 | 0.00 | −0.15 | −0.02 | −0.01 | −0.01 | −0.06[a] | 1.00 | | | | |
| X20 Peers' sexual behavior | −0.36 | −0.21 | −0.12 | 0.25 | 0.27 | 0.21 | −0.33 | −0.16 | −0.23 | −0.07 | 0.08 | 0.04 | 0.03 | 0.04 | 0.17 | 0.07 | 0.11 | −0.09 | −0.05 | 1.00 | | | |
| X21 Peers' educational performance | −0.30 | −0.34 | −0.13 | 0.24 | 0.32 | 0.20 | −0.16 | −0.14 | −0.14 | −0.02 | 0.26 | −0.04 | 0.05 | 0.17 | 0.15 | 0.20 | 0.31 | −0.06[a] | −0.10 | 0.39 | 1.00 | | |
| X22 Stress | 0.12 | 0.06 | 0.07 | −0.01 | 0.00 | −0.03 | 0.08 | −0.10 | 0.05 | 0.03 | −0.06 | −0.05 | −0.03 | −0.15 | −0.01 | −0.07 | −0.03 | −0.01 | 0.25 | −0.15 | −0.10 | 1.00 | |
| X23 Delinquent behavior index | 0.17 | 0.14 | 0.11 | 0.03 | −0.02 | −0.02 | −0.07 | 0.05 | 0.06 | −0.01 | −0.13 | 0.00 | −0.09 | −0.23 | −0.05 | −0.28 | −0.14 | 0.05 | 0.02 | −0.19 | −0.18 | .13 | 1.00 |

*Note*: Correlations greater than |0.06| are significant at the 0.05 level, two-tailed test, except those (because of rounding) marked with superscripts "a".

while generally modest, are nonetheless consistent with expectations. Number of residential moves is significantly and inversely correlated with parental attachment ($r = -0.11$), parents' knowledge of children's friends ($r = -0.06$), peers' conservative sexual behavior ($r = -0.12$), and peers' favorable educational performance ($r = -0.13$), and significantly and positively correlated with self-reported loneliness ($r = 0.09$), stress ($r = 0.07$), and delinquency ($r = 0.11$). In contrast, the correlations between number of residential moves and parental control, school attachment, educational aspirations, and number of close friends are statistically non-significant.[5]

Third, the correlations between the hypothesized intervening variables and the dependent variables are also generally consistent with the hypotheses. For example, school attachment, educational aspirations, peers' sexual and educational behaviors, stress, and delinquency are correlated significantly and in the expected direction with both early sexual initiation and school dropout. Parental attachment and parents' knowledge of children's friends are significantly and inversely related to early sexual initiation, but not to dropping out of school. Loneliness is significantly and positively correlated with school dropout, but not with age at first intercourse. Number of friends is significantly and positively associated with having first intercourse before age 17, perhaps because included among these friends are boyfriends and girlfriends who serve as sexual partners.

Fourth, the correlations between residential mobility and the control variables provide an indication of how mobile youth differ demographically from their residentially stable counterparts. The strongest correlations are between number of residential moves, on the one hand, and both home ownership ($r = -0.20$) and family disruption ($r = 0.10$), on the other. These correlations reflect the much lower rates of migration and residential mobility among families that own rather than rent their dwelling (Long, 1988), and the higher rates of mobility among single-parent than among two-parent families (South, Crowder, & Trent, 1998).

Table 2 presents the results from a series of logistic regression models that evaluate the impact of the explanatory and control variables on the likelihood that a respondent experienced first sexual intercourse at age 16 or younger. Model 1 includes only the number of residential moves as an independent variable and, as in the correlation matrix, its coefficient is positive and statistically significant. Each residential move increases the odds of having early intercourse by about 5% ($5 = 100(e^{0.052} - 1)$). Model 2 adds the control variables. Of the controls, males report having had first intercourse significantly younger than females, and both parental education and respondent's self-reported class standing are significantly and inversely related to the likelihood of having sex by age 16. The racial difference in the timing of first intercourse is marginally significant ($p<0.10$, two-tailed test). These associations are consistent with prior research on the risk factors for early sexual intercourse. However, controlling for these background characteristics does nothing to attenuate the observed effect of residential mobility, relative to Model 1.

Models 3 through 12 of Table 2 add singly to Model 2 each of the potentially intervening variables. Five of these variables exhibit statistically significant net effects on adolescents' risk of having first intercourse prior to age 17: parental attachment (Model 4), school attachment (Model 6), and peers' conservative sexual behavior (Model 10) are all inversely related to the likelihood of having early intercourse, while higher levels of stress (Model 11), and more frequent delinquent behavior (Model 12) increase the likelihood of early intercourse. In addition, the coefficient for parental control (Model 3) is marginally significant ($p<0.10$, two-tailed test). Of these, however, only peers' sexual behavior and respondent's self-reported delinquency explain a non-trivial portion of the effect of residential mobility on age at first intercourse. Controlling for peer's sexual behavior (Model 10) reduces the observed effect of residential mobility (relative to Model 2) by about 30% ($0.30 = (0.052 - 0.036)/0.052$). Higher rates of delinquent behavior (Model 12) among mobile adolescents explain about 13% of the effect of residential mobility on early sexual intercourse ($0.13 = (0.052-0.045)/0.052$).[6] The third most important mediator is parental attachment (Model 4), but its inclusion in the model reduces the coefficient for residential mobility by only 6% ($0.06 = (0.052-0.049)/0.052$). Although less central to our purpose, it is also worth noting that controlling for respondent's attachment to school (Model 6) reduces substantially the inverse effect of class standing on the timing of first sexual intercourse (relative to Model 2), and in fact drives the coefficient for class standing to statistical non-significance.

In order to assess the degree to which the potential mediators as a whole can account for the observed impact of adolescent residential mobility on the timing of first intercourse, Model 13 of Table 2 includes as predictors those intervening variables whose inclusion in Models 3 through 12 served to reduce the impact of mobility, however slightly. These variables are parental attachment, school attachment, peers' educational performance, stress, and the delinquent behavior index. Of these five variables, peers' educational performance, stress, and delinquent behavior take on statistically significant coefficients. Including all five of these possible mediators simultaneously reduces the coefficient for residential mobility by 44% ($0.44 = (0.052-0.029)/0.052$) and drives this coefficient to statistical

Table 2. Logistic Regression Analysis of the Likelihood of Having First Sexual Intercourse Age 16 or Younger: National Survey of Children ($N = 1{,}105$).

| Variables | 1 | 2 | 3 | 4 | 5 | 6 | 7 | 8 | 9 | 10 | 11 | 12 | 13 |
|---|---|---|---|---|---|---|---|---|---|---|---|---|---|
| Number of residential moves | 0.052*** (0.016) | 0.052** (0.017) | 0.054** (0.017) | 0.049** (0.018) | 0.053** (0.017) | 0.051** (0.017) | 0.052** (0.017) | 0.052** (0.017) | 0.054** (0.017) | 0.036* (0.018) | 0.050** (0.018) | 0.045* (0.018) | 0.029 (0.019) |
| Family income | | −0.037 (0.048) | −0.039 (0.048) | −0.034 (0.048) | −0.038 (0.048) | −0.050 (0.048) | −0.036 (0.048) | −0.038 (0.048) | −0.039 (0.048) | −0.044 (0.050) | −0.045 (0.048) | −0.054 (0.048) | −0.063 (0.051) |
| Parental education | | −0.106*** (0.029) | −0.107*** (0.029) | −0.108*** (0.029) | −0.106*** (0.029) | −0.104*** (0.029) | −0.101*** (0.029) | −0.101*** (0.029) | −0.105*** (0.029) | −0.069* (0.029) | −0.109*** (0.029) | −0.104*** (0.029) | −0.074* (0.029) |
| Home ownership | | −0.268 (0.186) | −0.270 (0.187) | −0.264 (0.187) | −0.270 (0.187) | −0.249 (0.187) | −0.264 (0.187) | −0.273 (0.187) | −0.282 (0.187) | −0.214 (0.195) | −0.264 (0.188) | −0.272 (0.189) | −0.215 (0.197) |
| Black | | 0.322 (0.180) | 0.330 (0.181) | 0.351 (0.181) | 0.331 (0.184) | 0.344 (0.181) | 0.334 (0.181) | 0.340 (0.181) | 0.328 (0.181) | −0.077 (0.185) | 0.277 (0.183) | 0.403 (0.183) | 0.000 (0.181) |
| Male | | 0.521*** (0.131) | 0.534*** (0.132) | 0.542*** (0.132) | 0.525*** (0.132) | 0.496*** (0.132) | 0.519*** (0.131) | 0.507*** (0.131) | 0.517*** (0.131) | 0.303* (0.138) | 0.572*** (0.133) | 0.497*** (0.133) | 0.342* (0.141) |
| Family disruption | | 0.022 (0.185) | 0.015 (0.185) | 0.015 (0.185) | 0.022 (0.185) | 0.010 (0.185) | 0.029 (0.185) | 0.012 (0.185) | 0.017 (0.185) | −0.076 (0.194) | −0.007 (0.187) | −0.070 (0.188) | −0.150 (0.197) |
| Number of siblings | | 0.063 (0.055) | 0.061 (0.055) | 0.062 (0.055) | 0.062 (0.055) | 0.069 (0.057) | 0.062 (0.055) | 0.058 (0.055) | 0.065 (0.055) | 0.064 (0.057) | 0.057 (0.055) | 0.059 (0.055) | 0.064 (0.058) |
| Class standing | | −0.151* (0.072) | −0.153* (0.073) | −0.127 (0.073) | −0.152* (0.073) | −0.081 (0.078) | −0.139 (0.075) | −0.151 (0.072) | −0.154* (0.073) | −0.146 (0.076) | −0.134 (0.073) | −0.108 (0.074) | −0.069 (0.082) |
| Number of imputations | | −0.276 (0.175) | −0.282 (0.176) | −0.298 (0.177) | −0.276 (0.175) | −0.264 (0.179) | −0.281 (0.175) | −0.277 (0.176) | −0.276 (0.175) | −0.211 (0.183) | −0.243 (0.173) | −0.274 (0.177) | −0.207 (0.184) |

| | (1) | (2) | (3) | (4) | (5) | (6) | (7) | (8) | (9) | (10) | (11) |
|---|---|---|---|---|---|---|---|---|---|---|---|
| Parental control | | | 0.037 (0.021) | | | | | | | | |
| Parental attachment | | | | −0.043** (0.016) | | | | | | | −0.024 (0.017) |
| Parent knows child's friends | | | | | 0.017 (0.069) | | | | | | |
| School attachment | | | | | | −0.076* (0.032) | | | | | −0.032 (0.035) |
| Educational aspirations | | | | | | | −0.047 (0.068) | | | | |
| Number of friends | | | | | | | | 0.008 (0.460) | | | |
| Loneliness | | | | | | | | | −0.101 (0.085) | | |
| Peers' sexual behavior | | | | | | | | | | −0.338*** (0.038) | −0.308*** (0.039) |
| Stress | | | | | | | | | | | 0.086* (0.042) |
| Delinquent behavior index | | | | | | | | | | | 0.039* (0.016) |
| Constant | −0.708*** | 1.130** | 1.157* | 1.060* | 1.078* | 0.916* | 1.183** | 0.994* | 1.379* | 0.863 | 0.755 |
| Degrees of freedom | 1 | 10 | 11 | 11 | 11 | 11 | 11 | 11 | 11 | 11 | 15 |
| Model $\chi^2$ | 10.724 | 90.584 | 93.691 | 98.034 | 90.643 | 96.139 | 91.071 | 93.166 | 91.979 | 175.278 | 194.6 |

Wait, Model χ² values: 10.724, 90.584, 93.691, 98.034, 90.643, 96.139, 91.071, 93.166, 91.979, 175.278, 104.676, 115.446, 194.6

*Note*: Entries are logistic regression coefficients with standard errors in parentheses.
*$p<0.05$;
**$p<0.01$;
***$p<0.001$.

non-significance. As indicated above, most of this mediation is accomplished by the index of peers' sexual behavior and, to a lesser extent, the delinquent behavior index. The effects of both variables are sizable. For example, net of the effects of the other predictors, a one standard deviation difference in the index of peers' sexual behavior translates into an almost 50% reduction in the odds of having experienced first sexual intercourse prior to age 17 ($0.54 = e^{(-0.308)(2.02)}$). And, a one standard deviation difference in the delinquent behavior index translates to a 20% increase in the odds of having first sex by this age ($1.20 = e^{(0.039)(4.60)}$).

Table 3 presents the results from a parallel series of logistic regression models that evaluate the impact of the explanatory and control variables on the likelihood that a respondent ever dropped out of high school. Model 1 shows the significantly positive bivariate effect of number of residential moves, and Model 2 adds the control variables. Of the controls, parents' education, home ownership, and the respondent's class standing are all significantly and negatively associated with the risk of dropping out of school. Controlling for these background characteristics attenuates only slightly the effect of residential mobility on school dropout; the coefficient for number of residential moves decreases from 0.116 in Model 1 to 0.103 in Model 2, and remains statistically significant in the latter model.

Model 2 shows that, even net of the controls, residential mobility exerts a substantial influence on adolescents' risk of dropping out of school. Each residential move increases the odds of dropping out of school by about 11% ($11 = 100(e^{0.103}-1)$). Put another way, these estimates imply that, compared to residentially stable adolescents, adolescents who move four times during childhood (approximately the sample mean) are about 50% more likely to drop out of high school ($51 = 100(e^{(0.103)(4)}-1)$).

Models 3 through 12 of Table 3 add to Model 2 each of the variables that potentially account for the effect of residential mobility on school dropout. Of these mediating factors, school attachment (Model 6), educational aspirations (Model 7), peers' educational performance (Model 10), and self-reported delinquency (Model 12) exert significant net effects on the risk of dropping out of school. The positive coefficient for perceived loneliness (Model 9) is marginally significant ($p < 0.10$, two-tailed test). However, only peers' educational performance (Model 10) explains even a modest amount of the observed impact of residential mobility on school dropout. Controlling for peers' educational performance reduces the impact of number of residential moves by about 17% ($0.17 = (0.103-0.086)/0.103$). After peers' educational performance, the next most important mediator is the index of delinquent behavior (Model 12), but its inclusion in the model diminishes the coefficient for residential mobility by only 4% (0.04 = (0.103−0.099)/0.103). The other hypothesized mechanisms do even less to explain the effect of residential mobility on the risk of dropping out of high school.

The final model of Table 3 (Model 13) includes as predictors the four potential mediators (loneliness, peers' educational performance, stress, and the delinquent behavior index) whose inclusion in Models 3 through 12 attenuated in any amount the observed effect of adolescent residential mobility initially observed in Model 2. Of these four variables, only the coefficient for peers' educational performance is statistically significant when the effects of the other variables are controlled. As in Table 2, this effect is moderate in strength. A one standard deviation in the index of peers' educational behavior translates into approximately a 50% reduction in the odds of dropping out of school ($0.47 = e^{(-0.332)(2.22)}$). The coefficient for the delinquent behavior index is statistically significant at a borderline level ($p<0.10$, two-tailed test). More importantly, including all four possible mediators as predictors of school dropout reduces the coefficient for residential mobility relative to Model 2 by about one-fifth (0.19 = (0.103−0.083)/0.103). As indicated by Model 10, however, virtually all of this mediation can be attributed to the role of peers' educational performance. When compared to the results in Table 2, these findings demonstrate that the mechanisms hypothesized to explain the detrimental impact of residential mobility on adolescent behavior do a better job of accounting for the effect of mobility on the timing of first sexual intercourse than on the probability of dropping out of school.

## ADDITIONAL ANALYSES

To explore further the relationships between adolescent residential mobility and the timing of first intercourse and school dropout, we performed several additional analyses with these data. Two are worth mentioning. First, we estimated the models separately for females and males. Broadly speaking, because females tend to attach greater importance to their friendship relationships and to derive more emotional support from these relationships (Aukett, Ritchie, & Mill, 1988), relational problems or the loss of relationships may be more disruptive for females than for males. Because residential and school mobility often means the elimination or reduction of close friendship ties, females who experience mobility may be at a more severe disadvantage than male adolescents experiencing mobility. If this is the case, then residential and school mobility may be more problematic and lead to

*Table 3.* Logistic Regression Analysis of the Likelihood of Dropping Out of High School: National Survey of Children ($N = 1,105$).

| Variables | 1 | 2 | 3 | 4 | 5 | 6 | 7 | 8 | 9 | 10 | 11 | 12 | 13 |
|---|---|---|---|---|---|---|---|---|---|---|---|---|---|
| Number of residential moves | 0.112*** (0.019) | 0.103*** (0.021) | 0.103*** (0.021) | 0.103*** (0.021) | 0.104*** (0.021) | 0.103*** (0.022) | 0.104*** (0.021) | 0.103*** (0.021) | 0.101*** (0.021) | 0.086*** (0.023) | 0.102*** (0.021) | 0.099*** (0.022) | 0.083*** (0.023) |
| Family income | | 0.028 (0.070) | 0.027 (0.070) | 0.028 (0.070) | 0.023 (0.070) | −0.007 (0.071) | 0.039 (0.070) | 0.028 (0.070) | 0.031 (0.070) | 0.055 (0.070) | 0.025 (0.070) | 0.011 (0.070) | 0.043 (0.071) |
| Parental education | | −0.179*** (0.040) | −0.180*** (0.040) | −0.179*** (0.040) | −0.183*** (0.040) | −0.180*** (0.041) | −0.142*** (0.042) | −0.178*** (0.040) | −0.182*** (0.040) | −0.127** (0.043) | −0.183*** (0.040) | −0.178*** (0.040) | −0.133*** (0.043) |
| Home ownership | | −0.556* (0.236) | −0.555* (0.236) | −0.556* (0.236) | −0.565* (0.236) | −0.514* (0.239) | −0.530* (0.238) | −0.556* (0.236) | −0.534* (0.235) | −0.417 (0.246) | −0.559* (0.236) | −0.561* (0.237) | −0.421 (0.247) |
| Black | | −0.157 (0.259) | −0.151 (0.260) | −0.157 (0.260) | −0.108 (0.263) | −0.087 (0.260) | −0.039 (0.263) | −0.151 (0.260) | −0.183 (0.261) | −0.183 (0.267) | −0.188 (0.261) | −0.081 (0.262) | −0.165 (0.270) |
| Male | | 0.152 (0.190) | 0.153 (0.190) | 0.151 (0.190) | 0.176 (0.191) | 0.094 (0.192) | 0.109 (0.192) | 0.148 (0.190) | 0.171 (0.190) | −0.058 (0.200) | 0.178 (0.191) | 0.130 (0.191) | −0.041 (0.202) |
| Family disruption | | 0.294 (0.249) | 0.291 (0.249) | 0.294 (0.249) | 0.291 (0.249) | 0.257 (0.252) | 0.340 (0.253) | 0.290 (0.249) | 0.312 (0.249) | 0.375 (0.256) | 0.272 (0.249) | 0.209 (0.251) | 0.317 (0.259) |
| Number of siblings | | 0.061 (0.077) | 0.061 (0.077) | 0.061 (0.077) | 0.058 (0.077) | 0.085 (0.078) | 0.063 (0.078) | 0.060 (0.077) | 0.054 (0.077) | 0.074 (0.079) | 0.058 (0.077) | 0.059 (0.077) | 0.069 (0.080) |
| Class standing | | −0.418*** (0.104) | −0.419*** (0.104) | −0.419*** (0.105) | −0.425*** (0.104) | −0.246* (0.111) | −0.342** (0.107) | −0.418*** (0.104) | −0.415*** (0.104) | −0.255* (0.106) | −0.408*** (0.104) | −0.377*** (0.104) | −0.238* (0.106) |
| Number of imputations | | 0.184 (0.204) | 0.182 (0.204) | 0.184 (0.204) | 0.180 (0.206) | 0.228 (0.204) | 0.147 (0.202) | 0.184 (0.204) | 0.188 (0.205) | 0.200 (0.202) | 0.206 (0.203) | 0.196 (0.204) | 0.208 (0.203) |
| Parental control | | | 0.011 (0.029) | | | | | | | | | | |
| Parental attachment | | | | 0.001 (0.023) | | | | | | | | | |

| | | | | | | | | | |
|---|---|---|---|---|---|---|---|---|---|
| Parent knows child's friends | | | | 0.094 (0.095) | | | | | |
| School attachment | | | | | −0.178*** (0.044) | | | | |
| Educational aspirations | | | | | | −0.364*** (0.094) | | | |
| Number of friends | | | | | | | 0.002 (0.007) | | |
| Loneliness | | | | | | | | 0.223 (0.117) | |
| Peers' educational performance | | | | | | | | | −0.351*** (0.047) |
| Stress | | | | | | | | | |
| Delinquent behavior index | | | | | | | | | |
| Constant | −2.350 | 1.338* | 1.349* | 1.340* | 1.056 | 0.799 | 1.753 | 1.302* | 0.795 |
| Degrees of freedom | 1 | 10 | 11 | 11 | 11 | 11 | 11 | 11 | 11 |
| Model $\chi^2$ | 35.088 | 110.379 | 110.509 | 110.381 | 111.368 | 127.002 | 125.565 | 110.462 | 114.000 |

| | | | |
|---|---|---|---|
| | | 0.126 (0.125) | |
| | | | −0.332*** (0.048) |
| | 0.085 (0.054) | | 0.021 (0.058) |
| | | 0.052** (0.018) | 0.034 (0.018) |
| | 1.371* | 1.278* | −0.398 |
| | 11 | 11 | 14 |
| | 112.815 | 118.760 | 175.468 |
| 170.662 | | | |
| −0.179 | | | |

*Note*: Entries are logistic regression coefficients with standard errors in parentheses.
*$p<0.05$;
**$p<0.01$;
***$p<0.001$.

greater negative behavioral outcomes for female than male adolescents. We might also expect a larger mediation of this effect by peer relationships for females than for males. However, although we did observe slightly stronger effects of mobility on the timing of first intercourse among females than among males, this difference was not statistically significant. Moreover, the effect of residential mobility on school dropout was actually slightly stronger for males than for females (though again, a non-significant difference), and for both outcomes the effects of the mediating variables were generally similar for the two sexes. Nonetheless, the possibility that there are important gender differences in either the effect or residential mobility or in the mechanisms that transmit those effects may be a profitable area for future study.

Second, we explored an alternative operationalization of residential mobility. By measuring residential mobility as the number of moves made prior to the wave 3 interview, it is possible that some of the association we observe may be due to the effect of early intercourse or school dropout on subsequent residential mobility. Unfortunately, the NSC does not contain exact dates for residential moves, so it is not possible to determine the relative timing of residential moves, first sexual intercourse, and school dropout with absolute certainty. As a check on possible biases, we reestimated the models measuring residential mobility as the number of moves made prior to the wave 2 interview. Because very few respondents had experienced first intercourse or dropped out of school prior to the wave 2 interview, this strategy largely ensures the proper temporal ordering of the key variables. This is likely to be a conservative strategy, because those residential moves occurring closest in time to the outcome behaviors (first intercourse and school dropout) are likely to have stronger effects than moves in early childhood, and these moves will not be counted in the measure of mobility only through wave 2. However, the results from these analyses were generally similar to those reported above. Thus, it does not appear that our findings are reflecting an influence of intercourse timing or school dropout on the frequency of subsequent adolescent residential mobility.

## DISCUSSION AND CONCLUSION

Although several recent studies have observed noteworthy effects of frequent residential mobility on potentially problematic adolescent behaviors, the mechanisms through which these effects operate have gone largely unexplored. This analysis of longitudinal data from the NSC suggests that the sexual behavior and educational performance of peers may be key mechanisms linking frequent residential mobility to adolescents' timing of first sexual intercourse and the risk of dropping out of school. We find that about one-third of the observed effect of residential mobility on the initiation of intercourse, and about one-fifth of its effect on school dropout, can be explained by the sexual and educational behaviors of peers. Thus, part – though by no means all – of the reason why frequent residential mobility is associated with a younger age at sexual initiation and with dropping out of school is that mobile youth are more likely than their residentially stable counterparts to have friends whose own behaviors and attitudes discourage delayed intercourse and higher levels of educational attainment.

Despite their centrality to theories linking residential mobility to adolescent behavior, we find little evidence that youth's relations with their parents or schools, parents' knowledge of children's friendship cliques, adolescents' actual or desired number of friends, or psychosocial stress can explain the impact of frequent mobility on the timing of sexual initiation or school discontinuation. Several of these variables are significantly associated with residential mobility, age at first intercourse, and/or school dropout, and some of the effects of the predetermined background characteristics appear to operate through these mediators. For example, the impact of students' class standing on the timing of first intercourse and the risk of school dropout occurs partly because low-performing students are less attached to their schools. Accordingly, intervention strategies that encourage greater school attachment among low-performing students might help to dampen performance-related differences in early sexual activity and school discontinuation. Yet, these characteristics of parent–child and child–school relationships are generally unable to account for the impact of residential mobility on early sexual activity and school dropout.

Our findings are consistent with extant research on the general importance of peer networks for shaping adolescent problem behaviors (Matsueda, 1982; Kandel & Davies, 1991; Thornberry, Lizotte, Krohn, Farnworth, & Jang, 1994; Akers, 1985; Warr, 2002) and they reaffirm the relevance of peers for explaining the impact of residential mobility on adolescent behavior (Humke & Schaefer, 1995). However, in contrast to some theoretical accounts, it is not the paucity of close friends, or even the desire for more friends, that explains the effect of mobility on the timing of first intercourse and the risk of dropping out of school. Rather, the *composition* of peer networks, and in particular, the greater acceptance of early sexual activity and weak educational performance among the friends of highly mobile adolescents that – of the mechanisms considered here – is most responsible for transmitting the effects of mobility. Perhaps friendship cliques predisposed toward these non-normative behaviors are more accepting of newcomers (i.e., residentially mobile adolescents) than are peer groups whose members delay sexual initiation and value educational success. Students' reputational status in the school hierarchy is often based on being known by other students (Eder, 1985), which is likely to place mobile students at a disadvantage. Social groups more accepting of early sexual activity and weak educational performance are also probably lower overall in social status (Eckert, 1989). Mobile students' attraction to, or acceptance into, such networks thus might reflect considerable similarity in their relative positions in the school status hierarchy. Once immersed in such networks, mobile adolescents appear to adopt the sexual and educational practices of their newfound peers. In colloquial terms, "new kids in town" may find it harder to join the ranks of the most popular students, among whom problematic behaviors are at least moderately devalued, than to enter the networks of "burn-outs" (Eckert, 1989) and "headbangers" (Kinney, 1999), among whom such behaviors are tolerated, if not outwardly encouraged.

Admittedly, none of the potentially intervening processes that we are able to measure can explain more than a fraction of the observed impact of residential mobility on adolescent sexual initiation or school dropout. Future research in this area might attempt to explore other possible mechanisms linking residential mobility to these youth outcomes. Richer measures of social capital, including connections between adolescents and their schools, between parents and schools, and between parents and other parents, might prove useful in this regard. The very rich (and more recent) data on adolescents' friendships contained in the National Longitudinal Study of Adolescent Health (or *Add Health*) might prove particularly useful in determining how youths' peer networks mediate the impact of geographic mobility and school transitions (Haynie & South, 2002). Future research might also profit by distinguishing long- from short-distance moves, by distinguishing residential moves from school changes (e.g., Pribesh & Downey, 1999), by examining the cumulative impact of mobility (Kerbow, 1996), and by exploring how long the effects of a residential move last.[7] It is also possible that the effects of residential mobility – and the processes that transmit those effects – differ by race, ethnicity, or gender. Finally, the long-term impacts of childhood residential mobility warrant greater attention. Indeed, recent research suggests that the effects of childhood residential mobility are not transitory, but rather extend through the young adult years (Haveman et al., 1991; Myers, 2000) and even middle age (Bures, 2003). A comprehensive assessment of the impact of residential mobility on adolescent behavior thus awaits further research.

## NOTES

1. In contrast, network density among children's parents does not appear to enhance children's academic achievement (Morgan & Sorenson, 1999).

2. Since the collection of the NSC, rates of both teenage sexual activity (Grunbaum et al., 2002) and school dropout (U.S. Department of Education, 2000) have tended to decline, as have rates of residential mobility (Fischer, 2002).

3. Residential moves are, of course, not synonymous with school moves since either type of move can occur without the other. Unfortunately, because the NSC does not contain data on the number of school changes experienced by the respondents, it is not possible to examine the possible impact of school mobility on the risk of early intercourse or school dropout. Pribesh and Downey (1999) find that both residential and school mobility have independent effects on school performance.

4. We recognize that this and some of the subsequent scales exhibit reliabilities that are, at best, marginally acceptable. Accordingly, we also estimated models that included the individual scale items as potentially mediating variables. The results of these analyses were virtually identical to those that employ the scales.

5. With a two-tailed $p$-value of 0.054, the correlation between number of residential moves and parental control just barely fails to attain statistical significance.

6. Ideally, we would perform a test of the statistical significance of the difference between the two partial regression coefficients. Unfortunately, there exists no universally accepted procedure for making this comparison (Allison, 1995; Clogg, Petkova, & Haritou, 1995).

7. Unfortunately, the NSC does not contain detailed information on the distance of residential moves. However, Tucker et al., (1998) suggest that short-distance moves may be as disruptive as long-distance moves for adolescent school life and subsequent educational attainment.

## ACKNOWLEDGMENTS

This research was supported by grants to the first author from the National Institute of Child Health and Human Development (RO1 HD35560) and the National Science Foundation (SBR-9729797), a grant to the third author from U.S. Department of Justice (97IJCX0028), and grants to the University at Albany Center for Social and Demographic Analysis from NICHD (P30 HD32041) and NSF (SBR-9512290). We thank David Kinney, Nancy Tuma, and anonymous reviewers for helpful comments on an earlier draft.

## REFERENCES

Adler, P. A., & Adler, P. (1998). *Peer power: Preadolescent culture and identity*. New Brunswick, NJ: Rutgers University Press.

Akers, R. L. (1985). *Deviant behavior: A social learning approach*. Belmont, CA: Wadsworth.
Allison, P. D. (1995). The impact of random predictors on comparisons of coefficients between models: Comment on Clogg, Petkova, and Haritou. *American Journal of Sociology, 100*, 1294–1305.
Astone, N. M., & McLanahan, S. S. (1994). Family structure, residential mobility, and school dropout: A research note. *Demography, 31*, 575–584.
Aukett, R., Ritchie, J., & Mill, K. (1988). Gender differences in friendship patterns. *Sex Roles, 19*, 57–66.
Baumer, E. P., & South, S. J. (2001). Community effects on youth sexual activity. *Journal of Marriage and Family, 63*, 540–554.
Bures, R. (2003). Childhood residential stability and health at midlife. *American Journal of Public Health, 93*, 1144–1148.
Clogg, C. C., Petkova, E., & Haritou, A. (1995). Statistical methods for comparing regression coefficients between models. *American Journal of Sociology, 100*, 1261–1293.
Cohen, J., & Cohen, P. (1983). *Applied multiple regression/correlation analysis for the behavioral sciences*. Hillsdale, NJ: Erlbaum.
Coleman, J. S. (1988). Social capital in the creation of human capital. *American Journal of Sociology, 94*(Suppl.), S95–S120.
Coleman, J. S. (1990). *Foundations of social theory*. Cambridge, MA: Harvard University Press.
Eckert, P. (1989). *Jocks and burnouts: Social categories and identity in the high school*. New York: Teachers College Press.
Eder, D. (1985). The cycle of popularity: Interpersonal relations among female adolescents. *Sociology of Education, 58*, 154–165.
Elliott, D. S., Wilson, W. J., Huizinga, D., Sampson, R. J., Elliott, A., & Ranjkin, B. (1996). The effects of neighborhood disadvantage on adolescent development. *Journal of Research in Crime and Delinquency, 33*, 389–426.
Entwisle, D. R., Alexander, K. L., & Olson, L. S. (1997). *Children, schools, and inequality*. Boulder, CO: Westview Press.
Fenzel, L. M. (1989). Role strain in early adolescence: A model for investigating school transition stress. *Journal of Early Adolescence, 9*, 13–33.
Fischer, C. S. (2002). Ever-more rooted Americans. *City & Community, 1*, 175–193.
Grunbaum, J. A., Kann, L., Kinchen, S. A., Williams, B., Ross, J. G., Lowry, R., & Kolbe, L. (2002). Youth risk behavior surveillance – United States, 2001. *Morbidity and Mortality Weekly Report, 51/SS-5*, 1–68.
Hagan, J., MacMillan, R., & Wheaton, B. (1996). New kid in town: Social capital and the life course effects of family migration on children. *American Sociological Review, 61*, 368–385.
Haveman, R., Wolfe, B. L., & Spaulding, J. (1991). Childhood events and circumstances influencing high school completion. *Demography, 28*, 133–157.
Haynie, D., & South, S. J. (2002). Friendship networks of mobile youth. Paper presented at the annual add health workshop, Bethesda, MD.
Hendershott, A. B. (1989). Residential mobility, social support, and adolescent self-concept. *Adolescence, 24*, 217–232.
Hoffman, J. P., & Johnson, R. A. (1998). A national portrait of family structure and adolescent drug use. *Journal of Marriage and the Family, 60*, 633–645.
Humke, C., & Schaefer, C. (1995). Relocation: A review of the effects of residential mobility on children and adolescents. *Psychology: A Journal of Human Behavior, 32*, 16–24.

Ingersoll, G. M., Scamman, J. P., & Eckerling, W. D. (1989). Geographic mobility and student achievement in an urban setting. *Educational Evaluation and Policy Analysis, 11*, 143–149.

Jencks, C., Smith, M., Acland, H., Bane, M. J., Cohen, D., Gintis, H., Heyns, B., & Michelson, S. (1972). *Inequality: A reassessment of the effect off family and schooling in America.* New York: Harper & Row.

Kandel, D. B., & Davies, M. (1991). Friendship networks, intimacy, and illicit drug use in young adulthood: A comparison of two competing theories. *Criminology, 29*, 441–469.

Kerbow, D. (1996). Patterns of urban student mobility and local school reform. *Journal of Education for Students Placed at Risk, 1*, 147–169.

Kinney, D. A. (1999). From "headbangers" to "hippies:" Delineating adolescents' active attempts to form an alternative peer culture. In: J. McLellan & M. J. Pugh (Eds), *The role of peer group stability and change in adolescent social identity, new directions for child and adolescent development,*, (Vol. 84, pp. 21–36). San Francisco, CA: Jossey-Bass.

Long, L. (1988). *Migration and residential mobility in the United States.* New York: Russell Sage Foundation.

Matsueda, R. L. (1982). Testing control theory and differential association. *American Sociological Review, 47*, 489–504.

McLanahan, S., & Sandefur, G. (1994). *Growing up with a single parent: What hurts, what helps.* Cambridge, MA: Harvard University Press.

Moore, K. A., & Glei, D. (1995). Taking the plunge: An examination of positive youth development. *Journal of Adolescent Research, 10*, 15–40.

Morgan, S. L., & Sorenson, A. B. (1999). Parental networks, social closure, and mathematics learning: A test of Coleman's social capital explanation of school effects. *American Sociological Review, 64*, 661–681.

Myers, S. M. (1999). Childhood migration and social integration in adulthood. *Journal of Marriage and the Family, 61*, 774–789.

Myers, S. M. (2000). Moving into adulthood: Family residential mobility and first-union transitions. *Social Science Quarterly, 81*, 782–797.

National Research Council. (1987). *Risking the future: Adolescent sexuality, pregnancy, and childbearing.* Washington, DC: National Academy Press.

Pittman, J. F., & Bowen, G. L. (1994). Adolescents on the move: Adjustments to family relocation. *Youth & Society, 26*, 69–91.

Portes, A. (1998). Social capital: Its origins and applications in modern sociology. *Annual Review of Sociology, 24*, 1–24.

Pribesh, S., & Downey, D. B. (1999). Why are residential and school moves associated with poor school performance? *Demography, 36*, 521–534.

Raviv, A., Keinan, G., Abazon, Y., & Raviv, A. (1990). Moving as a stressful life event for adolescents. *Journal of Community Psychology, 18*, 130–140.

Rumberger, R. W. (1995). Dropping out of middle school: A multilevel analysis of students and schools. *American Educational Research Journal, 32*, 583–625.

Rumberger, R. W., & Lawson, K. A. (1998). Student mobility and the increased risk of high school dropout. *American Journal of Education, 107*, 1–35.

Sampson, R. J. (1997). Collective regulation of adolescent misbehavior: Validation results from eighty Chicago neighborhoods. *Journal of Adolescent Research, 12*, 227–244.

Sampson, R. J., & Groves, W. B. (1989). Community structure and crime: Testing social-disorganization theory. *American Journal of Sociology, 94*, 774–802.

South, S. J., & Baumer, E. P. (2000). Deciphering community and race effects on adolescent premarital childbearing. *Social Forces, 78*, 1379–1408.
South, S. J., Crowder, K. D., & Trent, K. (1998). Children's residential mobility and neighborhood environment following parental divorce and remarriage. *Social Forces, 77*, 667–693.
Stack, S. (1994). The effect of geographic mobility on premarital sex. *Journal of Marriage and the Family, 56*, 204–208.
Sucoff, C. A., & Upchurch, D. M. (1998). Neighborhood context and the risk of childbearing among metropolitan-area black adolescents. *American Sociological Review, 63*, 571–585.
Swanson, C. B., & Schneider, B. (1999). Students on the move: Residential and educational mobility in America's schools. *Sociology of Education, 72*, 54–67.
Teachman, J. D., Paasch, K., & Carver, K. (1996). Social capital and dropping out of school early. *Journal of Marriage and the Family, 58*, 773–783.
Thornberry, T. P., Lizotte, A. J., Krohn, M. D., Farnworth, M., & Jang, S. J. (1994). Delinquent peers, beliefs, and delinquent behavior: A longitudinal test of interactional theory. *Criminology, 32*, 47–84.
Tucker, C. J., Marx, J., & Long, L. (1998). 'Moving on': Residential mobility and children's school lives. *Sociology of Education, 71*, 111–129.
U.S. Department of Education. (2000). *Dropout rates in the United States: 1999*. Washington, DC: National Center for Health Statistics.
Vernberg, E. M. (1990). Experiences with peers following relocation during early adolescence. *American Journal of Orthopsychiatry, 60*, 466–472.
Vernberg, E. M., Abwender, D. A., Ewell, K. K., & Beery, S. H. (1992). Social anxiety and peer relationships in early adolescence: A prospective analysis. *Journal of Clinical Child Psychology, 21*, 189–196.
Warr, M. (2002). *Companions in crime: The social aspects of criminal conduct*. Cambridge: Cambridge University Press.
Wood, D., Halfon, N., Scarlata, D., Newacheck, P., & Nessim, S. (1993). Impact of family relocation on children's growth, development, school function, and behavior. *Journal of the American Medical Association, 270*, 1334–1338.
Zill, N., Furstenberg, F. F. Jr., Peterson, J., & Moore, K. (1990). *National survey of children: Wave I, 1976, Wave II, 1981, Wave III, 1987* [Computer File]. Washington, DC: Child Trends, Inc., 1988 [producer]. Inter-university consortium for political and social research, 1990 [distributor].

# APPENDIX

A brief description and summary statistics used in our analysis are outlined in Table A1.

*Table A1.* Description and Source of Variables Used in Analysis: National Survey of Children.

| | Description | Wave | Mean | Standard Deviation |
|---|---|---|---|---|
| *Dependent variables* | | | | |
| Initiation of sexual activity | Whether R had first sexual intercourse age 16 or younger (1 = yes) | 3 | 0.38 | 0.48 |
| High school dropout | Whether R dropped out of high school for more than 1 month (1 = yes) | 3 | 0.14 | 0.34 |
| *Independent variables* | | | | |
| Number of residential moves | R's report of the number of residential moves through wave 3 | 1, 2, 3 | 3.75 | 3.84 |
| Family income | Parent's report of family income on an 8-point scale (1 = less than $5,000, 8 = $50,000 or more) | 2 | 4.50 | 1.93 |
| Parental education | Years of schooling reported by R's more educated parent | 2 | 13.03 | 2.89 |
| Home ownership | Whether R's parents own home (1 = yes) | 2 | 0.81 | 0.39 |
| Black | Whether R is black (1 = yes) | 1 | 0.20 | 0.40 |
| Male | Whether R is male (1 = yes) | 1 | 0.49 | 0.50 |
| Family disruption | Whether R lives without both biological parents (1 = yes) | 2 | 0.25 | 0.43 |
| Number of siblings | R's number of siblings residing in same household | 2 | 1.78 | 1.24 |

Table A1. (Continued)

| | Description | Wave | Mean | Standard Deviation |
|---|---|---|---|---|
| Class standing | R's report of class standing on a 5-point scale (1 = near bottom of class, 5 = one of the best students in class) | 2 | 3.43 | 0.91 |
| Number of imputations | Number of independent variables for which value is imputed from valid mean or mode | N/A | 0.12 | 0.40 |
| Parental control | Five item standardized scale comprised of R's reports of how much it is like R's mother and father to want to know R's whereabouts and activities, and whether family has rules regarding keeping parents informed about R's whereabouts, doing homework, and dating and going to parties ($\alpha = 0.60$) | 2 | 0.00 | 3.12 |
| Parental attachment | Seven item standardized scale comprised of R's reports of how often R argues with parents, does enjoyable things with parents, whether parents spend enough time with R, how much affection parents give R, how close R is to parents, how much R wants to be like parents, and how much parents love and are interested in R ($\alpha = 0.68$) | 2 | 0.00 | 4.13 |
| Parent knows child's friends | Primary parent's report of the number of R's friends known to parent by sight and by first and last name (1 = none; 2 = only a few; 3 = about half; 4 = most of them; 5 = all of them) | 2 | 3.88 | 1.00 |

| | | | | |
|---|---|---|---|---|
| School attachment | Three item standardized scale comprised of R's report of how much R likes school, interest in schoolwork, and satisfaction with schoolwork ($\alpha = 0.58$) | 2 | 0.00 | 2.21 |
| Educational aspirations | R's report of what R would like to do about school (1 = quit school as soon as possible; 2 = finish high school; 3 = get some college or other training; 4 = finish college; 5 = take further training after college) | 2 | 3.56 | 1.04 |
| Number of friends | A count of R's close friends | 2 | 12.16 | 12.40 |
| Loneliness | R's response to the question, "Do you feel lonely and wish you had more friends?" (four response categories range from never to often) | 2 | 2.39 | 0.77 |
| Peers' sexual behavior | Three item standardized scale comprised of R's report of the number of R's friends who had become parents by age 16, the number of friends who had had sex by age 16, and a dichotomous variable indicating whether friends encouraged R to have sex during the teen years ($\alpha = 0.43$) | 3 | 0.00 | 2.02 |
| Peers' educational performance | Three item standardized scale comprised of R's report of the number of R's friends who, when R was 16, planned to go to college, received good grades, and had dropped out of school ($\alpha = 0.58$) | 3 | 0.00 | 2.22 |
| Stress | Two item scale comprised of R's report of how often R feels "nervous, tense, or on edge" and how often R feels "unhappy, sad, or depressed" (four response categories range from hardly ever to very often, $\alpha = 0.39$) | 2 | 0.00 | 1.67 |

**Table A1.** (*Continued*)

| Description | Wave | Mean | Standard Deviation |
|---|---|---|---|
| Delinquent behavior index | Eight item standardized scale comprised of R's reports of the frequency during the past year that R hurt someone badly enough to need bandages or a doctor, taken something from a store without paying for it, damaged school property on purpose, gotten drunk, and skipped a day of school without permission; and whether in past 2 weeks R used alcohol, marijuana, or other drugs ($\alpha = 0.71$) | 2 | 0.00 | 4.60 |

# BUILDING DEMOCRACY, PROMOTING TOLERANCE: ADOLESCENT RESPONSIVENESS TO SOCIAL MOVEMENT MESSAGES

Greg Scott and Julie E. Artis

## INTRODUCTION

Social movement scholars conventionally neglect high school students and settings. This elision stems in part from the fallacious assumption that high schools constitute a segment of society traditionally immune to conflict and in equal part from a failure to appreciate the political agency of high school-aged youth. When scholars do concern themselves with youth social movements, they tend to privilege large-scale, epochal protests on college campuses. In this study, however, we document a significant level of "social movement behavior" among actors who rarely see the light of scholarly print: suburban high school students.

The youth featured in this paper participate in social movement activities geared toward advancing a social justice agenda whose eventual accomplishment may subvert their own status interests. Specifically, we explain how and why mostly white, suburban, reasonably affluent adolescents get involved in school-centered efforts to combat the white separatist movement,[1] and how and why others do not. The answer, we find, lies not so much in personal psychology, peer relations, socioeconomic status, or the intergenerational transmission of prejudice through parenting. Rather, we find that one of the key explanatory variables is whether or not youth feel supported by those who control resources: the adults in the school and in the community.

To explain adolescent responsiveness to social movement messages we modify McAdam, McCarthy, and Zald's (1988) notion of a "micro-mobilization context." In essence, we introduce the relational mid-range variable of intergenerational social capital, arguing that an individual student's sympathy for political messages and the presence of like-minded peers, while necessary for mobilization, are by themselves insufficient catalysts. To initiate and develop a school-based social movement, the motivated and peer-supported students must also perceive and make effective use of the social ties that connect them with adults in the school setting and in the surrounding community.

Within this framework, we analyze quantitative data gathered from youth surveys, field observations, and telephone interviews. In effect, the youth who exhibit high levels of tolerance, but low levels of adult support, tend to remain politically inert, whereas those with lower (but still relatively high) levels of tolerance and high levels of adult support tend to engage in more pro-movement behavior, however minor. These data, while preliminary, suggest that three predictors explain student involvement in the anti-white power movement: favorable attitudes toward movement ideologies, perceptions of peer support for movement engagement, and the perceived presence of supportive adults with access to school- and community-based resources necessary for sustaining a social movement organization.

Our analysis is based on preliminary data and builds toward the development of testable theory regarding variation within social networks and contexts through which social movement participation is catalyzed. Our findings suggest the need to revise and test theory of how action networks are hierarchically arranged and how movement actors use these networks in receiving and acting on movement messages.

## SOCIAL MOVEMENTS AND YOUTH: WHERE ARE THE ADOLESCENTS?

The preponderance of empirical research on youth participation in social movements focuses on protest-type activities among college-aged students (e.g., McAdam, 1988; Park, 1993; Polletta, 1998; Soule, 1997; Van Dyke, 1998; Yang, 2000). Researchers in this tradition tend to concern themselves with such epic phenomena as the civil rights movement, the anti-war movement, and the women's movement of the 1960s and 1970s (McAdam, 1988; Paulsen, 1991; Sherkat & Blocker, 1994; Van Dyke, 1998). These studies conventionally posit university characteristics – socioeconomic, cultural, and/or historical – as key predictors of student social movement participation. Other studies account for the influence of individual-level student characteristics, such as social class, religious beliefs, race, and gender (Paulsen, 1991; Sherkat & Blocker, 1994).

A handful of projects, however, have taken up the study of less academically scrutinized events, including shantytowns of the 1980s (Soule, 1997), the 1989 Chinese student movement (Yang, 2000), student protest participation and civic engagement in general (Park, 1993), and urban renewal protests waged by economically and culturally disenfranchised street youth (Lees, 2003). But these studies, and parallel studies of high school student involvement in political action, construe youth not as activists, but instead as members of civic society in general or student organizations in specific (Youniss, McLellan, & Mazer, 2001). Theoretically speaking, these studies classify student civic engagement as a function of identification with a particular subculture or peer groups (Irwin, 1999; Youniss et al., 2001). Furthermore, social movement scholarship implies that youth and adults occupy completely separate, mutually exclusive orbits that more often than not attempt to derail each other.

*Adults and Youth Together, but Mostly Apart*

How adults and youth connect (or do not connect) with each other in the context of movement activities remains, for the most part, a social science mystery. In general, studies seem to agree that youth and adults possess distinct worldviews. Most of the seminal studies of 1960s youth movements, for instance, cast young people as alienated, marginalized, disconnected, independent, and/or ostracized from adults (see Oppenheimer, 1968; Polletta, 1998; Van Dyke, 1998). An even more extreme – though not entirely unique – view manifests in Orcutt and Fendrich's (1980) research wherein adult–youth relationships are defined primarily by the youths' fear that adults will punish them. In another line of research that combines space and culture, Katz (1998) argues that youth-controlled, adult-free ecologies appear to be on the wane, a development that may spell the eventual demise of youth-directed culture. From Katz's perspective, adults interfere with youth decision-making. Below we illustrate the contrary: In some instances, adult support may be a necessary ingredient for the creation of a sustainable, youth-driven social movement.

Other studies present a more benign but still bifurcated view of the adult–youth nexus. Sociologists of education show how schools and families influence youth activism. Studies by Saha (1994) and Van Dyke (1998), for example, demonstrate how youth learn political activism from adults and how their learning in turn fosters the genesis and maturation of an "active political culture." However, youth in most of these studies seem to possess little, if any, human agency (e.g., Paulsen, 1991; Granvold & Saleebey, 1980). Our study offers a contrast by emphasizing a more robust conception of youth agency, one that at least allows for the possibility that youth construct themselves as social movement actors through the "interplay between cultural constraints and artful agency" (Broad, 2002, p. 317).

Several recent studies have documented social movement activity that focuses on exploited, abused, neglected, marginalized, or otherwise disadvantaged youth/children (e.g., Broad, 2002; Dewees & Klees, 1995; Minow & Weissbourd, 1993; Rodgers, 2003). For example, Rodgers (2003) examines children (generally pre- or peri-adolescent) as social movement participants. In her study the activities of children as social movement actors fall into one or more of three categories: (1) as symbolic participants in that they appear as images to induce sympathy and outrage in prospective adult participants; (2) as participants by "default" through merely physical proximity to their adult care providers who participate actively in a movement; and (3) as active, willful, and knowing participants. This latter category of youth participants is the most relevant to our study. Rodgers notes, not incidentally, that a central difficulty children face is gaining support from adults who may not be sympathetic to the movement's ideology.

In this study, we find that perceived support from adults is relatively widespread and that it is positively correlated with political action. Even more critical, the absence of perceived support will quash the political ambitions of a sufficiently motivated youth. In other words, the relationships between adults and youth matter, and they are not always hostile. High school students' lives unfold in a maze of bureaucratic comings and goings. Because their teachers and school administrators control virtually every available material and symbolic resource for the promotion of social movement activity, they must learn to manipulate the organizational and bureaucratic environment to their individual and collective advantage. In the case at hand, student involvement in a political movement depends in great part on how well-connected to and supported by adults they are. "Responsiveness" to a social movement message has as much to do with relationships as with individual ideological sympathy.

## YOUTH RESPONSIVENESS TO SOCIAL MOVEMENT MESSAGES

Social movements arise from some sort of "stirring up." The success of any given social movement's initial overtures to prospective actors will depend upon the "responsiveness" of individual humans to these overtures. In general, the research literature on social movements that has accumulated over the past half-century implies a relatively linear model wherein a social movement sends some kind of message out to the environment and certain individuals predisposed favorably toward the message receive it and act on it. When all is said and done, what matters most in these models is the individual's sympathy for the message.

As Jasper and Poulsen (1995, p. 494) point out, "Recruitment of new members is probably the most studied aspect of social movements." Among studies that concentrate on what propels social movement actors to take action, three major analytical foci prevail – cognitive/emotional responses (e.g., Goodwin, 1997; Goodwin, Jasper, & Polletta, 2000; Jasper, 1998; Polletta, 1998; Yang, 2000), social background predictors (e.g., Paulsen, 1991) and social networks (see Diani & McAdam, 2003 for a collection of studies). Studies generally adopt one of these three perspectives. The present study leans more toward the social networks approach.

These social network studies usually focus on interorganizational connections (e.g., Soule, 1997) and/or peer-to-peer influences on civic engagement and political action (e.g., Youniss et al., 2001). Other studies acknowledge the crucial role that networks play in social movement activity, but then underscore the primacy of cognitive cultural messages (Jasper & Poulsen, 1995). Either way, these endeavors treat networks mechanistically, as mere conduit and thus present a one-dimensional view of the connections among social movement actors. In particular, they often fail to capture the dynamics of stratification within networks and thus fail to recognize that social movement networks themselves are political concerns fraught with power inequities and conflict over scarce resources. In the research on student political action, it is rare to find a study that captures the differential distribution of resources within the action networks. Instead, this work concentrates on the peer-to-peer contacts out of which political action grows and matures. But in a high school, peer-to-peer contacts may be a necessary but insufficient causal condition when someone else – i.e., the adult authority structure – controls the resources necessary for action to occur. Below we document the centrality of youth–adult connections in the promulgation of student political activity and, moreover, show that network stratification may work in favor of student political action as much as against it.

## DEVELOPING INTEGRATED THEORY: YOUTH–ADULT CONNECTIONS IN MICRO-CONTEXTS

Several "schools" of social movement scholarship – each with its own assumptions, theoretical devices, methods, and analytical darlings – now animate the discipline of sociology. The conceptual framework in which we conduct the present analysis is a modification of McAdam et al.'s (1988) concept of the "micro-mobilization context." This perspective emphasizes how macro and micro contexts come together in the production of social movements and their constituent organizations. McAdam et al.'s (1988) work integrates social psychological models (e.g., relative deprivation theory) and structural-institutional models (e.g., resource mobilization theory) of social movement activity.[2]

The micro-mobilization context refers to "any small group setting in which processes of collective attribution are combined with rudimentary forms of organization to produce mobilization for collective action" (McAdam et al., 1988, p. 709). So, micro-mobilization contexts are organizational units in which insurgency is incited and cultivated. These social contexts are crucial in the processes of forming, defining, maintaining, and mobilizing a social movement. In these environments, the main activity is the articulation and aggregation of interests as they get transmitted into the broader political system. They serve as the bridge that connects individuals with personal concerns to collectivities hoping to engage social change (Abrahams, 1996; McAdam, 1982; McAdam et al., 1988; Offe, 1985; Scott, 1990).

Contexts qualifying for inclusion in this conceptual scheme include church settings, student support groups, campus political and social organizations, trade unions, outreach centers, state welfare offices, informal personal relationship networks, and schools. Micro-mobilization contexts, as dense networks of associations and informal contacts underwritten by ties to viable institutional resources, provide an arena for the "framing" of personal troubles as public issues via the application of a movement ideology.

We modify McAdam's approach by focusing more on the social context of the networks themselves. In the school environment, for instance, one can imagine networks or clusters of students sympathetic to a particular social movement's ideology, but their participation in the movement is stymied because the success of the network's mobilization depends in large measure on how well it mobilizes school-based resources. In school settings, the adults (namely faculty and staff) by and large control organizational resources. This means that networks of sufficiently enlivened youth will succeed only to the extent that they (a) perceive support from adults in the school and (b) effectively capitalize on that support to advance the movement's cause.

A final modification to McAdam's micro-mobilization context draws upon the work of Emirbayer and Goodwin (1996), who view "ties and transactions" as the appropriate unit of analysis in social movement studies. Central to their analysis is the "social-structural level," which includes social networks or "patterns of social relationships that comprise an interpersonal or interorganizational setting of action" (Emirbayer & Goodwin, 1996, p. 367). Circulating through these networks are money, information, affective energy, and other resources for social action. Perhaps more importantly, they build *asymmetry* into their conceptualization of networks: "flows are often 'directional' in content and intensity, with significant implications for actors' differential access to resources," (Emirbayer & Goodwin, 1996, p. 367) as well as disparities in the ability to control both the resources and the constitution of the networks. Their formulations obviously relate to our own assessment of student–teacher–adult network ties in the fomenting, initiating, and/or sustaining of social movement action, even though the current analysis is predicated on the individual student as the unit of analysis. This puts the final piece in place for us: Micro-mobilization networks are themselves political concerns exhibiting a differential capacity for social-change oriented political mobilization. See Fig. 1 for a graphical depiction of our theoretical model.

This model – specifically its focus on youth activism and adult support in a high school setting – is consistent with Fine's (2004) inquiry into the lives of high school debaters. His interactionist perspective holds that "adolescents shape their actions in light of how they are viewed and treated by adults and adult institutions, how they are viewed and treated by their peers, and how they desire to view themselves" (p. 2). Fine emphasizes "the ability

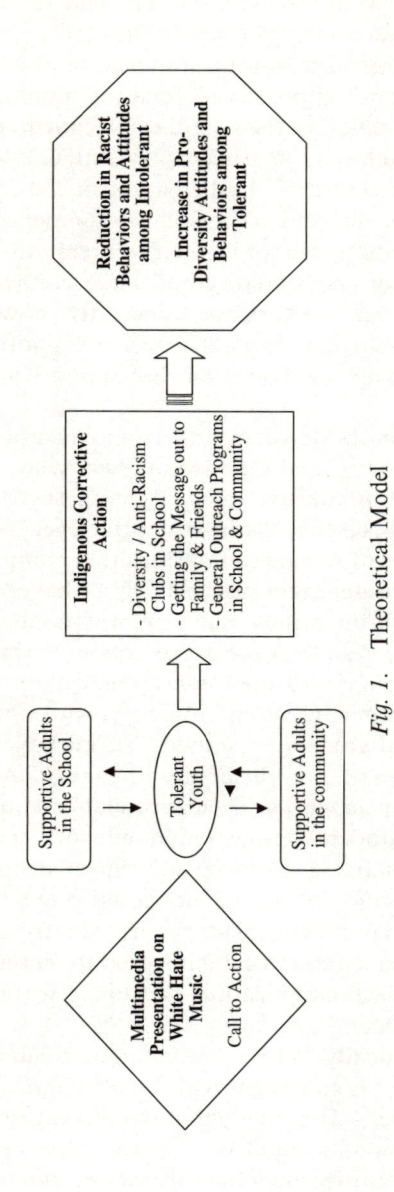

*Fig. 1.* Theoretical Model

of adolescents to justify themselves to adults, to peers, and to themselves" (p. 2). Fine borrows Ann Swidler's (1986, p. 273) notion of the "cultural toolkit" to elucidate how youth develop personal and collective identities using cultural devices, strategies, rhetorics, and logics shaped (if not controlled) by adults in their lives. Fine states succinctly: "The behavioral and identity choices of adolescents are situated amid adult claims to the authority and the moral responsibility to monitor these choices" (Fine, 2004, p. 14).

To summarize, our integrated model makes the following contributions to the field of social movement studies: First, we put adolescents at the center of the analysis as we attempt to understand them as social change agents rather than as passive recipients of authoritative exertion. Second, we acknowledge their situatedness in the school context, where virtually all substantial material and symbolic resources rest under the control of adults. Third, we problematize youth connections with adults without making the a priori judgment that these associations always work against youth involvement in the social movement in question. Fourth, we broaden the orthodox conception of political action beyond high profile protests and instead concentrate on small-scale political action, such as conveying knowledge to friends, family, and adults in the school.

## MOBILIZING CHICAGO-AREA YOUTH AGAINST WHITE SUPREMACY

With this integrated micro-mobilization framework in mind we embarked in the summer of 2002 on a 2-year endeavor to collect survey and telephone interview data from Chicago-area youth who participate in a tolerance-promoting and democracy-building program offered by the Center for New Community (CNC), a non-profit organization located in the Chicago area. Conceived as an evaluation study, the project yields data whose study may answer some of the questions posed above regarding responsiveness to social movement ideology and institutional support of social movement organization (SMO) development. This program, called "Turn It Down" (TID), comprises four distinct but interrelated "interventions" into the lives of high school-age youth in the City of Chicago and its surrounding suburbs.

The interventions comprising TID aspire to minimize hostility and prejudice related to differences of race, ethnicity, religion, gender, and sexual orientation while maximizing tolerance along these same dimensions. They also seek to mobilize students to take "corrective social action" individually and collectively in their own lives, especially in the school and community. Such action may include organizing students against racism in general or purveyors of racist materials in specific, setting up school- and/or community-based organizations (i.e., SMOs) to promote diversity, and convincing the school to sponsor pro-diversity events. More prosaically but no less significantly, the interventions attempt to effect change in how youth relate to each other and to adults both culturally and politically.

The first, and most general, intervention in the TID package is the "educational event," consisting of a single 1-h session in which a CNC staff person delivers a multi-media presentation on white power music to a general assembly of high school students. This event serves as a kind of "hook" or springboard for mobilizing corrective social action among a select group of youth. In the language of the relative deprivation model, CNC staff frame or package white power music as a grievance, attempting to convey to students the idea that hate-breeding groups represent a menace to democratic civil society. The youth targeted by the event are (by necessity and design) those most likely to take action as a result of being exposed to the presentation. Ideologically, CNC believes that the problem of white racism lies within white society and therefore targets for mobilization the white suburban youth who already hold leadership positions in their respective schools.

The educational event intends to inspire the less "at-risk" youth (i.e., the relatively more tolerant youth) to work toward changing their less tolerant, less politically committed, less knowledgeable, and less-well-supported peers. The educational event marks the beginning of what CNC hopes will be a long sequence of social change projects carried out in large part by the youth best-positioned and most likely to take action. From these general assembly populations, CNC recruits highly motivated students to attend a voluntary half-day or whole-day peer leadership-training institute, the second prong of the TID intervention. The institute offers interactive training sessions that provide students with the skills and knowledge necessary to create and sustain youth-directed, school-based organizations whose mission centers on maximizing the school's tolerance of diversity along lines of race, ethnic, class, gender, religious, and sexual orientation. Some of these highly motivated students continue to meet with CNC organizing staff at least once a month. Their monthly meetings constitute TID's third intervention, called "Night at the Center." This even smaller subset of students continually utilizes CNC's ongoing support to engage in democracy-building projects within their own schools and communities.

## Music and Youth Social Movements

The CNC operates its program on the empirically confirmed premise that music plays a crucial role in adolescent life and development. Quantitatively, music matters in that the average teenagers listen to over 5 h of music each day (Mueller, 1999). In more qualitative terms, social scientists have shown that music serves as a key peer group organizer for teenagers (Frith, 1981), which in turn affects the development of identity, norms, values, and status orientation (Christenson & Roberts, 1998). Contemporary music figures heavily into the shaping of the adolescent moral universe (Leming, 1987). Adolescent culture turns on the currency of music and its power to resolve or at least explain some of the tensions surrounding teens' liminal status, their position between the dependence of childhood and relative autonomy of impending adulthood (Weinstein, 1983). Changes in music often point to changes in youth culture (Irwin, 1999; Willis, 1990) as youth frequently use music to demonstrate their significance in the world.

In their presentation to high school students, the CNC uses tracks of hate music to inspire youth to "fight fire with fire." Like so many anti-white power movement organizations, CNC appreciates the white power movement's long and incredibly successful history of using youth-oriented music to breed hate-mongering among teenagers and young adults.[3] Indeed, hate music has become one of the greatest revenue streams and youth recruitment ploys for the world's most powerful white supremacist outfits, including the National Alliance, which now owns the largest global distributor of recorded white power music, Resistance Records. Bands playing hate music transcend genres and more often than not (but not always) adopt a subtle approach that speaks to youth anxiety over identity and community.[4] No one understands or articulates this anxiety – the bread and butter of hate-propagating musical groups – than Matti Sundquist, singer for the Swedish band Svastika:

> I'm totally convinced that the music is the best way to awaken the young and make them understand that they have a value, despite what the society and the media states.... In the music of White Power, we have a force that can grow to an undreamed strength. A force that is constantly growing and becoming more professional. The fact that more and more record stores around the world have begun to sell our products, means that we are constantly reaching new listeners, who in most cases are convinced that we present them with the truth.... If Adolf Hitler our spiritual leader was alive today, I'm convinced that he would not run around in shoulder belt or riding trousers. Every era has its own strategy for the struggle and today our weapon is the music and our White skin is our uniform. (Quoted in Center for New Community, 1999)

By playing this often aesthetically pleasing music for students, and exposing its message, CNC hopes to inspire youth to be motivated to incorporate anti-racism into their musical culture. In effect, CNC works hard to "make hate uncool," as one of its program staff has said many times. Accomplishing this objective requires CNC to identify and capitalize on what and who is "cool" among youth, which of course means determining what and whom youth admire, prize, and value, culturally speaking. In sum, CNC wants to infuse youth culture – especially the cultural places that involve music – with political ideology, and make it fun for youth to propagate a politicized culture centered on pro-diversity and pro-tolerance beliefs, norms, and practices.

## THE PRESENT STUDY

According to CNC's logic model and intervention plan, high school students in the target population need certain resources to respond favorably – both cognitively and behaviorally – to CNC's message. First, they need to exhibit a relatively high degree of social tolerance. Second, those who are relatively more tolerant (i.e., the "choir") need to perceive and actually have solid adult support systems in the school itself and in the school's surrounding community. Third, the socially tolerant teenagers need to believe that white power music is a problem, as this is the "hook" used to capture the attention of the proximal target population. To explain tolerance, we examine a variety of variables, including legal cynicism, hostility, and demographic features, including age, gender, race, and level of parents' education.

Our key objective is to discern the causes and correlates of "corrective social action." That is, we are attempting to identify the individual-level attributes associated with student involvement in CNC-supported social movement enterprises *as well as* the organizational features (school, peer, and community support systems) correlated with SMO developments. Our prediction is that the students most likely to engage in SMO development and maintenance are those who (a) exhibit a relatively high degree of tolerance for differences of race and sexual orientation, (b) report high levels of adult support *in the school*, (c) indicate a low degree of hostility, and (d) display a low degree of cynicism toward the prevailing legal and normative order.

# METHODS

## Data: Surveys and Telephone Interviews

Since the study's inception in July 2002, we have distributed self-administered surveys to 823 high school and college students in the Chicago metropolitan area. Students complete the questionnaire in the context of a school assembly, just prior to receiving CNC's multimedia presentation on the dangers of white power music and its ideological lineage. The instrument generates numeric data on demographic items and on students' attitudes, beliefs, knowledge, and self-reported behaviors, including questions about tolerance for differences of race and sexual orientation, social responsibility, views of the legal system, perceived levels of social support, and hostility. For the purposes of this paper, we excluded a significant portion of the respondents ($N = 357$) who participated in a "pre-test" phase. This version of the survey did not include questions about adult support, one of our primary variables of interest. We also excluded college students ($N = 52$). In this paper, we focus only on high school students because the social contexts and resources available to them differ markedly from those available to college students. The total number of remaining cases is 414.

After data cleaning, we also excluded cases with missing values ($N = 89$), resulting in a sample size of 325 respondents. Of these 89 cases, 21 were dropped due to missing demographic information about the student's age, sex, or race. The remaining 68 cases were dropped because students did not respond to survey questions about tolerance, hostility, or legal cynicism. To examine whether and how the 68 cases dropped due to lack of response to survey items are different from the respondents, we conducted a series of analyses (not shown) to ascertain whether the non-respondents and respondents differed on demographic indicators. There are no significant differences in respondents and non-respondents in terms of age or gender. However, there are significant differences in regard to race and parents' education. Non-respondents were more likely to be non-white and were more likely to have parents without a college degree. For this reason, the reader should exercise caution when interpreting the findings we present in our later discussion of how key predictors seem to vary (or not) by race.

An additional caveat regarding the survey data merits consideration. Because survey data were collected during school assemblies where students sat in close proximity to one another, the potential for data contamination arises. While we do expect that some responses may have been influenced by peers, because the student population within each high school tended to be homogeneous, we doubt that their peers may have severely affected overall ratings of tolerance, hostility, legal cynicism, and adult support. One of the authors (Scott) attended approximately 75% of the sessions in which the survey was administered. These venues tend to be educational presentations occurring in the auditorium, with each classroom's students and teacher present (therefore accomplishing roughly the same teacher–student ratio as exists in the individual classrooms). Students tend to approach the session as they would in an ordinary classroom situation, mostly deferring to the authority of their teachers. Field observations indicate that students complete the survey in "test-taking mode" – quietly and independently, with very little discussion between or among them. These observations lead us to conclude that peer influence exerts a minimal effect on survey responses.[5]

Students who complete the survey at the educational event have the opportunity to self-select into our study's follow-up telephone interview component. Once a student chooses to be interviewed, a researcher contacts him or her roughly 30 days following the educational event. Telephone interviewers administer a 30-min schedule of open- and closed-ended questions, the latter including but not limited to the tolerance scale (i.e. quick discrimination index). The telephone interview component helps us to achieve many objectives: (1) assess variation across time in self-reported social tolerance; (2) determine what students remember and learned from the presentation; (3) solicit student input on how to improve the presentation; (4) gather data on student perceptions of school-based adult support for student-led social movement activity; and (5) discern how the presentation has affected students behaviorally, with particular attention to their relationships with peers and adults inside and outside of the school setting. The latter objective is the one most relevant to this paper.

To date, we have conducted 28 follow-up telephone interviews of high school-age youth (20 females, 8 males). The point of the follow-up interview is to discern the kind and degree of "corrective social action" students take in response to receiving CNC's clarion call for political mobilization. These interviews yield additional quantitative and qualitative data concerning student involvement in social movement activity generally and SMO development more specifically.

Owing to the non-random selection of interviewees and the formative nature of our data gathering efforts, our conclusions should be considered suggestive rather than determinative. Our analysis of the telephone interview data focuses mainly on indicators of student satisfaction and learning, how students convey their newly gained political knowledge to peers and adults close to them, and how the educational event prompts changes in students' everyday customs.

**Table 1.** Descriptive Statistics ($N = 325$).

| Variable | Description | Range | Mean | Sd |
|---|---|---|---|---|
| Tolerance scale | 20-item scale; high score = more tolerance | 2.29–4.76 | 3.59 | 0.44 |
| Adult support at school scale | 3-item scale; high score = more support | 1–3 | 2.16 | 0.56 |
| Higher than average tolerance and support | Higher than median score on tolerance and adult support scale = 1 | 0–1 | 0.22 | 0.42 |
| Age | Student's age | 14–19 | 16.31 | 1.25 |
| Female | Female = 1; male = 0 | 0–1 | 0.75 | 0.43 |
| White | White = 1; other race = 0 | 0–1 | 0.58 | 0.49 |
| Parent has college education | One parent has a B.A. or higher = 1; less than a B.A. degree = 0 | 0–1 | 0.68 | 0.47 |
| Legal cynicism scale | 5-item scale; high score = more cynicism | 1–5 | 2.83 | 0.73 |
| Hostility scale | 6-item scale; high score = more hostility | 1–5 | 2.57 | 0.98 |

*Measures*

In our analyses of the survey data, the dependent variables are drawn from two standardized scales designed to assess the two key characteristics that CNC uses to identify students who are likely to become involved in the development and maintenance of a social movement against white power music in their school: (1) tolerance and (2) the perception of adult social support within the school. Descriptive statistics on all independent and dependent variables are shown in Table 1.

*Tolerance* is measured using the quick discrimination index (QDI) (adapted from the scale initially validated by Ponterotto, Burkard, Rieger, & Grieger (1995)). Students respond to 20 items that assess their level of tolerance of racial and ethnic difference. Responses to QDI statements are five-point Likert-scaled: strongly disagree, disagree, neither agree nor disagree, agree, and strongly agree. Some example items include, "I feel I could develop a close and personal relationship with someone from a different race," "I think White people's racism toward racial minority groups is a major problem in America today," and "I think the school system, from elementary through college, should promote the values of many different and diverse cultures." High scores on this scale indicate higher levels of tolerance. This measure has a high level of scale validity ($\alpha = 0.798$).

*Adult support at school* comprises a scale of three items drawn verbatim from the nine-item "Vaux Social Support Record" (Vaux, 1988).[6] Higher values indicate greater support. Respondents indicate whether they have "not at all," "some," or "a lot" of support in different areas of their lives, including (and especially) the school setting. Items include, "At school, there are adults I can talk to, who care about my feelings and what happens to me," "At school, there are adults I can talk to, who give good suggestions and advice about my problems," and "At school, there are adults who help me with practical problems, like helping me get somewhere or helping me with a project." In our own analysis the adult social support scale exhibits a high level of internal validity ($\alpha = 0.814$).

Finally, we have created a third, dichotomous variable by combining the tolerance and adult support scales just described. Because the CNC targets students who have higher levels of tolerance *and* adult support, we created a dummy variable identifying students who have over the median scores on both of these variables.

Key independent variables include legal cynicism, hostility, and a series of demographic characteristics. The *legal cynicism* scale consists of five items with which respondents report their level of agreement: "Laws were made to be broken," "It's okay to do anything you want as long as you don't hurt anyone," "To make money, there are no right and wrong ways anymore, only easy ways and hard ways," "Fighting between friends or within families is nobody else's business," and "Nowadays a person has to live pretty much for today and let tomorrow take care of itself." This scale was developed by Sampson and Bartusch (1998), who modified Srole's (1956) anomie scale. There is a moderately high level of scale validity for these items ($\alpha = 0.677$).

*Hostility* is a six-item scale measuring the frequency with which students feel angry and inclined toward violence.[7] We drew this scale verbatim from the work of Derogatis, Rickels, and Rock (1976). High scores on this scale indicate higher levels of hostility. Items include "How often do you have temper outbursts you cannot control?" and "How often do you shout or throw things?" This scale has a high level of internal validity ($\alpha = 0.852$).

Other measures include demographic information. *Age* is a continuous variable. *Female* is a dummy variable. Given the small sample size at this point, we measure *race* as a dummy dichotomous variable distinguishing white from non-white students. For the same reason, we measure *parent's education* as a dichotomous dummy variable indicating whether one parent has a college education.

# RESULTS

## Surveys of High School Students

Given the Center for New Community's interest in identifying students who have higher than average levels of tolerance *and* who report high levels of adult support at school, we begin with bivariate analyses, comparing the characteristics of the students in this group to those who report lower than average levels of tolerance and/or support (see Table 2). In terms of the demographic indicators, we find that students who report higher levels of tolerance and support are more likely to be female and to have parents who are college educated. Interestingly, there is no significant difference in terms of age or race between students who report higher levels of tolerance and support and those who do not.

We also compare these two groups in terms of their beliefs about the legitimacy of law (legal cynicism) and how often they report being hostile and angry. Students who report higher levels of tolerance and support are significantly less likely to exhibit legal cynicism. Moreover, these students indicate less frequent hostile feelings when compared to those who report lower levels of tolerance and/or support. These bivariate analyses suggest that these two groups of teens have quite different characteristics. However, we are not able to tell from this bivariate analysis, which variables best explain tolerance and support net of other explanations.

Hence, we must utilize multivariate analyses to assess competing explanations and examine adult support and tolerance separately. Our question here is: What factors best explain, net of other characteristics, the level of

*Table 2.* Comparison of Means ($N = 325$).

| Variable | Students Who Report Higher than Average Levels of Tolerance and Support | Lower than Average Levels of Tolerance and/or Support |
|---|---|---|
| Age | 16.35 | 16.30 |
| Female | 0.82 | 0.73* |
| White | 0.60 | 0.58 |
| Parent has college education | 0.72 | 0.67* |
| Legal cynicism scale | 2.64 | 2.88* |
| Hostility scale | 1.94 | 2.22* |

*$p<0.05$, 2-tailed *t*-test.

*Table 3.* OLS Regression Predicting Adult Support at School ($N = 325$).

|  | Adult Support at School | |
|---|---|---|
|  | Model 1 | Model 2 |
| Age | 0.009(0.027) | 0.009(0.027) |
| Female | −0.058(0.081) | −0.458*(0.203) |
| White | −0.033(0.071) | −0.267(0.195) |
| Parent has college education | −0.050(0.072) | −0.037(0.072) |
| Legal cynicism | 0.034(0.046) | 0.030(0.046) |
| Hostility | −0.160**(0.038) | −0.317**(0.076) |
| Hostility × female |  | 0.155*(0.069) |
| Hostility × white |  | 0.099(0.069) |
| Constant | 2.416 | 2.841 |
| Adjusted $R^2$ | 0.043 | 0.055 |

Standard errors in parentheses.
*Significant at 5%.
**Significant at 1%.

adult support at school? In Model 1 of Table 3, we explore the effect of demographic and attitudinal variables on adult support. Interestingly, *none* of the demographic variables are significantly related to adult support at school and legal cynicism is also insignificant. It appears that the *only* variable that significantly predicts adult support is hostility. Hostility is inversely related to level of adult support.

Given the importance of hostility in predicting adult support in school, we next examined whether this relationship differed by gender and race. Model 2 in Table 3 adds two interaction terms to the model to explore this possibility. Although gender is not significant in the main effects model, the relationship between hostility and adult support appears to differ by gender. Specifically, this relationship appears to be stronger for males than for females. The interaction term for race was not significant.

Next we construct a multivariate model to predict the amount of tolerance students reported (see Table 4). Female students have significantly higher levels of tolerance, net of other factors, while white students report lower levels of tolerance. However, the other demographic variables are not significantly related to tolerance. In terms of attitudinal variables, legal cynicism is marginally significant and negatively related to tolerance. Hostility is significant and also negatively related to tolerance. White students

Table 4. OLS Regression Predicting Tolerance ($N = 325$).

|  | Tolerance | |
| --- | --- | --- |
|  | Model 1 | Model 2 |
| Age | −0.012(0.021) | −0.010(0.020) |
| Female | 0.149*(0.062) | −0.279⁺(0.153) |
| White | −0.117*(0.055) | 0.266⁺(0.147) |
| Parent has college education | −0.027(0.055) | −0.017(0.054) |
| Legal cynicism | −0.058⁺(0.035) | −0.047(0.035) |
| Hostility | −0.085**(0.029) | −0.099⁺(0.057) |
| Hostility × female |  | 0.150**(0.052) |
| Hostility × white |  | −0.134*(0.052) |
| Constant | 4.144 | 4.120 |
| Adjusted $R^2$ | 0.089 | 0.133 |

Standard errors in parentheses.
⁺Significant at 10%.
*Significant at 5%.
**Significant at 1%.

have significantly lower tolerance scores compared to non-white students, net of other factors.

To further explore the effect of hostility on tolerance, we examined how the relationship between hostility and tolerance might be moderated by race and gender. The interaction effect between hostility and gender is significant, as is the interaction between hostility and race. These variables are displayed in Model 2 of Table 4. The significant interaction effect between hostility and gender suggests that the relationship between hostility and tolerance is significantly different for males and females. Males display a stronger inverse relationship between hostility and tolerance than do females. Similarly, students differ by race. There is a stronger, negative relationship between hostility and tolerance for white students than for non-white students.

*Telephone Interviews*

In terms of race, these 28 student respondents represent the CNC's ideal "targets" for intensive intervention, with most of them (23) being white (four Hispanic, one Asian). The modal grade level (10 students) is sophomore (8 juniors, 5 seniors, 5 freshmen). This sample is representative of the students whom CNC wants to mobilize in developing local SMOs that in turn plan and execute "corrective social action."

Overall, students report a high level of satisfaction with the educational event. On a scale of 1–10 (with 10 being excellent), the average quality rating is 8.55. Students also self-report a great deal of learning. Again on a 1–10 scale (10 being "learned a lot"), the mean score is 7.995. Students generally find the presentation itself to be quite compelling and comment favorably on the presenter's use of various media, including sound, audio, video, and still photography. We have found that every student can recall the presentation with exceptional clarity and detail. As this young man told us, the presentation resonates well with young people: "I thought it was really informative. I like the way it was presented. It was something I could relate to because it dealt with music and it made it easy for teens to relate to."

More relevant to our concern with student mobilization outcomes, we find that the educational event inspired all 28 of these students to convey what they had learned to a total of 256 other people (an average of nine contacts per youth) (Fig. 2). The most frequently reported contact impelled by the educational event was peer-to-peer, with 17 interviewees saying that they had shared with school peers what they had learned from the event, and 12 saying they had conveyed information to non-school peers. In total, these students reached out to 184 school peers and 18 non-school peers. When asked what she had shared with a non-school peer, one young woman offered this emblematic response: "The fact that their school lacks racial diversity, although they still need to be aware of all this stuff, because it might appeal to the students who aren't exposed to racial diversity and how not to stereotype and be aware of all comments." Such a phenomenon obviously merits further inquiry, since it flags the potential for connecting anti-white power movements across high schools.

The second most frequently cited contact was with adults outside of school, usually a parent: 22 interviewees reported sharing their newfound knowledge with a total of 35 adults outside of school. Most commonly these students shared what they had learned with a parent, either a mother or father (with an equal likelihood of sharing with each). This sharing took the form of showing them the handouts from the presentation but also of talking about what they had learned. Characteristically, students informed their parents of the "bottom line," as did the young man who said "I just was telling my dad how you can't judge people how they look on the outside, and that you have to learn how to get along with everyone, no matter who they are."

Finally, 16 students indicated that they had relayed information to a total of 19 teachers or other adults in the school. It is significant that youth respondents were more likely to have shared what they learned with adults outside of school than with any other group, and that they were just as likely

Building Democracy, Promoting Tolerance 73

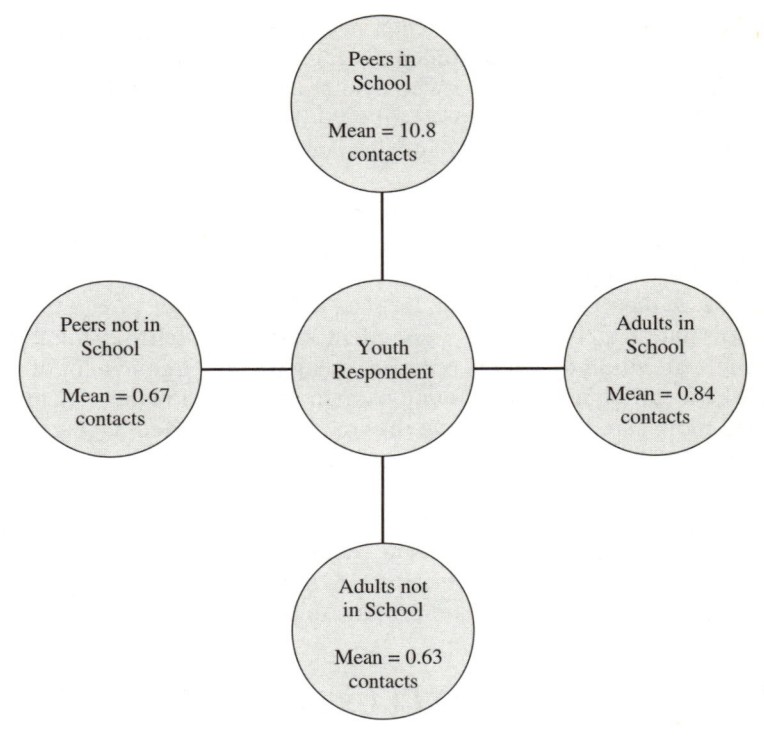

```
                    ┌─────────────┐
                    │  Peers in   │
                    │   School    │
                    │ Mean = 10.8 │
                    │  contacts   │
                    └─────────────┘
                           │
┌─────────────┐    ┌─────────────┐    ┌─────────────┐
│ Peers not in│    │    Youth    │    │  Adults in  │
│   School    │────│  Respondent │────│   School    │
│ Mean = 0.67 │    │             │    │ Mean = 0.84 │
│  contacts   │    │             │    │  contacts   │
└─────────────┘    └─────────────┘    └─────────────┘
                           │
                    ┌─────────────┐
                    │ Adults not  │
                    │  in School  │
                    │ Mean = 0.63 │
                    │  contacts   │
                    └─────────────┘
```

*Fig. 2.* Youth Conveyance of Political Information

to have shared with at least one adult in school as with multiple peers in school. (Clearly, though, the preponderance of information exchanges occurs between peers.) Typically, exchanges with teachers occurred in the classroom setting, following attendance at the presentation. One young man's recollection exemplifies the norm: "We talked about the overview of the presentation and the distinction between the music I listen to versus what was played at the program." In the best case, students and teachers discussed white power music in such a way that youth were able to make these comparisons with the music they themselves listen to. A few students reported encountering significant resistance in their overtures toward teachers, the most extreme case being this report from a young woman: "I talked with my teacher and some school friends. This teacher doesn't believe that white supremacy even exists, or that the Holocaust even happened for that matter. Some people you just can't convince, they're so set in their ways."

Most ($N = 22$) of the students interviewed by telephone reported active involvement in school-based student organizations. Those with the most involvement tended to be those who also reached out to adults with information. Of these 22 students, 45% indicated that the presentation motivated them to somehow change their involvement in their respective organizations.

Also noteworthy is our realization that 15 of the interviewees reported changes in their sensibilities and sensitivity to the issues raised in the presentation. For instance, several said that they now question the symbols appearing on their peers' clothing, lockers, notebooks, etc., or else they have "gone on hate watch," as one respondent said: "I watch out for it more. I pay more attention to what people are saying because I go to a lot of shows and I like metal bands." One young woman said, quite plainly: "I am now listening more carefully to my own music." Others reported having stopped listening to a musical group whose recordings they now know to be hate-laden, and still others report more significant lifestyle changes, such as actively seeking out new experiences and new friends: "I've been trying to make friends with people of different races. There is so much I can learn from them." Finally, many of these 15 indicated that they have been "spreading the word" about hate-propagating music.

## CONCLUSION

The central goals of the CNC's "Turn It Down" program are to educate youth about the dangers of white power music and to inspire youth-led activities against the intolerant messages in this type of music. Our research project attempts to evaluate whether the CNC program achieves these goals. More broadly, this study speaks to an issue of fundamental interest to scholars of social movements: what attitudes and resources are necessary to galvanize social movement activity among adolescents in a high school setting?

In pursuing this question, we build toward an integrated theory of how youth use connections with adults to advance their own pursuit of youth-driven social movement organizations. We extend micro-mobilization theory by emphasizing the social context in which the network is embedded (e.g., school settings) and by explicitly accounting for power asymmetry in the network (e.g., adults in schools). Our theoretical model uses a multi-level approach, considering not just the student's attitudes, but also the student's peer network, relationships with adults in the school, and with adults at home and in the community. Each of these levels is crucial to understanding student responsiveness to the anti-racist message promulgated by the CNC.

An important feature of this theoretical model is that the child is viewed as an agent of social change. While acknowledging that high school students do not have control over certain aspects of their lives or over school resources, we avoid characterizing these adolescents as passive. Instead, in our model, it is the students who must cultivate relationships with adults in order to engage in school-based action after viewing the CNC presentation. Thus our model is consistent with recent developments in the sociology of childhood that sees children as actors in their own right whose voices and perspectives need to be heard (Corsaro, 1997; Thorne, 1987).

The intent of this paper is not to test this integrated theoretical model, but instead to examine whether the preliminary data we have collected provide suggestive evidence that supports its various components. The key findings here emerge from the telephone interviews. Preliminary analyses of 28 follow-up telephone interviews with teens who attended the CNC educational program illustrate some important outcomes. Students reported that they discussed this presentation with others, most frequently with peers, teachers, and parents. Each student "spread the word" about the hate messages contained in white power music to, on average, 12 other people. Primarily, students had discussions with their peers in school, but it is notable that they also talked with peers outside of their school, teachers, school administrators, parents, and other family members. Perhaps more importantly, the telephone interviews revealed that some students said that they have altered their own patterns of behavior – for example, by being more careful in their music choices or by changing their involvement in school-based student organization – as a result of the presentation.

Our analyses of the survey data examine the correlates of student attitudes. We find that when explaining tolerance and adult support the most important explanatory variable is hostility. Furthermore, the relationship between hostility and each of these variables is different for male and female students. In the models explaining tolerance, we also note differences in hostility by race. The CNC would be well-served to craft its message and target its audience with the understanding that variation in tolerance and support can be attributed to the few key variables described above. When trying to reach the tolerant and well-supported students, CNC needs to recognize the importance of hostility, for it is the most powerful predictor of where students fall on the support-tolerance continuum. We would be remiss, however, if we were to fail in issuing a caveat: Because our data do not allow us to establish time order, we cannot conclude either that hostility induces intolerance and low support, or vice versa. Causal pathways may function in one direction or the other, or perhaps even both.

Although our theoretical model was developed to understand how youth respond to the anti-hate music message of the CNC, it certainly may be transferable to understanding youth responsiveness to the messages of other social movement organizations. Future research on youth and social movements can build upon the present study by considering the manifold role of adults in the social networks of youth activists. Rather than assuming that adults interfere with adolescent social movement participation, more exploration in this area would help us understand when and how adults can support youth activism.

## NOTES

1. We concur with Dobratz and Shanks-Meile (1997), who document in painstaking detail the emergence and growth of white power in the United States, that indeed white separatism constitutes a social movement.

2. A relative deprivation approach accentuates the pre-movement attitudes and behaviors of people who become activists. The main assumption is that individuals believe their own primary reference group to be disadvantaged, or handicapped, relative to some other group. People take part in movements not because they want to acquire better material standing but rather because they desire the psychological reassurance that comes from associating and identifying with others who feel similar misery (see Aberle, 1966; Davies, 1963; Feieraband, Feieraband & Nesvold 1969; Gurr, 1970; McAdam, 1988; Oberschall, 1973). In contrast, the resource mobilization model posits that social movements sprout in existing institutions dedicated to facilitating social change and/or civic development (e.g., the educational system). Resource mobilization theorists, according to McAdam (1988, p. 697), underscore the "constancy of discontent and the variability of resources in accounting for the emergence and development of insurgency." The key to any particular movement's success, then, depends upon its SMOs' adeptness at deploying resources rather than how ardently its supporters work for the causes of the organization or what kind of psychological profile the participants exhibit (Turner & Killian, 1987).

3. For probing accounts of the international hate music movement and its relationship to white supremacy and anti-Semitism, see Lowles and Silver (1998) and Center for New Community (1999).

4. Some of the more well-known "hate-core" bands include the Midtown Bootboys, Mudoven, Intimidation One, Aggressive Force, and Iron Youth. Because many bands change their names and venues chameleonically in response to social control efforts, protest, and other negative attention, compiling a definitive list is infeasible.

5. To guard against teacher-influenced data contamination, where students feel as though they may be sanctioned negatively for either not completing the survey or for responding in a particular way, we attempted to defuse teacher authority a bit by asking that all adults present also complete the survey.

6. Scale taken from Dahlberg, Toal and Behrens (1998). Internal consistency on initial target group of elementary school students, grades 1–6.
7. Scale taken from Dahlberg et al (1998). Internal consistency on initial target group of African-American males aged 12–16.

## ACKNOWLEDGMENTS

The authors wish to thank Monique Urganus, Jennifer Michals, Susan Agruss, Shanon Lersch, and Abra Johnson for their data management assistance on this project. Thanks also go to Elizabeth Gregory for her research on youth music consumption habits. We also extend our gratitude to anonymous reviewers and to editors Kate Rosier and David Kinney for their incisive and helpful comments on earlier drafts of this article.

Funding for this project was provided in part by the Righteous Persons Foundation. In addition, each of the authors received research support from DePaul University. Artis received a summer research grant from the Faculty Research and Development Program, College of Liberal Arts and Sciences, DePaul University and a research leave from the University Research Council, DePaul University. Scott received a paid research leave from the University Research Council, DePaul University. Points of view, statements, or opinions contained in this article belong to the authors and do not necessarily represent the official positions or policies of the Righteous Persons Foundation, DePaul University, or the Center for New Community.

## REFERENCES

Aberle, D. (1966). *The peyote religion among the navajo.* Chicago: Aldine.
Abrahams, N. (1996). Negotiating power, identity, family, and community: Women's community participation. *Gender & Society, 10,* 768–797.
Broad, K. L. (2002). Social movement selves. *Sociological Perspectives, 45,* 317–336.
Center for New Community. (1999). *Soundtracks to the white revolution: White supremacist assaults on youth music subcultures.* A publication of The Center for New Community in cooperation with The Northwest Coalition for Human Dignity, Chicago, IL.
Christenson, P. G., & Roberts, D. F. (1998). *It's not only rock and roll: Popular music in the lives of adolescents.* Cresskill, NJ.: Hampton Press.
Corsaro, W. (1997). *The sociology of childhood.* Thousand Oaks, CA: Pine Forge Press.
Dahlberg, L. L., Toal, S. B., & Behrens, C. B. (1998). *Measuring violence-related attitudes, beliefs, and behaviors among youths: A compendium of assessment tools.* Atlanta, GA: Centers for Disease Control and Prevention. National Center for Injury Prevention and Control.
Davies, J. C. (1963). *Human nature in politics: The dynamics of political behavior.* New York: Wiley.

Derogatis, L. R., Rickels, K., & Rock, A. F. (1976). SCL-90 and the MMPI: A step in the validation of a new self-report scale. *British Journal of Psychiatry*, *128*, 280–289.

Dewees, A., & Klees, S. J. (1995). Social movements and the transformation of national policy: Street and working children in Brazil. *Comparative Education Review*, *39*, 76–100.

Diani, M., & McAdam, D. (Eds) (2003). *Social movements and networks: Relational approaches to collective action*. Oxford: Oxford University Press.

Dobratz, B. A., & Shanks-Meile, S. L. (1997). *The white separatist movement in the United States: White power white pride*. London: Twayne Publishers.

Emirbayer, M., & Goodwin, J. (1996). Symbols, positions, objects: Toward a new theory of revolutions and collective action. *History and Theory*, *35*, 358–374.

Feierabend, I., Feierabend, R., & Nesvold, B. (1969). Social change and political violence: Cross national patterns. In: H. D. Graham & T. R. Gurr (Eds), *Violence in America: Historical and comparative perspectives*. Washington, DC: Government Printing Office.

Fine, G. A. (2004). Adolescence as a cultural toolkit: High school debate and the repertoires of childhood and adulthood. *The Sociological Quarterly*, *45*, 1–20.

Frith, S. (1981). *Sound effects: Youth, leisure and the politics of rock and roll*. New York: Pantheon.

Goodwin, J. (1997). The libidinal constitution of a high-risk social movement: Affectual ties and solidarity in the Huk rebellion, 1946–1954. *American Sociological Review*, *62*, 53–69.

Goodwin, J., Jasper, J. M., & Polletta, F. (2000). The return of the repressed: The fall and rise of emotions in social movement theory. *Mobilization*, *5*, 65–84.

Granvold, D. K., & Saleebey, M. D. (1980). Adolescents as change agents: Culture at the crossroads. *Social Development Issues*, *4*, 44–57.

Gurr, T. (1970). *Why men rebel*. Princeton, NJ: University Press.

Irwin, D. D. (1999). The straight edge subculture: Examining the youths drug-free way. *Journal of Drug Issues*, *29*, 365–380.

Jasper, J. M. (1998). The emotions of protest: Reactive and affective emotions in and around social movements. *Sociological Forum*, *13*, 397–424.

Jasper, J. M., & Poulsen, J. D. (1995). Recruiting strangers and friends: Moral shocks and social networks in animal rights and nuclear protests. *Social Problems*, *42*, 493–512.

Katz, C. (1998). Disintegrating developments: Global economic restructuring and the eroding of the ecologies of youth. In: T. Skelton & G. Valentine (Eds), *Cool places: Geographies of youth cultures*. London: Routledge.

Lees, L. (2003). The ambivalence of diversity and the politics of urban renaissance: The case of youth in downtown Portland, Maine. *International Journal of Urban and Regional Research*, *27*, 613–634.

Leming, J. (1987). Rock music and the socialization of moral values in early adolescents. *Youth and Society*, *18*, 423–522.

Lowles, N., & Silver, S. (Eds) (1998). *White noise: Inside the international Nazi skinhead scene*. London: Searchlight.

McAdam, D. (1982). *Political process and the development of black insurgency, 1930-1970*. Chicago: University of Chicago Press.

McAdam, D. (1988). *Freedom summer*. New York: Oxford University Press.

McAdam, D., McCarthy, J. D., & Zald, M. N. (1988). Social movements. In: N. J. Smelser (Ed.), *Handbook of sociology*. Newbury Park, CA: Sage.

Minow, M., & Weissbourd, R. (1993). Social movements for children. *Daedalus*, *122*, 1–29.

Mueller, W. (1999). *Understanding today's youth culture*. Wheaton, IL: Tyndale House.

Oberschall, A. (1973). *Social conflict and social movements.* Englewood Cliffs, NJ: Prentice-Hall.
Offe, C. (1985). The new social movements: Challenging the boundaries of institutional politics. *Social Research, 52,* 817–868.
Oppenheimer, M. (1968). The student movement as a response to alienation. *Journal of Human Relations, 16,* 1–16.
Orcutt, J. D., & Fendrich, J. M. (1980). Students' perceptions of the decline of protest: Evidence from the early seventies. *Sociological Focus, 13,* 420–434.
Park, B. (1993). An aspect of political socialization of student movement participants in Korea. *Youth and Society, 25,* 171–201.
Paulsen, R. (1991). Education, social class, and participation in collective action. *Sociology of Education, 64,* 96–110.
Polletta, F. (1998). 'It was like a fever...' narrative and identity in social protest. *Social Problems, 45,* 137–159.
Ponterotto, J. G., Burkard, A., Rieger, B. P., & Grieger, I. (1995). Development and initial validation of the quick discrimination index (QDI). *Educational and Psychological Measurement, 55,* 1016–1031.
Rodgers, D. (2003). Children as social movement participants. Paper delivered at the annual meetings of the Midwest Sociological Society, Chicago: IL.
Saha, L. J. (1994). Student activism and education: An overview. Paper delivered at the International Sociological Association Conference.
Sampson, R. J., & Bartusch, D. J. (1998). Legal cynicism and (subcultural?) tolerance of deviance: The neighborhood context of racial differences. *Law and Society Review, 32,* 777–805.
Scott, A. (1990). *Ideology and the new social movements.* London & Boston: Unwin & Hyman.
Sherkat, D. E., & Blocker, T. J. (1994). The political development of sixties' activists: Identifying the influence of class, gender, and socialization on protest participation. *Social Forces, 72,* 821–842.
Soule, S. A. (1997). The student divestment movement in the United States and the Shantytown: Diffusion of a protest tactic. *Social Forces, 75*(3), 855–883.
Srole, L. (1956). Social integration and certain corollaries: An exploratory study. *American Sociological Review, 21,* 709–716.
Swidler, A. (1986). Culture in action: Symbols and strategies. *American Sociological Review, 51,* 273–286.
Thorne, B. (1987). Re-visioning women and social change: Where are the children? *Gender & Society, 1,* 85–109.
Turner, R. H., & Killian, L. M. (1987). *Collective behavior* (3rd ed.). Englewood Cliffs, NJ: Prentice-Hall.
Van Dyke, N. (1998). Hotbed of activism: Locations of student protest. *Social Problems, 45,* 205–219.
Vaux, A. (1988). *Social support: Theory, research, and intervention.* New York: Praeger.
Weinstein, D. (1983). Rock: Youth and its music. In: J. Epstein (Ed.), *Adolescents and heir music: If it's too loud, you're too old* (pp. 3–24). New York: Garland Publishing.
Willis, P. (1990). *Common culture: Symbolic work at play in the everyday cultures of the young.* Cambridge, MA: Westview Press.
Yang, G. (2000). Achieving emotions in collective action: Emotional processes and movement mobilization in the 1989 Chinese student movement. *The Sociological Quarterly, 41,* 593–614.
Youniss, J., McLellan, J. A., & Mazer, B. (2001). Voluntary service, peer group orientation, and civic engagement. *Journal of Adolescent Research, 16,* 456–468.

# THE MESSY NATURE OF DISCIPLINE AND ZERO TOLERANCE POLICIES: NEGOTIATING SAFE SCHOOL ENVIRONMENTS AMONG INCONSISTENCIES, STRUCTURAL CONSTRAINTS AND THE COMPLEX LIVES OF YOUTH

Linda M. Waldron

## INTRODUCTION

I began my research at two suburban high schools in the spring of 2000, shortly after the one-year "anniversary" of the Columbine High School shootings in Littleton, Colorado. On April 20, 1999, Dylan Kelbold and Eric Harris entered their school and killed 10 classmates and 1 teacher, wounded 23 others, and then took their own lives in the library. It was the worst mass murder ever to take place on school grounds in the United States. I was particularly interested in looking at suburban schools during this time period because statistics showed juvenile crime, and in particular violence within the school systems, was on the decline, yet the perception of school violence seemed unrelated to these statistics (Brooks, Schiraldi, & Ziegenberg, 2000; Cook, 2000; Glassner, 1999). Following the widespread national attention given to the Columbine shootings,[1] public polls showed 71% of Americans believed a school shooting was likely to happen in their community (Brooks et al., 2000). A month after the Columbine shootings, a Gallup Poll found 52% of parents still feared for their children's safety at school (Brooks et al., 2000). I was interested in learning how this perception of violence and fear shaped the everyday lives of kids going to schools throughout the United States. I wanted to know how schools dealt with issues of violence and safety at the local level, and in particular, how discipline and punishment was thought about, practiced, and negotiated within public-school settings.

In order to study these issues, I looked specifically at what kids[2] at two suburban high schools had to say about school rules and discipline policies. I examined their lives in relation to how some vice-principals, counselors, and teachers understood and dealt with these issues. In addition to people at each school, texts, such as policies, disciplinary forms, hall passes, signs on the walls, and local, state, and federal laws, also organized "school safety." Yet, although the schools were organized around these texts, they did not determine the practices of both adults and youth. This chapter explores the relationship of these texts to the practices and actions of kids and adults in the school. In this paper, I address the following questions:

- How did the institutional arrangements of each school shape discipline and punishment? How did youth and adults manage structural constraints that affected this?
- How did the practices of kids and adults reflect meanings of the texts? How was the struggle between power and resistance negotiated?
- How did kids, administrators, resource officers, and counselors create, negotiate, and try to sustain a "safe school"?

Theoretically, my work is aligned with other researchers who study children from an interpretive perspective. This perspective claims children are active social agents, both creating and resisting dominant structures of society as well as being influenced by them (Ambert, 1986; Best, 2000; Corsaro, 1997; Currie, 1999; Jarrett, 1997; Prout & James, 1997; Thorne, 1993; Van Ausdale & Feagin, 2001; Waksler, 1991; Wulff, 1995). In my research, I paid close attention to the struggles that youth identified and prioritized, and investigated their understandings of social life. I focused on the dialectical relationship between young people, adults, school policies and institutional arrangements, in an attempt to better understand how safety was negotiated and maintained at these public-school systems.

## The Historical Context

In many regards, what is going on in schools today is not unconnected to the origins of the public educational system. The development of public schools coincided with the economic and social transformation of North America (Katz, 1980). Public schools were developed to mediate and facilitate both the social transformation of the country as well as the emergence of a commercially based and industrial capitalist society (Katz, 1968, 1980). Given this, public schools were as much places for kids to socialize and learn, as they were agencies of social control, training students in the ideals of efficiency, and productivity to help create a potential labor supply (McNeil, 1986; Noguera, 1995). As the public educational system continued to develop, several things began to characterize its organization. Administrators tended to function more as business leaders than educators, curriculum was differentiated by track according to a students' social class and expected job future, and emphasis was on testable "outputs" rather than long-term learning (McNeil, 1986; Noguera, 1995). School promoters argued that this model of order, efficiency, and control would give youth access to social mobility and hence future wealth (Katz, 1980).

The creation of public schools was also intricately tied to concerns over violence and crime. In the latter part of the 19th century, "motivated by a combination of benevolence related to child welfare and fear related to the perceived threat of crime and delinquency" (Noguera, 1995, p. 194), government officials and educators shaped a public-school system that they argued could alleviate social problems (Casella, 2001; Katz, 1980; McNeil, 1986; Noguera, 1995). Urban schools in particular were looked upon by educators, politicians, and business leaders as a place to "save" poor rural children, "Americanize" recent immigrants, and get "idle youth" off the streets (Katz, 1980; McNeil, 1986). The first targets of this "Americanization" were Catholics from Ireland in the 1840s, and later Catholics from Italy (Casella, 2001; Katz, 1968, 1980). Poor farmers from rural areas seeking work in factories would also bring their children to these urban schools. Yet, middle-class parents also wanted to ease their own anxieties about adolescence, and educate their children near their homes (Katz, 1980). By the late 1800s, the development of compulsory education laws and the

Juvenile Court Act of 1899 gave the state power to act in loco parentis for delinquent youth (Casella, 2001). And by 1900, most states had enacted some form of compulsory education laws (Casella, 2001).

By the 1960s and 1970s, the relationship between school systems and violence regained national attention. But this time, the focus began to shift from looking at schools as an institution to solve violence in society, to actually examining violence within the schools. During this time period, "students' insubordination and aggression toward teachers was becoming increasingly common, and violence within schools, especially among students, was widely seen as the norm" (Noguera, 1995, p. 197). Educators and politicians connected this difficulty to the political turmoil that accompanied desegregation and civil rights protests throughout the US against the social and economic injustices (Casella, 2001; Noguera, 1995). Although the 1954 Brown vs. Board of Education case declared segregation unconstitutional, the decision of how to enforce the new requirement had been put off and segregation remained largely intact for a full decade after the decision (Orfield, Eaton, & The Harvard Project on School Desegregation, 1996). It was not until the 1964 Civil Rights Act that rapid and dramatic changes were made. And with those rapid changes, came more turmoil within the school system.

Federally mandated desegregation campaigns, compensatory education programs, and antipoverty programs combined to give rise to serious discussions about violence in schools. In response to the perception of increased violence and vandalism in schools, the US Congress mandated a "Safe School Study," which was conducted by the National Institute on Education. The study analyzed quantitative data on discipline problems from 4,000 schools, did on-site surveys with 642 schools, and conducted intense qualitative studies with 10 schools. The results were released in 1978 and revealed "shocking" statistics regarding violence in American schools (Elliott, Hamburg, & Williams, 1998). The report indicated that approximately 282,000 students and 5,200 teachers were physically assaulted every month in secondary schools (Elliott et al., 1998). With this report, the US Congress determined that school violence was a justifiable concern (Casella, 2001).

*Contemporary Schools*

The legacy of order, efficiency, discipline, and control that guided the development of public-school systems continues to define how most contemporary public schools are organized (Eckert, 1989; McNeil, 1986; Noguera, 1995). By the late 1980s, several federal mandates helped facilitate a "get tough policy" as the preferred method for creating "safe schools." These Zero Tolerance Policies emerged in schools out of a combination of the 1986 Comprehensive Drug Reform Act and the 1994 Gun-Free Schools Act (The Advancement Project and Civil Rights Project, 2000; Casella, 2001). The Drug Reform Act mandated there was a "drug-free zone" around each school in the US, specifying that juvenile drug offenders on campus would be tried as adults, with the potential of prison sentences ranging from 10 months to life. In 1994, US Congress passed the Gun-Free Schools Act, which required each school in the United States to enact some form of a Zero Tolerance Policy for weapons, or risk the loss of federal funding. "The act required not only that such policies exist within school districts, but that all gun incidents be reported by districts to their state education agencies, and that state and local laws regulating weapons in public schools be strengthened" (Brooks et al., 2000, p. 26).

Many states later expanded Zero Tolerance Policies to include a wide variety of behaviors, with some states employing sweeping interpretations of the federal law (The Advancement Project and Civil Rights Project, 2000). For example, some states have considered aspirin, Midol, and even Certs as drugs, and paper clips, nail files, and scissors as weapons. In the strictest sense, these policies provide non-discretionary punishment guidelines. But despite the increase of these types of policies, the value of them has consistently been brought into question. "Overall, there is little evidence that Zero Tolerance Policies are working to reduce violence, or increase safety in schools" (The Advancement Project and Civil Rights Project, 2000, p. 15). In fact, the National Center for Educational Statistics found that schools that use Zero Tolerance Policies are less safe than those without such policies (The Advancement Project and Civil Rights Project, 2000).

Along with these harsher policies has come the escalation of mechanisms of surveillance (Casella, 2001; Devine, 1996; Noguera, 1995). For some schools, this has included the installation of metal detectors and video cameras, the elimination of lockers, mandatory ID cards, and the use of police officers and security guards to monitor the hallways (Noguera, 1995).

Despite concerns over increasing levels of violence in schools, research has shown that juvenile crime has actually been on the decline. The Federal Bureau of Investigations Uniform Crime Reports indicated a 56% decline in juvenile homicide arrests from 1993 to 1998 (Brooks et al., 2000). During that same time period, the number of youths under 18 arrested for rape declined by 29%, for robbery 47%, and the total juvenile crime rate was dropped by 30%. Overall, only about 13% of all violent youth crimes occurred in schools, and most were considered minor assaults (Elliott et al.,

1998). The Centers for Disease Control found a 9% decline in school fights, and a 30% decline in students carrying a weapon to school from 1993 to 1998. They also found that children had less than a one in a million chance of being killed at their school on any given day.

As concerns over school violence continued to take center stage in political, educational, and mediated debates, I became more and more interested in what it meant to be a teenager in public schools during this historical moment.

## METHODS

My research consists of a qualitative, ethnographic study of two suburban schools that are both approximately 20 miles outside of a metropolitan area; one in the northeast and the other in the southeast. Although both schools were geographically suburbs, they differed demographically.[3] North Central High School was approximately 83.6% White, 10% Asian American, 1.3% African American, 4.9% Latino, and 0.1% Native American. Over 94% of their graduates went to college, and less than 1% of their students received reduced-cost or free lunch. In contrast, South River High School was 98.8% African American, 0.3% White, 0.1% Latino, and 0.2% Asian American. Approximately, 47% of the student population was eligible for free or reduced-cost lunch, and less than half of their graduates went on to college. Also significant was the fact that South River referred to itself on its website as an "urban school located in a suburban area," which signified not only how kids and school officials thought of their school, but how race and social class influenced the meaning of urban and suburban.

The demographic differences between these two schools are not uncommon. School segregation by race and social class has been increasing since the 1980s, particularly in the south (Orfield et al., 1996). Although desegregation law remained relatively stable through the 1980s, the struggle over the meaning of the law was ongoing.

> Opposition to the mandatory desegregation reached a new intensity during the Reagan Administration. Although desegregation orders were still sufficiently well rooted to prevent a clear trend toward resegregation, the shift toward a 'separate but equal' philosophy manifested itself at the end of the 1980s. (Orfield et al., 1996, p. 16)

By the 1990s, despite the increase in minorities moving into predominantly White suburban areas, a pattern of segregation for suburban Black and Latino youth intensified. National data show schools with a majority

African-American and Latino student population are dominated by poor children. In contrast, 96% of White schools have middle-class majorities (Orfield et al., 1996). Such segregation becomes problematic because it continues to exist in conjunction with a lack of resources for many poor students and students of color. Research has shown that schools with large numbers of impoverished students tend to have much lower test scores, higher dropout rates, and a lower percentage of students who will eventually finish college (Orfield et al., 1996). In this regard, the two schools in my study represent not only the national trend in suburban demographics, but also its correlation to academic performance.

A snowball sampling method was used to select participants for this study. Several adult informants were essential in helping me to obtain participants. I began my research at South River High School in May 2000 and conducted interviews through the end of the school year in June.[4] Mr. Sutton, a White, middle-class teacher, and Rita Davis, an African-American resource and police officer at the school, helped identify kids that may be interested in speaking with me. At North Central High School, Mr. Wind, a White, middle-class teacher, provided me with similar assistance. I began my interviews at North Central in September and stayed through late October, although I returned for a few times throughout the winter months for some follow-up interviews. Although these informants helped me gain initial access into the schools and with the students, after being at each school for a couple of weeks, students also began to recommend other possible participants. On a few occasions, students who heard about my research project also came to me directly and asked to be interviewed.

Overall, I interviewed 31 teenagers across a diverse range of race, class, and gender backgrounds. All of my participants were seniors at the time of the interview and between 16 and 19 years of age. I focused on seniors because when I began this research at South River, the principal preferred that I only interview students who were at least 18 years of age, so in order to be consistent, I followed this structure at North Central.

At South River High School, I interviewed nine African-American females, six African-American males, and one Asian-American male. About half of these students self-identified as either poor or working class, the other half was mainly middle class, with two students who identified as being upper class. At North Central High School, my participants included five White females, five White males, two Latino males, one Asian-American female, two Asian-American males, and one African-American female. Over half of these kids were middle class, with four being working class and three coming from upper-class backgrounds. Although I selected kids with some attention to their race, class, and gender biographies, I knew I could not represent every perspective at the school. Instead, I tried to focus on how these particular kids thought and gave meaning to the issues we discussed.

I generally began my interviews by trying to get a sense of "who" my kids were. I asked them questions about where they lived, their families, and what they wanted to do when they graduated. I asked them what it was like to go to school, and what they thought about the kids, teachers, and administrators there. To get at issues of discipline and punishment, I also questioned them about the kinds of things kids did to get in trouble for, and how the school dealt with those problems. Since I was interviewing the kids in the wake of the anniversary of the Columbine shootings, I also asked them what they felt about the incident, and how they thought it affected their own school. Finally, I questioned them about what they perceived as possible solutions for the problems at their schools. Although I had an interview guide going into each interview, I kept my questions open ended in order to give the participants considerable latitude to pursue a range of topics and to give them the ability to shape the subject matter we talked about (Bogdan & Biklen, 1992).

I interviewed kids anywhere between 40 min and $2\frac{1}{2}$ h, although the majority of interviews lasted around 1 h. The interviews took place in either the school library or guidance office during one of the student's 55-min-class periods, although some interviews ran longer than one period. These interviews were audio-taped and fully transcribed.

In order to explore how decisions got made about school safety, which included how regulation and surveillance of youth was achieved, I also interviewed administrators and staff at each school. Although I was hoping to start with the principals, both declined interviews several times, explaining that I should talk to the assistant principals, who they argued were "in charge of discipline." At North Central, there was just one White, middle-class woman named Ms. Kelly Ann O'Brien. At South River, there were three assistant principals, two of who dealt with discipline and one with scheduling. The two assistant principals were "in charge" of different grade levels, so I focused on interviewing the one in charge of seniors, the grade level of my participants. This was Dr. Marcia Cooper-Abdul, a middle-class African-American woman. At South River there were also three police officers that monitored the hallways, and I interviewed Police Officer Rita Davis who was the "senior resource officer" and the one most frequently cited by the kids I spoke with.[5]

At both schools, problems often got characterized as either "counseling" or "discipline" issues, so I was also interested in speaking with some counselors.

My informants at each school recommended a counselor who I eventually interviewed. At South River I spoke with Ms. Mary Huntington, a White, middle-class woman, who had worked at the school for 15 years. At North Central I spoke with Mr. Norm Calhoun, a White, middle-class man, who had been at the school for almost 30 years.

Each of these interviews took place in the staff's office and took about $1\frac{1}{2}$ h, with the exception of Officer Davis. Each attempt to sit down with Officer Davis and conduct some type of "formal interview" generally ended abruptly with a school situation that she needed to attend to. So instead, I took to having brief conversations with her as we walked a kid down the main office, as she monitored the cafeteria during lunchtime, or when she was able to take a quick break in the teacher's lounge. I also spent a 7-h day "shadowing" her as she went through her daily activities. During this time period, I asked her questions that were included in my interview guide, in order to ensure that I was gathering comparable data with the other staff. I also collected fieldnotes during the time I spent with her.

When I sat down with the adults at the school, I followed similar methodological techniques as I did with the children. I asked them about the school and the problems they saw occurring. I wanted to know why they thought kids got in trouble at their school, what were some of the barriers to dealing with the problems at their school, and what type of solutions they thought were possible.

# FINDINGS

## School Rules and Zero Tolerance

Schools use a range of practices to monitor and manage kids in order to create a safe school environment. School rules, disciplinary policies, video cameras, metal detectors, police officers, hall passes, teachers, administrators, staff, and the kids all play a role in trying to maintain a safe school in order for education to take place. Although all of these things play an important part in the overall organization of the school, rules were the things that most explicitly defined student conduct and behavior.

Within the local setting of each school, student handbooks outlined the rules for students. As Ms. O'Brien at North Central described, student handbooks provided kids "in black and white" with a list of the rules regarding student conduct and discipline policies. Disciplinary rules at both schools generally consisted of three different categories of rules: rules governing where a student should be; rules governing what they can and cannot say; and rules about what they can and cannot do. Rules about where a student was supposed to be included restrictions on being in the parking lot and hallways during certain time periods as well as more general rules about being late or absent from class, or school in general. Rules about what kids can and cannot say included restrictions on obscene language and cursing, insubordination, and calling in a bomb threat. What a student can and cannot do during the school day consisted of rules restricting behavior such as bringing a weapon to school, smoking, assaulting a peer or adult, using or selling drugs and alcohol, theft, or damaging property. This also included rather extensive dress code policies at both schools.

As outlined in the student handbook, breaking rules carried specific consequences. As Dr. Cooper-Abdul of South River noted, "Sometimes they will think before they act because they don't want another punishment. Because even if they can get their assignments, when they are suspended, it still is an impediment on learning" (Interview #32: 5). For each offense, penalties ranged from detention,[6] to in-school suspension,[7] to out-of-school suspension, and finally expulsion. The handbook outlined each offense with its subsequent penalty, for example cursing may get you a detention for the first offense, but a suspension for a repeated offense. Both schools ran under a progressive punishment standard, which was, do something once you get detention; do it twice you get suspended. But there were also certain things that garnered immediate expulsion. At South River, a countywide tribunal, run by the board of education, reviewed all "critical" problems before a student could be transferred or expelled. Overall, a transfer to an alternative school or an expulsion usually entailed part of each school's "Zero Tolerance Policies."

Both North Central and South River had state laws that mandated Zero Tolerance Policies for students who possessed firearms or who committed violent acts with weapons other than firearms. According to state law, these students were supposed to be expelled from the regular education program for a period of 1 year and be placed in alternative schooling. North Central's state laws included zero tolerance for continued and willful disobedience, assault, vandalism, theft, trespassing, or knowing possession or consumption of alcohol or dangerous substances. South River's state Department of Education specifically required schools to adopt codes of conduct that included, "Zero Tolerance – There will be consequences for serious drug, weapon and youth gang/hate group offenses on school property or at a school activity, function or event."

Although principals, assistant principals, resource officers, and even the librarians informed me that each school had Zero Tolerance Policies, nowhere in the student handbooks was the phrase "zero tolerance" explicitly used. The policies in the handbook were written up in such a way that there was certainly zero tolerance for certain acts that could garner immediate expulsion. For example, at North Central, possession of a weapon did carry the possibility of expulsion and the guarantee of police intervention. At South River, this guaranteed immediate county tribunal, where expulsion was both possible and likely.[8] But for the most part, each school's Zero Tolerance Policies tended to be vague.

The discourse of discipline that ran through the school handbooks was not unconnected to the practices in the schools. At times, youth and adults alike looked at these policies as templates for what the consequences were for certain behaviors. But although certain acts were clearly "not tolerated" according to written policies, the lack of explicit Zero Tolerance Policies "on the books" seemed to imply some understanding that issues were not always as cut and dry as Zero Tolerance Policies presumed. The fact that certain rules got written up (or not) did not determine what happened next; it only organized it. In this regard, the rules and punishment were hardly in "black and white" and were rather quite messy.

### Differential Treatment

> It basically depended on how the administration feels about you. Like, if you haven't gotten in trouble before, and this is your first altercation, then you probably won't get that big of a penalty. (*Zakiya, a working-class African American, South River*, Interview #4: 6)

In practice, rules and punishment never quite got played out in the neat way that they were organized in the student handbooks. Kids often cited administrators and teachers as the source of such inconsistencies. As Zakiya discussed, if you were a "good kid" you tended to get less penalties than a "bad kid," even for the same offense, reinforcing the idea that schools reproduced societal hierarchies (Eckert, 1989).

Often, these societal hierarchies were connected to race and social class. At North Central, many of the students connected "bad" kids to the White, working-class "skaters" and "punks."

> Like I have a reputation here at North Central, whatever. Crap, like I'm just a kid. That's the bottom line. Okay, so mothers of the other kids see me smoking cigarettes, bla bla bla, whatever. Couple years back I broke into the community pool and sat on the lifeguard posted. That's all you need to have a reputation, in a small town like Thomasville. Like any other school, rumors, you know, the shit hits the fan, everybody

hears about it. I don't like taking crap from teachers. (*Drew, White, working class, North Central*, Interview #20: 12)

At South River, "bad" kids were generally referred to as "hood-raised," "thugs", or "ghetto kids," essentially lower-income Black kids.

> The people who get in trouble, are the most, I don't want to label them as ghetto children, but they are people who aren't from the middle class or the upper, middle class. The people who are in the um, who stay in like the projects or apartments. I mean I guess they just haven't had the upbringing that most of the other students had, so they don't know what they should and should not be doing. So they are most of the people who get into altercations. (*Zakiya, African American, working class, South River*, Interview #4: 4)

> Like I was saying, I was a bully, so no one really judged me (laughs). Everyone was like speaking to me, greeting me and stuff. They kind of make me feel like a queen or whatever. But I know some of them looked at me probably like, she's ghetto or something like that. Like I said though, I didn't really care about what other people think about me, because I was popular. (*Sharifa, African American, low income, South River*, Interview #13: 8)

Overall, the rules tended to be followed more strictly for students with a "bad" social status, than those with a "good" one.

To some degree, "good" kids were more likely to be involved in school-sanctioned activities. Joy, a White, middle-class youth at North Central, and Qwame, a Black, middle-class youth at South River were both student body presidents, and both admitted they walked the halls frequently without passes, and rarely got asked to show one. Even though they were breaking a school rule, neither got reprimanded. On the other hand, Drew, a self-proclaimed "troublemaker" and "skater," said he was constantly asked to show a hall pass and account for where he was supposed to be, and essentially was monitored more than "good kids." Students like Drew were constantly referred to as going "against the system," because they are "always trying to defy the rules you know, trying to skip class or walk around with a bad attitude, because they're someone that doesn't really care about the school" (Deonté, middle-class, African American, South River, Interview #1: 11). And to some degree, kids that were considered "bad" did express feelings of disenfranchisement and despair.

> I believe that teachers might look at me and say, that's a bad, little girl, that's a bad little girl. But to me, I didn't really care how people looked at me, because I just always did my stuff. (*Sharifa, low income, African American, South River*, Interview #13: 7)

In addition to "good" students, athletes, and in particular male athletes, were often not subjected to the typical practices of discipline and punish. Describing why he never was suspended, even though he had frequently talked about being in fights, Vincent, an African-American football player at South River, simply stated, "That's why I have coaches." Hector, a Latino student at North Central who played varsity football and track, also admitted that coaches frequently got him out of after school detentions, so he would not miss practice. Marcus, a working-class Black athlete at South River said this about being an athlete:

> It's easy to slide by. You play any sport, you slide by easily. It ain't even hard. It's like, I want to do this or do that, 'Okay, you don't have to come to class today.' I mean they don't care. (Interview #11: 6)

At a football game I attended at South River, a more poignant incident was revealed. As I stood in the food line with a teacher, I overheard him and another student remarking about Troy playing tonight, and I noticed the female student rolling her eyes. After we sat down, he pointed to the field and said, "That's Troy, the quarterback. He punched a girl in the face today at school." Somewhat surprised, I asked why he was not suspended. The teacher responded, "Oh he is suspended. Starting on Monday." The fact that his suspension for assaulting a female student was delayed to ensure that he could play in that night's game was indicative of how rules were inconsistently enforced for male athletes.

At South River, students also frequently talked about a star football player, Travis, who "can't get in trouble." During the time of my study, he had gotten into a fight with Joseph, a student with a "reputation for being in trouble." Since both students had gotten suspended for fighting before, their case went directly to tribunal. Two coaches, the gym teacher and a former teacher of Travis, came to the tribunal on his behalf, arguing that not only did he have potential to go onto college as an athlete, but that he was diagnosed with an Emotional Behavior Disorder, and his athleticism was the only thing that got him out of special education. Travis was allowed to return to South River; Joseph, who was a special-education student, was transferred to an alternative schooling program.

### *Keeping Problems "Hush Hush"*

Although the social status of the student often came into play when deciding who received punishment, and who did not, sometimes problems were simply kept "hush hush" (as one teacher described), in an effort to maintain a reputation of a "good school system." During my research, Mr. Wind told a story about several students who had gotten into a serious car accident during the weekend. He said he had heard it had to do with alcohol, but "that will never surface," because North Central does not want to be perceived as a "bad school." Another North Central teacher talked about how a student came to the school drunk one morning, so an administrator took her to an emergency medical office to get tested, rather than the school nurse's office. In this way, he believed, "It's less likely to become part of an official record."

Kids also felt that administrators often deliberately tried to hide school problems. At South River, Vanessa talked about how the schools tried to "act like nothings happening" when it came to serious problems, like fighting or bringing weapons to school. Ashleigh at North Central described the same thing when she said her school tried to keep serious problems "low key." In this regard, consequences for breaking the rules were sometimes subverted and concealed.

Overall, each school seemed to be somewhat invested in maintaining the image of a "good school."[9] Although adults and youth at both schools recognized that problems existed, once they became part of an official "record," it was more likely to alter the public perception that others had of their school. For example, when a case surrounding a teacher who sexually molested students occurred, Ms. Huntington had asked the police officer if he would help keep it out of the media. She said she was happy when the case was only marginally referred to at the end of the local evening newscast. Although Ms. Huntington's intention was to protect the students and avoid having their painful experiences exploited, not all school officials wanted to keep problems hidden out of benevolence to safeguard the kids' welfare.

Some teachers felt a more common reason for keeping problems "hush hush" was more "self-serving." This was best exemplified at North Central, when the superintendent requested a state monitoring report. Several teachers said the request in itself was purely out of self-interest because the superintendent was looking to move to a better school, so he wanted to ensure he had a good school on his record. In "preparation" for this, teachers were literally encouraged by the principal to try and keep the number of penalties down for school offenses and to keep their record "as clean as possible." Additionally, months in advance they were given a list of scripted answers for multiple scenarios that they were told to learn if any state monitors talked with them. Yet, they were also strongly advised in multiple meetings to not initiate any conversation with the monitors, just to address questions if they were directly asked, and more importantly, to follow the script. Mr. Wind, a teacher at North Central, described his frustration with the process, particularly when he discovered the monitoring itself proved to be of little value.

> For months they had been planning for this and the teachers were required to do so much work. They finally came to the school and, I didn't even see them in the hallway. And you know the only recommendation they made? They said that doorstops were a fire hazard. Can you believe that shit? So all of the teachers in protest are going to be tying our doors open to lockers and using other methods to keep our doors open. All of the hell they put us through and all's we get are no doorstops as the recommendation. (Fieldnotes October 11, 1999, pp. 22–23)

South River had a similar situation, but for them it followed 26 bomb threats in a 2-month period. The state Alcohol, Tobacco, and Firearms division was sent in to evaluate the school, and teachers were advised by administrators to not talk with ATF officials, if at all possible. Teachers expressed their frustration with this, particularly because they felt the request came in contrast with a genuine concern to get at the root of the problem. Instead, they said the principal's "job was on the line," and they believed keeping it was given a greater priority, than finding out why bomb threats were made to the school.

These incidents exemplified the extent to which schools would go to in order to ensure the presentation of a good image. Yet, covering up problems certainly did not get at the root of them or necessarily maintain a safe school environment. Rather, it just maintained the perception of one.

### Playing the System

In many regards, students were quite aware of the inconsistencies and differential treatment when it came to school rules and punishments. At North Central, Lee, an Asian–American middle-class student, described inconsistencies regarding detentions for being late to school. "You get like Saturday school for like four lates. And sophomore year I had like 23. Bad news. Because that year my brother drove me and like his teacher didn't give him lates but mine did" (Interview #28: 19). For Lee, ramifications for breaking the tardiness rule relied more on whether or not a teacher would enforce it, than whether the rule actually existed. Priscilla, a White, working-class youth, described a similar inconsistency in regards to the rule on profanity.

> Profanity, we do that all the time. And some teachers don't even care. And like some of the older teachers, they care because you're like disrespecting them, which is true. So you get a Saturday [detention]. (Interview #21: 9)

At North Central, Todd, a White, working-class student, talked about how he "smokes cigarettes at this school everyday," even though there were strict rules against it. Todd discussed how the previous assistant principal would often just give him warnings about smoking, what he called his "get out of jail free" cards. He said he was more likely to "get out of jail free" if no one else was around when he was caught.

Often inconsistencies regarding rules and punishment actually followed some kind of pattern, and youth were quick to pick up on the pattern in order to "play the system." They learned who they could curse in front of, or who would let them wear a hat to class. Todd said he avoided smoking with friends because he knew he was less likely to get in trouble when he was alone. Students also seemed to recognize that "good" kids didn't get in a lot of trouble and some used this to "play the system."

> You have to understand that when you are talking to the principal that you're wrong and you're sorry. And then you're out the door. (*Todd, White, lower-middle class, North Central*, Interview #20: 14)

As Todd described, one way to avoid consequences was to say what you thought a particular administrator wanted to hear and admit you were wrong, hence giving legitimacy to the rule.

In general, students seemed to be able to "play the system" if their behavior was perceived as non-confrontational. A teacher at South River talked about one male student who was literally always roaming the hallway. When teachers approached him, he tended to be silly and playful, joking about where he was supposed to be, always claiming to "have a pass" and be on his way to class. The teacher said staff consistently struggled to get him where he needed to be. But since his nature was non-confrontational, there seemed to be "less of an urgency" to remove him from the hallways.

Kids also seemed likely to ignore rules if they felt they could get away with it. This came up most frequently in regards to the dress code. Priscilla, a working–class White youth at North Central, talked about getting away with "hiding" her outfit. "No mid-riff shirts. I always used to wear them. You can't anymore, but I'm still going to wear it. We hide it. Like girls are able to hide it" (Interview #21: 11). At South River, although there were strict rules against gang-related clothing, a group of African-American boys at the school bought sweatshirts with "Turner Park Clique" airbrushed across the front. Most of these boys considered themselves to be part of a gang, or at least a group that would "represent their turf" in Turner Park, but the administration was unable to punish them, because technically airbrushed sweatshirts and "cliques" did not violate the school rules.

Although most of the students I spoke with described peer mediation as an effective tool available to deal with school problems, a few peer mediators at South River felt some students took advantage of the program.

This was because students who agreed to go to peer mediation to resolve their problems would generally not receive standard punishment (i.e. in-school suspension for verbal fighting, etc.). Although mediators did not believe that students did this often, Michael feared a few kids who came to him for mediation did not want to sincerely solve their dispute, and instead were just "copping out," and taking advantage of a good program, just to avoid a detention or suspension.

Some students also felt you could easily "play the system" by learning more about surveillance at the school. This tended to be brought up in reference to the video cameras. Deonté said, "You know where the camera is, so if you want to do something, don't do it right in front of the camera." And for the most part, kids recognized exactly where the cameras were located – the front of the building, the parking lot, the cafeteria, the office, a few stairwells – and where they were not located. Many spoke of literally moving a fight, or even engaging in sexual relations in areas of the building where they knew they were not under the watchful eye of the camera. Most kids also believed the cameras were not being monitored all the time, and in fact, they were not.

*Rules Becoming "Lax"*

Students tended to stop following rules if they thought they were no longer being strictly enforced, or as they described, administrators became "lax." This was exemplified in the hallway "sweeps" at South River. Randomly, when a "sweep" was announced, any student caught in the hallway without a hall pass received an automatic in-school suspension. At the beginning of the school year, they were frequent and students believed effective. Yet by the end of the school year, school sweeps rarely were executed. Kids recognized the inconsistency of this, rendered hallway sweeps ineffective, and therefore discussed becoming more "lax" themselves when it came to hall passes, getting to class on time, or going to class at all.

A similar situation existed at North Central. Following the Columbine shootings in particular, the kids at North Central perceived that things got "stricter." As Lee described, "My friend was just like joking around with a girl, like they are just friendly, they are friends. And he wrote this fake death threat. But it was just, like make-believe, messing around. And he got called down to the principal and stuff. They called his parents" (Interview #28: 6). Richard, a White, middle-class youth at North Central, said he got called to the main office following Columbine because of a slide presentation for his

English class that contained a reference to cannibalism. "My mom said, you know you can't do this 'cause you know what people will think, with the whole Columbine thing. But I was like how does this show that I'm screaming for help?" (Interview #17: 10).

Students soon began to test the consistency of this Zero Tolerance Policy. "So I came out and I said to someone, I'm gonna kill you! And no one said anything, and I'm like, so why aren't you enforcing that" (Interview #21: 24)? Gina, an upper-class White student at North, felt this rule was not being uniformly enforced. And in general, the farther away from the Columbine incident it got, kids noticed that they got in less trouble for "joking" about violence or making references to it in their school work.

Once rules became more lax, and students saw there were fewer ramifications, they tended to break the rules more frequently. For example, following the Columbine shootings, North Central also began a single-entry policy, which meant all doors were locked except the main entrance. This entrance was on the complete opposite side of the student parking lot. Gina described her way around this rule. "Yeah, they lock all the doors. And we have late arrival and we come in at like 8:45 and the doors are locked and we're like, ok. So we just cut through the janitors' room" (Interview #24: 19). She had never been penalized for this, so she made it her daily routine. Additionally, Priscilla talked about how students were required to have parking permits, but since she had never gotten one, and administration had yet to do anything about it, she failed to see the importance of following this rule. Overall, if students saw there were no ramifications for breaking a rule, they continued to break it.

Sometimes students challenged rules because they felt they were infringements on their personal rights. Jada refused to do anything about the tinted windows on her car because she claimed that the Assistant Principal had them on her car. She questioned why administrators could have such features, but she could not. At South River, students who were caught cutting lunch to go to McDonald's told the principal after being caught that it was "their right" to eat a good meal since the cafeteria food "sucked." One student argued that if he was "old enough to vote," he should be old enough to leave school when he wanted to. Plus, he argued, that teachers were allowed to leave school campus if they wanted to, so why could not students? In this regard, students recognized the power imbalances between adults and youth, and therefore challenged rules that had apparent age-based discrepancies.

## Structural Constraints

Administrators tended to be aware of some of these inconsistencies, and struggled with structural constraints and lack of stability that they felt made consistency difficult. At South River, not only did the principal change four times since these seniors had been in school, but there were just as many changes with assistant principals and counselors. Additionally, they had about 15 new teachers that year, which tended to be the norm. North Central had fewer changes in their administration and faculty. For the staff at both schools, they understood that stability was a privilege that only some public schools, the ones who could pay faculty and staff higher salaries, could afford.[10] Without stability, being consistent was difficult. As a counselor, Ms. Huntington described, "There's no structure that is followed through, day by day by day. And if our kids don't know what to expect and they have no structure, they don't feel secure" (Interview #33: 5).

Staff at both North Central and South River talked about some of the problems as being inherent in a bureaucracy. Administrators frequently talked about wanting to spend more time with their students, but always being caught up with paperwork. As South River's assistant principal, Dr. Marcia Cooper-Abdul described, "too many disciplinarian referrals and not enough time to do other things." North Central's assistant principal, Kelly Ann O'Brien, voiced similar concerns. "All you really do all day is deal with problems and you have little student contact. Like I don't mind doing lunch duty, because that's the only time I get to see all the kids."

Teachers and administrators found themselves being inconsistent about some rules when it came to certain students, because some parents were more involved with the school, and sometimes more difficult to deal with.

> You know some kids would get sent down, two kids for the same thing, but they didn't get the same consequences. A desire to take the path of least resistance. Like if you had a child who you knew the parent was a difficult parent, they tended to not come down hard on those kids, because they just didn't want the hassle with the parent. And uh, those were the kids that would really take advantage of a situation. (*Ms. Kelly Ann O'Brien, Assistant Principal, North Central,* Interview #35: 3)

At some level, this too was related to social status, and issues of race and social class.[11] Ms. O'Brien's secretary felt that "rich kids' parents" most persistently called the school over the "slightest little problem." One North Central teacher said he was asked by the principal to excuse a kid from detention because the student had to "catch a flight to Bermuda for a family vacation." In contrast, at South River a teacher was told by one administrator not to worry about handing out detentions to a student, because "it's not like his ghetto mom would ever call." For some, it was not just whether or not a parent would challenge a child's punishment, but whether or not the administration would support their decision to discipline the child. Ms. O'Brien said she was in a tenuous position when it came to parent complaints about punishment, because she said, the administrators in charge of the school were more likely to side with the parents, no matter what the situation.

This rigid hierarchy that organized the school, and more specifically, the lack of collaboration within the hierarchy, was often cited as part of the problem. For example, when a new assistant principal came to South River, Officer Davis tried to stress the importance of using teachers as extra monitors in the cafeteria, auditorium, and bus ramp during the mornings. But the new principal failed to take her advice.

> There was this pepper spray incident this year also. I told the VP that we needed two teachers and one officer in the auditorium, in the cafeteria, and at the buses each morning to monitor the kids. The administrative assistant said the same thing several times to him. But the new VP says we only need one. Well one day the teacher is out. Who's there to watch them in the morning if you only have one person there? So this pepper spray goes off, and the kids who sprayed it goes to tribunal. Well it gets thrown out. If they don't have supervision, then how can they say it's their fault? This is my point. PLUS, the administrative assistant also said to him, when he said we only needed one person watching, that we needed someone to at least check to make sure the teachers got there every morning. So she was doing this on her own. But he told her to stop doing it. And on the morning she stopped, this happened. This is what I mean. (Interview #34: 19)

As exemplified in this story, often the people who were closest to the kids and who seemed to understand their social situations the best, were most frequently disregarded by administrators when it came to creating ways to ensure the safety of the kids. In fact, the rules themselves were not created in collaboration. Instead, at both schools, the board of education created the rules, with very little input from the assistant or head principals, and certainly no input from teachers or students. A counselor who had been at South River for over a decade said the board of education would pay "lip service" to grand ideas, which were so far removed from what was "real" at their school.

> It's great to think outside the box. It's great to want to do programs and all this stuff. But I think for the most part, many teachers want to talk about what is real, and what are the real problems of this school. Our real issues are kids getting to class on time, kids coming prepared, and academic reports. If you take care of that and get a good grip at

the discipline, then maybe you look at other problems. (*Ms. Huntington, Counselor, South River*, Interview # 33: 5)

The structure itself of a countywide tribunal system best exemplified how those who knew the least about students where the ones who dealt with them after they committed the worst rule violations. For example, one case involved an African-American male student who assaulted a teacher. It happened one day after he was sent out of the classroom to the office. As he was refusing, another teacher approached and agreed to escort the student to the office, so the teacher could continue with instruction. When this teacher asked him to head to the office, the student punched him in the face. Officer Davis arrived moments later, and as the two tried to hold the student down in order to put handcuffs on him, the student proceeded to bite the hand of the teacher. As the case headed to tribunal, more information regarding the student's personal history began to emerge.

> He was banned from every school in the area he used to live, so he moved here to live with his Aunt. He had a learning disability that the mother or aunt didn't inform the school about because the parents, you know, often they're too embarrassed about that and don't like their children to be labeled at a new school. (*Officer Rita Davis, Resource Officer, South River*, Interview #37: 13)

Yet there was strong support by the principal to "get rid of the kid," despite the circumstances of his background, and the principal made it clear that he planned to make sure tribunal would kick him out of the school. The teacher who was assaulted decided to not press charges after he learned more about the student, and actually went to the tribunal hearing in the student's defense, hoping administrators would consider placing him in the school's special-education program. But the kid was expelled anyway. This teacher, who was also a special-education teacher himself, told me later, "I don't think that the school should have thrown him out, because that's obviously been a pattern that hasn't helped him out. Clearly, it's been making him worse." Overall, once a problem at South River got to the level of the county tribunal, teachers, administrators and counselors agreed, there was very little that could be done at the local level to help keep the kid in their school system.[12]

## DISCUSSION AND POLICY IMPLICATIONS

School rules themselves are not inherently "bad," and I am not arguing that they need to be eliminated by any means. Having clear consequences for acts of violence or things that disrupt the educational process are important. Responsible steps are certainly needed to protect students from weapons, violence, and illegal drugs. Yet this does not mean that the rules, or how they are enforced, are not also problematic. Paying close attention to how rules get interpreted and practiced illuminates important issues that can help schools create policies that sustain safe school environments.

### Understanding the Complex Lives of Youth

I would argue that one of the biggest problems with having rules in "black and white" is that there is so much messiness that is part of the everyday lives of youth. Having particular punishments for rule violations leaves little room for understanding the complex lives of youth, and as Ms. Huntington, a counselor at South River stressed, "I think the biggest thing is to know our kids." This involves learning about youth's everyday experiences in their homes and neighborhoods, and seriously considering how these experiences are connected to the kids' social behavior within the school system.

My data include several examples during my research that stressed how knowing more about the complex lives of youth created opportunities for teachers and administrators to address problems in more effective ways. At South River, a teacher had one student who was chronically sleeping in class. In talking with the student he discovered that the student's family of six was kicked out of their home, and was now sharing just one room at a motel. The student claimed that sleeping in that type of environment was nearly impossible. Knowing more about the student's reason for sleeping in class gave the teacher an opportunity to call the family, and help them try and find alternative housing for the student while he was in school.

At North Central, counselor Norm Calhoun talked about the importance of not only knowing your students, but also effectively communicating this with other staff at the school.

> Last year there was a case where a kid was coming in late to school, fairly frequently. There was uh you know, he was getting into some minor difficulties here at school. And I was able to inform the vice-principal that the mother in that house is an alcoholic. The parents are in the process of going through a divorce. The police have been called to that house several times because of domestic violence issues. So this kid is dealing with a lot. So I'm not saying that it is okay for him to be late to school. And I'm not saying it's okay for him to act out once he gets here. But there is a reason for it. And knowing that background, I think she was able to be a little more lenient with him, and a little more understanding with him then she might be with somebody else. (Interview #36: 9–10)

## The Messy Nature of Discipline and Zero Tolerance Policies 103

At South River, taking a moment to talk with one student gave a teacher the chance to get at the root of why he was refusing to go to a pep rally. On the day of the rally, several teachers walked through the hallways on their way to the football field, gathering students who were "straggling behind." As they passed a group of male students sitting on an outdoor stairwell, teachers told the students to "get going to the pep rally" and most got up and complied with the request, except for one student, Devon. Devon stared at the ground as teachers tried to redirect the group, and would not head down to the field. One teacher told him he "had no choice – pep rallies were mandatory." Yet Devon insisted, he was not going. Another teacher interjected, it was "either the pep rally or ISS [In-school Suspension]." But Devon said he did not care. Finally, one teacher approached the youth and said, "Look we're not trying to give you a hard time, but you got to go to the pep rally. If you can give me one good reason of why you're refusing to go, you can sit here for the pep rally." Devon looked up at the teacher and said, "My cousin shot himself in the head last night." Such examples paint a complicated picture of youth and the violence they experience. Devon's ability to negotiate what he had to do during the school day was directly tied to how he was able to manage the rest of the things that went on in his life, including the sudden and tragic death of a close relative. Understanding his behavior in relationship to his life experiences gave one teacher an opportunity to look beyond the rule-breaking behavior, and respond to the student's needs.

Understanding the complex nature of kids' lives sometimes requires moving beyond rules and punishment to building relationships with the students that foster trust and support. Chai Son, the only Asian-American student in his graduating class at South River, talked about the resource officers in a way that resonated with many of the kids I talked with.

> Resource officers are friendly; they show you the ropes. Basically they clear the hallway when the bells ring and stuff like that. Make sure everybody is safe at school. Guide you in a positive way, not a negative way. Always keep your hopes up. (Interview #8: 4)

Although their bodies were covered with symbols of control and punishment (police jackets, badges, guns, and batons), the resource officers at South River, and in particular Officer Davis, were often spoken about in a positive manner. Officer Davis was described as down-to-earth and caring, and she would "help you with any problem you had." For the "Mother/ Daughter" lunch she took three female students with her – one who had an abusive and alcoholic mother, another whose mother was in a mental hospital, and another who did not have a mother – to ensure that they did not feel left out of the event. Students frequently talked about how thankful they were when she would break up a fight. Zakiya characterized her as "dedicated to helping students."

Another integral part of knowing kids involves knowing the language that they use. As Lisa Delpit has argued, "When a significant difference exists between the students' culture and the school's culture, teachers can easily misread students' aptitudes, intent, or abilities as a result of the difference in styles of language use and interactional patterns" (1995, p. 167). Kids would use terms like "mean muggin'," "flexing," "nutting up," or "rainbow parties." If you were mean muggin', you were staring someone down, letting the person know you were ready to fight. Flexing meant you were showing off your weapon, like a gun or knife. Nuttin' up generally referred to students who were "freaking out," or essentially having some kind of mental health breakdown. And if a rainbow party was taking place in the locker room, this meant girls (wearing different shades of lipstick) were performing oral sex on several boys. Knowing the language and slang kids use is essential if teachers and administrators are to understand what is going on in their schools, and more effectively deal with the problems at hand.

At the beginning of every school year at South River, administrators would take all the new teachers on a bus ride into the neighborhoods where the students lived. Demographically, South River was predominantly African American, and the social class of their students ranged from poor to wealthy. The principal would "tour" the new teachers through the Canoe Brook Housing Project, to the gated communities of the West side. The point of this exercise was to give the new teachers some understanding of the diverse group of students they would soon be teaching. Although the teachers and principal never actually got off of the bus and went into the communities they traveled through, the exercise itself is a useful starting point and example of the kinds of things that schools can do to better understand the complex nature of the every day lives of their students.

Taking the time to sit down and talk with students about what is going on in their lives and why they may not be following a school rule is sometimes time consuming, as assistant principal Ms. O'Brien revealed:

> To nip it in the bud, when something is small. I had girls in here last week come up and spend an hour. It's very time consuming, like I spent an hour and half with them. But if it's gonna avoid a confrontation down the line, then it's worth investing the hour and a half. (*Kelly Ann O'Brien, Assistant Principal, North Central*, Interview #35: 4)

So "nipping it in the bud" can often ensure that small problems do not escalate into larger ones.

Research has shown that violent acts diminish within an environment of familiarity and connectedness (Delpit, 1995; Epp & Watkinson, 1997; Noguera, 1995). Noguera (1995) found that teachers, who lacked familiarity with their students, were more likely to misunderstand and fear them. At a very basic level, I believe that gaining familiarity and fostering the type of relationships and understanding that is needed to maintain a safe school environment begins by reducing classroom and school size. At both South River and North Central, there were more than 30 students in the regular education classrooms. South River had over 1,200 students in their building, and North Central had nearly 800. Dr. Marcia Cooper-Abdul at South River said she had teachers who would send her discipline forms about particular students with only their first name on the form, "because the teacher didn't even know the kid's last name." Taking the time to talk with a student about why he is not going to a pep rally, or bringing two girls who are constantly fighting into your office to discuss the conflict they are having is difficult to do if you have large numbers of students, and very few faculty and staff to work with them.

I believe that having more team-taught classes could also help foster an environment where both learning and relationship building could take place. At South River, team-taught classes were sometimes created when several special-education students were integrated into a classroom. Teachers that worked in these environments generally spoke about their ability to give kids more attention during the school day. And if a problem did occur, they said one teacher could address the problem while the other continued with the curriculum. In this regard, the process of learning did not have to be interrupted.

Becoming more familiar with your students could also be better achieved if there was more consistency among the teachers that students had throughout their 4 years of high school. At both schools, students would get assigned one counselor during their freshman year and they would keep that counselor until they graduated. In this regard, the counselor was able to get to know the student and better understand their background, know the challenges they faced, and know the goals they had. Yet with teachers, it does not work this way. Teachers were generally grade-specific, that is, you are a 9th grade English teacher. But there is the potential for teachers to also stay with students during their 4 years at the school. I do not think this needs to be, or even could be applied to every single subject matter or class in which a student is enrolled, but moving toward more consistency among teachers could help build those connections that are essential to creating a safe school environment.

Developing and maintaining a cadre of teachers at any one particular school is difficult when resources are scarce. At South River, the teacher turnover rate was much higher than at North Central. Although a systematic examination of the factors related to this issue are beyond the scope of this study, decreasing expenditures per pupil, relatively low faculty wages, and increasing class size may be relevant factors. To deal with these issues, vast changes in local, statewide, and national public school funding are clearly necessary.

Beyond policy changes dealing with classroom size and teacher assignment, I think understanding kids' lives can happen at an informal level. Ms. Huntington referred to this as the "tennis shoe thing," which she saw as far more important than most of the rules and mechanisms of surveillance that existed at school.

> We used to laugh at this, because it's the tennis shoe thing. They need to see you with jeans and tennis shoes on after school, doing something, supporting them and their interests. It cuts down on the discipline in the classroom. It would cut down on a lot of stuff. And it seems real hokey, but it's very true. (Interview #33: 6)

Undoubtedly, getting to know your students is the best way to ensure a more humanizing school environment.

### Collaborating on Rule Making

In general, I found the youth I spoke with were generally invested in creating safe school environments. They did not want fights going on in their hallways, or kids disrupting their classrooms. When they saw trouble occurring, youth would often look to the adults they trusted at the school.

> When it gets to that level, generally someone is gonna tell on somebody, for whatever reason. Whether it is out of fear or retaliation or I'll fix him. They may not tell if you're in a group, but they'll come by later. (Dr. Marcia Cooper-Abdul, Assistant Principal, South River, Interview #32: 8)

During my time at each school, I saw kids come to teachers about graffiti on the walls, or tell a counselor about a friend who was depressed, drinking alcohol frequently, or even suicidal. Some female students came to Officer Davis about girls having sex in the auditorium and locker rooms, in particular because they felt these girls were being "taking advantage of [by boys] because they were freshmen." This "monitoring" of each other only occurred, though, in situations where kids trusted adults enough to bring these problems to their attention.

Kids also looked to each other to solve the problems at their school. Sometimes this happened at an informal level. For example, several male students I spoke with prided themselves in breaking up fights, "to help administrators out." This also happened at a more formal level, with peer mediation at South River and student outreach at North Central. As Imani described, "If you have two teenagers trying to help you solve your problem, they probably have been where you are, and can talk it out with you. Instead of just an administrator saying, okay, you did this and you did that, and we're going to give you an in school or out-school suspension for it" (Interview #6: 20). Sharifa, who admitted she was consistently in trouble while at South River, said, "I think peer mediation would have helped me as far as fighting. Just to talk things out" (Interview #13: 10). Mr. Calhoun, a counselor at North Central, felt a combination of peer mentors and guidance counselors worked best to solve problems at their school.

> I don't know one could replace the other, but I think both are needed. I think kids for years have always been getting advice from other kids, and at many times are more willing to go to other kids than to a professional person. But I think we're the professionals and we can intervene. Or if a kid goes to another kid with something really serious, if we have a good relationship with them, sometimes the kid will come to me and say, hey my friend is having this problem. (Interview #36: 9)

In part, I believe that both kids and teachers need to be a more integral part of the rule-making process at the school. When video cameras at South River were installed in the hallways, kids said they began to meet in the parking lot to fight. After several months of having fights outside of the school building, administrators created a rule restricting students from going to the parking lot at all during the day, with disciplinary tribunal as the ramification for being caught. When this rule was instituted, Qwame said that "It took them long enough to figure that one out. If they just asked the kids what was going on, fighting in the parking lot could have ended months ago."

Each school's student handbook began with a mission statement that was clearly about collaboration. The words "community," "cooperative," "democratic," and "partnership" were included in the mission statement of each school. Yet in general, rules were not made in collaboration among teachers, administrators, students, and staff. In fact, many of the rules themselves were created in complete isolation of the local school setting. At both schools, the board of education, guided by state laws regarding zero tolerance and in loco parentis, created most of the rules and punishments for each school. Overall, kids had no say about the rules that were created, and therefore, I would argue, were less invested in them. They also questioned the validity and vagueness of some rules.

> Like you can't wear anything that's offensive to someone else. Like I don't know how that can work, because anything can be offensive to someone else. (*Hector, middle class, Latino youth*, Interview #16: 11)

Teachers often admitted that they themselves did not follow rules that they thought were petty or useless. If rules were truly made in collaboration, students and teachers would likely come to see the value of them and respect the importance of them.

In general, an overall critique is needed of how disciplinary rules at both schools were strictly about controlling and constricting student behavior, not adult. As previously discussed, youth were often aware of the power-imbalances of the rules and challenged them because of it. It would be useful if students not only knew about rules that teachers and administrators had to follow, but also helped create these rules. At South River, there were signs that hung throughout the school that read "No Guns, No Gangs, No Violence." It might be equally useful to hang signs regarding student conduct alongside signs regarding adult conduct, or even more general signs regarding rules for the entire school community.

### *Limited Options for Punishment*

I argue that the types of punishment available in schools today are very limited. Detentions, suspensions, and expulsions are the most common method of dealing with school problems. Administrators often perceived that there was little else to do but "get rid of" problem students, if they needed to ensure the safety of the majority of students.

> I guess nobody ever wins when we have to get to the point of tribunal. But if a kid is making an environment where the teacher can't teach and other kids can't learn, or it's not safe, he needs to go. (*Dr. Cooper-Abdul, Assistant Principal, South River*, Interview #32: 7)

Yet "getting rid of" kids, whether it be by kicking them out of class or expelling them from school, seems to come in contradiction with the overall philosophy of education. As Zakiya at South River cogently stated:

> If we're having a hallway sweep today, and you get caught in the hallway without a pass, you get suspended. You get sent home. I don't agree with it. 'Cause I don't feel that if you are late to class that you should be penalized like that. Like maybe you should get a

detention but I don't think you should get suspended. They're supposed to encourage education, not hinder you from getting your education! (Interview #4: 7)

As noted educator Paulo Freire (1970, p. 73) has argued, "Any situation in which some men [and women] prevent others from engaging in the process of inquiry is one of violence. The means used [to prevent someone from learning] are not important; to alienate men [and women] from their own decision-making is to change them into objects."

Other research has suggested that "getting rid of troublemakers" at schools needs to be seriously examined (The Advancement Project and Civil Rights Project, 2000; Bowditch, 1993; Brooks et al., 2000; Fine, 1986; Noguera, 1995). Studies have long found that "getting rid" of kids is closely tied to issues of race, social class, and learning disability. In 1998, there were more than 3.1 million students who were suspended in the US and another 87,000 expelled (The Advancement Project and Civil Rights Project, 2000). Among those youth suspended and expelled, research has found some significant disparity among African-American, Latino, and Native American students (The Advancement Project and Civil Rights Project, 2000; Brooks et al., 2000; Noguera, 1995). In 1997, the US Department of Education found that although African Americans made up only 17% of overall school enrollment, they made up 32% of the school suspensions. This report also noted that one out of eight Black students was suspended during the school year, as compared to one out of 30 White students. A study by the Applied Research Center (1999) found Black children, particularly Black males, were disciplined more often and more severely than any other minority group. And in general, Zero Tolerance Policies were more likely to exist in predominantly Black and Latino school districts.

The Advancement Project and Civil Rights Project also found that, "Zero Tolerance Policies are also having a profound impact on children with special needs" (2001, p. 8). Although the Individuals with Disabilities Education Act was amended in 1997 to ensure that a child would not be punished for behavior characteristic of her/his disability, evidence has revealed that children with disabilities have been negatively impacted by Zero Tolerance Policies. Research has also shown a strong correlation between being suspended and dropping out of school. One survey showed 28% of special-education students stated the reason for dropping out of school was directly related to discipline problems they were having at school (Brooks et al., 2000; Wagner, 1991).[13]

Although I agree that there should be zero tolerance of weapons, drugs, and violence in schools, it is troubling how zero tolerance philosophies have become the dominant ways to deal with additional problems in school. And this way of dealing with problems is often very removed from the everyday lives of students. For example, teachers are often the first link in the discipline process, but as previously noted a principal, board of education, or disciplinary tribunal generally becomes involved. Subsequently, these officials tend to follow the non-discretionary punishment guidelines and ultimately decide what happens to the student. I believe this system needs to change and teachers need to become a more integral part of the process. But in order for the system to change, more training of teachers is needed. The Advancement Project and Civil Rights Project found that teachers are often ill equipped to deal with conflict resolution and classroom management. Providing teachers the tools they need to deal with the problems when they occur could help improve school safety.

Addressing the problem of school violence should also involve more consistent and deliberate collaboration with parents, guardians, and the community. At South River, counselor Mary Huntington said, "Grandmothers and church are the biggest influences in these children lives. Those 9th graders, I guarantee you all I have to say is, 'Do I need to call your grandma? Do I need to tell her how you're acting?' And that's it. That's all it takes" (Interview #33: 7). Organizations like the Parent, Teacher, Student Association (PTSA) have already been established, but unfortunately, as Mr. Wind at North Central described, "All the PTSA does is organize the prom." Involving an organization like this in the discipline and safety at the school could prove useful. Pedro Noguera noted that some schools he visited during his research hired adults who lived within the community to tutor or coach students. And at one school, rather than hiring security guards, a grandmother from the surrounding community was hired to monitor students.

> Instead of using physical intimidation to carry out her duties, this woman greets children with hugs, and when some form of punishment is needed, she admonishes them to behave themselves, saying that she expects better behavior from them. ...Such measures are effective because they make it possible for children and adults to relate to one another as human beings, rather than as anonymous actors playing out roles (Noguera, 1995, p. 206).

Schools also need to monitor disciplinary referrals and punishment decisions. Monitoring this could expose instances when, for example, athletes are being given preferential treatment, or when special-needs students are getting in trouble for things that are consistent with their disability. As other researchers have suggested, "Where teachers overuse disciplinary referrals, additional training should be provided. As a result, students will not be singled out, and they will ultimately have faith that the system of punishment is just" (The Advancement Project and Civil Rights Project, 2000, p. 17).

More creative punishment techniques could also be explored. One teacher I spoke with suggested that rather than "letting the kid rest his head on the desk during an hour of detention," that the student who gets a detention for profanity could actually spend the hour writing an essay about profanity. The teacher suggested this could be applied to other subjects. For example, if he began cursing in math class, he could calculate the percentage of time he wasted in class. A task like this would provide the student with a chance to actually consider their social behavior, and give them some agency in explaining why they chose to do such a thing. One teacher I spoke with talked about a school where she had previously taught, where several students who were caught writing graffiti on the bathroom walls actually had to create a mural in one of the hallways. With the students involved in this project, she saw the amount of graffiti decrease significantly.

In this way, violence prevention becomes a part of the instruction curriculum and a violence-free ethic becomes part of the entire school culture. School policies then become less about controlling kids and more about giving diverse groups of youth a place to invest positive energy, so safe school environments and productive learning can flourish.

## NOTES

1. It was not just Columbine that was in the headlines. In general, there was widespread political and media attention to random acts of violence in White, middle-class suburban and rural communities, fueled by Columbine as well as shooting sprees in Pearl Mississippi and West Paducah, Kentucky, where five students were killed (Glassner, 1999).

2. As Barrie Thorne has argued in her work *Gender Play*, "Several of the group in question insisted that 'children' was more of a put-down than 'kids.' ...I found that when I shifted to 'kids' in my writing, my stance toward the people in question felt more side-by-side than top-down" (1993, p. 9). For similar reasons, I use "kids" frequently to describe my participants. As Best suggested (1998), the use of "kids" captures a sense of unity as a group. I also use the term "youth" to maintain a similar methodological concern. On occasion, I use "teens" because that is how many of my participants referred to themselves, although I would try to use this infrequently, given its origins in the developmental models of childhood that I was trying to transcend (Best, 1998).

3. The names of the school systems as well as that of the participants are given pseudonyms to protect their identity.

4. I did return to the school in September to conduct some follow-up research.

5. At North Central High School, there were no police officers that specifically monitored the hallways, but there was one particular officer that the town assigned to the school. If there was any occasion that the police needed to come to the school grounds, this police officer was generally in charge of the investigation.

6. At North Central, they also had Saturday detentions that were given for 2–4 h at the school. Generally, this type of detention was given after regular detention was exhausted, or for chronic rule violation that involved tardiness, insubordination, or profanity.

7. In-school suspension required students to spend the school day in a specific ISS room with an assistant who monitored behavior. The student was required to work on school activities during the suspension. ISS was generally given to repeat offenders who had already received teacher and office detentions several times, such as students with chronic tardiness, or several cases of insubordination or profanity. Since state law also prohibited special education students from having more than
10 days of out-of-school suspension, in-school suspension was also used in cases where a special education student had exceeded their 10 days out-of-school.

8. At South River, once infractions became "chronic" or if they were considered "critical," the county handled the situation through a disciplinary tribunal hearing ran by the Superintendent and a panel selected by the countywide board of education. Although each school in the county could develop their own school rules and discipline cycle, each school in the county had to follow the same countywide disciplinary cycle for certain things. In contrast, North Central's school administrators handled all of the punishment that was given, although they were governed by their board of education that supervised the high, middle, and elementary schools in the district.

9. I do not want to argue that these were "bad" schools by any means. On many levels these schools were in fact "good," depending on how this was measured. For example, both had low rates of weapons-related violent crimes, both had advanced placement classes, both had winning football teams, and both had at least half of their graduating class going on to higher education.

10. See Kozol (1992), Eckert (1989), and Devine (1996) for more evidence on the unequal distribution of public school resources.

11. In Eckert's (1989) work on Jocks and Burnouts, she argued that parents are part of the power structure within schools, and this structure is connected to social class. The middle-class parents of Jocks often attend school-related meetings, would monitor school programs, and the school's treatment of their children. Therefore, they tended to be able to exert pressure on the school on behalf of their children, whereas working-class parents generally did not have this privilege.

12. As other studies have shown, students with learning disabilities often suffer disproportional negative effects of Zero Tolerance Policies (The Advancement Project and Civil Rights Project, 2000).

13. Although these statistics are telling, most argue that record keeping and data availability on this issue are inadequate, and the extent of the disparities for youth of color and students with special needs is not fully known (The Advancement Project and Civil Rights Project, 2000).

## ACKNOWLEDGMENTS

I am beholden to the American Association of University Women and the American Fellowship Program for their generous support of this project. Dr. Assata Zerai, Dr. Debra Van Ausdale, Dr. Marj DeVault, Dr. Sari Biklen, and Dr. Arthur Paris also provided dedicated feedback throughout this research process. I am also extremely grateful to Christopher Kolloff, for his thoughtful insight and constructive criticism of the final draft of this paper.

## REFERENCES

The Advancement Project and Civil Rights Project. (2000). *Opportunities suspended: The devastating consequences of zero tolerance and school discipline policies.* Boston, MA: Harvard University Civil Rights Project.

Ambert, A. (1986). Sociology of sociology: The place of children in North American sociology. *Sociological Studies of Child Development, 1,* 11–31.

Applied Research Center. (1999). Making the grade: A racial justice report. Oakland, CA.

Best, A. (1998). *Schooling and the production of popular culture: Negotiating subjectivities at the high school prom,* Unpublished doctoral dissertation. New York: Syracuse University.

Best, A. (2000). *Prom night: Youth, schools, and popular culture.* New York: Routledge.

Bogdan, R., & Biklen, S. (1992). *Qualitative research for education: An introduction to theory and methods* (2nd ed.). Boston: Allyn and Bacon.

Bowditch, C. (1993). Getting rid of troublemakers: High school disciplinary procedures and the production of dropouts. *Social Problems, 40,* 493–509.

Brooks, K., Schiraldi, V., & Ziegenberg, J. (2000). School house hype: Two years later. Policy Report. Covington, Kentucky: Justice Policy Institute, Children's Law Center.

Casella, R. (2001). *Being down: Challenging violence in urban schools.* New York: Teachers College Press.

Cook, D. (2000). Childhood is killing "our" children: Some thoughts on the columbine high school shootings and the agentive child. *Childhood, 7,* 107–117.

Corsaro, W. (1997). *The sociology of childhood.* Thousand Oaks, CA: Pine Forge Press.

Currie, D. (1999). *Girl talk: Adolescent magazines and their readers.* Toronto: University of Toronto Press.

Delpit, L. (1995). *Other people's children: Cultural conflict in the classroom.* New York: New Press.

Devine, J. (1996). *Maximum security: The culture of violence in inner-city schools.* Chicago: University of Chicago Press.

Eckert, P. (1989). *Jocks and burnouts: Social categories and identity in the high school.* New York: Columbia University Press.

Elliott, D., Hamburg, B., & Williams, K. (Eds) (1998). *Violence in American schools: A new perspective.* Cambridge, UK: Cambridge University Press.

Epp, J., & Watkinson, A. (Eds) (1997). *Systemic violence in education: Promises broken.* Albany, NY: State University of New York Press.

Fine, M. (1986). Why urban adolescents drop into and out of public high school. *Teachers College Record, 87,* 393–409.
Glassner, B. (1999). *The culture of fear: Why Americans are afraid of the wrong things.* Washington, DC: Basic Books.
Jarrett, R. (1997). Resilience among low-income African American youth: An ethnographic perspective. *Ethos, 25,* 218–229.
Katz, M. (1968). *The irony of early school reform: Educational innovation in mid-nineteenth century Massachusetts.* Cambridge, MA: Harvard University Press.
Katz, M. (1980). Reflections on the purpose of educational reform. *Educational Theory, 30,* 77–87.
Kozol, J. (1992). *Savage inequalities: Children in America's schools.* New York: Harper Perennial.
McNeil, L. (1986/1999). *Contradictions of control: School structure and school knowledge.* New York: Routledge.
Noguera, P. (1995). Preventing and producing violence: A critical analysis of responses to school violence. *Harvard Educational Review, 65,* 189–212.
Orfield, G., Eaton, S. & The Harvard Project on School Desegregation. (1996). *Dismantling desegregation: The quiet reversal of Brown v. board of education.* New York: The New Press.
Prout, A., & James, A. (Eds) (1997). *Constructing and reconstructing childhood.* London: Falmer Press.
Thorne, B. (1993). *Gender play: Girls and boys in school.* New Brunswick, NJ: Rutgers University Press.
Van Ausdale, D., & Feagin, J. (2001). *The first r: How children learn race and racism.* Lanham, MD: Rowman and Littlefield.
Wagner, C. (1991). Educational renaissance: Our schools at the turn of the twenty-first century. *The Futurist, 25,* 41–42.
Waksler, F. (1991). Beyond socialization. In: F. Waksler (Ed.), *Studying the social worlds of children: Sociological readings* (pp. 12–22). New York: The Falmer Press.
Wulff, H. (1995). Inter-racial friendship: Consuming youth styles, ethnicity and teenage femininity in South London. In: V. Amit-Talai & H. Wulff (Eds), *Youth cultures: A cross-cultural perspective* (pp. 63–80). New York: Routledge.

# ATHLETICISM AND FEMININITY ON A HIGH SCHOOL BASKETBALL TEAM: AN INTERPRETIVE APPROACH

Janet Enke

## INTRODUCTION

Over 30 years have passed since the enactment of Title IX, the legislation that required all schools receiving federal aid to provide "equal opportunity for both sexes to participate in interscholastic, intercollegiate, intramural, and club athletic programs" (East, 1978, p. 213). Since 1972, girls' and women's sport participation has increased in high schools, colleges and universities, the Olympics, and professional sports. Researchers interested in the study of gender and sport have raised critical questions and conducted empirical research concerning the meanings of masculinity and femininity, the implications of sport participation, the meanings of heterosexuality and homosexuality, gender equity, and media coverage of sports (Dworkin & Messner, 2002). One persistent theme in the literature on girls' and women's sport participation is the connection between athleticism and femininity. Historically, researchers have used the role conflict perspective or the apologetic defense strategy to examine girls' sport participation. In this chapter,

I analyze athleticism and femininity on a high school basketball team using a third framework.

The role conflict perspective is one of the earliest and most prevalent frameworks used to analyze girls' experiences with athletics (Allison, 1991). The popular conception is that girls perceive and/or experience a conflict between their role as female and their role as athlete. In other words, societal images, definitions, and expectations of being a female collide with those of being an athlete (Allison & Butler, 1984). Yet, past research indicates that female athletes perceive and experience low levels of role conflict (Allison & Butler, 1984; Anthrop & Allison, 1983; Desertrain & Weiss, 1988; Goldberg & Chandler, 1991; Hoferek & Hanick, 1985; Jackson & Marsh, 1986; Sage & Loudermilk, 1979). Research conducted in the 1970s (Sage & Loudermilk, 1979) found that girls who participated in non-traditional sports such as basketball or hockey were more likely to perceive and experience role conflict than girls who participated in traditional sports such as gymnastics, tennis, or swimming; however, a more recent study found that role conflict was unrelated to type of sport (Desertrain & Weiss, 1988). In sum, Hall (cited in Allison & Butler, 1984) argues that researchers have reified the concept of role conflict while Allison (1991) suggests that the concept has outlived its usefulness.

Another framework that is used to analyze girls' sport participation is the apologetic defense strategy. This approach argues that girls experience a cultural contradiction between being a female and being an athlete. The female athlete fears being labeled as too athletic or too masculine. The defense is "a coping strategy that allows a woman to compensate for the perceived masculinizing effect of participating in sports by exaggerating her femininity" (Malcom, 2003, p. 1388). In other words, a female athlete downplays her athleticism, embraces her femininity, and expresses her desire for heterosexual relationships. Past research indicates that female athletes have used this strategy within the athletic context (see Malcom, 2003 for a review of the literature).

More recent research suggests that the strategy has changed over time. Female athletes embrace both their femininity and athleticism; however, they still must be appropriately feminine. Thus, they continue to exaggerate and overemphasize feminine behaviors (Festel, 1996; Shakib & Dunbar, 2002; Theberge, 2000). Shakib (2003) analyzed how basketball players constructed the meanings of athleticism and femininity within the peer context using semi-structured interviews. Players reported emphasizing their femininity (appearance) to keep playing sports and to increase their heterosexuality desirability to peers. Griffin (1998) and Broad (2001) suggest that female athletes may currently use the apologetic defense to avoid being labeled a lesbian.[1]

While the apologetic defense provides a powerful explanation for female athletes' continued display of exaggerated feminine behaviors, Malcom's (2003) study of a recreational softball team illustrates how girls successfully combine femininity and athleticism without employing the apologetic defense. She argues that girls' display of exaggerated feminine behaviors (clothing, jewelry, makeup, hair, and discussions of boys) is motivated by a desire to prove their maturity. Overemphasized femininity is an age-related phenomenon with younger girls (12–13) displaying more exaggerated displays of feminine behavior than older girls (14–16).

In sum, some girls and women may feel a tension between athleticism and femininity, but they do not experience the tension as a role conflict. Some female athletes employ the apologetic defense, while others combine athleticism and femininity without employing the strategy. One limitation of both the role conflict perspective and the apologetic defense strategy is the focus on individual behavior and individual coping strategies. Few studies of girls' sport participation have examined collective processes.

This chapter analyzes athleticism and femininity on a high school basketball team using the interpretive approach to socialization and the construction of culture. "From this perspective, children enter into a social nexus and, by interacting and negotiating with others, establish understandings that become fundamental social knowledge on which they continually build" (Corsaro & Eder, 1990, p. 200). In other words, children do not just individually internalize culture; they become part of the adult culture.

> Children creatively appropriate information from the adult world to produce their own unique peer cultures. Such appropriation is creative in that it both extends or elaborates peer culture (transforms information from the adult world to meet the concerns of the peer world) and simultaneously contributes to the reproduction of the adult culture (Corsaro & Eder, 1990, p. 200).

This process of creative appropriation is called interpretive reproduction (Corsaro, 1992).

Corsaro (1992, p. 162) defines peer culture as "a stable set of activities or routines, artifacts, values, and concerns that children produce and share in interaction with peers." An essential element of the interpretive approach is children's participation in cultural routines (Corsaro, 1992). Routines such as gossip, funny stories, and teasing provide opportunities for displaying and creating cultural knowledge because of their predictable, underlying structure (Goffman, 1974). They are public and collective processes, which have cognitive, behavioral, and affective components (Corsaro, 1992).

Using the interpretive approach, this chapter analyzes (1) how young women interpret and negotiate cultural meanings of athleticism and femininity within the peer culture of the basketball team and (2) how players grapple with the meanings collectively through the cultural routines of gossip, funny stories, and teasing. Thus, the chapter "emphasizes the collective, public nature of developing cultural meanings" (Eder, Evans, & Parker, 1995, p. 7).

Ethnographic data reveal that the interpretive reproduction of female athleticism is complex. Data analysis uncovered the complicated emotional dynamics that occurred among team members and an unexpected finding regarding the content of the cultural routines. The routines focused primarily on physical appearance. Through the focus on collective processes, the interpretive approach to socialization and the construction of culture provides a fresh way of seeing the enduring concern with women's femininity within the context of athletics.

## RESEARCH METHODOLOGY

The findings reported in this chapter are from a qualitative study of peer culture and social relations on girls' high school athletic teams. The study was conducted in the late 1980s and early 1990s. The methods included in-depth interviewing, observations, and audiotaping of naturally occurring talk. I collected secondary data in the form of articles from the local newspaper and high school yearbooks. I also collected a limited amount of data from adults in the field (informal conversations at athletic events). The research setting was a high school (grades 9–12), which enrolled approximately 1,600 students. While most of the students in the high school were White, a small number of students of color were enrolled. The school was selected because some of the students participated in a qualitative study of peer culture and social relations in middle school conducted by Eder and her research team (see, e.g., Eder, 1985; Eder, Evans, & Parker, 1995; Eder & Parker, 1987). The rich and detailed data from Eder's study served as a point of reference for understanding girls' middle school experiences and their subsequent high school experiences. The school was located in a medium-size midwestern community and enrolled students from a wide range of socioeconomic backgrounds, including students from middle class, working class, and lower class families. A state university employed a large percentage of the adult population in the community in professional and blue-collar jobs. There were also a number of factories, quarries, and farms located in or around the surrounding community. Many of the activities in the community revolved around the university. The local newspaper highlighted the sport programs at the university, particularly men's basketball and football.

## Data Collection and Data Analysis

The institutional review board at the university approved the project and the principal granted access to the school.[2] While I entered the setting with an interest in young women's friendships, the specific focus of the study emerged in conjunction with data collection and analysis, and continued to be refined as part of the ongoing qualitative research process (Taylor & Bogdan, 1998). Although I did not enter the setting with a predetermined time frame for collecting data, three identifiable phases emerged that coincided with three academic school years.

### Phase One

I spent the first year of fieldwork observing a variety of extracurricular activities, clipping articles from the local newspaper on high school activities, and conducting a few unstructured interviews about friendship. I discovered that friendship networks were more complex than I had anticipated. I was repeatedly asked in interviews, "Which friends do you want me to talk about?" After analyzing my field notes and transcripts, I decided to focus my research on the peer culture and social relations of young women who participated in varsity athletics. I was impressed with the camaraderie I observed among players during basketball, volleyball, and softball games. Moreover, athletics provided a specific context for collecting data. The high school offered the following nine sports for females: basketball, cross-country, golf, gymnastics, softball, swimming, tennis, track, and volleyball.

### Phase Two

During the second year of fieldwork, I observed practices and games of the nine sports offered at the high school, conducted unstructured interviews with athletes, clipped sport articles from the local newspaper, and began interacting with the girls' athletic director, the varsity basketball coach, and a few parents at basketball games. I discovered during this phase of research that athletics brings young women together and is a basis for friendship; however, the competitive nature of sports places stress on those friendships. The camaraderie I observed during games was often a performance. As I became more familiar with the setting, I noticed subtle behaviors during games (e.g., basketball players not throwing the ball to an open teammate under the basket). Sensitizing concepts (Blumer, 1969) that began to emerge included friendship, competition, tension, and conflict.

*Phase Three: In-depth Interviews*

After analyzing my field notes and interview transcripts from the second year of fieldwork, I designed a semi-structured interview guide to conduct additional interviews with athletes. The interviews focused on participants' sport history including responses from others regarding their athletic participation, social relations on the team, peer group affiliation within the school, involvement in other extracurricular activities, and free time activities with friends. I used a guide to ensure comparability across interviews. At the same time, I gave participants the opportunity to voice their experiences and concerns in their own words.

I used information collected from observations, newspaper articles, and another researcher's study (Kinney, 1990, 1993, 1999) to select players to be interviewed in all three phases of data collection. I also asked participants for suggestions on persons to interview. At least three varsity players from each of the nine sports offered at the school were interviewed. A high status player, a medium status player, and a low status player were selected. In this context, status refers to athletic ability. Indicators include playing time, starting positions, and performance (e.g., average number of points, rebounds, assists, or blocked shots, individual scores or times). I also interviewed athletes who either quit during the season or chose not to go out for the sport as a senior. I employed this strategy of selecting players by status to search for cases that did not fit the emerging themes. The athletes I interviewed in the second year of fieldwork were players who held starting positions. I wanted to establish whether competition and friendship were concerns for any player, regardless of status.

I established rapport with participants by drawing on my knowledge of the school, activities, and participants. For example, I often mentioned a specific game or meet at the beginning of interviews. I initially contacted participants at school in conjunction with the attendance office. A typed note was sent to the student's last class period or the class period before lunch. The note contained a brief statement about the project and asked the student to remain after class. I introduced myself, briefly explained the nature of the project, and asked the student if she would be interested in being interviewed at a later date. If the student agreed to be interviewed, I gave her a consent form, a self-addressed, stamped envelope, and set up a time for the interview. Participants were interviewed in the school library during a free period or in public places after school.

Overall, I conducted 38 in-depth interviews with athletes (including the athletes interviewed in phase two). All interviews were audiotaped and ranged in length from 30 to 150 minutes. During transcription, I did some light editing (added punctuation).

### Phase Three: Ethnography of the Basketball Team

While interviews generate rich and detailed data, there are limitations to the method. Interviews are verbal accounts of how people act and feel; they are not firsthand observations of what people say and do in social life (Taylor & Bogdan, 1998). I conducted an ethnography of the varsity basketball team to explore peer culture and social relations as they emerged over the course of a single season (November–February). I attended practices, games, related events (party in player's home, meeting at coach's house, and sports banquet), and rode on the bus with the team to away games (games played at the school of the opponent). Sensitizing concepts that emerged from the ethnographic data included physical appearance, conflict, femininity, and athleticism.

During the first two phases of the study, I was primarily a nonparticipant observer at sporting events. I chatted with a few adults and spoke to players I had met, but I primarily observed the events. I started thinking about how to study the basketball team during the second phase of data collection. I attended many of the games and approached the varsity basketball coach toward the end of the season with my desire to study the team the following year. While she did not consent to the study at this time, she invited me to travel with the team to a game in another city. I rode on the bus with the team and sat with the varsity players in the bleachers during the junior varsity game. They were telling jokes and stories. The coach heard me laughing with the players and commented that I should not be laughing.

Clearly, I was an adult in her eyes. I did not assume the role of an authority figure with the players though. I continued to laugh with the team. This experience gave me a preview of the difficulties I would face as a participant observer.

Accessing the basketball team for the third phase of the project was relatively straightforward. I obtained verbal permission from the principal, the athletic director for girls' sports (a woman and former coach at the school), and the basketball coaches. I obtained written consent from the basketball players and their parents. Developing rapport with participants and establishing my role in the group proved more challenging. Unlike other researchers who have accessed peer groups in natural settings, I could not simply avoid or distance myself from adults (see, e.g., Bettie, 2003; Corsaro, 1985; Eder, 1985; Kinney, 1990). Adults were part of the team. In fact, the varsity coach introduced me to the players at a practice. Thus, I had to develop alternative ways of managing the youth/adult divide (Bettie, 2003).

Initially, I emphasized my university graduate student role with the basketball players and my researcher role with adults. As I spent more time in the field, the distinction became meaningless. I had information about the basketball players: adults wanted access to the knowledge. For example, the varsity coach asked if I would alert her to conflicts on the team since the players did not always discuss their concerns with her. Some parents wanted to know more about their daughters' thoughts and feelings. The athletic director wanted to hear about my findings as I was collecting data. At the same time, the players knew I interacted with adults and were concerned I might repeat information I had learned from them. I responded to all inquiries in a direct manner and established my boundaries. I told adults that I could discuss general trends with them, but I would not discuss individual players or conflicts on the team. I explained the reasons for maintaining confidentiality. I told the basketball players that I would not tell adults what I observed or heard. However, I stressed that their experiences would eventually be written up under pseudonyms. After the season was over, I received unexpected feedback on my actions. I went to a softball game to watch several of the basketball players play softball. They introduced me to other members of the softball team and commented, "Janet's cool, she never gave the tapes to the coach."

Another factor that made the fieldwork challenging is the fact that the team was not an established peer group. The players did not hang out together as a team during lunch, after games, or on weekends. Therefore, I had to initially build rapport with individual players rather than developing a role in the group. Like Bettie (2003), I relied on personal dialogue. I

## Athleticism and Femininity on a High School Basketball Team 123

initially talked about safe topics such as games and events at the school because I did not want to align myself with any one player. In December, the varsity coach commented that the team wondered why I was so reserved around them and added that the team wanted to get to know me. I relaxed after hearing the feedback and discussed more topics with the players.

Some indicators of rapport were non-verbal. For example, I often looked at players when the coach yelled at them. No words were communicated, but there was an acknowledgment of the situation communicated through our eyes. Other indicators of rapport were verbal. For example, I was taping a conversation among four players on the back of the bus after a game. One of the players teased me about my enthusiasm through her comment, "Janet's over there thinking, this is good stuff." We all shrieked with laughter. I acknowledged those were my exact thoughts. One particular example illustrates the level of rapport I developed with the varsity coach. I was taping the players in the locker room after a game. The coach entered the locker room. She was angry that the team had lost the game. I asked if I should leave; the coach said no. I left the tape recorder running as the coach expressed her anger with the team. I later asked the coach if she wanted me to destroy the tape. She responded, "No, because I know you will not hurt me." I affirmed that I would not intentionally hurt her or the team with the data I collected.

In January, an unforeseen chain of events brought the team together and established my rapport with the group as a whole. The team played seven games in 12 days, including four away games. The schedule was grueling; however, the players also had to take final exams. The team spent hours together, including a 10-hours day when the team traveled to a distant city for a game. I attended many of the practices and all of the games. During this time period, the coaches and players invited me into the locker room. Previously, I had sat in the bleachers during practices, before/after games, and during half time. I also received consent to audiotape the team in the locker room and on the bus. The coach asked if I would record the statistics for individual players during games. I declined because the activity would interfere with my ability to collect data.

On the evening of the sectional game, the last game the team played, the coach stated that she felt like the players had become a team in January and that I had become a member of the team. We hugged in the locker room after the game. I was relieved the season was over due to the intensity of the experience. At the same time, I knew I would miss seeing the team. The players asked if I planned on attending the banquet and if they would see me again. I told them I planned on attending the banquet and the crowning of the winter court queen and king (a basketball player was crowned queen). I also expressed my interest in conducting interviews with individual players. In the end, I was not a coach, an authority figure, a mentor, or a peer. I was simply Janet, a graduate student from the university, who shared the season with the team.

In regard to the mechanics of data collection, field notes were constructed from keywords and memory. During the first phase of the project, I took notes on the program during the sporting event. When parents began to notice my behavior at games during the second phase (they asked if I was a scout), I quit taking notes during games. Instead, I sat in a bathroom stall during halftime and jotted down notes. Bettie (2003) used the same strategy for note taking in her study of young women. I also took notes in the car after games. I rarely took notes in public during the third phase of data collection with the basketball team; I did not want my presence to be perceived as intrusive. I kept a small notebook in my coat pocket and continued the practice of writing notes in the bathroom and in my car. When I returned home, I emptied my thoughts into a computer file. The next day, I organized and further expanded upon the notes. I adopted Corsaro's (1985) scheme for recording notes and organized the text under the headings field notes, theoretical notes, methodological notes, and feeling notes.

The amount of time I spent with the team varied across events and the season. Initially, I attended practices approximately twice a week. As the season progressed, I spent more time at practices and related events, although the exact number varied each week. I attended almost all of the 19 games, and spent 5–10 hours with the team per game when they traveled to another city. I audiotaped approximately 15 hours of conversation in a variety of locations including the locker room, bus, gymnasium, and the coach's house. The technical quality of these tapes varies due to background noise (e.g., bus motor) and the size of the group. The clearest tapes tend to be conversations involving 2–5 speakers. I interviewed seven of the eight varsity players several months after the season ended. They are included in the sample of 38 interviews mentioned previously. The findings presented in this chapter are based primarily on fieldwork with the basketball team over the single season. Selected excerpts from field notes, interviews, and audiotapes are used to illustrate points and support interpretations of the data.

*Reflexivity*

I have learned, through my training and experience that qualitative research is not a one-way process. While I am committed to understanding young women's lives from their point of view, I acknowledge that my gender, race, class, and physical appearance provide a lens through which I interpret the social world. Overall, my social location had a positive effect on the research process. My background is similar to the participants. I am a White woman of working-class origin who was raised in the midwest. The study was conducted in the midwest and most of the participants were White and from middle or working class backgrounds.[3] While my class location has shifted to the middle class, I still identify with my working class roots. Thus, I used my experiences in both class locations to develop rapport with some of the participants.

My awareness of the reflexive nature of research prompted me to reflect on my background, experiences, and feelings as I was collecting and analyzing data. Like many scholars, my interests are rooted in personal experience. During my adolescence, I looked to peers for emotional support. I experienced trust, intimacy, and solidarity in my friendships with other working class women. I also experienced anger, jealousy, and conflict as we dealt with the realities of daily life. My experiences with friendship prompted me to study social relations among young women. I wanted to contribute to the growing body of empirical work on girls and young women. I did not enter the field with the intention of studying female athletes. My interest in athletics developed as I collected and analyzed data.

I participated in a wide variety of extracurricular activities during middle school and high school, including athletics (swim and track teams). While I received both criticism and support for playing sports, I quit competing in high school due to drug and alcohol use. In my mid-20s, I started running and swimming again. I also took aerobic classes and cycled. Although I did not compete in any of these activities, I was in excellent shape during graduate school. Players and parents often asked if I participated in athletics as a young woman. I mentioned my past experiences on the swim and track teams and also commented on my current physical activities. Both sets of experiences provided another means of developing rapport with participants.

I was in my late 20s when I conducted the study and looked somewhat younger than my age. I wore a few pieces of jewelry and dressed casually (name brand jeans, tailored pants and shirts, and comfortable shoes). I did not wear athletic attire (t-shirts, sweatshirts, and athletic shoes) or try to mimic the clothing styles adopted by high school students. I never sensed that my age or clothing was an issue for participants. However, I sensed my body size and shape was an issue. I felt obligated to provide some players with an explanation for my slender, toned body (active life style and high metabolism).

My awareness of the reflexive nature of research also prompted me to reflect on my background, experiences, and feelings as I produced texts from the study. The analysis of the basketball team is grounded in the data (Glaser & Strauss, 1967), but the text is structured by my interpretations and voice (Stacey, 1988). In this chapter, I integrate a discussion of subjectivity with the findings from the study.

## RESEARCH SETTING

### The High School and Community

In order to understand the peer culture of the basketball team, it is important to consider the social and cultural context of the high school and community in more detail. There were two public high schools in the community. I refer to the schools as East High School and West High School. I conducted the study at East High School. The girls' athletic program began at the high schools in the 1970s. Teams had few resources in the early years. Funds for equipment and clothing were limited. Players had to be driven to games by their parents. According to adults who attended high school in the community, young women were stigmatized for participating in athletics during the early years. Athletes were labeled unfeminine, particularly players who participated in non-traditional sports like basketball. The varsity basketball coach commented that she never went out on a date during high school (she attended East High School and played basketball). This observation that sports participation was accompanied by stigma and the possible loss of femininity, particularly for athletes who participated in non-traditional sports, is supported by research conducted during the 1970s (Snyder & Kivlin, 1977; Snyder & Spreitzer, 1978).

Young women were not stigmatized for playing sports during the years I collected data in the school. In fact, they were encouraged to participate in athletics by coaches, parents, and peers. Players had a positive outlook on sport participation. Many discussed how athletics had prepared them for life by teaching them discipline, the value of hard work, and how to get along with others. Athletics also gave them the opportunity to meet young women they might not have met otherwise. A few players commented that sports allowed them to get dirty and play rough.

Coaches, parents, and players felt that support for the girls' athletic program from the school and community was inadequate. While parents and siblings frequently attended games and meets, peer attendance was low.

Typically, the students who attended the games and meets had friends or girlfriends on the team. In contrast, the boys' basketball, football, and to a lesser degree baseball games were well attended. Cheerleaders sometimes showed up for the volleyball and basketball games. However, they often sat in the stands in their uniforms rather than cheering in front of the crowd. Many of the female athletes were angry that the cheerleaders actively supported the boys' teams but not the girls' teams. The pom–pom squad sometimes performed during half time at girls' basketball games; the squad always performed at boys' basketball and football games.

Coverage of high school sports in the media varied by gender, sport, and athletic ability. The local newspaper routinely printed pictures and detailed articles about the boys' football, basketball, and baseball games. The newspaper also ran feature articles about the coaches and players on these teams regardless of the team's record. In addition, the paper printed a summary article at the end of the season, which commented on the prognosis for next year's teams. In contrast, girls' sports and boys' minor sports (golf, cross country, and tennis) were poorly represented in the local newspaper unless the team produced a winning season. Outstanding players were recognized in newspaper articles and a radio program. The local radio station picked a male and female athlete of the week during each of the sport seasons. Three schools participated in this program, including the two public high schools in the community and a public high school in an adjacent community. Each of the coaches nominated a player from their team. The same players were typically nominated week after week. Thus, only a few individuals received visibility in the media.

Since the basketball team did not produce a winning season, they received little recognition in the press. However, one evening the basketball team beat an opponent who had the state's leading scorer on their team. We all expected to see an article in the paper highlighting the athletic accomplishments of the team. However, the writer chose to focus on the state's leading scorer. This incident upset parents, players, and the coaches. One parent was so irate he wrote the following letter to the editor:

> To the editor: On Jan. 15, the East High school girls' basketball team upset Marshall, 57-53. Marshall has the state's leading scorer on their team and they had just defeated Craig, which was a highly ranked team.... I have watched Coach Jan Snyder, Assistant Coach Chris Hall and all the members of the team struggle the last two years attempting to put together winning combinations of players and teams on the floor. The coaches and the players have never given up and have consistently given 110 percent towards the effort. I was totally amazed when I opened the sports section of the Gazette Tuesday. One of the two hometown teams in Greenland had won but you decided to devote most of the front page to the opposing team that had lost. Marshall and the state's leading

scorer deserve coverage but not on the night the home team won. It is not unusual for Kick Saunders to receive 21 points and grab 14 rebounds. She is also one of the five seniors on the team who are playing their last year for the team. They deserve recognition from the hometown newspaper. Jan Snyder played on the university team and was a star when she played at East. Chris Hall was a star at West. Wouldn't a picture of Kick Saunders talking to the winning coaches have been far more appropriate on the front page? As for that matter, you can count on one hand the number of times the Gazette has published any pictures of our Greenland girls' high school basketball teams, East or West. But, no, your opening paragraph is 'East's Kick Saunders and her East's girls' basketball teammates got the right bounce of the ball Monday night', accompanying a picture of the losing coach and the state's leading scorer. The Gazette should back the Greenland teams and provide them the coverage they deserve. Huntsville already has a newspaper that covers their home team.[4]

## The Varsity Basketball Team

East High School had a freshman, junior varsity, and varsity basketball team. The purpose of the freshman team is to teach young women the necessary skills for playing the sport and to provide playing experience. The junior varsity team (freshmen, sophomores, and some juniors) gives athletes an opportunity to further develop and refine their skills. Athletes typically played on the varsity team as juniors and seniors. If a player had exceptional talent, then she could be placed on the varsity team as a freshman or sophomore. I met the freshman coach and attended a few games, but I did not study the freshman team. The junior varsity and varsity teams practiced at the same time and held their games on the same evenings; however, my research focused on the varsity team.

There were eight players on the varsity basketball team: Kala, Kick, Jenny, Melissa, Laurie, Cassi, Katie, and Pam. Kala, a senior and starter, was a confident and poised young woman who was highly visible in the school. She stood out among her peers in numerous ways. Kala was an excellent basketball player and a varsity cheerleader. She was voted captain of the basketball team by her teammates, Player of the Week by sportscasters at a local radio station, voted captain of the cheerleading squad, crowned Winter Court Queen, and voted the senior female with the loudest mouth. Kala had hair down to the end of her back, a toned body, and dressed in stylish clothes. I was intimidated by Kala's presence when I started the ethnography of the basketball team. The varsity coach admitted Kala had intimidated her when she first started coaching the team. However, she added that Kala would respond well if I approached her and made an effort to get to know her. Despite her strong presence, Kala was well liked by her teammates.

Kick was a senior and 4-year varsity player.[5] She was voted most valuable player by her teammates at the end of the season, selected as one of the state's top 100 senior basketball performers, and received a scholarship to play basketball at a small college. Kick was a co-captain of every game, typically with Kala. The leadership style of these two young women was quite different. Kala brought her cheerleading experience to the team and used her loud mouth to lead the group. Kick's leadership style was subtle. She had more experience playing varsity basketball than any of her teammates. Kick set an example for her teammates to follow through her actions rather than through her voice. She had an amazing ability to keep cool and calm under pressure. Kick was a walking encyclopedia of information about girls' basketball. She remembered details about games and players that took place 2 years ago. Players always directed me to Kick if I had questions. I particularly enjoyed Kick's dry sense of humor. While Kick was the most committed player on the team, her whole identity was not invested in basketball.

The third starter for the team was Jenny, a junior. Jenny was a dedicated athlete and competitive player. She played volleyball, basketball, and softball, although she chose not to go out for volleyball her junior year. Jenny was on the Winter Court during her freshman and junior years, and she was crowned Winter Court Queen during her senior year. Jenny was nicknamed bargain shopper by her peers. She was also teased for being gullible. In some ways, Jenny was the most diverse player on the team. She could relate to many of the players on an individual level. Jenny talked about sports and basketball with Kick, and she discussed guys and winter court dresses with Kala. The only player Jenny did not get along with was Cassi. They competed for positions and playing time in both basketball and softball. I personally had a better rapport with Jenny than any of the other players. I had watched Jenny play sports since her freshman year and interviewed her during her sophomore year. While I simply knew her longer than the rest of the team, we were able to talk about a wide variety of subjects. Jenny was friends with Melissa and Laurie.

Melissa, a starter and junior, was another player I had observed since her freshman year. She played basketball and volleyball during her freshman year but only continued with basketball as a sophomore and junior. I was quite intrigued with Melissa. She was insightful and perceptive but very reserved. I always wanted to know what Melissa was thinking because her eyes and body communicated a great depth. Players frequently commented on Melissa's behavior during interviews. Melissa never said much to her teammates unless she was mad during a game.

The fifth and final starter on the team was Laurie. She was a senior and 2-year varsity basketball and softball player. Laurie was well liked by her peers. She was a gentle, kind, and intelligent young woman. Laurie was quiet but often engaged in lively conversations with Jenny and several of the junior varsity players on bus trips. Laurie's performance was inconsistent during her senior year.

Cassi, a junior, was a softball and basketball player. She was a starter for the softball team but not for the basketball team. Cassi liked to have a good time when she was not playing sports. The other players commented on Cassi during interviews; they felt she had a bad attitude. Pam and Katie were also varsity players, but they did not receive much playing time. They were both seniors. Pam played on the varsity team as a junior while Katie played on the junior varsity team. Both of these players had peripheral roles on the team.

Dawn was a freshman who was moved up to varsity later in the season. She was a talented and dedicated athlete. It is sometimes difficult for younger players to be on varsity teams but this was not the case for Dawn. She was respected and well liked by the varsity and junior varsity players because she worked hard. Her teammates called her monkey arms because she has long limbs. There were three junior varsity players that received some varsity playing time toward the end of the season: Terri, Anne, and Liz. All three were sophomores. Terri was the younger sister of Kala. While Terri was just as physically striking as her older sister, she did not have an intimidating presence.

The varsity coach, Jan Snyder, was in her early 30s. She had played basketball for East High School and the university located in the community. Jan was a teacher at East and married with two children. This was her second year as varsity coach. Jan frequently told me how much basketball and the team meant to her although it was hard for her to communicate this to the team. She felt she had to be an authority figure and disciplinarian. Both Jan and the girls' athletic director felt that the current generation of female athletes did not appreciate the availability of resources or social support for girls' athletics. Chris Hall was the junior varsity coach. She was in her late 20s and had played basketball for West High School. Chris was married and had two children.

## THE EMERGENCE OF A PEER CULTURE

The tension between competition and cooperation was the most salient theme to emerge from the interview data during the first and second phases of the study. An analysis of the data revealed that a concern for affiliation and friendship shaped the way young women competed. At the same time, however, a concern for excellence and winning shaped the way young women interacted with peers. I argue that conflicts emerged on teams from the tension created by simultaneously competing against and cooperating with peers on athletic teams. Thus, managing the tension was a significant aspect of the athletic experience for young women.

Given the theme that emerged from the interview data, I anticipated observing and recording cultural routines that basketball players used to manage the tension between competition and cooperation. As I collected data, I noticed that my field notes contained many references to physical appearance. I doubted these notes would be relevant to the study, but I kept recording them. Moreover, I did not see much evidence of a peer culture on the team. I began to question why I wanted to study one team in depth. As mentioned earlier, the team played seven games in 12 days during the month of January. The sheer number of hours the players spent together during this time period brought them together as a team: a peer culture developed. Teasing, funny stories, and gossip emerged as salient cultural routines in the peer culture.

## CULTURAL MEANINGS OF ATHLETICISM

There were multiple meanings of athletic participation on the basketball team including competitiveness, teamwork, and toughness. The team interpreted and negotiated the meanings through social interaction. The varsity coach encouraged the players to develop their athleticism. She often praised her players after games, as the following excerpt from an audiotape indicates:

> Hey we may be up but I am not going to take anything from ya (someone claps). You played to win, and you fought back, real guts, real guts. When it came down to whether or not you knew you could do it, you knew you could and you did it cause you had to. There were no choices. There were no choices involved ... I'm not gonna go into the things we didn't do. We won. We came through when we had to. W is W (meaning a win is a win). This is the time of the year where winning is winning and that's all that counts. Good job, way to work together. Odd combinations of people, way to work together, good job.

In this passage, the coach emphasizes displays of toughness (you fought back), teamwork (way to work together), and competitiveness (you played to win).

The coach also expressed her frustration with the team's performance after games. One exchange I observed was particularly intense. The team had just finished playing their 7th game in 12 days. They had the potential to win the game, but they were unable to pull together as a team and lost. The coach was very upset with the team for losing the game. Her feelings turned to anger when she entered the locker room and heard the players joking and laughing as they changed clothes. She accused them of not caring about losing and proceeded to yell at them, as the following field note illustrates:

> This is anger, this is sheer anger ... it is not ok to lose ... and all you accept the fact that you lose, and you're not losers. Bullshit situations that force you to lose. I want you to remember what you all feel, or you're gonna hear this same thing again. We have worked our tails off. We're winners. We know how to win. We know how to work.

The laughter quickly turned to silence and nonverbal exchanges between the young women and me. For example, I looked players directly in the eye and raised my eyebrows and shoulders as if to say, "What's her problem?" In turn, they shrugged their shoulders as if to say, "I don't know." Other players gazed back at me with looks of anger that seemed to say, "There she goes again."

For the coach, competitiveness included a cognitive component (desire to win) and a behavioral component (playing to win). Jan also expected the team to be emotionally invested in basketball; she had a difficult time understanding why the team was not more invested in basketball. In other words, the coach wanted the players to cultivate a winner's attitude. The emphasis on winning is a complex issue for girls' athletic programs. Winning teams receive more media coverage. Spectators are more likely to attend girls' sporting events if the team has a winning record. Winning seasons are also a factor in budget allocations and college scholarships for talented players.

At the end of the season, Jan shared some changes she was going to make the following year. The coach decided that the players needed to build more teamwork if they were going to produce a winning season. Thus, she encouraged the players to start lifting weights and conditioning in the fall, rather than waiting until the season began. Several of the players expressed their resentment at being asked to condition before the basketball season even began. Some of the seniors commented that the players would be burned out of basketball and sick of seeing each other before the season started. The players were not opposed to lifting weights or building some muscle. In fact, the team made fun of a senior who could not handle conditioning at the beginning of the season. They called her a baby, particularly after she quit the team. However, most of the players resented being asked to devote so much of their time and energy to the sport. The lives of the young women were multi-faceted. Many of the athletes were good students. They were involved in a variety of activities and had active social lives with friends. Some of the players dated or were in steady relationships with male peers. The basketball players also wanted to win, but they did not want the sport to consume their lives throughout the school year.

Another meaning of competitiveness that was interpreted and negotiated within the peer culture concerns the display of cocky behavior (acting like you are a hot player). Many of the varsity basketball players disliked Cassi because of her attitude. However, attitude was only part of the problem. Kala articulated the team's perception of Cassi in an interview conducted several months after the season ended:

> I don't know. I think. I can't explain how it was. She was like. She sometimes. She acts like she was so good you know and she could get the job done and everything. But when it came really came around to it, she lacked the concentration or something and she didn't get the job done when we needed her to. And I think. I don't know what. I don't really know what it was but it made everyone so mad at her. And I think it was cause sometimes she was cocky. I don't know but she. It would have been different if she was cocky and she could do it. But she was cocky and she couldn't do it and and that's what made us mad I think. So we were all, oh we would all talk, oh Cassi whoa, why is she doing that oh great. And Kick and I would that's when we'd talk. That's the person we would always talk about the most cause we'd be down there, oh well she just traveled again, shoot another one Cassi, shoot another (brick) we'd say and turn and walk off. But I mean at the end of the year I was friends with Cassi and I was glad because the whole year ... I think I was kinda mean to her but sometimes she deserved it.

The meaning that begins to emerge from Kala's description is that the display of cocky behavior is appropriate if you perform well and consistently. Cassi was cocky, but inconsistent in her performance. While team members gossiped about Cassi and expressed their frustration with her performance, they also tried to support her. I recorded a conversation between Cassi, Jenny, and Kick on the bus one afternoon. Jenny and Kick verbally supported Cassi as she struggled to understand the coach's behavior and her lack of playing time. They encouraged Cassi to develop her athletic skills through hard work. In other words, Jenny and Kick displayed teamwork off the court.

Many of the parents who attended games supported the basketball players' displays of athleticism. Fathers often shouted instructions to their daughters during games or halftime. They encouraged them to be tough as the following field note indicates:

> The parents were loud today. I heard Kala's father yell, 'Hold your position.' He was trying to tell her what to do when they were in a huddle by the bench and also right after

the half. He kept trying to instruct her. I don't know if Kala really listened to him or not. I heard Dawn's father yell, 'Help her, pick up the tempo.'

The players also interpreted and negotiated the meaning of toughness within the peer culture. In the following passage, Jenny tells a story about an event that occurred during a game. A player on the opposing team was hustling (intentional elbowing or shoving) Melissa on the court. Jenny thought the player was going to hit Melissa so she used nonverbal intimidation to confront the player. Kick comments that Melissa would have hit the player if she struck her first.

Jenny: That's what happened tonight this girl she was standing right there [ ] piss on you (others chuckle) and she didn't say anything (Jenny laughs) and I hate it. You know what I really hate is when somebody tries to pick a fight. That really ticks me. That's why I got down there and got in that girl's face cause I wouldn't let her hit Melissa

Kick: She wouldn't [ ] Melissa would hit her right back.

Jenny: I know Melissa's [but] my buddy and everything and I wouldn't want somebody doing that to somebody on my team.

The meaning that begins to emerge from the conversation is that aggressive behavior is appropriate if it is used to defend one's self or a teammate against a player on another team.

As noted in the yearbook, the team's biggest accomplishments were their wins over the 19th ranked team in the state and a rival team in an adjacent community. Two players were quoted in the yearbook. Kick commented, "I thought we worked together well. When we won, everyone won, if we lost, we all lost. We didn't blame each other." According to Laurie, "Everyone achieved something this season, but there were a few who stood out." Kick finished her senior year with an average of 18.9 points per game, a career high of 29 points, and a school record of 12 blocked shots in one game. Kala averaged 7.6 rebounds per game and led the team with 35 assists for the season. The team ended their season with a record of 8–11.

## CULTURAL MEANINGS OF FEMININITY

There was only one meaning of femininity on the basketball team: physical appearance. The basketball players openly displayed their femininity. For example, all of the players had shoulder length hair or longer. Some players wore stylish clothes and many wore jewelry off the court. The femininity of basketball players shows on the court by virtue of the fact their uniforms are shorts and shirts (Watson, 1987). The players in this study wore sleeveless jerseys and shorts. They also prepared themselves to be on display for their physical appearance during games by shaving their legs and armpits at home and wearing make-up in some cases. The players did not change clothes or shower at the gym after home games. They simply put on sweat pants over their shorts and showered when they got home.

I observed the young women "checking out" the physical appearance of other players. This behavior entails a nonverbal gaze of another person's body. The gaze can be subtle or blatant and often involves an evaluation of another woman's clothes, body, and/or weight. I found myself checking out the physical appearance of players while I observed games. I was also conscious of being checked out by the basketball players. This nonverbal behavior often turned into the verbal activity called gossip.

Gossip is "evaluative talk about a person who is not present" (Eder & Enke, 1991, p. 494). The activity became a routine element of the peer culture. The team frequently gossiped about the physical appearance of players on other teams, as the following examples illustrate:

(1) Kala and Jenny were arguing in the locker room about Megan Anderson's (player on opposing team) skirt. She had a white mini skirt on. You could see her panty lines. Jenny was arguing she should wear a slip. Kala said she cannot wear a slip under a skirt like that. Chris (junior varsity coach) commented she never thinks about these things. I told Chris I do. Like Jenny, I do not like to see panty lines under skirts.

(2) The players were talking about Megan Anderson's hair again, a player for Skillman. Kala commented that Megan would look good no matter what she wore or did. Her hair is long but she has shaved off the sides. The varsity players kept calling some of the Skillman players Pentecostals. I didn't understand so I had to ask them what they meant. They were making fun of how straight-laced some of the players are with their long straight hair and their conservative style of dress. It is interesting to note that they were making fun of how the other players looked, e.g. appearance, not how they looked as they ran or shot baskets.

(3) The team was making fun of the players from other teams. A woman had a shirt with the nickname Brick House printed on it (she was a large, solid woman). Kala commented that she'd never wear a shirt like that. Jan (the coach) commented that she likes Megan Anderson. Chris said players talked about the appearance of other players when she played in

high school. Chris pointed out some jock-looking player on the court and said that's how a lot of the athletic women looked when she was in high school. Jan, Kala, and Chris were talking about the clothes they had on at particular games. Kala remembered the color of underwear she wore at a game. Jan commented that she was in great shape when she was younger, 5'9 and 140 pounds.

In all three examples, the players are interpreting and negotiating norms for physical appearance through the routine of gossip. Chris and I participated in the first episode of gossip about Megan's skirt. Kala and Jenny never reached an agreement about the skirt. The team members agreed that long straight hair and conservative clothes are not attractive in the second episode of gossip. The coaches join the gossip in the third example and also tell stories from the past. Kala did not think a large woman should draw attention to her size through text on a t-shirt. Chris felt that female athletes were not feminine in the 1970s. Kala, Jan, and Chris recalled specific clothes they wore at games, including the color of underwear. Ironically, the team was supposed to be watching the athletic performance of the Skillman team in order to prepare for the upcoming sectional game. Sometimes the team explicitly evaluated the appearance of female athletes on other teams (e.g., she's really cute).

The basketball players also gossiped about the physical appearance of Jill, a former student and athlete at the high school. Jill played three sports a year (golf, basketball, and track) and participated in city golf tournaments. She was a state champion in two different high school sports (golf and track-discus) and won numerous city golf tournaments. While the basketball players respected Jill's athletic ability, they negatively evaluated her bulky muscles. Supposedly, Jill could bench press as much as some of the male football players. Several players criticized Jill for wearing a prom dress with thin spaghetti straps; they said she looked silly in the dress. Some of the players negatively evaluated the muscular development in their own bodies. In particular, they complained about the size of their buttocks and thighs.

## FEMALE ATHLETICISM

While I have discussed the cultural meanings of athleticism and femininity separately for purposes of illustration, the meanings were often interpreted and negotiated simultaneously through social interaction. The following field note is from a game that was played in another city. The coaches and players were preparing for the game in the locker room. The team is simultaneously talking about physical appearance and athleticism.

> I went with the team into the locker room. We arrived pretty early. They were not even ready for us to be there yet. Kick forgot to bring an undershirt to wear under her jersey but she said she was not going to get upset or take it as a sign of bad luck. She was pushing a broom around the locker room. Jan and Chris (coaches) put up a few signs in the locker room. Jan was commenting on how attractive the team is and was saying they probably have the biggest breasts collectively of most teams. Jan read a letter from Claudia Eaton (athletic director) and a couple of poems. They were inspirational. One was about trying hard and succeeding against all odds. Kick had a can of hairspray. She was passing it around to the other players. I asked why they use hairspray. They responded to keep their hair out of their eyes when they play. Laurie didn't use any hairspray, she will be interesting to interview. I remember how shocked I was to discover at the Wheaton game that Kick permed her hair and used hairspray. It was my awakening to the salience of appearance. It was like I could no longer ignore it ... Jan was showing Kala and some of the players how she puts tape in her shoes to keep her nylons from running. Kick said she went through two pairs of nylons the day of the Rockville game.

Some of the talk and behavior regarding physical appearance was practical. The players wore undershirts beneath their jerseys to absorb the sweat. Tape prevents nylons from running. Hair can fall into a player's face if it is not tied back or held in place with spray.[6] However, the coach's comments about the attractiveness of her players and their breast size seem inappropriate for the context. At the same time, Jan tried to cultivate a winning attitude in her team through a pep talk before the game. She read a couple of poems and a letter from the athletic director to inspire the players to win. In other words, the coach encouraged the players to display their athleticism and their femininity.

One day the coach was teaching the players how to use visualization to improve their performance and win the sectional game against Skillman. She also suggested that they gross the other team out through body odor.

> Jan was telling the team to use visualization. She said take ten minutes a day to do this for yourselves, to do it for the team. She wants them to visualize performing well and beating Skillman. Jan suggested to the team that they don't shower or shave the day of the game. She said they could gross the other team out. The team responded no way! Jenny said we wouldn't be able to stand ourselves. Someone commented on one of the teams having bad body odor.

The players resisted the coach's suggestion. While Jenny comments that they would not be able to stand themselves, the players also seem concerned about how their physical appearance (unshaven legs and odor) would be evaluated by others.

Teasing and funny stories emerged as salient routines in the peer culture about halfway through the season. Teasing is an activity that "involves a target who is present and who therefore must respond in some way" (Eder, 1991, p. 183). Funny stories are a form of communication in which interactants take turns building a series of tales about events in their daily lives (Sanford & Eder, 1984).

One practice stood out in the minds of most of the players. Apparently, the junior varsity players teased the varsity players through imitations of their behavior (I missed the practice because I was home visiting family for the holidays). For example, they imitated Jenny going up for a shot and said, "This one's for David (her boyfriend)." The players teased Kick about her hair and use of spray. The junior varsity players teased all of the varsity players and told funny stories about the practice for weeks. However, the team's recollection of the day focused on how well Terri imitated Kala's behavior after she received a technical foul. Terri demonstrated how her sister stood defiantly with her hands on her hips as she whipped her long ponytail around her body. It is important to note that Kala was not teased for committing a technical foul. She was teased for her emotional and behavioral reaction to the foul.

Kala became a frequent target of teasing after this practice. Terri initiated many of the episodes of teasing. For example, the senior players and their parents were honored during halftime at the last home game of the season. Terri announced the players and parents as they walked across the gym.

> Next we have Kala and her parents, Donna and Tim. Kala's a two year varsity basketball player and a one year varsity track team member. Kala's also a two year varsity cheerleader captain. After graduation Kala plans to open a tanning booth (audience bursts out laughing, some of the students hoot and holler).

Kala actually planned to attend the university in the community and try out for the cheerleading squad. Terri seized the opportunity to tease her sister in a public arena. Since Terri and Kala are sisters, Terri may have felt more comfortable initiating the routines. Other players participated in the episodes though. Team members frequently teased Kala about using tanning booths. They told her she was going to have wrinkled skin by the time she was 30. Kala responded playfully to the teasing remarks.

Another memorable day for the team took place during a team dinner at the end of the season. The dinner was at Jenny's house. Several players told a funny story about Kala during dinner. The story is about an episode of teasing.

> Terri and Laurie told a story about Kala from some class. Apparently, Kala was flirting with some of the guys in the class. Someone, I don't remember who, convinced Kala that she had a booger hanging from her nose. At first she didn't believe them but then she grew concerned that she really did have a booger hanging from her nose. I guess it was pretty funny to watch Kala try to nonchalantly get rid of the apparent booger from her nose during class.

The story produced a roar of laughter among the players.

Jenny's younger brother taped the dinner using a camcorder. The players watched the tape after dinner.

> Jenny's brother had the camcorder out. I guess it's their grandparents. He was taping the players while they were eating and talking. A lot of the talk at the table centered on Kala and Jenny. They were also talking about Megan Anderson, the player for Skillman, particularly Kala. I sense some rivalry between Megan and Kala ... A lot of the shots were of the players putting food in their mouths. They were laughing and joking as the camera zeroed in on people. There was a good shot of Pam eating and many shots of Kala on the tape. There were numerous shots of people shoveling food in their mouths. The players were a bit self-conscious but not too much. They are used to seeing themselves on tapes from basketball games and Kala is quite used to performing in front of people given her cheerleader role.

This episode of teasing involved most of the team members because there were shots of all the players on the tape. Nevertheless, more of the attention was focused on Kala.

Why was Kala a frequent target of the team's teasing? One factor was Kala's display of feminine behaviors. She wore make-up both on and off the court, dressed in stylish clothes, and was tan from frequenting tanning booths. Occasionally, the players directly questioned or challenged Kala about her behavior. One instance was particularly interesting. We all met at the coach's house on a Saturday morning to review tapes for the upcoming sectional game. Most players wore comfortable, causal clothes to the event. Kala had styled her hair, put on make-up, and wore stylish clothes. Kick asked Kala why she was so made up on a Saturday morning. Kala responded, "You never know who you will run into." The team was silent. They did not tease Kala. On this particular morning, the players focused on the tapes of the opposing team.

A second factor was Kala's physical appearance. All of the varsity players were attractive; however, Kala's beauty, poise, and confidence set her apart from the rest of the team. I often heard young men comment on Kala's beauty. Sometimes the players heard the remarks. For example, a group of young men followed Kala to the door of the locker room at an away game and made comments about her appearance. While the players did not say anything about the incident, their nonverbal behavior communicated discomfort about the attention Kala was receiving for her physical appearance. After the game, Kala talked about the incident on the bus. She was flattered by the comments she received but seemed unaware of her teammates' discomfort with the discussion.

A final factor was Kala's cheerleading role. The coach felt the presence of cheerleaders on the team brought legitimacy to girls' basketball within the school (one varsity player and two junior varsity players). The activity of cheerleading involves displays of athleticism, but it is primarily a supportive role that emphasizes physical attractiveness (Davis, 1990).

In sum, through her behavior, appearance, and cheerleading role, Kala heightened the team's awareness of physical appearance. The team could not simply disregard her though. She was tough, competitive, and a team player. As mentioned earlier, Kala was one of two players who stood out on the team for her athletic performance. In other words, Kala was an excellent ball player and she was beautiful. Through the activity of teasing, the team released and collectively expressed underlying emotions (Eder, 1991).

Teasing is also a way to indirectly express positive feelings toward a group member (Eder, 1991). Kala was well liked by her teammates. In fact, several players expressed a desire to be friends with her outside the context of the team, but they never communicated this desire to her directly. Ironically, Kala did not know how to interpret the teasing by her peers. During an interview conducted several months after the season ended, Kala commented that she never took the teasing personal (e.g., she responded playfully). Yet, she was uncertain about her teammates' feelings until she received the captain's award at the sports banquet.

> I was thinking God who's going to get it you know Kick's gonna get B-Man (most valuable player) you know, but who's gonna get captain. I really kinda thought Laurie would. I don't know why. I kinda or I thought Kick would get both. I don't know which. When she said Kala, I, I was really, I was really surprised. I was like are you sure? I really. I think that probably is the most, probably was the most special because they, they voted and everything. And I don't know that, I don't know cause I cause like sometimes. I didn't feel like I, you know how I made other people feel uncomfortable at times made me feel like I didn't fit in with any of them. So I tried to fit in with them and everything and then I was really surprised that they would vote for me as their captain since I made them sometimes feel uneasy and everything so I guess that's that's probably the most special one (referring to awards she received) being captain of the basketball team I guess.

Kala and I also talked about the team's focus on her. While I initiated the discussion, Kala was willing and eager to discuss the issue because she had been thinking about it herself. I asked Kala why she thought the team focused on her. She thought it had something to do with her loud mouth and strong personality. Furthermore, Kala did not understand why her teammates were uncomfortable around her. "Sometimes I just got the feeling I was making a lot of people feel uncomfortable. I did get that feeling but I, I didn't know why." Kala did not see how her cheerleading role, her physical appearance, or her displays of feminine behavior affected social relations on the team.

During the last practice of the season, a conflict erupted on the team. The practice was short because the team planned on watching the first round of sectional games to be played that evening. While the players were practicing, a cake was delivered to the gym and placed on a table. It was a sheet cake wishing the team good luck in the sectionals. At the end of practice, the team gathered around the table to listen to a speech Kick had prepared. Kick stood on the table to deliver her speech. A cake fight began, distracting the team from Kick's speech. The following text is from an audiotape of the event.

| | |
|---|---|
| Coach: | Ok guys Kick Kick (a lot of chatter among players) Ok your up. |
| Kick: | Can I stand on the table? |
| Coach: | Kick. |
| Kick: | Alright. |
| ?: | Can I stand up there with you (one of coach's young daughters)? |
| Kick: | Sure if you want to, you won't, you won't know what I'm talking about, but that's alright. |
| Kick: | Well (more chatter taking place among players). |
| Kick: | Alright this is my story (players laughing) when I was a freshman at East, I know you probably, you probably all think I'm full of you know what. |
| ?: | Shit? |
| Kick: | Yeah but just listen to what I have to say and I mean so ok when I was a freshman at East our team, I didn't. I played varsity part of the time, part of the time I did well. At Christmas we were 4 and 5. We had a losing record alright, but we came back and we beat this certain team that was out there across the town called Skillman there by 10 points and they were supposed to be good right. They had won the sectional the year before alright they were supposed to be good and. |
| | (Someone starts laughing hysterically, cake fight begins here) |

Kala: Oh my god (some of the players are laughing)
?: Go on.
Kick: (Laughter dies down and Kick starts speaking louder) Alright, so anyways, so we had the sectional game the final of the sectional game.
(Kala suddenly screams, someone has thrown cake in her face)
Kick: And we beat West (some of the players are laughing and screaming, Kick makes a comment I cannot hear and then says softly to the coaches and I, they aren't listening, she then screams) you aren't listening, listen to what I have to say alright now, listen, alright so we. We played West. We beat West. We beat Skillman and then (raises voice even louder) the final game of the sectional we were behind by 17 points at half time.

I do not know who started the cake fight. My eyes had been focused on Kick. I later asked several players who started the cake fight, but I never received a definite answer. Given Kala's response, "Oh my God," it is unlikely she started the cake fight. She became a central target though. Kala's hair and face were covered with icing and cake. Kick's speech continued for several minutes. It was difficult to transcribe the tape after the cake fight started due to the laughter and screams; however, Jan and Kala tried to direct the team's attention back to Kick's speech. Kick ended her speech with the comment, "As long as we go out and give our best and give it all the heart we have, we'll win the goddamn game." The team hollered in support of Kick's comment. The coach praised the team for being a group of people who play well under pressure and adversity. Kala got up on the table and led the team in a cheer.

Only a few of the players participated in the cake fight but it distracted the entire team. Several of the players expressed negative comments about Kala's participation in the cake fight while the fight was taking place. The cake fight was also a topic of conversation before the team's sectional game the following evening. Kala told the varsity players she had to go home and shower and wash her hair. Jenny commented that the fight was stupid and she would not enjoy washing cake and icing out of her long hair. Kala expressed irritation with Jenny's attitude and commented that it is silly to worry about washing your hair. Kick expressed her overall frustration with the team.

The cake fight demonstrates the complex, ambiguous nature of teasing (Eder, 1991). Teasing had been a playful, verbal activity within the peer culture of the team, up to this point. Through the routine, the team expressed positive feelings toward Kala and collectively expressed emotions. The cake fight transformed the teasing into a physical act against Kala (and other players). On a symbolic level, Kala's beauty was temporarily marred by the cake and icing. While Kala interpreted the cake fight as playful, several of her teammates did not respond playfully, particularly Melissa and Kick. Teasing can disrupt the rapport of the group if it is done at the wrong time. Kick was the only member of the basketball team who had extensive experience playing in tournament games. Through her speech, Kick tried to inspire her teammates. She tried to cultivate a desire to win, against all odds. Teasing (in the form of the cake fight) was not an appropriate response to Kick's speech. I interviewed Kick several months after the season ended. She felt the team's attitude hurt their performance. Like the coach, Kick felt the players lacked a winner's attitude.

The team lost the sectional game. The players sat in the locker room and cried after the game, except for Kick. She remained in the gym to talk with friends. It is plausible that the cake fight affected the performance of the team. The conflict did not affect Kick's individual performance though. Her picture was printed in the local newspaper along with the following caption:

> TOWERING BEAR. East's Kick Saunders towers over Kim Roberts during Thursday's sectional semifinals at West. Kick nearly single-handedly beat the favored Vikings with 29 points, 8 rebounds and 4 blocks. Kim pulled down 8 boards for the Vikings, who advanced with a 52-47 win.

Kick's 29 points were a career high.

## DISCUSSION

Using the interpretive approach to socialization and the construction of culture, this ethnographic study of a high school basketball team illustrates the complexity of female athleticism. Findings from this study highlight collective processes, the content of cultural routines, and the emotional dynamics that occurred among team members. The findings resonate with, as well as contribute to, previous research on girls' sport participation and female adolescent culture.

Women's sport participation has been surrounded by a complex set of meanings for over a century. It is important to consider the social and historical contexts of these meanings before discussing the findings from the study reported here. Sociohistorical accounts have examined the connections between sport, femininity, and sexuality (Cahn, 1994; Lenskyj, 1986). The cultural tension between athleticism and femininity and sexual debates in sport emerged in the early 20th century, as women's access to and participation in sport increased (Cahn, 1994). "The perceived 'mannishness' of the female athlete complicated her reception, making the 'athletic girl' a cause for concern as well as celebration" (Cahn, 1994, p. 8).

As Cahn's (1994) trajectory outlines, between 1890 and World War I female athleticism was associated with mannishness.[7] Competition and vigorous activity posed a threat to women's health (motherhood) and morality (uncontrolled heterosexual desire). Therefore, physical educators advocated a philosophy of athletic moderation for women, which limited female physicality. Two competing images of the female athlete emerged in the late 1920s. The "wholesome, modest athlete" was juxtaposed with the "athlete as beauty queen" (Cahn, 1994, p. 57). Both images tried to eradicate the cultural concern with the mannish female athlete. By the 1930s, mannishness was associated with failed heterosexuality, rather than excessive heterosexuality. In the 1940s, as women athletes became more physical, the physical appearance of women athletes was emphasized. In the years after World War II, the mannish athlete was depicted as ugly and sexually unappealing, and she became explicitly linked with lesbianism. Female athletes felt pressured to prove their femininity and heterosexuality; many developed an apologetic stance about their athletic ability. The most acceptable athletes were those whose female beauty and sex appeal "compensated" for their athletic skill (Cahn, 1994, p. 183).

The feminist movement of the late 1960s and 1970s coupled with the fitness boom of the 1970s and 1980s (particularly body building and aerobic dance) revived the national interest in women's sports. However, the concern with lesbianism continued even as women's athletics grew in popularity and acceptance. As Lenskyj (1986) notes, during the 1980s advertisers promoted an image of female physical fitness. The ideal woman was attractive, lean, and muscular. In other words, she was fit and feminine.

A cultural shift began to occur in the 1990s. In their recent book, Heywood and Dworkin (2003) discuss the rise of the female athlete as cultural icon.[8] She is athletic, muscular, and powerful (female masculinity), and she is beautiful and sexualized (emphasized femininity). This image of the female athlete was novel in the early 1990s. The image gained momentum in 1996 (success and coverage of women in the Olympics) and 1999 (Women's World Cup Victory) and reached outright mainstream status by 2001. "Female athletes were once oddities, goddesses, or monsters, exceptions to every rule. Now the female athlete is an institution" (Heywood & Dworkin, 2003, p. xvi). Yet, Dworkin and Messner (2002) cite research that demonstrates the media coverage of women's sports is lacking in both quality and quantity. A recent analysis of nonsport magazines found that images in women's magazines emphasized pleasure-participation sports more than power-performance sports (Curry, Arriagada, & Cornwell, 2002). The images "... send the message that women are not primarily interested in the competitive success of women athletes but in how they manage to conform to standards of beauty in the context of the sport activity" (Curry et al., 2002, p. 409).

The basketball players in the study reported here are positioned between the cultural image of the mannish lesbian athlete and the female athlete as cultural icon. They were born after 1972 and the passage of Title IX, but played high school sports before the growth of professional leagues such as the Women's National Basketball Association (WNBA) in the 1990s. The young women's understanding of female athleticism reflects the social and historical context of women's athletics during the late 1970s, the 1980s, and the early 1990s. At the same time, the players actively developed cultural meanings of athleticism and femininity through social interaction and the production of a peer culture. As Corsaro (1992, p. 175) notes, "... socialization is not something that happens to children; it is a process in which children, in interaction with others, produce their own peer culture and eventually come to reproduce, to extend, and to join the adult world."

As the data indicate, the basketball players combined femininity and athleticism without employing the apologetic defense (they did not downplay their athleticism or exaggerate feminine behaviors). They were competitive, tough athletes, and attractive young women. Their understanding of female athleticism appears to be a precursor to the image of the female athlete as icon, which developed in the 1990s. However, the varsity coach's behavior suggests that she employed the "reformed" apologetic defense as an athlete. The coach was proud of the team's athletic accomplishments, and she pushed the players to be tough and competitive. At the same time, she seemed concerned about how others would view the athletic behavior of her team. Thus, to downplay her team's tough approach to basketball, she overemphasized the appearance of her players. Since the coach played high school and college basketball in the 1970s, she may have embraced cultural meanings for athleticism and femininity that reflected her experience with athletics at that point in history.

The findings of this study pose a challenge to the historic association between sport and sexuality in the academic literature (Blinde & Taub, 1992; Broad, 2001; Cahn, 1994; Griffin, 1998; Lenskyj, 1986, 1987; Shakib, 2003). Sexuality was not an explicit concern for the young women on the basketball team I studied. However, there are several factors that may explain why the team did not experience homophobia. First, the members of the basketball team were "appropriately feminine" when the season began (shoulder length hair or longer and moderate muscular development). Their bodies differed in size and shape, but none of the players were overweight. In other words, they were attractive by heterosexual standards of femininity (like the women on the 1999 World Cup Soccer Team). Second, one of the players was a cheerleader and two of the players were voted Winter Court Queen (both roles are indicators of heterosexuality desirability). Three, several of the players were in steady relationships with young men. Finally, the team had a losing record. If they had produced a winning season, the players may have behaved differently in response to others' evaluations of their success and athleticism. Nevertheless, this study suggests that additional frameworks are needed to understand girls' and young women's experiences with athletics.

An unexpected finding from the study concerns the content of the cultural routines. The routines focused primarily on physical appearance. The finding suggests that the team cared more about appearance than athleticism; however, this is not the case. How does one explain the content of the cultural routines? A broader discussion of appearance and female adolescent culture is needed.

The concern with women's appearance is deeply rooted in Western ideas about gender (Banner, 1983).[9] In regard to sport, women's physical beauty is emphasized more than athleticism in sport-related magazines (Duncan, 1994; Eskes, Duncan, & Miller, 1998; Leath & Lumpkin, 1992) and media representations of women athletes (Blinde, Greendorfer, & Shanker, 1991; Duncan & Hasbrook, 1988; Duncan, Messner, Williams, & Jensen, 1994; Feder-Kane, 2000; Kane, 1988; Kane & Greendorfer, 1994; Kane & Lenskyj, 1998).

Studies show that appearance is also a salient topic among girls and young women (Bettie, 2003; Eder, Evans, & Parker, 1995; Eder & Parker, 1987; Eder & Sanford, 1986; Griffin, 1985; Hey, 1997; McRobbie, 1978; Simon, Eder, & Evans, 1992; Thorne, 1993). Milkie's (1999) research suggests that media images have an indirect effect on girls through the peer culture. She studied the impact of beauty images on the self-concept of girls. Both Black and White girls saw the images as largely unrealistic; however, White girls were more likely to make negative social comparisons. Black girls were more satisfied with their appearance than White girls and their self-esteem was higher. Beauty images shaped the self-concept of White girls because the images were part of their peer culture. They believed that others evaluated them on the basis of the media ideals, particularly in regard to body shape and weight.

Bettie (2003, p. 29) suggests there is an unarticulated awareness of body image in girls' peer culture; "... girls this age (or perhaps women of almost all ages) are interminably and unfortunately aware of their body size and shape in relationship to unreasonable beauty norms and to each other." In other words, females "check out" the physical appearance of other females. If the awareness of body image is unarticulated, perhaps adolescent girls rely on indirect forms of communication to address their concerns. Moreover, talking about appearance may be an indirect way to discuss body image.

The basketball players in this study expressed their concerns through the cultural routines of gossip, funny stories, and teasing. All three routines are indirect forms of communication. The young women frequently discussed appearance (clothing, make-up, and hair styles), but they rarely discussed body image. While some players expressed dissatisfaction with the size of their legs or buttocks, they did not discuss how they felt about comparing their bodies to peers or media images. It is important to note that the young women did not discuss appearance, body size, or body shape in the interviews I conducted after the season ended. This also suggests that the awareness of body image was unarticulated and points to the importance of multimethod approaches to data collection.

Most studies of female adolescent culture have focused on informal peer groups. Few studies have examined appearance concerns within formal, structured activities like athletics.[10] As I watched the sectional game, I reflected on the season and the team's losing record. The varsity coach felt the team needed to build more teamwork if they were going to produce a winning season. Both the coach and Kick felt players lacked a winner's attitude. I pondered if appearance concerns affected teamwork and the competitive success of the team. There were times during practices when the basketball team was supposed to be watching the athletic performance of opponents to prepare for upcoming games. Instead, the team gossiped about the appearance of players on the other team. A cake fight distracted the team from Kick's speech during the last practice of the season. Kala's presence on the team and the coach's behavior may have heightened the team's awareness of appearance. Media images of the fit and feminine body may have influenced the players indirectly through the peer culture of the team. In other words, appearance concerns may have distracted the team.

There are many factors that affect teamwork and the competitive success of a team. The study reported here suggests that appearance concerns may be one of those factors. I wonder how the peer culture of the team would change if players could directly discuss their concerns and feelings about body image, beauty norms, and social comparisons. Could teams challenge and resist media images of females and female athletes? Could muscular development be interpreted as an indicator of strength and athletic achievement? Could players spend less time "checking out" the appearance of other players and more time on the development of skills and teamwork? In sum, could young women actively contribute to cultural change through the production of a peer culture? More research is needed on female adolescent culture across athletic settings. Research examining female adolescent culture within other formal, structured activities is also needed.

Finally, data analysis revealed the complicated emotional dynamics that occurred among team members. The basketball players did not hang out together outside of team-related events: only a shared interest in basketball brought them together. Many players negatively gossiped about Cassi during the season, but stated she was a friend by the end of the season. Several players expressed a desire to become friends with Kala in the interviews; however, they never shared this feeling with her. While Kala responded playfully to the teasing, she was not sure how the team felt about her until the sports banquet. In fact, she sat with the cheerleaders at the banquet rather than the basketball players. More research is needed on social relations within formal, structured activities like high school athletics.[11] Research examining the experiences of female athletes that crosses racial, ethnic, and class groups is also needed.

In summary, the basketball players appropriated information from the adult world to produce their own peer culture. They interpreted and negotiated cultural meanings of athleticism and femininity. Moreover, they created an understanding of female athleticism. Through the production of cultural routines (teasing, funny stories, and gossip), the players indirectly discussed their concerns, conveyed information about appropriate behavior, and expressed underlying emotions. In the end, they reproduced the cultural concern with femininity within the context of athletics. The findings underscore the salience of appearance in the lives of young, White women and the importance of studying collective processes.

## NOTES

1. In her review of the literature, Malcom (2003) refers to the first strategy as the "classic" apologetic defense and the second as the "reformed" apologetic defense.

2. The following notations are used in the presentation of data from interviews, field notes, and audiotapes: researcher comments are placed in parentheses; ellipses indicate that words have been omitted from a quote; and brackets indicate missing words or words that are hard to identify on the tape.

3. All of the varsity basketball players and the coaches on this team are White.

4. Blais' (1995) journalistic account of a girls' high school basketball team is from the same era as the study I conducted. While there are some similarities in our work, the team in her narrative differs in one important respect from the basketball team I studied: they were state champions.

5. I gave all of the players the opportunity to choose a pseudonym. Kick is the only player who chose a name.

6. An anonymous reviewer pointed out that sharing hairspray in the locker room before a game can also be viewed as a ritualistic activity to prepare for competition.

7. Cahn (1994) also discusses race and class in her historical account.

8. The athletic body has become a cultural ideal for women and men. Both genders are being marketed according to their physical appearance and sexual appeal. Using focus groups, the researchers explore how young people interpret recent images of female athletes.

9. Malcom (2003) cites research that documents racial differences in the construction of gender among adolescent females.

10. Eder and Parker (1987) studied the effects of extracurricular activities on peer-group culture. They found that cheerleading had the most influence on the female peer culture of early adolescents.

11. I am currently revising a paper on competition and cooperation among young, White women within the context of high school athletics.

## ACKNOWLEDGMENTS

I am indebted to my mentor and friend, Donna Eder, for her encouragement and feedback. I thank Steve Carlino for his unwavering friendship and Cathy Evans for her compassion. I am grateful for the care I receive from David Stussy at Kenwood Chiropractic Arts and Brian Calderon and Karla Mueller at Comprehensive Rehab, Inc. Bill Corsaro provided valuable feedback when I was working on the dissertation and the Woodrow Wilson National Fellowship Foundation provided a year of financial support. I wish to thank Monte Bute, Donna Blacker, an anonymous reviewer, and the editors of the volume for their comments and suggestions on earlier drafts of this chapter. Finally, I thank the young women and coaches for allowing me to enter their lives and share the basketball season with them.

## REFERENCES

Allison, M. T. (1991). Role conflict and the female athlete: Preoccupations with little grounding. *Journal of Applied Sport Psychology, 3,* 49–60.

Allison, M. T., & Butler, B. (1984). Role conflict and the elite female athlete: Empirical findings and conceptual dilemmas. *International Review for the Sociology of Sport, 19,* 157–166.

Anthrop, J., & Allison, M. T. (1983). Role conflict and the high school female athlete. *Research Quarterly for Exercise and Sport*, *54*, 104–111.
Banner, L. W. (1983). *American beauty*. Chicago: The University of Chicago Press.
Bettie, J. (2003). *Women without class: Girls, race, and identity*. Berkeley: University of California Press.
Blais, M. (1995). *In these girls, hope is a muscle*. New York: Atlantic Monthly Press.
Blinde, E. M., Greendorfer, S. L., & Shanker, R. J. (1991). Differential media coverage of men's and women's intercollegiate basketball: Reflections of gender ideology. *Journal of Sport and Social Issues*, *15*, 98–114.
Blinde, E. M., & Taub, D. E. (1992). Women athletes as falsely accused deviants: Managing the lesbian stigma. *Sociological Quarterly*, *33*, 521–534.
Blumer, H. (1969). *Symbolic interactionism: Perspective and method*. Englewood Cliffs, NJ: Prentice-Hall.
Broad, K. L. (2001). The gendered unapologetic: Queer resistance in women's sport. *Sociology of Sport Journal*, *18*, 181–204.
Cahn, S. K. (1994). *Coming on strong: Gender and sexuality in twentieth-century women's sport*. New York: The Free Press.
Corsaro, W. A. (1985). *Friendship and peer culture in the early years*. Norwood, NJ: Ablex.
Corsaro, W. A. (1992). Interpretive reproduction in children's peer cultures. *Social Psychology Quarterly*, *55*, 160–177.
Corsaro, W. A., & Eder, D. (1990). Children's peer cultures. *Annual Review of Sociology*, *16*, 197–220.
Curry, T. J., Arriagada, P. A., & Cornwell, B. (2002). Images of sport in popular nonsport magazines: Power and performance versus pleasure and participation. *Sociological Perspectives*, *45*, 397–413.
Davis, L. R. (1990). Male cheerleaders and the naturalization of gender. In: M. A. Messner & D. F. Sabo (Eds), *Sport, men and the gender order: Critical feminist perspectives* (pp. 153–161). Champaign, IL: Human Kinetics.
Desertrain, G. S., & Weiss, M. R. (1988). Being female and athletic: A cause for conflict? *Sex Roles*, *18*, 567–582.
Duncan, M. C. (1994). The politics of women's body images and practices: Foucault, the panopticon, and shape magazine. *Journal of Sport and Social Issues*, *18*, 48–65.
Duncan, M. C., & Hasbrook, C. A. (1988). Denial of power in televised women's Sports. *Sociology of Sport Journal*, *5*, 1–21.
Duncan, M. C., Messner, M. A., Williams, L., & Jensen, K. (1994). Gender stereotyping in televised sports. In: S. Birrell & C. L. Cole (Eds), *Women, sport, and culture* (pp. 249–272). Champaign, IL: Human Kinetics.
Dworkin, S. L., & Messner, M. A. (2002). Introduction: Gender relations and sport. *Sociological Perspectives*, *45*, 347–352.
East, E. R. (1978). Federal civil rights legislation and sport. In: C. A. Oglesby (Ed.), *Women's sport: Myth, reality, and social change* (pp. 205–219). Philadelphia: Lea and Febiger.
Eder, D. (1985). The cycle of popularity: Interpersonal relations among female adolescents. *Sociology of Education*, *58*, 154–165.
Eder, D. (1991). The role of teasing in adolescent peer group culture. *Sociological Studies of Child Development*, *4*, 181–197.
Eder, D., & Enke, J. L. (1991). The structure of gossip: Opportunities and constraints on collective expression among adolescents. *American Sociological Review*, *56*, 495–508.

Eder, D., Evans, C. C., & Parker, S. (1995). *School talk: Gender and adolescent culture.* New Brunswick, NJ: Rutgers University Press.

Eder, D., & Parker, S. (1987). The cultural production and reproduction of gender: The effect of extracurricular activities on peer-group culture. *Sociology of Education, 60,* 200–213.

Eder, D., & Sanford, S. (1986). The development and maintenance of interactional norms among early adolescents. *Sociological Studies of Child Development, 1,* 283–300.

Eskes, T. B., Duncan, M. C., & Miller, E. M. (1998). The discourse of empowerment: Foucault, Marcuse, and women's fitness texts. *Journal of Sport and Social Issues, 22,* 317–344.

Feder-Kane, A. M. (2000). A radiant smile from a lovely lady: Over determined femininity in ladies figure skating. In: S. Birrell & M. G. McDonald (Eds), *Reading sport: Critical essays on power and representation* (pp. 206–233). Boston: Northeastern University Press.

Festel, M. J. (1996). *Playing nice: Politics and apologies in women's sports.* New York: Columbia University Press.

Glaser, B. G., & Strauss, A. L. (1967). *The discovery of grounded theory: Strategies for qualitative research.* New York: Aldine.

Goffman, E. (1974). *Frame analysis.* Boston: Northeastern University Press.

Goldberg, A. D., & Chandler, T. J. L. (1991). Sport participation among adolescent girls: Role conflict or multiple roles? *Sex Roles, 25,* 213–224.

Griffin, C. (1985). *Typical girls? Young women from school to the job market.* New York: Routledge & Kegan Paul.

Griffin, P. (1998). *Strong women, deep closets: Lesbians and homophobia in sport.* Champaign, IL: Human Kinetics.

Hey, V. (1997). *The company she keeps: An ethnography of girls' friendships.* Philadelphia: Open University Press.

Heywood, L., & Dworkin, S. L. (2003). *Built to win: The female athlete as cultural icon.* Minneapolis: University of Minnesota Press.

Hoferek, M. J., & Hanick, P. L. (1985). Women and athlete: Toward role consistency. *Sex Roles, 12,* 687–695.

Jackson, S. A., & Marsh, H. W. (1986). Athletic or antisocial? The female sport experience. *Journal of Sport Psychology, 8,* 198–211.

Kane, M. J. (1988). Media coverage of the female athlete before, during, and after Title IX: Sports illustrated revisited. *Journal of Sport Management, 5,* 1–21.

Kane, M. J., & Greendorfer, S. (1994). The media's role in accommodating and resisting stereotyped images of women in sport. In: P. J. Creedon (Ed.), *Women, media, and sport: Challenging gender values* (pp. 28–44). Thousand Oaks, CA: Sage.

Kane, M. J., & Lenskyj, H. J. (1998). Media treatment of female athletes: Issues of gender and sexualities. In: L. A. Wenner (Ed.), *Media sport* (pp. 186–201). New York: Routledge.

Kinney, D. A. (1990). *"Dweebs," "headbangers," and "trendies": Adolescent identity formation and change within socio-cultural settings.* Unpublished doctoral dissertation. Indiana University, Bloomington.

Kinney, D. A. (1993). From nerds to normals: The recovery of identity among adolescents from middle school to high school. *Sociology of Education, 66,* 21–40.

Kinney, D. A. (1999). From "headbangers" to "hippies": Delineating adolescents' active attempts to form an alternative peer culture. In: J. McLellan & M. J. Pugh (Eds), *The role of peer group stability and change in adolescent social identity. New directions for child and adolescent development* (Vol. 84, 1pp. 21–36) San Franciso: Jossey-Bass.

Leath, V. M., & Lumpkin, A. (1992). An analysis of sportswomen on the covers and in the feature articles of women's sport and fitness magazines, 1975–1989. *Journal of Sport and Social Issues, 16*, 121–126.

Lenskyj, H. (1986). *Out of bounds: Women, sport and sexuality.* Toronto: Women's Press.

Lenskyj, H. (1987). Female sexuality and women's sport. *Women's Study International Forum, 10*, 381–386.

Malcom, N. L. (2003). Constructing female athleticism: A study of girls' recreational softball. *American Behavioral Scientist, 46*, 1387–1404.

McRobbie, A. (1978). Working class girls and the culture of femininity. In women's studies group: Center for contemporary cultural studies, Women take issue. (pp. 96–108), University of Birmingham, London: Hutchinson.

Milkie, M. (1999). Social comparisons, reflected appraisals, and mass media: The impact of pervasive beauty images on black and white girls' self-concepts. *Social Psychology Quarterly, 62*, 190–210.

Sage, G. H., & Loudermilk, S. (1979). The female athlete and role conflict. *Research Quarterly, 50*, 88–96.

Sanford, S., & Eder, D. (1984). Adolescent humor during peer interaction. *Social Psychology Quarterly, 47*, 235–243.

Shakib, S. (2003). Female basketball participation: Negotiating the conflation of peer status and gender status from childhood through puberty. *American Behavioral Scientist, 46*, 1405–1422.

Shakib, S., & Dunbar, M. D. (2002). The social constriction of female and male high school basketball participation: Reproducing the gender order through a two-tiered sporting institution. *Sociological Perspectives, 45*, 353–378.

Simon, R. W., Eder, D., & Evans, C. (1992). The development of feeling norms underlying romantic love among adolescent females. *Social Psychological Quarterly, 55*, 29–46.

Snyder, E. E., & Kivlin, J. E. (1977). Perceptions of the sex role among female athletes and nonathletes. *Adolescence, 12*, 23–29.

Snyder, E. E., & Spreitzer, E. (1978). Socialization comparisons of adolescent female athletes and musicians. *Research Quarterly, 49*, 342–350.

Stacey, J. (1988). Can there be a feminist ethnography? *Women's Studies International Forum, 11*, 21–27.

Taylor, S. J., & Bogdan, R. (1998). *Introduction to qualitative research methods: A guidebook and resource.* New York: Wiley.

Theberge, N. (2000). *Higher goals: Women's ice hockey and the politics of gender.* Albany: State University of New York Press.

Thorne, B. (1993). *Gender play: Girls and boys in school.* New Brunswick, NJ: Rutgers University Press.

Watson, T. (1987). Women athletes and athletic women: The dilemmas and contradictions of managing incongruent identities. *Sociological Inquiry, 57*, 431–446.

# WHO ARE THE EXPERTS? MEDICALIZATION IN TEEN MAGAZINE ADVICE COLUMNS

Janice McCabe

Teen magazines are ubiquitous in adolescent girls' lives, as evidenced by their high rates of readership – approximately 90 percent of U.S. adolescent girls read them at least occasionally (Currie, 2001; Evans, 1990; Milkie, 1995, 2002) – and by the large number of issues sold each month – the leading magazines *Seventeen* and *YM* each have circulation rates nearing three million (LaGuardia, Katz, & Katz, 2002). Advice columns are girls' favorite items to read in teen magazines (Currie, 1999) and one site where teenage girls turn for answers to their questions about what are "normal" bodily changes and feelings. Until recently, discussions of female adolescent sexuality and bodies were not routinely part of public discourse, including that in teen magazines. Sources on women's health, such as *Our Bodies, Ourselves for the New Century*, point to the importance – for both health and well-being – of women learning about their bodies and talking with other women about their bodies (Boston Women's Health Collective, 1998). Therefore, with their discussions of traditionally taboo topics and their information and advice to girls who are curious about these topics, teen magazine health advice columns may be an encouraging development for adolescent girls and their health and well-being. Although the presence of these columns is liberating, we know little about the messages they present to teenage girls.

Sociological theory on medicalization suggests that girls, women, and other less powerful groups are increasingly subject to medicine's authority over their bodies and their lives. Because at adolescence girls suffer a significant drop in self-esteem (American Association of University Women, 1991; Block & Robins, 1993; Bolognini, Plancherel, Bettschart, & Halfon, 1996; Brown & Gilligan, 1992; Martin, 1996; Orenstein, 1994; Polce-Lynch, Myers, Kliewer, & Kilmartin, 2001; Simmons & Blyth, 1987), teenage girls may be especially vulnerable to medicalization. Some researchers suggest this sudden drop in self-esteem may be due not only to teenage girls' changing bodies, but also to the negative discourse in our culture surrounding women's bodies and sexuality (Brumberg, 1997; Martin, 1996; Polce-Lynch et al., 2001). Many girls receive limited information about these bodily changes and often feel ambivalent about puberty (Martin, 1996). Health advice columns in teen magazines are one place where explicit discussions of girls' bodies, health, and sexuality take place.[1] Specifically, health advice columns represent one site where female youth may (or may not) come to respect medicine's pronouncements on how people should think about their bodies and what they should do with them. What kind of information and advice is being given in these columns?

Through a content and textual analysis of the health advice columns in *Seventeen* and *YM* (the two leading "mainstream" teen magazines) and those in *New Moon* and *Teen Voices* (two "alternative" teen magazines) from 1998 to 1999,[2] this paper analyzes the questions posed and advice given in the columns using the theory of medicalization to interpret the messages. The analysis suggests that mainstream advice columns present norms and standards for teenage girls through their focus on medical authority, medical language, citation of medical experts, and "normality," especially regarding sexuality and body issues. In contrast, the girls' advice in the alternative magazine is less medicalized, advocates multiple explanations and multiple authorities on the body, and occasionally recognizes problems as socially produced. Through a format where girls answer other girls' questions, girls are cultural producers in addition to being consumers of health and medical knowledge. While this paper highlights problems surrounding medicalization in teen magazines, it also attempts to illustrate the complexities in this process. For example, while columns in mainstream magazines bring adolescent girls' concerns about their bodies and sexuality into public discourse, they also privilege the medical professions' knowledge over that of other adults as well as adolescent girls through their use of doctor citations, doctor referrals, and medical language. In addition, these columns provide adolescent girls with information – albeit limited and medicalized information – about their bodies and health. In the next section, I explain the theoretical framework for this paper and consider research on the content of teen magazines and their potential effects on adolescent girls' behavior and perceptions of their bodies.

## BACKGROUND AND THEORY

### *Theoretical Framework: Medicalization*

Medicalization is the increasing social control of the everyday by medical experts. It is a key concept in the sociology of health and illness because it sees medicine as not merely a scientific endeavor, but a social one as well. Medicalization is a "process whereby more and more of everyday life has come under medical dominion, influence, and supervision" (Zola, 1983, p. 295); previously these areas of everyday life were viewed in religious or moral terms (Conrad & Schneider, 1980; Weeks, 2003). More specifically, medicalization is the process of "defining a problem in medical terms, using medical language to describe a problem, adopting a medical framework to understand a problem, or using a medical intervention to 'treat' it" (Conrad, 1992, p. 211). Sociologists have used this concept to describe the shift in the site of decision-making and knowledge about health from the lay public to the medical profession.

Many early writings regarded medicalization as a negative development in Western societies. Labeling something as a medical problem makes it an individual concern, thereby discouraging individuals from discussing their "problem" with others, recognizing non-medical solutions, or attempting to understand the social causes of their "problem" (Conrad & Schneider, 1980; Zola, 1972). Recently, researchers have questioned this simple characterization and, instead, have argued that medicalization is a complex process (Broom & Woodward, 1996; Conrad, 1992; Garry, 2001; Purdy, 2001; Riessman, 1983; Williams & Calnan, 1996). At times, medicalization is beneficial because it may be accompanied by research, medical interventions, and new treatments (Broom & Woodward, 1996; Conrad & Schneider, 1980). Medicalization is not only a top-down process as individuals sometimes embrace it (Foucault, 1979; Oinas, 1998; Riessman, 1983). Medicalization can have both constructive and destructive outcomes.

Medicine is an influential institution; medical knowledge both reflects and reproduces gendered social and cultural structures. Some scholars argue that women are especially at risk for medicalization and are the main targets in the expansion of medicine and the medical profession (Boston Women's Health Collective, 1998; Ehrenreich & English, 1979; Garry, 2001; Levy, 1992; Riessman, 1983; Weitz, 1998). Young women may be especially vulnerable to medicalization. Teenage girls are at an age where they experience many bodily changes and have to figure out what they mean. In recent years, many aspects of women's experiences have been medicalized: exercise and eating problems (Hesse-Biber, 1996), cosmetic surgery and body shaping (Sullivan, 1993), menopause (Bell, 1987; Coupland & Williams, 2002; Martin, 1987), premenstrual syndrome or premenstrual dysphoric disorder (PMDD) (Figert, 1996; Martin, 1987), and, most recently, female sexual dysfunction (Moynihan, 2003; Purdy, 2001). For example, the debate over the naming of PMDD and its inclusion in the Diagnostic and Statistical Manual of Mental Disorders (DSM) illustrates both the "positive" effects (e.g., the term legitimates and legitimizes a condition that many women report and it stimulates thought and research on the topic) and the "negative" effects (e.g., it may be stigmatizing since it is only women's – not men's – hormones that are seen to cause mental illness) of medicalization (Figert, 1996). While medicalization can serve to control bodies (especially those of women), it also can provide care (Morgan, 1998; Purdy, 2001) and be used for "genuine empowerment" (Morgan, 1998, p. 115). As stated earlier, medicalization is, at times, a constitutive process (Foucault, 1979; Oinas, 1998; Riessman, 1983) in which girls, in the case of teen magazine readers, may willingly participate to define "normal" female behavior. Therefore, advice columns in teenage magazines may offer particular insight regarding theories of knowledge, power, and gender.

*Girls and Teen Magazines*

Mainstream teen magazines are widely read and, through their focus on heterosexual romance and physical appearance, play a part in socializing adolescent girls to be "proper" young American women. Research finds that these magazines focus on the theme of self-improvement through fashion, beauty, and traditional heterosexual femininity (Evans, Rutberg, Sather, & Turner, 1991; McRobbie, 1991; Peirce, 1990). In her best-selling book *The Body Project*, Brumberg (1997) remarks that starting in the 1980s, information about contraception and protected sex (with the "right" boy and when the girl is "ready," following the magazines' dominant sexual script) is included in *Seventeen*'s advice columns. Brumberg argues that although this adolescent sexual behavior is not new, it was, until recently, excluded routinely from public discourse.[3] Research shows that the sexual scripts in mainstream teen magazines frame sexuality in terms of heterosexual romance rather than girls' sexual desire, portraying girls, not as sexual subjects, but as the gatekeepers of sex (Carpenter, 1998; Durham, 1998; Fine, 1988). No sociological research has focused on the content of alternative magazines, such as *New Moon*, and few on teen zines (Kearney, 1998; Schilt, 2003), although a few scholarly pieces have noted their growing popularity and have applauded the alternative femininities they offer girls (Bayrl, 2000; Gonick, 1997). These researchers have noted the need for examinations of the texts that girls produce as well as those created for them to consume (Kearney, 1998; Schilt, 2003).

Regardless of mainstream teen magazines' general focus on heterosexual romance, fashion and beauty, some researchers find that politicized and/or feminist subtext and positive images, while limited, are present in these magazines as well (Budgeon & Currie, 1995; Currie, 1994; Peirce, 1990; Schlenker, Caron, & Halteman, 1998). Budgeon and Currie (1995, p. 175) argue that although teen magazines seem to naturalize and reinforce traditional gender roles for girls who read them, the messages are not all traditional or all negative. Instead, they found that some of these images promote non-traditional roles for women, although there are few direct references to feminism or the women's movement. Still, these authors do not address the role that health advice columns specifically play in reinforcing traditional or non-traditional gender norms, or whether this range of images is present in these columns.

Studies on the readers of teen magazines find that the influence these magazines have over girls is not total. Girls do not just passively accept teen magazines' discourse about what it means to be an adolescent girl. Meaning is negotiated in a wider cultural context; therefore, not all young women internalize the same messages to the same extent (Bordo, 1993; Currie, 1999; Duke & Kreshel, 1998; Gonick, 1997; McRobbie, 1991; Milkie, 1994, 1995, 1999). Certainly, reading these magazines feels like a pleasurable, rather than oppressive, act for many girls and women (Budgeon & Currie, 1995; Currie, 1999; Fiske, 1989; Hollows, 2000; McCracken, 1993; Winship, 1987). Nonetheless, even when girls are critical of magazines' images and messages, these images negatively affect girls' self-esteem according to both qualitative and quantitative examinations of the consequences of girls' media interpretations (Milkie, 1995, 1999). In summary, research on youth and magazines suggests that the content of these messages is complex, thus inviting further detailed examination.

### *Magazine Advice Columns*

Although health advice columns are present in many girls' and women's magazines, very little research has been conducted on them. In one of the few studies that examine advice columns in teen magazines, McRobbie (1991, p. 155) observes that the "problem page" – an advice column in British teen magazines for girls such as *Just Seventeen, Jackie, Patches, Blue Jeans,* and *My Guy* – is appealing because it promises confidentiality and advice for girls' "problems" and concerns. Furthermore, the problem page is important to study because it provides girls with "the strongest definitions of teenage femininity" (McRobbie, 1991, p. 165). Through a content analysis of teen magazines and individual and focus group interviews with teenage girls about "teenage fashion culture," Currie (1999, 2001) found that girls identify "questions and answers" as their favorite item to read in teen magazines. Approximately, three-quarters of 13- and 14-year-old girls read advice pages and that increases to nearly 90 percent of 15- and 16-year olds. Currie attributes part of their popularity to the framing of advice as "problems" rather than information, although she also notes that girls consider questions and answers to be "useful information" (Currie, 1999, pp. 166–168). Questions and answers are "useful information" not only for learning how to solve one's individual problems, but also for illuminating what types of problems are common among their peers, thereby serving a normative function as well. Chow's (1999) focus groups with girls about health advice in mainstream teen magazines also point to the normative functions of "health secrets."

Through her interviews with young readers, Currie (2001, p. 277) found that "the rejection or creative rewriting of advice texts was the exception rather than the rule." More often, girls compare their behavior "against the normalcy constructed by the text." Currie's (1999, 2001) interviews and focus groups with adolescent readers suggest that many girls take magazine advice constructions as "truth."[4] Currie briefly discusses the content of health advice columns and notes that the magazine "often directs the reader to male professionals employing patriarchal definitions of womanhood" but does not discuss how these same references can function to socialize girls to respect medical authority over their bodies (Currie, 1999, pp. 183–184). In the only published empirical study that focuses on health or medical advice columns in popular magazines, Oinas (1998) analyzed letters concerning menstruation answered by doctors in Finnish health, youth, and women's magazines in 1991. Oinas found that the questions written by young women are seldom medical in nature; rather, they express concerns about normality. The doctors, on the other hand, answer the questions with assurances that the young women need not worry because the medical profession can and will handle their problems and concerns. These findings point to the importance of a systematic study of the content of teen magazine health advice columns.

This paper explores the multiple messages present in health advice columns addressing a broad range of questions about health and bodies in U.S. teen magazines. In these magazines, girls' questions are not answered by doctors, but by other girls in the alternative magazines and by columnists in consultation with medical "experts" or doctors in the mainstream magazines. The questions this paper addresses are threefold. First, what topics and what questions are included in these columns? Second, what do columnists' (i.e., girls' in *New Moon* and *Teen Voices*) responses to girls' questions reveal about the multiple messages offered in teen magazine health advice columns? In other words, what information is presented to adolescent girls in these columns and how do they advise girls to solve their "problems"? Third, how is expert knowledge conveyed in the columns? Who is presented as an "expert" on girls' bodies, health, and sexuality? Specifically, how are physicians, other medical experts, and the medical profession represented in these columns? What is the relationship between the presentation of medical knowledge (including medical language) and lay understandings of girls' bodies in these columns? To answer these questions, I analyze both the manifest content – the characteristics of the messages presented in the columns – and the latent content – the meaning of these messages – (Holsti, 1969) in mainstream and alternative teen magazine advice columns.

## METHODS

### Sample

I chose four teenage magazines for analysis based on their circulation rates and their inclusion of a regular advice column aimed at adolescent girls addressing mental and physical health issues. The first, *Seventeen*, published since 1944, has approximately 2.4 million yearly subscriptions and sells over

450,000 copies from newsstands (Carr, 2003; LaGuardia et al., 2002, p. 1438; Striplin, Banks, Joseph, & Rasberry, 2002, p. 1905). According to their website, "Seventeen is a leading magazine for women, ages 12–24, each month reaching 14.45 million readers nationwide" so that one in every two female teens reads *Seventeen* (The Hearst Corporation, 2004). *Seventeen*'s monthly health advice column is called "sex + body." The second magazine, *YM: Young & Modern*,[5] reaches 9.1 million teens (G & J USA Publishing, 2004), has over 2.2 million yearly subscriptions and sells nearly 600,000 copies from newsstands (Carr, 2003; LaGuardia et al., 2002, p. 1439; Striplin et al., 2002, p. 1096). *YM* publishes ten issues per year; double issues are published in December/January and June/July. In 1998, *YM*'s advice column was called "ask anything: the lowdown on life, sex, and your bod." In 1999 the title was changed to "ask anything: the lowdown on sex and your bod."[6] In both magazines, a columnist (a young woman) in consultation with doctors and other medical experts answers readers' questions on health and body issues. Beyond circulation rates and the data presented earlier about readership of these columns, the magazines themselves reveal the extent to which girls rely on this advice. That the pages of these advice columns were often torn out of the magazines to such an extent that I had to travel to multiple public and university libraries to compile a complete set of columns for this 2-year period also confirms their popularity.

The third magazine, *New Moon: The Magazine for Girls and Their Dreams*, is an "alternative" magazine for girls. At about 30,000 readers, *New Moon* – a non-commercial magazine for girls and edited by girls[7] with girls from "all over the world" as contributors – has a much lower circulation rate than *Seventeen* and *YM* (LaGuardia et al., 2002, p. 351; Striplin et al., 2002, p. 1905). *New Moon* has won many prestigious awards including the Parent's Choice Award and the National Organization for Women's Woman of Courage Award. *New Moon*'s approach, with their "Ask a Girl" column, differs from the format used in *Seventeen* and *YM*'s advice columns. According to *New Moon*: "Ask a Girl is an advice column for you and by you. We help each other and take our problems seriously. Here's how it works: We publish letters that ask for help or advice. In later issues, we publish your replies – advice or personal experiences you can share." Unlike the format used in the mainstream magazines, many of the questions in *New Moon* are printed with multiple answers.[8]

The fourth magazine, *Teen Voices*, is another "alternative" teen magazine edited and written by, for, and about girls and young women with circulation rates similar to *New Moon*. According to their website, most readers are girls 13–19 years old (Teen Voices Online, 2004). Women Express, Inc., a non-profit organization, publishes *Teen Voices* four times a year. Magazine content is written by "girls from all over the world" and is edited by Boston-area teens in their journalism-mentoring program. Teens are matched with interns/volunteers, who are usually college students, and each team edits an aspect of the magazine. Unlike *New Moon*, *Teen Voices* includes ads "for products and services that enhance the reader's life, education, and/or entertain," but, unlike the mainstream magazines, has a policy to only accept advertisements that "do not exploit their audience through graphics or text." According to Alison Amoroso, a prior editor-in-chief of *Teen Voices* and co-founder of Women's Express, *Teen Voices* was established to "cut down on alienation, so common among teen girls, and provide good information in a helpful way, instead of through an uninspiring public health brochure" (Norton, 2001/2002). Their advice column was called "Dear Debbie" until 1998 when it became "Dear D." Like *New Moon*, questions are answered by girls, but there are many differences in this process between the alternative magazines. *Teen Voices*' advice column typically is focused around a theme. A team (often one or two teens advised by an intern) selects a topic from the submissions they have received from teens, they select material to appear in the column (often a couple of letters and a poem), and they compose a response. After the team has written an answer, it is sent to a social worker, who gives them feedback on the column (Ellyn Ruthstrom, 2004, *Teen Voices*' Managing Editor, personal communication).

Initially, I chose only the two mainstream magazines for analysis because they are the two most popular teen magazines, based on their circulation rates and wide readership. I had planned to compare *Seventeen* and *YM*; however, my analysis suggested the advice columns were operating in ways that were more similar than different. After my initial analysis, I was surprised by the extent of medicalization in the advice, regardless of the topic. I showed the paper to several colleagues and was struck by their reactions, particularly that they did not see the medicalized nature of the advice as problematic. Therefore, I felt it was important to seek out other comparisons and delve into the emerging market of alternative teen magazines. The problem became the lack of advice columns in such publications. *New Moon* and *Teen Voices*, however, fit the criteria for inclusion: they are aimed at teenage girls and each has an advice column. They also are two of the most established alternative magazines in the U.S. teen market. Unfortunately, during the 2 years of this analysis, the advice column in *Teen Voices* was not included in every issue, most likely because the column was transitioning from "Dear Debbie" (up through 1997) to "Dear D" (included in 1 issue in 1998, 2 issues in 1999, and nearly every issue thereafter). Because of the small number of questions and answers published during these 2 years (six questions and answers), I include 3 years of *Teen Voices*. Therefore, my analysis encompasses the 15 questions, 11 answers, 3 poems, and 1 essay included in *Teen Voices*' advice column in 1997–1999. I also analyzed the 41 answers and 60 questions[9] that appeared in the 12 issues of *New Moon* in 1998 and 1999 as well as the 175 questions and answers that appeared in the 44 issues – 24 issues of *Seventeen* and 20 issues of *YM* – of the "mainstream" magazines published in 1998 and 1999.

*Coding Categories*

Systematic analyses and close readings of advice columns in teen magazines are important because implicit messages can be overlooked easily. Budgeon and Currie (1995, p. 175) argue that, when they were teenagers, their own readings of teen magazines suggested that multiple discourses exist in teen magazines and many layers, including alternative interpretations, are overlooked when researchers do not fully examine the context of these magazines but rather analyze them by "simple counting without reading." Their conclusions, as well as my own experiences with reading teen magazines as a teenage girl, encouraged me to combine content and textual analysis and led me to develop a detailed coding system for this study. I used both inductive and deductive theory as an analytical approach when coding the columns. Guided by the theory of medicalization, deductive reasoning was used to develop coding categories, such as "doctor citation," "doctor quotation," "doctor referral," "other expert referral," and "medical terminology." Feminist theory guided the development of codes, such as "offer self-solution" and "ask/talk to other women." Other codes such as "structural explanation," "slang," "slang and medical language," and "explicit focus on normality" were developed inductively, based on the data.

Further illustrating the systematic nature of the content analysis, the question was coded as having an "explicit focus on normality" if it included a phrase or sentence such as "Am I normal?," "Am I weird?," or "Is something wrong with me?" Examples of words categorized as medical terminology are included in the appendix; the medical terminology found in these advice columns was cross-referenced with and validated by comparison to several medical dictionaries, including *Dorland's Illustrated Medical Dictionary* (1994), *Gould Medical Dictionary* (1979), *Mosby's Medical, Nursing, and Allied Health Dictionary* (1998), and *Webster's New Explorer Medical Dictionary* (1999). Theory was further refined through the use of negative cases. For example, the three doctor referrals in *New Moon* magazine, described later, were initially negative cases. Through additional textual analysis, these three exceptions to a general pattern led to the development of more nuanced codes such as "multiple experts" and "relates personal experience," which then enriched theoretical understandings of expert knowledge and medicalization. The idea of multiple experts on the body emerged and the coding categories of "non-medical expert" and, more specifically, "counselor," "guidance counselor," "peer," and "friend" emerged as separate, but related categories, which expanded my initial category of "ask/talk to other women," mentioned above.

In addition, using lists of key words for each topic, questions were placed in a main topic category. Secondary topics addressed in the question were also noted. These categories and the key words for each category were based on my preliminary analysis of question topics in teen magazine health advice columns. The ten categories are: (1) appearance; (2) dating; (3) relationships with peers, friends, and parents; (4) sex, pregnancy, contraception, and virginity; (5) menstruation; (6) sexually transmitted diseases (STDs); (7) vaginal discharge or odor; (8) smoking, drinking, and drugs; (9) visit to a doctor or gynecologist; and (10) other topics. Topics falling into the "other" category include depression and mood swings in *New Moon*, tattoos, thumb sucking and constipation in mainstream magazines, and nutrition in both types of magazines. Through analyzing the manifest and latent content of these columns, I examined the topics and content of the questions and answers, focusing on which solutions were and were not offered. The goal here is not to determine whether the advice given is right or wrong, but to examine what messages are offered.

## RESULTS

Consistent with analyses of the overall content of leading teen magazines, which suggest that these magazines are more alike than different (Evans et al., 1991), this content analysis indicates that *YM* and *Seventeen's* health advice columns address similar issues. For example, questions about sex and appearance are the most popular topics published in both mainstream magazines. Slightly more than one-fourth of the answers involve questions about sex, such as virginity, pregnancy, contraception, and masturbation. Approximately one-fifth of the questions asked in these columns concern the girls' appearance, such as body image or body hair. The content analysis suggests that similar topics are covered in both magazines and the messages conveyed in the answers are similar; however, the textual analysis suggests that medicalization occurs in slightly different ways in the two magazines. Although differences between the two mainstream magazines' approaches will be discussed, this paper focuses primarily on the similarities between the mainstream magazines, comparing and contrasting them with the alternative magazines.

The alternative teen magazines address comparable issues although the most popular topics are different than those in the mainstream magazines. For example, *New Moon* and *Teen Voices* print more questions/answers on relationships with peers, friends, and parents than either *YM* or *Seventeen* and focus less on sex and appearance-related issues. During this 2-year period, *New Moon* occasionally published questions whose main topic included dating or a doctor visit; however, there was no mention of menstruation, STDs, or vaginal discharge even as secondary topics. Compared to *New Moon*, *Teen Voices* covers a wider range of topics, including menstruation, vaginal discharge, sexual intercourse, and masturbation. The topic differences do not account for the greater medicalization in mainstream magazines; the same patterns are present when examining only the most medical or health-related issues in both groups of magazines (see later discussion). The implications of the differences between the types of magazines will be discussed later in the paper. The most striking difference in the answers, however, is in whether the message is medically oriented or not.

Five themes regarding medicalization, expert knowledge, and the body emerged from the content and textual analysis which I identify as: (1) the use of medical language and medical experts; (2) physicians as *the* authority or one of many; (3) seeking non-medical help; (4) self-help; and (5) normality and structural versus individual explanations.

## *"Are We Getting Too Textbookish on You?": Use of Medical Language and "Expert" Citations*

Medical terms are used extensively in both mainstream magazines. For example, in response to the question "How long does pubic hair grow? Do you need to shave it?" the answer reads:

> You can relax ... All the hair on your body has a growth cycle with three distinct phases: *anogen* (growing), *teelogen* (resting) and *catogen* (falling out). Hair growth depends on the longevity of the anogen phase; pubic hair has a shorter anogen phase than your head hair but a longer one than, say, your eyebrow hair. Pubic hair falls under the category of sexual hair – that is, hair that begins to grow at the onset of puberty. Pubic hair may, at

first, be a little coarser and lighter in color than nonsexual hair, but within a few years, it darkens, thickens, becomes coarser and covers the entire area, even extending onto the inner thighs ... You don't have to shave (or even trim) your pubic hair as you might your legs. (*Seventeen*, May 1998, p. 107, emphasis in original)

In this example, the issue of pubic hair is addressed through medical language describing the phases of hair growth. In fact, the columnists in a few instances explicitly acknowledge this language use: one answer in the October 1998 issue of *Seventeen* reads, " ... (Are we getting too textbookish on you?)." Medical terms are also used to answer a question on endometriosis:

This genetic condition, which affects 15 percent of American females, occurs when the tissue that lines the uterus (endometrial tissue) also grows on other parts of the body, like on the surface of the uterus, the bladder, the large intestine or the ovaries, as well as outside the fallopian tubes. But unlike the uterine lining which sheds – resulting in your period – this tissue and blood remain trapped in your body, causing cramping and pain in the lower pelvic area ... Early detection is key, because if left to progress for years, endometriosis can make it difficult to conceive. As always, it's important to pay careful attention to your body and know how it works. (*Seventeen*, February 1999)

This example, regarding a clearly medical topic (endometriosis), uses medical language to describe the problem and discusses medical treatments for endometriosis, yet also encourages girls to explore and better understand their bodies. Over three-quarters of the answers to the adolescent girls' questions in mainstream magazines contain at least one example of medical language. Because the answers use medical terminology to describe and define the young women's "problems," the use of medical language in these columns is an example of medicalization, according to Conrad's (1992) definition. On the other hand, the use of medical language is not entirely negative; the answers cited above provide information about hair growth and endometriosis to young women curious about their bodies. Additionally, not all of the medical terms are as foreign to most teenage girls as "anogen" or "endometriosis" (see the appendix for examples of medical terminology).

Medical language was used much less frequently in *New Moon* and *Teen Voices*; about 10 percent of the answers included at least one medical term. One such answer is a response to a girl concerned about her best friend who eats very little:

Your friend has an eating disorder. Hers seems to be anorexia, a self-starvation process. I recently ended my struggle with bulimia. I'm 13 now and started my battle at 10 ... I lost over 77 pounds in 3 years, until my esophagus ruptured. The full 10 or so inches from my mouth to my stomach on the left side ripped. I had been home alone. My aunt came home to find me running down the stairs coughing up blood. I had three surgeries after that. Eating disorders usually deal with control. Your friend might have some troubling things happening in her life. I started after my mother, who was a model, got brain cancer. I wanted to be as beautiful as I could before she died. Didn't happen ... (*New Moon*, May/June 1998, p. 11)

This answer takes a medical approach by labeling the girl's problem as a medical condition and through describing the writer's own experiences with medical treatment of bulimia. The answer above also relates personal experience and offers advice about talking with the girl's friend and listening to her. Even among the most medically oriented questions in all magazines (those where appearance, sex, or other mental or physical health issues are the main topic), the differences between the magazines are stark: more than three-quarters of answers in mainstream magazines use medical terms, compared to nearly 30 percent of those in alternative magazines. This suggests that differences in the use of medical language between the two types of magazines are not attributable to less frequent discussions of medically oriented issues in the alternative magazine.

Along with the use of medical language, the citation of medical experts is another implication of the choice of writers between alternative and mainstream magazines (e.g., teenage girls or professional columnists in consultation with medical experts). Quoting or citing a doctor in the body of the answer privileges the medical profession's authority and knowledge because, presumably, the "experts" give the answers authority. Doctors are cited for a variety of medical and non-medical concerns in mainstream magazines. In each issue, *Seventeen* visibly lists the medical experts consulted for that month's column,[10] and medical experts and doctors are listed, even if they are not cited directly. *YM* cites or quotes "experts" or doctors in nearly two-thirds of the answers. Although they are not prominently displayed, *YM* lists its medical experts consulted for that issue in the binding of the magazine. *New Moon*'s advice column, in contrast, contained no doctor or expert citations or quotations in their answers. Although this is a notable difference, it is not entirely surprising since girls, rather than columnists in consultation with doctors or other medical experts, answer girls' questions. However, *Teen Voices*'s column, which is written by girls in consultation with a professional expert – a social worker – contains only two expert citations. The first references a study done by the School of Medicine at the University of California at San Francisco, showing that while 58 percent of girls thought they were overweight, only 15 percent were (*Teen Voices*, Fall 1997, p. 7). The second citation, "P.S. Therapists do edit *Teen Voices* – we take our responsibility to you very seriously!" was in response to a letter which began "I know you're not a therapist or anything, but ... " (*Teen Voices*, Winter 1999, p. 55). That professionals are consulted for the column in *Teen Voices* as they are in mainstream magazines suggests that the sheer volume of expert citations in mainstream magazines is the result of more than their consultation with medical professionals in writing the column.

One mainstream magazine question asks, "I've never had sex, but I've done some serious body-bonding. Does that mean I'm still a virgin?" The answer reads, "Elliot Levine, M.D., a Chicago gynecologist, says a girl remains a virgin until she's had intercourse, meaning penis-in-vagina penetration" (*YM*, April 1998, p. 52). The doctor's name appearing in this answer serves to give legitimacy to the answer. On the other hand, without the expert's name in the answer, would *YM*'s authority be in danger of being doubted by teenage girls? The frequency with which doctors are cited and listed in mainstream teen magazine advice columns reinforces the belief that the young women should believe the advice because doctors possess the ultimately true and right answers. *YM* cites medical doctors in the answers when what they are stating could be doubted, but they consult doctors for every question in every issue (Chandra Czape, 2000, *YM*'s Features Editor, personal communication). In a second example, in response to the question, "Even when my period's heavy, it hurts to put in a tampon. Why?" the answer cites a medical doctor on how to put in a tampon:

> Here, some plug pointers from Bonnie Dattel, M.D., a professor of gynecology at Eastern Virginia Medical School in Norfolk: Take a few deep breaths. Then put one foot on the toilet and slightly bend your other knee while you insert the little bugger. If you meet resistance, stop and readjust the angle. And if you're using cardboard-applicator tampons, try plastic for improved glide-ability. (*YM*, September 1999, p. 44)

In the answer, a medical doctor is cited when, presumably, the columnist, a young woman, could answer the letter herself based on personal knowledge and experience. Through responses such as the one discussed above, medical authority and knowledge is privileged over other adults' knowledge and over youth's knowledge of their bodies, perhaps because the authors of the column think girls accept medical authority.[11] Although the advice columns' reliance on medical terms can inform girls about their bodies, it, as with the citation of medical experts, signifies medicalization.

### "When in Doubt, Get a Doctor's Opinion": Physicians as The Authority or One of Many

There were also striking differences between the types of magazines in the solutions proposed, especially regarding doctor referrals. In response to the questions asked in the column, the answers can relate a range of messages depending on which bodily authority the columnist wishes to promote. One alternative is to refer the teenage girl to see a doctor who knows best, thereby implying that the body always is, at least potentially, sick. A doctor referral occurred in nearly half of the answers in mainstream magazines. In one issue, a girl asked "I have small bumps on my nipples. Can I get rid of them?" The answer begins:

> We all have bodily imperfections that we would love to see disappear. But before taking action, you need to determine whether these are normal physical characteristics and whether it's safe to remove them. When in doubt, get a doctor's opinion. In this case, what you're referring to as your nipple is probably the darker circle of skin around it called the areola ...
> (*Seventeen*, August 1999, p. 170)

In this answer the young woman's own ability to judge and assess her own body is not given much credit. Examining this answer through the lens of medicalization, the message implicit behind "When in doubt, get a doctor's opinion" is that a teenage girl never can be quite sure if everything is all right; therefore, it is always good to let an "expert" take a look. Another example illustrates this point more clearly: the columnist recommends, "[Y]ou should call your doctor ... Whenever you have *any* question, pick up the phone!" (*Seventeen*, July 1998, p. 55, italics in original). Because of liability concerns, magazines may refer a girl to see a doctor to protect themselves from giving wrong or inadequate advice, such as telling a girl she is "normal" when she has a condition that requires medical attention. And, certainly, doctors can be a good source of information on some topics. The frequency with which mainstream magazine columnists refer young women to see a doctor, for a range of medical and non-medical concerns, points to the centrality of medical authority in these columns.[12]

The answers in the alternative magazines also suggest doctor or health referrals, but do so less frequently (i.e., in only five responses) than mainstream magazines. Moreover, the context of the referral is often quite different. The following example uses medical language and includes a health referral, yet informs the girl about what may occur after the referral through relating personal experience, implicitly telling the girl that she is not alone. A 14-year-old girl wrote to *New Moon* about feeling lonely and depressed. One girl responded:

> It is 2:30 in the morning, and I can't sleep. I thought about your letter, and decided to write to you. I don't know if I can help you, but I'll sure try. The reason I am up in the middle of the night is because I have a disease called depression. I can't sleep, I can't eat, and I cry a lot. Sometimes I don't even want to get out of bed. I have been depressed for a year and a half. In that time, I have attempted suicide twice. The most important thing to recover from depression is to get help ... Especially if you are suicidal like me, you

need to see a counselor ... Like you, I didn't feel comfortable telling my parents that something was wrong, so I talked to the counselor at school ... If and when you go to a counselor or other mental health person (which I strongly suggest), you will probably start with talk therapy. You and your counselor will chat about how you feel, why you feel that way, your past, and your relationships with other people ... You may also be put on antidepressant medication, of which Prozac is the most famous. I'm going to be starting one next week. I'm not thrilled about taking a "happy" pill, but if it will make me feel better, then I guess it's worth it. Also, to find out more about depression, there is a book that really helped me: *Overcoming Depression*, by Demitri and Janice Papolos. It talks about everything – feelings, treatment, medication, hospitalization (only in extreme cases), insurance, etc., etc., etc ... " (*New Moon*, May/June 1998, p. 11)

The girl answering the question couches her answer in terms of her personal experiences, and advocates the same solution as many of the answers in *YM* and *Seventeen*: go see a professional (in this case, "go to a counselor or other mental health person"). On the one hand, this answer suggests that lay people are encouraging respect for the authority of medicine, which reflects how pervasive medicalization is in our culture. As discussed earlier, medicalization is not only a top-down and uniformly negative process. On the other hand, the answer is qualitatively different from those in mainstream magazines because the girl answering the question suggests multiple explanations and multiple authorities on the body. She does not just briefly empathize with the questioner and move on to offer advice. She describes, in depth, her own experiences with depression and seeking help, informing the questioner (and other readers) about what she can expect during this process. Additionally, she recommends a book "that really helped me" where the girl can turn for further information – a suggestion never offered by the columnists at *Seventeen* or *YM*, yet offered in 10 percent of the answers in *New Moon* and in all but one of the columns in *Teen Voices*. Furthermore, the *New Moon* response above, rather than referring the girl to a doctor or a psychiatrist, proposes both a medical ("mental health person") and a non-medical expert (a counselor) on the body. This difference between the two types of magazines will be explored in more depth in the next section.

In addition to offering more context surrounding the doctor or medical expert referral, the answers in the alternative magazines suggest a less hierarchical view of the doctor-patient relationship. For example, in response to a girl's question about her sudden mood swings, Emma explains how her best friend went through something similar: "She found out that she has Reactive Hypoglycemia, which is where your blood sugar levels drop dangerously low. If these major mood swings continue, you might want to talk to your doctor" (*New Moon*, May/June 1999, p. 10). Suggesting that the girl "might want to talk to [her] doctor" gives the reader the choice of what action to take. This difference in wording (like that in the previous example, "If and when you go to a counselor ... ") recognizes the girl's agency in her decision to visit a doctor and in what occurs once she is with the doctor. In comparison, the advice in mainstream magazines advocates "call your doctor," "go see a doctor," or "get a doctor's opinion," implying that the girl has less of an active role in deciding whether to consult a doctor. In a second answer to the same question about mood swings, Anna tells how she "went through the same thing," describes how she worked to control her mood swings, and recommends, "if you continue having them, talk to a counselor. If you don't have a counselor at school, ask your parents to take you to a psychiatrist or pediatrician." By suggesting that a girl first talk to a counselor and that she should ask her parents to take her to a doctor if she does not have a counselor at school, the answer encourages girls to connect with others (a counselor, parents, a psychiatrist, or pediatrician). In addition, the answer presents doctors as one authority on the body (along with some adults, counselors, and the girl herself) without asserting that doctors are *the* authority on the adolescent female body.

### *"You Need to Talk to Someone":* Seeking Non-Medical Help

Not all of the answers offer a medicalized view of girls' bodies. An alternative to referring the young woman to see a doctor is to encourage her to trust her own knowledge or to actively learn about her body and talk to other women about their experiences. For example, a young woman writes, "It seems to me that I really stink 'down there.' I know a little smell is normal, but this is horrible. I wash a few times a day, and I've even tried baths instead of showers, but nothing works. Is something wrong?" The answer advises the young woman: "Here's one way to put your worries to rest: Ask your mom (or another close female relative) if she's ever noticed that you have an odor problem" (*Seventeen*, February 1998, p. 62). Another answer recommends that a girl concerned about her sweaty hands and feet ask her family members if they sweat a lot, and if so it might be hereditary (*Seventeen*, September 1998, p. 128). By encouraging the young woman to ask someone else – specifically, non-medical or non-professional help – about her concern, the columnist suggests a solution that encourages her to gain information about her body through connecting with and relying on the experiences of another person, a lay person. However, very few answers (i.e., only nine out of the 175 answers printed in 2 years) in mainstream magazines encouraged the girl to ask or talk to her peers, her mother, or another adult about her concern.

In contrast to the infrequent occurrence in mainstream magazines, over half of the answers in the alternative magazines encourage girls to talk to, tell, or ask a non-professional about their concerns. For example, one reader's advice to a girl whose best friend eats little includes, "Look, talk to your friend. Confront her with the facts, then listen to her. If she insists she's OK, and you know otherwise, tell an adult. Call her parents. Get her help. Anything. Love and support." (*New Moon*, May/June 1998, p. 11). This answer offers multiple solutions that fall into this category: talk to your friend and listen to her, if that does not work, then "tell an adult," such as her parents. Another reader advises a girl whose friends tease her and call her "Heather the feather" because of her weight to tell her friends that she does not like it (*New Moon*, September/October 1999). By suggesting that the girl address her concerns to the people doing the teasing – her friends – this response encourages the girl to connect with those around her.

More specifically, nearly two-thirds of these responses in the alternative magazines encourage girls to specifically *talk to* or *talk with* someone else, whereas nearly half of the responses in this category (i.e., consult a non-professional) in the mainstream magazines encourage girls to *ask* someone (as in the examples above, ask your mom if she's noticed your odor or if your family sweats a lot). *Teen Voices* counsels a reader, "If you are still friends with your best friend, you should talk to her about how you feel if you haven't already" (*Teen Voices*, Summer 1999, p. 43). A *New Moon* reader advises a girl with mood swings: "You need to talk to an adult. Is there someone you are close to, like an aunt or guidance counselor? You might want to talk to them. They can take you to see someone or even try to help you out themselves ... " (*New Moon*, March/April 1999, p. 11). Another reader suggests that a girl who is depressed should "stop denying how you feel ... You need to talk to someone" (*New Moon*, March/April 1998, p. 11). These answers do not suggest medical authorities on the body, but that girls talk with adults (such as family members, teachers, or guidance counselors), peers (such as friends), or just someone, particularly someone you are close to or someone you trust. Advising girls to begin addressing their problem themselves, through talking with others about their "problem," advances the idea – supported by the women's health movement – of multiple experts on the body.

### *"Do the Confident Girl Thing"*: Self-Help

Another alternative or supplement to doctor referrals is self-efficacy solutions.[13] For example, in response to a question about belly button odor, the answer suggests, "While you're in the shower, use an antibacterial soap ... and rinse. Pat your navel dry with a towel. You can also clean out lingering lint by gently swabbing your navel with a warm, soapy Q-tip" (*Seventeen*, November 1999, p. 91). This solution provides the girl (and other readers) with practical suggestions on how she herself can address her concern about belly button odor. Advice that acknowledges the girls' concerns and offers solutions that girls themselves can do, if appropriate, is one alternative to doctor referrals. These solutions range from general suggestions, such as advising a girl unsatisfied with her small breasts to "start loving the ones [breasts] you're with" (*YM*, June/July 1999, p. 30), to the more concrete, such as advising a girl who is too embarrassed to buy tampons to "do the confident girl thing and buy 'em [your tampons] yourself" (*YM*, May 1998, p. 52) or suggesting padding to make a girl's breasts appear more even in size (*Seventeen*, July 1998, p. 56). Although mainstream magazines offer self-solutions, they are recommended more frequently (in nearly nine-out-of-ten answers) in alternative magazines. Moreover, alternative magazines are more likely to suggest many types of self-solutions in the same answer. For example, in response to a girl concerned about her weight, *Teen Voices* advises a range of self-efficacy solutions including, "Don't let that little voice (or the voice of the media) put you down" and "Accept all parts of what make you who you are," while also providing suggestions for healthy lunches to bring to school and types of exercise "to let go of stress and tension" (*Teen Voices*, Fall 1997, p. 7).

A mainstream magazine responds to the question "Both of my ex-boyfriends were grossed out by my saggy breasts. I don't know why I have old-woman boobs, 'cause I'm only 16. Help!," by advising, "To help you see that you're not a freak, just check out the chests on your girlfriends and classmates." (*YM*, August 1998, p. 62). This solution encourages the adolescent girl to take a more active role in learning about her body and to perhaps discover for herself the large variation in girls' bodies. However, the next sentence in the answer states, "Or as Dr. Carll suggests, ask your doc if he or she thinks they're normal for your age." By suggesting that a doctor is the final authority on the adolescent female body, the omnipotence of medical knowledge and the medical profession is still the underlying message of this answer. Citing a doctor to legitimate the doctor referral further emphasizes medical authority. In mainstream magazines, multiple solutions are rarely offered without a doctor referral included as one of these choices; this never occurred in *Seventeen* during the 2 years studied and only occurred three times in *YM*. Although a doctor referral is one among several solutions, the doctor is presented as expert, often as the ultimate authority on the adolescent female body. For example, the answer to the question above about belly button odor begins, "ask someone close to you for a second opinion about the source of the smell, and see your doctor to make sure you don't have an infection" (*Seventeen*, November 1999, p. 91).

Although advice columns can provide girls with information and can encourage them to understand, and perhaps even solve, their own "problems," the columns in mainstream magazines (and less frequently those in alternative magazines) also may offer medicalized understandings of the "problems" and medical solutions, in the form of doctor referrals, doctor citations, and/or medical language. Furthermore, as illustrated previously, when mainstream magazines offer multiple solutions, a doctor's visit is almost always encouraged. In this way, the medical profession still appears as the primary source of power and control over girls' bodies. Recommending girls begin addressing their concern themselves, through self-efficacy solutions or talking with other women about their bodies, advocates a different expert on the body than does including medical language, doctor referrals, and doctor citations in the answers. The answers in alternative magazines (and less frequently those in mainstream magazines) offer multiple perspectives on who are the authorities on the adolescent female body by more often suggesting solutions that girls can do themselves and encouraging girls to talk with others about their concerns.

## "Am I Normal?": Normality and Structural versus Individual Explanations

The health advice columns in teen magazines may discipline girls' bodies, behaviors, and attitudes, not only through socializing women to respect medicine's authority over their bodies, but also in how they define and refer to "normal" appearance, behavior, and attitudes for adolescent girls. Regarding normality, 25 of the 175 answers in mainstream magazines include an answer where the columnist disapproves of the girls' questions, concerns, or actions, or reprimands the girl for what she has done or is considering doing, while only two of the 52 answers in alternative magazines disapprove of the girls' actions. A girl writes to *New Moon* concerned about her mood swings and the answer advises, "Don't ignore this" (*New Moon*, March/April 99, pp. 10–11). The other example, in *Teen Voices*, advises a girl who is debating between her heart and her friends in deciding whether to date a specific boy to "Remember that if you don't follow your heart, then you might live to regret it – and your heart is usually right" (*Teen Voices*, Summer 1999, p. 43). In contrast, the following example is more characteristic of the responses of this type in mainstream magazines. A columnist responds to one girl's question about how to not laugh when she sees unclothed men on TV and in movies: "And, hey: We don't want to dis your crowd, but ... oral sex should never directly follow kissing on the make-out scale. Would a baseball player cut across the field from first base to third? No ... We say, let a whole lotta time elapse between kissing a guy and engaging in some serious foreplay with him" (*Seventeen*, September 1998, p. 128).

Sex or sexuality is the topic of 14 of the 25 answers in which the mainstream magazines' columnists explicitly tells readers what not to do, while neither of the answers in alternative magazines deal with sexuality.[14] As in the answer above, most of the columnists' answers involving sex explicitly advise girls to follow a sexual script (as explained above, not jump from first to third base). In another example, a girl asks, "I'm afraid my boy will decide my body's ugly if we have sex and he sees me in the nude. Should I do it with him anyway?" The columnist first empathizes with the girl: " ... it's understandable that you're self-conscious about it. Unfortunately, tons of chicks think their so-called imperfections will turn a guy off." Then, she advises the girl, " ... I'd hold off on doing anything sexual until your insecurities go away," but fails to acknowledge that most, if not all, women have insecurities. The answer encourages the girl to reconsider her decision and wait. After all, "You have a lifetime ahead of you to have sex" (*YM*, February 1998, p. 44). Although these answers probably are comforting to parents, they also act to direct girls' behavior by encouraging them to follow traditional gender role expectations, keep their hormones in check, and act as the gatekeepers to sex.

According to Broom and Woodward (1996), medicalization diminishes the importance of social factors and implies that the person's "problem" is an individual matter. The mainstream magazines' advice columns never discussed (during the 2 years of this analysis) the social causes of girls' problems. For example, in a question/answer previously mentioned about virginity, the columnist addresses the controversial definition of virginity with a definite answer:

> You're still a virgin after: your boyfriend touches you down there (yes); you masturbate (yes); your guy comes on your underwear (yes); you get your period for the first time (yes); you've had cybersex (yes!) ... Elliot Levine, M.D., a Chicago gynecologist, says a girl remains a virgin until she's had intercourse, meaning penis-in-vagina penetration. You've either done the deed or you haven't. (*YM*, April 1998, p. 52)

The answer fails to acknowledge that not all doctors or "experts" agree on the definition of virginity.[15] The answer presents the definition of virginity as a medical fact; therefore, the answer does not suggest that the definition of virginity is socially produced. In other words, the answer ignores how the term is socially constructed and historically contingent. The answer also contains a heterosexual bias; according to this definition, people can only "lose" their virginity if they are heterosexual. In a second example a girl wrote, "I get teased all the time 'cause my front teeth seriously stick out. My parents can't afford to get me braces. What can I do?" (*YM*, April 1998, p. 52). While the answer comforts the girl and empathizes with being teased in school, missing from the response is an examination of social factors. It does not question the standards of beauty in our society, or the idea that everyone would and should want to be beautiful. Through the implicit and explicit focus on normality in these columns, teenage girls find themselves subject to standards and norms surrounding the ideal female body that are constructed and defined for them.

In these ways, mainstream teen magazine advice columns often contribute to an unfortunate reality of social life for adolescent girls: that although "problems" are socially produced, people rarely experience them this way. Magazines exacerbate this problem. In fact, none of the mainstream magazines' responses encouraged girls to change the society that creates their anxieties, fears, and insecurities. Furthermore, very few of the answers even acknowledge that it is society, not the girls themselves, that creates their anxieties, fears, and insecurities. For example, a girl wrote in wondering if she could "take a dip with a maxi pad" because using tampons is painful. Rather than problematizing society's taboos about menstruation, the columnist provides "cool excuses" that girls can use to "fool" their friends and not swim while menstruating (*YM*, August 1998, p. 62). The pattern found throughout the mainstream magazine's columns is that regardless of whether the columnist tells the girl that she is normal (or even that she is not normal), what is not questioned is the idea of normality itself. In contrast, they validate girls' concerns by constructing them as individual, medical problems through the use of medical language, doctor referrals, and doctor citations. The columns are not informed by a sociological analysis, which would suggest that many of the "problems" that girls write in about are not individual problems, but social conditions that can, and possibly should, be changed.

In contrast, the answers in the alternative magazines occasionally treat social conditions and society as problematic. For example, a *New Moon* reader offered advice to a question about depression: "If you're still too shy to talk to anyone, talk to yourself! Be your own therapist, or even use a stuffed animal! You could tape-record yourself, or even write it down... Don't think your feelings have to be justified, and don't try to justify them ... there's no such thing as a wrong feeling. You have the right to your feelings, no matter what they are." (*New Moon*, March/April 1998). The answer implies that many girls think their feelings are not normal and believe their concerns need to be justified; however, according to the girl's response, "you have a right to your feelings" even if society does not condone them and perhaps even creates these anxieties, fears, and insecurities. Similarly, another reader advises a girl who is upset because her friends tease her and call her "Heather the feather": "What's important is how YOU feel about yourself, not how others feel about you. I think your problem is your friends, not your size" (*New Moon*, September/October 1999, p. 11). This suggests that her problem is not primarily an individual one, but begins to hint at a social explanation for the "problem."

*Teen Voices* is more explicit in the structural explanations they offer. For example, in response to a series of three questions about friendships and romantic relationships, the answer reads, "In this society, young women are raised to value romantic relationships with guys more than anything else, including education, hobbies, or other relationships. Don't fall into this trap ... " (*Teen Voices*, Winter 1997, p. 7). In another issue, sexuality is discussed in a framework very different from that in mainstream magazines:

> Many adults out there, including those at Teen Voices, don't want teens to have intercourse because we want to protect you. But what is often missing are conversations and discussions about the normal, sexual feelings that teenagers have. Not too long ago in the United States, teens used to get married and have kids, and this is still the norm in many parts of the world. Now in the U.S. you are almost guaranteed to live and raise your children in poverty if you have kids while you're a teenager. But just because the economy has changed, and more and more people, especially young women are educated doesn't mean our sexuality has changed. It's still controlled by our hormones. (*Teen Voices*, Summer 1997, p. 7)

This answer discusses structural reasons for adults' and teenagers' actions and feelings. Additionally, it places concerns of teenage sexuality in context both in the present day and historically, relating it to economic and societal changes, while also mentioning the role of biology. Later in the answer masturbation is discussed not only as a source of pleasure, but also in the context of gender relations in society at large: "This will make you less dependent on men and less likely to act on sexual urges without fully considering the consequences" (*Teen Voices*, Summer 1997, p. 7). *Teen Voices* also explains relations among women through a sociological lens. In response to a 13-year-old girl who wrote about problems with popularity and friends, the answer explains, "Because there is power and safety in numbers, members of cliques sometimes find it easy to be mean to others"

(*Teen Voices*, Spring 1997, p. 8). On a similar theme, another answer asserts, "Society has set up these standards that make it really impossible for women to look at each other and not feel threatened. The media also makes it very hard to love ourselves and others around us for who we are and not what the media says we represent" (*Teen Voices*, Winter 1999, p. 55). Another answer encourages "Moms (and dads!)" to explore with their daughter why she is worried about her weight. The column proposes a range of options to do together including, "Analyze the television shows, commercials, and magazines you see. What messages about being happy does she absorb? Where did she learn what the best weight is? What standards is she judging herself by?" (*Teen Voices*, Fall 1997, p. 7). These answers, like many others in the "alternative" magazines, explain how structural forces – such as the media, dominant heterosexual culture, and adolescent peer dynamics – can cause problems for teenage girls. While the mainstream columns are not informed by a sociological analysis – which would suggest that most of the "problems" that girls write in about are not primarily individual, but rather social conditions that can, and perhaps should, be changed – the alternative magazine's advice column illustrates that this is possible in a magazine advice column format.

## DISCUSSION

In summary, mainstream teen magazine health advice columns frequently cite doctors and medical experts as authorities on young women's bodies. These columns use medical language[16] to define the girls' "problem" as primarily an individual, medical one. Medicalization is further promoted because young women are referred to see a doctor in nearly half of the published answers. While the columns often propose solutions the girl can do herself without or in addition to medical interventions; they almost always are combined with suggestions to seek a doctor's opinion as well. In these ways, medical authority is privileged in these columns, and the power and control the medical profession can exert over girls' bodies remains unquestioned. Health advice columns would seem to play a role in the "disciplining" of girls' bodies, perhaps turning them into "docile bodies" (Foucault, 1979, p. 138), bodies of "a certain size and general configuration" with "a specific repertoire of gestures, postures, and movements" and displayed "as an ornamented surface" (Bartky, 1998, p. 27). In these ways, the health advice columns in teen magazines may serve to discipline girls' bodies, behaviors, and attitudes through socializing women to respect medicine's authority over their bodies and through their implicit and explicit discussions of "normal" appearance, behavior, and attitudes for adolescent girls.[17]

On the other hand, the alternative magazines' advice columns less frequently include doctor citations, doctor referrals, and medical language in answering girls' questions. Through the format where girls answer other girls' questions, girls are cultural producers as well as consumers of health knowledge. Instead of, or perhaps in addition to, medicalizing girls' concerns, the alternative magazines present different, and multiple, perspectives on who is the authority on girls' health and bodies. Encouraging girls to talk to others about their bodies and their concerns is also consistent with advice on increasing health and well-being according to sources on women's health (e.g., Boston Women's Health Collective, 1998) and on the benefits of peer advice (e.g., Turner, 1999). The sheer number of doctor referrals in mainstream magazines stands in stark contrast to the heterogeneity in explanations and bodily experts in alternative magazines. Similarly, the primarily fashion and beauty advertisements prevalent in *Seventeen* and *YM* stand in contrast to the lack of advertisements in *New Moon* and the focus on educational and political organizations in *Teen Voices*'s advertisements.

Some people argue that the medicalization of people's life experiences is negative; for example, discussions over the recent medicalization of women's sexuality through the creation of "female sexual dysfunction" have criticized the medical model for its "mind–body split, biological reductionism, focus on diseases rather than people, and reliance on norms" (Moynihan, 2003, p. 46). In contrast, others view the expansion of medicine as not primarily negative because it is accompanied by increased discussions, increased funding for research, new treatments or interventions, and a recognition of the condition as a medical (therefore, legitimized) concern. For example, naming something a medical concern (e.g., bulimia or depression) rather than an individual deficiency, can be helpful for individuals receiving treatment and is one positive effect of medicalization. Moreover, they argue that medicine offers more liberal solutions to people's problems than had previous authorities on the body – such as religious or lay solutions. Regardless of which perspective on medicalization is privileged, the results of this study illustrate that medicalization is present in media targeting youth, although this may not be the intention of the magazines' editors and writers.

Mainstream magazines also use slang to address girls' questions and concerns; for example, a question about pubic hair uses some medical vocabulary and incorporates the use of slang terms: "You know, those mini-butterfly clips are a lovely accessory. Kidding! Pubes grow during your teen years when your bod pumps up the hormones. While some believe that pubic hair serves to keep genitals warm and help protect them from harmful bacteria, others say the curlies have zippo practical function ... " (*YM*, October 1999, p. 44). The use of slang in the answer makes the advice sound more like it is coming from a friend and less like it is coming from a doctor or a medical textbook. When some slang terms are included in the answer, the advice becomes more accessible to teenage girls, which is one of the goals of these columns (Chandra Czape, 2000, *YM*'s Features Editor, personal communication). This combination, as illustrated above, can inform girls about the more technical aspects of their "bods" without the advice being entirely medicalized.

The use of some slang terminology might provide intimacy with readers, but the overuse of slang can discourage girls from being able to communicate their problems with adults and medical experts who may not be familiar with these terms. The overuse of slang may also trivialize girls' concerns. For example, magazines use terms such as "down there," which cloud girls' reproductive parts in mystery, particularly when used by the columnist and not the girl writing the question (for example, see *YM*, February 1999, p. 36) and slang terms with a negative connotation such as "icky leakage" to refer to what the girl describes as a "white discharge" (*YM*, March 1999, p. 24). In contrast, *Teen Voices* never used slang and *New Moon* only used one slang term ("the happy pill") and it was used along with medical language ("antidepressant medication" and "Prozac"). Perhaps because adolescent (and sometimes preadolescent) girls write the answers to these questions (and select which answers appear in each issue), the answers do not need to include slang terms to create intimacy and trust with girls who are the readers of the magazine. In sum, while slang can help foster a connection to teenagers and empower them, it also can trivialize girls' concerns, obscure the physiology of girls' reproductive organs, and make them appear negative (e.g., "icky").

As discussed earlier, the nature of the advice is different, to some extent, between the two types of magazines: the mainstream magazines focus on sexuality and body issues while the alternative magazines discuss more general issues, particularly relationships. However, even examining only the most medically oriented questions (those on sex, appearance, and other mental and physical health issues),[18] the considerable differences between the two groups of magazines are consistent with the findings presented earlier. As previously mentioned, over three-quarters of the answers on these more medical topics in mainstream magazines use medical terms, compared to less than one-half of those in alternative magazines. Of these answers in mainstream magazines, approximately 40 percent include doctor referrals and nearly 90 percent doctor citations. Half of these answers in *Teen Voices* include doctor referrals and citations, while none of the answers in *New Moon* include doctor citations and just over ten percent include doctor referrals. Additionally, in response to these more medically oriented questions, self-efficacy solutions were proposed in approximately 90 percent of the answers in alternative magazines compared to less than 70 percent of those in mainstream magazines.

As noted by Oinas (1998) in her study to Finnish magazines, this analysis of advice columns in *Seventeen*, *YM*, *New Moon*, and *Teen Voices* reveals that most of the readers' questions are not necessarily medical in nature. They could be answered by, or at least asked of, almost any woman or teenage girl. For example, consider the use of a medical doctor to describe how to use a tampon, as previously discussed (*YM*, September 1999, p. 44). The alternative magazines, however, provide a twist to the typical way that "expert" knowledge has been theorized, particularly through the lens of medicalization. Through a format where girls answer other girls' questions, girls are cultural producers in addition to being consumers of health knowledge. Moreover, in addition to occasionally including medical language or referring other girls to see a doctor, the advice that girls give each other often provides solutions girls can do themselves, offers multiple (including structural) explanations for girls' concerns, and recognizes multiple bodily experts – including non-medical experts.

The issue of power regarding medicalization in mainstream magazines is even more complex than just a negotiation between the medical profession and adolescent girls. Although the girls have the freedom to ask about any questions or concerns, the magazine editors have the power to select what gets published and what advice and information to dispense. In these ways, the editors (whether they be adults or teenage girls) possess power for social control; they decide what girls ought to worry about. Therefore, it is possible that the frequency of topics included in these advice columns, particularly in mainstream magazines, is not representative of teenage girls' actual questions and concerns.[19] However, the questions and answers published signal to girls what concerns are common (or "normal") among teenage girls (Currie, 1999). The magazine editors choose the language and terminology used in these columns and provide the girls with advice –"how they are meant to feel, how they are meant to act" (McRobbie, 1991, p. 164). What stake do magazines and magazine editors have in giving medicalized advice? While it is possible that teen magazines would be in alliance with doctors or the medical profession to keep a monopoly on advice giving, it seems more likely that they are building or maintaining trust with girls who already accept medical authority and are protecting themselves from giving inadequate or incorrect advice, with the medical experts' names in the column legally protecting them as well as providing legitimacy to their advice. Regardless of the reason, through the use of doctor referrals, doctor citations, and medical language, these columns suggest to girls to respect medical authority over their bodies.

Although the questions and answers in the alternative magazines focus more on relationships with friends, peers, and family and less on sex and appearance than those in *Seventeen* and *YM*, there is no reason to believe that an "Ask a Girl" format would not work in mainstream teen magazines, either separately or in conjunction with current more medically oriented columns. In an article discussing her difficulties in interesting minority girls in Canada in "alternative" teen magazines such as *Sassy* and *New Moon*, Gonick (1997) concludes that revolutionizing the content and discourse of teen magazines causes girls to reject these magazines and their messages outright. Gonick's solutions to providing girls with alternative images of femininity in teen magazines while still keeping their interest suggests taking small steps in changing the messages in teen magazines rather than drastically changing their entire layout, look, content, and discourse. Including the "Ask a Girl" or "Dear D" format in mainstream teen magazines is consistent with Gonick's solution. These columns could also rely on women or older peers (either instead of or in addition to other girls) as alternatives or supplements to columnists and medical experts. Research on peer educators and peer support has established the value of peer advice on topics such as health and sexuality, particularly the short-term value for teens on both sides of the peer-advice relationship (Hendrin, 1987; Kohler & Strain, 1990; Rickert, Jay, & Gottlieb, 1991; Turner, 1999).[20] The strength of such answers lies in their heterogeneous explanations and recognition of multiple experts.

Much research on this topic is left undone. Future research should continue examining the multiple and heterogeneous messages both within and between teen magazines. Similar health advice columns in women's fashion and beauty magazines could be analyzed. Do these magazines convey the same messages? Future research could also examine why men's and boys' magazines do not contain corollary columns, and to what extent magazine health advice columns vary (and are similar) internationally. Focus groups with teen girls who read these columns would be a fruitful method for future research, as meanings (about the messages in these magazines) are typically made in peer groups (Milkie, 1995). Currie's (1999, 2001) research suggests that few girls reject the advice in teen magazine columns. Nevertheless, future research should examine what messages within health advice columns girls are most likely to accept and/or resist, as well as how the context of the reading and the girls' class, race, and sexuality may influence their readings. How do girls accept and/or resist doctor referrals or doctor citations, since they are writing to the magazine about their concerns rather than discussing them with a doctor in the first place? How do they accept/resist the columnists' other advice – such as solutions that the girl can do herself and those that suggest that the girl talk to peers or women about her concerns – or the information itself? Finally, how do alternative forms, such as those in *Teen Voices* and *New Moon*, influence how girls interpret these messages? *Teen Voices* has changed the format of their advice column several times; for example, in recent issues they include a follow-up letter from the girl who asked for advice discussing how/if the advice worked for her (e.g., see *Teen Voices*, Fall 2003, p. 21). They often include poems and essays from girls in the columns. How do these unconventional components of advice columns influence girls' interpretations?

Future research should explore the meanings girls make from the messages presented in these columns as well as what purposes these columns serve for teenage girls. Particularly because this analysis of health advice columns revealed little class- or race-based content, research should continue to explore how girls in different social locations (e.g., race, class, age, sexual preference) interpret magazine advice (Bordo, 1993; Currie, 1999; Duke & Kreshel, 1998; Gonick, 1997; McRobbie, 1991; Milkie, 1994, 1995, 1999) and explore how these identities influence their reading of these columns. It is unclear how, or even if, reading these columns affects girls' self-esteem, either negatively – through privileging the medical profession and medical experts' understandings of girls' lives or bodies – or positively – through offering multiple experts on girls' bodies and empowering the girls to further their own health and well-being. Future research also should focus on editors' choices and intentions as they have the power to decide what questions and advice get published and on doctors and other medical "experts" as they are consulted in the answers to adolescent girls' questions in mainstream magazines. Additionally, more research is needed on media where girls are cultural producers, such as in "alternative" teen magazines and zines like *Teen Voices* and *New Moon*. Finally, while more than 70 percent of 15- to 17-year-olds report using the Internet to find health information (Rideout, Richardson, & Resnick, 2002), we know little about the content of such sites and the messages they present to teens about their bodies and health.

# CONCLUSION

In conclusion, this analysis shows the importance of revealing the complex processes through which medicalization operates in teen magazine health advice columns. These results illustrate that medicalization is present in media targeting youth, although this may not be the intention of the magazine's editors or columnists. This analysis shows that advice in teen magazine health advice columns, particularly those in mainstream magazines, is medicalized; they use medical language, doctor citations, and doctor referrals in their framing of girls' concerns as individual medical problems. Answers in mainstream teen magazines rarely analyze, or even acknowledge, the societal conditions that cause girls' concerns. Medicalization is pervasive in our culture; this analysis suggests that even laypeople (such as the columnists and teen girls themselves) respect the authority of medicine. However, these columns offer support for girls as well as discussions of, information about, and advice on topics of importance to teenage girls. One of the goals of the women's health movement is to make women full and active participants in their health, yet as women's health centers became mainstreamed they were co-opted by the capitalist system, thus revealing a conflict between feminist goals and capitalism (Thomas & Zimmerman, 2003). Similarly, health advice for teens is no longer absent from public discussion, yet it is influenced by this same tension between empowering women and surviving in a market-based system. However, pockets of resistance do exist, particularly where girls are cultural producers as well as consumers. This analysis shows two such sites, both alternative magazines, where girls offer less medicalized advice in which structural explanations and a range of "expert" knowledge – like that of peers, counselors, parents, and other adults in addition to doctors and other medical experts – are recognized.

# NOTES

1. Neither similar columns nor similar magazines are targeted to teen boys in the U.S.
2. Due to irregular publishing of their advice column during 1998 and 1999, 3 years (1997–1999) of *Teen Voices* magazine were selected for analysis. This decision will be discussed in more depth later in the paper.
3. My preliminary analyses of approximately 20 years (1978–1999) of *Seventeen*'s advice column – first called "Staying Well," then "Sex & Your Body," and during the years of this analysis (1998–1999) "sex + body" – showed similar patterns to those Brumberg (1997) found. The first time "Staying Well" was a regular feature in *Seventeen*, the topic was "What to believe about biorhythms: Scientists reveal how

*your* biological clocks may help you predict your future" (May 1978, p. 90). The next issue discussed "Bon voyage – but be careful! Helpful hints that can make your trip healthier and happier" (June 1978, pp. 92, 96). In comparison, the subtitles for the questions in the December 1999 issue include, "Can I get rid of spider veins? ... I love being naked ... My vagina swells ... There's hair on my bottom." This preliminary analysis suggests that over the past two decades, the advice column appears to have come to focus less on strictly medical matters and health issues and more on appearance, normality, and sexuality; changes in the title of the column ("Staying Well" to "sex + body") reflects these changes in content. The presence and current character of the columns seem to suggest an openness about (previously taboo) body and sexuality issues.

4. According to Currie, girls grant the text truth value because the "rejection of textual constructions in favour of experiential knowledge requires girls to place themselves outside the normalcy constructed by the text" so they were more likely to reject their own self-construction than the advice given in the text (Currie, 2001, p. 277). However, as stated earlier, Currie's study did not focus on health advice columns and she notes, "[r]egrettably, very little discussion appears in interview transcripts on this aspect of adolescent magazines [the body]" because her "research assistants were advised to avoid sensitive topics, such as sexual activity" (p. 273). Currie's conclusions, along with the findings presented here, point to the need for reception studies of health advice in teen magazines.

5. *Young & Modern* first appeared in 1954 as *Young Miss* and is currently known as *Your Magazine*.

6. *YM*'s advice column also includes one question per issue titled "guy trauma," which is a question from an adolescent male. This question was excluded from my analysis because it is outside an examination of health advice for young women.

7. *New Moon* has a "Girls' Editorial Board" consisting of 15 girls, 8- to 14-years old, who work with the Managing Editor and the Assistant Managing Editor to produce the magazine and to decide what is included in each issue. They were highlighted in a *Ms.* Magazine article on "Women Who Made a Difference in 2001" (Velasquez, 2002, p. 69) and in an article about girls' publications in *Women's Studies Quarterly* (Bayrl, 2000).

8. Over half of the questions answered in 1998 and 1999 were answered by more than one girl (55 percent were printed with more than one answer, 18 percent with three answers) and one answer was composed and submitted by a group, "The YMCA Teens" from Carlisle, Pennsylvania (*New Moon*, July/August 1999, p. 10).

9. Nineteen questions and 41 answers (and corresponding questions) were printed in *New Moon* in 1998–1999.

10. For example, the last few lines of the October 1999 column state, "Medical experts consulted for this month's column: Ann Davis, M.D., assistant professor of obstetrics and gynecology at Harvard Medical School; Leslie Kantor, vice president for education at Planned Parenthood, New York City." Additionally, *Seventeen* cites or quotes an "expert" or doctor in the text of two answers from 1998 to 1999.

11. *YM* uses doctor citations to "back us up" when the answer includes information that the magazine thinks girls may question (personal correspondence, Chandra Czape, *YM*'s Features Editor). This suggests that the columnists do not

question girls' acceptance of medical authority. An examination of the columnist's intentions is beyond the scope of this content analysis, but the discourse in these responses is important to examine and analyze due to its potential impact on the reader. In the example above, it is interesting that the columnist does not choose another young woman to explain the "plug pointers" rather than citing a doctor, even if the columnist herself does not use tampons.

12. The rate of doctor referrals is particularly puzzling, and seemingly ironic, as these girls are writing to the magazine presumably because they do not want to see a doctor.

13. In this paper, self-efficacy and self-help are used interchangeably although I recognize analytical differences between the two terms.

14. The other answers in mainstream magazines deal with appearance ($N = 2$), tattoos and piercings ($N = 4$) and miscellaneous topics ($N = 5$), such as illegal and over-the-counter drug use or abuse.

15. An answer about virginity in *Seventeen* offers a similar (but simpler) answer, "a virgin is a person who has never had sexual intercourse. Period." (November 1998, p. 80). One issue of *YM* (September 1999, p. 44) does mention that the definition of virginity is contested, but does not point out that it is heterosexist or question the notion that all girls (or all readers of teen magazines) are heterosexual.

16. Or medical language in combination with slang.

17. At times the magazine articulates this focus. For example, the "sex + body" column in the August 1998 issue of *Seventeen* is devoted to the question, "Am I Normal?" The description below the title reads: "This is a question many of you ask yourselves as your bodies grow and develop. Sometimes these physical changes are too embarrassing to discuss with your mom or even with your best friend. But you're not afraid to ask *us* these urgent questions. So read on for our reassuring advice about your most common problems."

18. The most medical questions/answers in these magazines are in three main topic categories – Appearance; sex, pregnancy, contraception, and virginity; and other topics, such as depression, mood swings, constipation, and nutrition. Numbers presented here are based on this restricted sample (mainstream magazines $N = 115$, alternative magazines $N = 18$).

19. This is difficult to assess. Very rarely have survey researchers asked teen girls to identify their concerns. In one recent exception, an American Psychological Association task force asked a racially diverse group of 733 adolescent girls to write down six questions they would like to ask an "expert." The task force was surprised to find that girls were more concerned about their future career and finances than with marriage and children (Murray, 1998). Other frequent concerns expressed by girls parallel those in teen magazine advice columns, particularly those about normal bodily changes and feelings, sex, and eating disorders. The most frequently asked questions were answered by experts in a book for teens and parents titled *The Inside Story on Teen Girls* (Rubenstein & Zager, 2002).

20. Although the teens answering questions in *New Moon* and *Teen Voices* have not received formal training in peer support or peer education (as have most peer support programs studied), these are established youth programs and the editorial boards (including adult advisors) are responsible for choosing which letters to print in each issue.

## ACKNOWLEDGMENTS

Earlier versions of this paper received a 2004 Society for the Study of Social Problems (SSSP) Graduate Student Paper Competition Award in the Health, Health Policy & Health Services Division and a 2003 Midwest Sociological Society Graduate Student Paper Competition Award. Portions of this paper were presented at the annual meeting of the Midwest Sociological Society, Milwaukee, Wisconsin, April 2002 and the annual meeting of the American Sociological Association, Chicago, Illinois, August 2002. I wish to thank the editors of this volume, Kate Rosier and David Kinney, and Donna Eder, Jeff Dixon, Emily Fairchild, Jane McLeod, Brian Powell, Rob Robinson, Sarah Smith, Jenny Stuber, Jeremy Vida, and members of the Spring 2004 and Fall 2001 S700 seminars at Indiana University for their helpful suggestions on earlier drafts of this paper.

## REFERENCES

American Association of University Women. (1991). *Shortchanging girls, shortchanging America : A nationwide poll to assess self esteem, educational experiences, interest in math and science, and career aspirations of girls and boys ages 9–15*. Washington, DC: The Foundation.

Bartky, S. L. (1998). Foucault, femininity, and the modernization of patriarchal power. In: R. Weitz (Ed.), *The politics of women's bodies: Sexuality, appearance, and behavior* (pp. 25–45). New York: Oxford University Press.

Bayrl, K. (2000). Mags, zines and gURLs: The exploding world of girls' publications. *Women's Studies Quarterly, 3, 4*, 287–292.

Bell, S. E. (1987). Changing ideals: The medicalization of menopause. *Social Science and Medicine, 24*, 535–542.

Block, J., & Robins, R. W. (1993). A longitudinal study of consistency and change in self-esteem from early adolescence to early adulthood. *Child Development, 64*, 909–923.

Bolognini, M., Plancherel, B., Bettschart, W., & Halfon, O. (1996). Self-esteem and mental health in early adolescence: Development and gender differences. *Journal of Adolescence, 19*, 233–245.

Bordo, S. (1993). *The unbearable weight: Feminism, western culture, and the body*. Berkeley: University of California Press.

Boston Women's Health Collective. (1998). *Our bodies, ourselves for the new century: A book by and for women*. New York: Touchstone.

Broom, D. H., & Woodward, R. V. (1996). Medicalisation reconsidered: Toward a collaborative approach to care. *Sociology of Health & Illness, 18*, 357–378.

Brown, L. M., & Gilligan, C. (1992). *Meeting at the crossroads: Women's psychology and girls' development*. Cambridge: Harvard University Press.

Brumberg, J. J. (1997). *The body project: An intimate history of American girls.* New York: Vintage Books.
Budgeon, S., & Currie, D. H. (1995). From feminism to postfeminism: Women's liberation in fashion magazines. *Women's Studies International Forum, 18,* 173–186.
Carpenter, L. M. (1998). From girls into women: Scripts for sexuality and romance in Seventeen magazine, 1974–1994. *Journal of Sex Research, 35,* 158–168.
Carr, D. (2003). After successfully reducing debt, Primedia explores sale of Seventeen. New York Times. Retrieved February 6, 2003 from http://www.nytimes.com/2003/02/06/business/media/06MAG.html
Chow, J. D. (1999). Wanna know a secret? *Advances in Nursing Science, 22*(2), 49–61.
Conrad, P. (1992). Medicalization and social control. *Annual Review of Sociology, 18,* 209–232.
Conrad, P., & Schneider, J. W. (1980). *Deviance and medicalization: From badness to sickness.* St. Louis: C.V. Mosby Company.
Coupland, J., & Williams, A. (2002). Conflicting discourses, shifting ideologies: Pharmaceutical, alternative and feminist emancipatory texts on the menopause. *Discourse & Society, 13,* 419–445.
Currie, D. H. (1994). Going green: Mythologies of consumption in adolescent magazines. *Youth & Society, 26,* 92–117.
Currie, D. H. (1999). *Girl talk: Adolescent magazines and their readers.* Toronto: University of Toronto Press.
Currie, D. H. (2001). Dear Abby: Advice pages as a site for the operation of power. *Feminist Theory, 2*(3), 259–281.
Czape, C. (2000). Personal communication.
Dorland's illustrated medical dictionary. (1994) (28th ed.). Philadelphia: W.B. Saunders Company.
Duke, L. L., & Kreshel, P. J. (1998). Negotiating femininity: Girls in early adolescence read teen magazines. *Journal of Communication Inquiry, 22,* 48–71.
Durham, M. G. (1998). Dilemmas of desire: Representations of adolescent sexuality in two teen magazines. *Youth & Society, 29,* 369–389.
Ehrenreich, B., & English, D. (1979). *For her own good: 150 years of the experts' advice to women.* Garden City: Anchor.
Evans, E. D. (1990). Adolescent females' utilization and perception of contemporary teen magazines. Paper presented at the meeting of the Society for Research on Adolescence, March, Atlanta, GA.
Evans, E. D., Rutberg, J., Sather, C., & Turner, C. (1991). Content analysis of contemporary teen magazines for adolescent females. *Youth & Society, 23,* 99–120.
Figert, A. E. (1996). *Women and the ownership of PMS: The structuring of a psychiatric disorder.* New York: Aldine de Gruyter.
Fine, M. (1988). Sexuality, schooling and adolescent females: The missing discourse of desire. *Harvard Educational Review, 58,* 29–53.
Fiske, J. (1989). *Understanding popular culture.* London: Unwin Hyman Ltd.
Foucault, M. (1979). *Discipline and punish: The birth of the prison.* New York: Vintage.
G & J USA Publishing. (2004). ym. Retrieved April 5, 2004 from http://www.gjusa.com/ym.cfm.
Garry, A. (2001). Medicine and medicalization: A response to Purdy. *Bioethics, 15,* 262–269.
Gonick, M. (1997). Reading selves, re-fashioning identity: Teen magazines and their readers. *Curriculum Studies, 5,* 66–69.

Gould medical dictionary. (1979) (4th ed.). New York: McGraw-Hill Book Company.
Hendrin, D. (1987). Students as teachers: A tool for improving school climate and productivity. *Social Policy, 17*(3), 42–47.
Hesse-Biber, S. (1996). *Am I thin enough yet? The cult of thinness and the commercialization of identity.* New York: Oxford University Press.
Hollows, J. (2000). *Feminism, femininity and popular culture.* Manchester, UK: Manchester University Press.
Holsti, O. R. (1969). *Content analysis for the social sciences and humanities.* Reading, MA: Addison-Wesley Publishing Company.
Kearney, M. C. (1998). Producing girls: Rethinking the study of female youth culture. In: S. A. Innes (Ed.), *Delinquents and debutants: Twentieth-century American girls cultures* (pp. 285–310). New York: New York University Press.
Kohler, F. W., & Strain, P. S. (1990). Peer-assisted interventions: Early promises, notable achievements and future aspirations. *Clinical Psychology Review, 10*, 441–452.
LaGuardia, C., Katz, B., & Katz, L. S. (Eds) (2002). *Magazines for libraries*, (11th ed.). New Providence, NJ: R. R. Bowker.
Levy, K. B. (1992). *The politics of women's health care: Medicalization as a form of social control.* Las Colinas, TX: Ide House.
Martin, E. (1987). *The woman in the body: A cultural analysis of reproduction.* Boston: Beacon Press.
Martin, K. (1996). *Puberty, sexuality, and the self: Boys and girls at adolescence.* New York: Routledge.
McCracken, E. (1993). *Decoding women's magazines: From Mademoiselle to Ms.* New York: St. Martin's Press.
McRobbie, A. (1991). *Feminism and youth culture.* Boston: Unwin Hyman.
Milkie, M. (1994). Social world approach to cultural studies. *Journal of Contemporary Ethnography, 23*, 354–381.
Milkie, M. (1995). The social psychological impact of gender images in media: A multi-level analysis of girls, peer networks, and media organizations. Ph.D. dissertation, Department of Sociology, Indiana University, Bloomington, IN.
Milkie, M. (1999). Social comparisons, reflected appraisals, and mass media: The impact of pervasive beauty images on black and white girls self-concepts. *Social Psychology Quarterly, 62*, 190–210.
Milkie, M. (2002). Contested images of femininity: An analysis of cultural gatekeepers' struggles with the real girls critique. *Gender & Society, 16*, 839–859.
Morgan, K. P. (1998). Contested bodies, contested knowledges: Women, health and the politics of medicalization. In: S. Sherwin (Ed.), *The politics of women's health: Exploring agency and autonomy* (pp. 83–121). Philadelphia: Temple University Press.
Mosby's Medical Nursing, and Allied Health Dictionary. (1998) (5th ed.). St. Louis: Mosby.
Moynihan, R. (2003). The making of a disease: Female sexual dysfunction. *British Medical Journal, 326*, 45–47.
Murray, B. (1998). Survey reveals concerns of today's girls. *APA Monitor, 29*(10). www.apa.org/monitor/oct98/girls.html (accessed 30.3.2005).
Norton, B. (2001/2002). When is a teen magazine not a teen magazine? *Journal of Adolescent & Adult Literacy, 45*(4), 296–299.
Oinas, E. (1998). Medicalisation by whom? Accounts of menstruation conveyed by young women and medical experts in medical advisory columns. *Sociology of Health and Illness, 20*, 52–70.

Orenstein, P. (1994). *School girls: Young women, self-esteem, and the confidence gap.* New York: Doubleday.
Peirce, K. (1990). A feminist theoretical perspective on the socialization of teenage girls through Seventeen magazine. *Sex Roles, 23,* 491–500.
Polce-Lynch, M., Myers, B. J., Kliewer, W., & Kilmartin, C. (2001). Adolescent self-esteem and gender: Exploring relations to sexual harassment, body image, media influence, and emotional expression. *Journal of Youth and Adolescence, 30,* 225–244.
Purdy, L. M. (2001). Medicalization, medical necessity and feminist medicine. *Bioethics, 15,* 248–261.
Rickert, V. I., Jay, M. S., & Gottlieb, A. (1991). Effects of a peer counseled AIDS education program on knowledge, attitudes and satisfaction of adolescents. *Journal of Adolescent Health Care, 12,* 38–43.
Rideout, V., Richardson, C., & Resnick, P. (2002). See no evil: How internet filters affect the search for online health information. A Kaiser Family Foundation Study Executive Summary, December 2002, 14pp.
Riessman, C. K. (1983). Women and medicalization: A new perspective. *Social Policy, 14*(1), 3–18.
Rubenstein, A., & Zager, K. (2002). *The inside story on teen girls.* Washington, DC: American Psychological Association.
Ruthstrom, E. (2004). Personal Communication.
Schilt, K. (2003). 'I'll resist with every inch and every breath': Girls and zine making as a form of resistance. *Youth & Society, 35*(1), 71–97.
Schlenker, J. A., Caron, S. L., & Halteman, W. A. (1998). A feminist analysis of Seventeen magazine: Content analysis from 1945 to 1995. *Sex Roles, 38,* 135–149.
Simmons, R. G., & Blyth, D. A. (1987). *Moving into adolescence: The impact of pubertal change and school context.* New York: Aldine deGruyter.
Striplin, D., Banks, B., Joseph, M., & Rasberry, D. (Eds) (2002). *The standard periodical directory,* (25th ed.). Baltimore, MD: Oxbridge Communications, Inc.
Sullivan, D. (1993). Cosmetic surgery: Market dynamics and medicalization. *Research in the Sociology of Health Care, 10,* 97–115.
Teen Voices Online. (2004). Advertise: Facts about *Teen Voices* readers. Retrieved April 27, 2004 from www.teenvoices.com/issue_current/weadvertise2.html#facts.
The Hearst Corporation. (2004). Seventeen. Retrieved April 5, 2004 from www.hearstcorp.com/magazines/property/mag_prop_seventeen.html.
Thomas, J., & Zimmerman, M. (2003). 'Beauty and biology': Another repackaging of women's health care. Paper presented at the annual meeting of the Society for the Study of Social Problems, August, Atlanta, GA.
Turner, G. (1999). Peer support and young people's health. *Journal of Adolescence, 22,* 567–572.
Velasquez, S. (2002). Women who made a difference. *Ms, XII*(1), 66–72.
Webster's new explorer medical dictionary. (1999). Springfield, MA: Federal Street Press.
Weeks, J. (2003). An unfinished revolution: Sexuality in the 20th century. In: S. LaFont (Ed.), *Constructing sexualities: Readings in sexuality, gender and culture* (pp. 376–386). Upper Saddle River, NJ: Prentice-Hall.
Weitz, R. (Ed.) (1998). *The politics of women's bodies: Sexuality, appearance, and behavior.* New York: Oxford University Press.
Williams, S. J., & Calnan, M. (1996). Modern medicine and lay populace: Theoretical perspectives and methodological issues. In: S. J. Williams. & M. Calnan (Eds), *Modern medicine: Lay perspectives and experiences.* London: UCL Press.

Winship, J. (1987). *Inside women's magazines.* London: Pandora.
Zola, I. K. (1972). Medicine as an institution of social control. *Sociological Review, 20,* 487–504.
Zola, I. K. (1983). *Socio-medical inquiries.* Philadelphia: Temple University Press.

Magazines Cited

*New Moon: The Magazine for Girls and Their Dreams* (Duluth, MN: New Moon Publishing) March/April, May/June 1998; March/April, May/June, July/August, September/October 1999.
*Seventeen* (New York: Primedia Consumer Magazines) May 1978; February, May, July, August, September, October, November 1998; February, August, October, November, December 1999.
*Teen Voices* (Boston: Women's Express, Inc.) Spring, Summer, Fall, Winter 1997; Summer, Winter 1999; Fall 2003.
*YM: Young & Modern* (New York: Gruner & Fahr USA Publishing) February, April, May, August 1998, February, March, June/July, September, October 1999.

# APPENDIX

*Examples of medical terms:*

| | | |
|---|---|---|
| Anus | Hymen | Psychologist |
| Cellular | Infection | Pubertal |
| Chlamydia | Infertility | Sclerotherapy |
| Chronic pain | Inflammation | Screening |
| Culture | Intestinal | Scrotum |
| Dermatologist | Irritation | Self-mutilation |
| Diagnosis | Labia majora | Semen |
| Digestive system | Labia minora | Sexual intercourse |
| Discharge | Menstrual cycle | Sexually transmitted disease (STD) |
| Ejaculation | Menstruate | Sperm |
| Erogenous zones | Microorganisms | Sweat glands |
| Estrogen | Nocturnal emissions | Symptoms |
| Fallopian tubes | Ovaries | Syphilis |
| Flatulence | Ovulate | Testosterone |
| Gynecologist | Ovulation | Trichomoniasis |
| Gynecological | Penetration | Urinary tract infection (UTI) |

Hemorrhoids
Hereditary
Hormonal
Hormones
Human papilloma
  virus (HPV)

Penis
Pre-ejaculation
Progesterone
Psychogenic

Urination
Uterine
Vagina
Vaginitis
Vulva

# THE INTERSECTION OF PRIVATE AND PUBLIC EXPERIENCE AMONG FAMILIES ADOPTING ROMANIAN CHILDREN

Roberta Goldberg

## INTRODUCTION

The experience of adoption has private and public contexts, which intersect in complex ways as families develop over time. The purpose of this study is to examine these contexts, and the relationship between them, that is, the intimate experience of family life as it impacts and is impacted by larger social institutions. This qualitative study utilizes data gathered from a small cohort of mothers of children adopted from Romania. Through an analysis of in-depth interviews conducted over time, we can see with greater clarity how adoptive families are socially constructed around their private and public worlds.

At the outset, the private context of adoption may be one of crisis: an unplanned pregnancy, an infertile couple wanting children, or a child's medical, developmental, or psychological condition. In the case of international adoption, personal crises may be compounded by social crises such as war, revolution, or economic instability, which impact on the ability or willingness of birth parents to raise their children. Recent historic examples include the adoption of children in the aftermaths of the Korean War and the Vietnam War. In the last decade, children have increasingly been adopted from countries experiencing rapid political and economic change. Since the breakup of the Soviet Union, thousands of Russian and other children from Eastern Europe, including Romania, have been adopted internationally. In China, economic conditions coupled with a one-child policy have led to the adoption of thousands of infant girls by Americans.

Despite the social and political factors that affect adoption, most current research approaches adoption as a solely private, internal family experience, and utilizes a clinical approach, as the body of research is found mostly in the fields of social work and psychology (Melina, 1989; Smith & Howard, 1999). This limited scope is useful in understanding problems associated with adoption, but not the experience of adoption on the whole. Even most research on international adoption is typically limited to several narrow areas associated with adjustment of children to their adoptive families: the effects of institutionalization, medical concerns, and cultural and racial issues (Haugaard, 1997; Tizard, 1991; Bartholet, 1997; Watkins & Fisher, 1993; Miall, 1996; Bascom & Mckelvey, 1997; Verhults, Althaus, & Versluis-Den Bieman, 1992; Marcovitch, Cesaroni, Roberts, & Swanson, 1995; Wilkinson, 1995). This research does little to develop an understanding of family dynamics over time as children grow and the family interacts with the wider society. Nor does it address the complex societal attitudes regarding adoption. In fact, little attention is given to the interaction between family and social institutions except in the popular, "how-to" literature shared by adoptive families. On the whole, in the scholarly arena, adoption is viewed as crisis-driven, and that can distort our understanding of the actual experience of adoptive families for whom life has become mostly "normalized" after the initial adoption process is completed. What can provide balance to this trend in research is a sociological examination of the structure of adoptive family life, most of which is only indirectly associated with the crises that may have precipitated the adoption in the first place. This paper is an attempt to contribute to that sociological understanding of adoption.

Perhaps the most clear-cut recent example of a social crisis impacting international adoption is that of Romania. The revolutionary overthrow of the Ceausescu dictatorship in 1989 revealed a nation in deep economic and political crisis. Ceausescu's family policies, in place since the 1960s, included bans on abortion and birth control as well as a pro-natalist policy requiring Romanian women to bear large numbers of children while their fertility was publicly monitored (Harsanyi, 1994; Kligman, 1998; Nicolaescu, 1994).

These policies set in motion the practice of poor families placing some of their children in institutions (known as children's homes) so as to be able to feed and care for the other family members. The post-revolution media attention given to institutionalized children alerted the West to the untenable conditions to which many of these children were subjected.

In the U.S., changes in pregnancy and parenting practices, availability of abortion, acceptance of single parenting, and the practices of family preservation have limited the availability of domestic children for adoption (Taylor, 1992; Serrill, 1991; Daly, 1988; Feigelman & Silverman, 1983). Families experiencing their own personal crises of infertility, sought out these very children languishing in Romanian institutions. Thus, a series of private and public experiences dynamically converged as American (and other Western) families adopted Romanian children. The vast majority of these children were adopted in 1991, after significant legal changes were made in adoption procedures. In 1991, for example, 2,552 children were adopted from Romania, compared to 121 in 1990 (Defence for Children International and International Social Service (DCI/ISS), 1991, p. 8). In 1992, the number of adoptions declined to 145 (National Council for Adoption, Inc., 1993, p. 11). Subsequent to those years, Romania has stabilized politically, and established new adoption policies that have resulted in curtailing international adoption. The continuing economic problems and limited attention given to the needs of institutionalized children indicates that children continue to be abandoned, however, they are less likely to be adopted outside of Romania (Groza, Ileana, & Irwin, 1999). It has been more than a decade since the largest group of Romanian children was adopted by Americans. In 1999, 895 visas were issued by the State Department for children adopted from Romania (National Adoption Information Clearinghouse, 2000). By 2002, only 168 visas were issued (United States Department of States, 2003).

## METHODS

This paper utilizes data from two related studies done on a small cohort of families whose children were adopted in 1990–1991 (Goldberg, 1997, 2001). Respondents in both studies were eight mothers who originally were members of a support group of families with Romanian children, known as the "mothers group." The "mothers group" formed shortly after the children came to the U.S. in their infancy, between 2 and 18 months old. While most respondents were first-time parents, one had previously adopted a child, and another was completing an adoption of another child at the same time. Each respondent was interviewed in depth on two separate occasions. All of the interviews were conducted in person, with the exception of one that was conducted through e-mail. Names and identifying information have been eliminated to protect the confidentiality of the participants. The first interviews took place when the children were toddlers, and focused on the choices and risks involved in the decision to adopt a child from Romania (Goldberg, 1997). The second set of interviews with the same eight mothers took place when the children were around 7 years old. These interviews focused on the social construction of adoption within these families in relation to private and public experiences (Goldberg, 2001). This current article utilizes the data from both sets of interviews to explore further the private and public contexts in which adoptive family life takes place.

While the adoptions themselves may have been precipitated by crises, the present lives of the families in this study are anything but crisis-driven. Nevertheless, as the findings will show, adoption remains central to family identity. How the day-to-day world of these families informs our understanding of adoption is central to this research. Understanding how families navigate the public world while constructing their private family lives is the purpose of this study.

## FINDINGS

Analysis of the interviews reveals three distinct stages through which families become socially constructed. The dynamic between the public and private experience of adoption plays out in each stage, with the families making decisions at each juncture that ultimately contribute to their understanding of themselves as a family unit, and to their place in the larger society. The first stage, Initiation, was characterized by public activities associated with creating these new families, and adoption was central to everyday life. The second stage, Stabilization, found families still in the early stages of formation, but life had settled down. Specific adoption experiences continued to dominate family life. In the third stage, Integration, adoption has become less dominant, and family life is immersed in a variety of public activities unrelated to adoption. At this stage, the ways in which adoption impacts private and public activities are highly complex. Following is an in-depth discussion of each stage, with an emphasis on integration.

## Initiation

It was apparent from the first phase of the study that the public crises of political and economic upheaval in Romania had a profound effect on the decisions of families to adopt from there. Interest in Romania was precipitated by widespread media exposure of the conditions of orphanages. Up to that point in time, respondents had no direct connection to or special interest in Romania as a country from which to pursue adoption. Respondents became aware that the very public crises that attracted them to Romania could involve a certain amount of risk in regard to the health and developmental status of the children they would adopt. The political and economic conditions in Romania and the international media exposure of orphanage conditions found families facing life-changing decisions for themselves and their prospective children while under considerable pressure to make those decisions quickly. Ironically, the appeal of Romania as a source of adoptable children precipitated a secondary crisis arising from publicity about black market adoptions. This was followed by a crack down by both the Romanian government and the American Embassy in Bucharest, which threatened to halt many of the pending adoptions. Indeed, adoptions were curtailed as the process came under greater internal and international scrutiny. The risks and choices faced by the families as they traveled to Romania, met their children, and formally adopted them are covered in detail in an earlier paper (Goldberg, 1997).

While in the initiation stage, parents weighed the risks associated with the adoption of their children. There were few reliable records on their children's health status or physical or mental development, so the decision to adopt required parents to decide with little useful information. The children were too young to be cognizant of the changes taking place in their lives, thus they faced risks, but had no choices. Risk, however, is central, since their prospects, had they stayed in the children's homes, were bleak. Only as they got older could they begin to assess the circumstances by which they came to be adopted into their families. Indeed, questions children later asked their parents were directly tied to their early lives: Who were their birth families? Where were they from? Why were they adopted?

The public nature of these very personal experiences heightened the awareness of the respondents regarding the understanding that the creation of their families depended on the particular conditions in Romania and the international response to children languishing in orphanages. For example, how "orphan" was defined, whether visas would be issued by the U.S. Embassy, and increased suspicion regarding baby-selling all affected whether and when the children would be adopted. Thus, rapid political change coupled with economic upheaval affected the adopting families, the institutions housing the children, and most dramatically, the children themselves. Their vulnerability was pronounced, given the lack of basic necessities and the limited stimulation that could affect their health and growth. Out of these most public circumstances, families were formed.

*Stabilization*

Once at home with their children, the respondents faced important adoption-related decisions that bridged their public and private lives: whether to apply for U.S. citizenship and whether to re-adopt in the U.S. All of the respondents reported that they applied for, and the children have received U.S. citizenship, a process of considerable effort, time, and expense. (Since the time of the interviews, a new law was enacted, which conveys automatic citizenship to internationally adopted children.) Motivation was high. As one mother put it, "The gift of citizenship is a door to the rest of the world." Pragmatically, citizenship protects against the possibility of deportation in the future. In addition, all but one family re-adopted their children after adopting them in Romania. While the adoptions that took place in Romania were considered legal in both countries, most families chose to re-adopt in the U.S., going through the formal procedures of their home states. These were the last formal, legal steps in the adoption process, and they mostly took place soon after the children arrived home. These public acknowledgments of belonging to both their families and their new country were highly significant in a personal way, beyond the legal or political ramifications. One respondent saw these as a purposeful, public way to connect her child to the family:

> We just thought it was another ceremony to bond him not just to us, but to extended family, and we made the big ceremony, and my mother-in-law came down, and as many people have, we added this to another ceremony to incorporate into our family.

In addition to formally and publically acknowledging their families, the period of stabilization involved regular discussions about adoption within families and introducing basic information about Romania and its culture to the children.

During stabilization, children were still too young to understand the nature of the changes that had taken place in their lives, but they were now formally members of a new family, and their identity with that family began to solidify. Parents, recognizing the importance of the new formal ties, wanted to help their children see these as causes for celebration and identification, hence the ceremonies and parties were geared toward increasing the child's awareness of his/her new, permanent status. These events also served to publically confirm the child's right to family membership. Additionally, this stage marked the beginning of the children's awareness of their unique status as adoptees from Romania. Encouraged by their parents, the children were given opportunities to explore their culture of origin and adoption through various public and private activities. Children's responses to these efforts varied widely, including embracing and rejecting the culture, as well as indifference. The young age of the children and their limited numbers renders these findings impossible to interpret, but it is evident that the families attempted to help their children understand the uniqueness of their identity.

The arrival of these children and the settlement into their new families marked a transitional stage in the adoption process where families often thought about and talked about the circumstances that led them to Romania. Acute awareness of the political and economic crises, the conditions of Romanian orphanages, and the multiple risks involved in choosing to adopt a child under those circumstances remained vivid to the parents as they constructed their families and thought about their adoptions in the early stages. The intersection of public and private affirmation was found throughout this period, including various ceremonies and cultural activities. To understand this stage in the lives of these families is to see the developing dynamic between the private and public contexts.

*Integration*

The second phase of this study addressed more directly how families managed the often dichotomous private/public experiences as they developed their own unique family structure (Goldberg, 2001). As the children grew older, the task defined by most of the respondents was to find ways to acknowledge their origins while having their children not be overwhelmed by them. Respondents were keenly aware of the social stigma attached to adoption, and sought ways to help their children cope with it. This process has taken on increased significance as children have become more cognizant of the meaning of adoption, and at the same time have begun to make their way in the public world. Thus, over time, these families have worked to integrate their unique origins with ordinary daily life.

The social construction of adoptive families shares many similarities with biologically based families, so much so, that respondents consistently reported that adoption issues often took a back seat to more immediate issues as children entered the public world of school and related social arenas. The critical events associated with the origins of these families seem to fade into the background, not forgotten, but irrelevant to daily life. As one respondent recalls:

> We reminisce once in a while. It was indeed an experience in our lives, but it has faded as our lives have gone on, and the joys of watching [her] grow and learn and turn into such a wonderful person have turned the event of her adoption into appreciation. We marvel at being blessed with such a child!

Adoption remains relevant, although indirectly, as another respondent explains:

> It's not particularly relevant ... more of the issues now that I'm focusing on is learning ... health issues ... I guess I've outgrown some of those concerns, but in terms of being adopted, it's more ... is there any history of allergies – sort of the unknown things. With no medical history, you tend to question things a lot more than you probably would with your own child, and you could say, well, I had those. I don't think about it on a daily basis. I think more about the learning problems.

Despite the fact that the initial experience of adoption had little influence on daily life after a few years, the period of integration presented the most striking evidence of the importance of the intersection of the private and public worlds adoptive families navigate. Integration is marked by attention to several distinct areas where private and public life converge. In particular, findings on the topics of communication about adoption, race, ties to Romania, and connections to birth mothers inform us about the intersection of the two arenas. Following is a discussion showing how respondents have developed their understanding of these issues as the families have moved toward integrating their private and public experiences.

*Communication about Adoption*

Respondents uniformly reported that the facts of their children's adoptions and their status as adoptive families are less relevant in their social encounters as time goes by. Over time, these families have reconsidered what private information about the adoptions to share, and with whom, narrowing the field of people with access to this information. At the same time, the children, as they get older, are becoming more aware of the meaning of adoption, and are more articulate and, in some cases, interested in discussing it with family and friends. What to share and with whom and under what circumstances can become complicated. Each decision about sharing information is tied to the degree to which a family feels it is appropriate or necessary to allow public discourse about their private world to take place. Interacting with new friends adds to the complexity, as experienced by this respondent:

> I share less and less with acquaintances. In the beginning we shared a lot, but I don't even tell people we have adopted ... He's not an adopted child. He is a child that came into our family who happens to be adopted. But again, I don't see that at this point as an issue. Now, we haven't had any genealogical searches, and I haven't had a lot of issues that may bring this up, but even with new friends because I have made some new friends in the neighborhood, we do share the fact that he is adopted. But unless the details of how we did it or what we went through, I don't share, unless it comes up ... Family knows, obviously, but new friends less and less the details, because it's not what I'm thinking about.

The following respondent demonstrates the many layers of complexity involved in sharing of information, including the input from her child's friends:

> I would say people who are close to us know everything. People who are a little bit further know that she is adopted and from Romania. People farthest out and are not local don't know. I don't make a point of telling everybody, and since she looks a lot like us, I mean, it's not real noticeable. People don't tend to think that [she is adopted]. But her close friends know. In fact her closest buddy, she has one friend in particular, who is intrigued by this whole thing. And she has a lot of friends who are intrigued by it, and they discuss it all the time. And I never initiated that she should talk to her friends about it. But she has done that on her own.

A third respondent simultaneously regards adoption as less important over time while reacting uncomfortably to an acquaintance's curiosity and attribution of altruism on her part:

> It has become less important as the years go by to mention that [she] is adopted. I did say something to one of her friend's mother over the summer and she was quite impressed by it, giving me more credit for saving a child than I deserve. She questioned [my daughter] about it a little too, which made me uncomfortable.

Not only do families have to figure out who to tell, but also to provide a context for both the child and the recipient of this new knowledge. The search for context demonstrates the potential for tension between the private life of adoptive families and their comfort level with public awareness of their status. This respondent was untroubled by revealing most of the facts of her child's adoption:

> [Her] adoption was under, I guess, what seems was the best of circumstance ... a very young unmarried woman who clearly was in no position to raise a child. I mean it's a

story that makes people feel that it was appropriate circumstances to place a child for adoption, and it's nothing that she feels uncomfortable about.

This same respondent also reported that parts of the story of her daughter's adoption were too sensitive for public consumption and remain private. Deciding who and what to tell is an important part of socially constructing these families. An additional source of public conversation is with others who are considering adoption themselves, or who are interested in Romania. This respondent is comfortable sharing details about her family when interest in adoption is part of the conversation:

> The people I find who ask more questions about adoption are the ones who either seriously considered adoption or have thought about a little bit more on the issues of Romania, or had sort of a general interest. And if they've got an interest, then I will fill things in, but most people ... are more interested in the sort of children as they are now, rather than when we adopted them.

School is a particular arena where parents must carefully assess the significance of revealing the adoptive status of their children. Respondents were of two minds. Most believed it was irrelevant for school personnel to know, and feared their children might be labeled as a result. Several believed it was important to tell teachers, on the assumption that the child may discuss it and the teacher would need to be prepared to respond, especially if other children view adoption negatively. Both views are a response to fears of stigma associated with adoption. Stigma is discussed further in an earlier paper (Goldberg, 2001). The issue of schools and stigma represents the first formal public arena that the adoptive child must navigate, and the decisions the family makes regarding the revelation of their adoptive status set the stage for potential tension or conflict between the public and private spheres. This is a significant juncture in the social construction of these families for it is the first clear-cut moment when the children are in a position to respond independently to the public scrutiny of their identity.

This stage marks the period of greatest intellectual maturity for the children as well as their first important forays into the public world, as mentioned above. Because the children were not interviewed, their experience of this stage can only be seen through the respondents, their mothers. While the mothers viewed this stage as being less relevant to adoption issues, the children faced the dilemma of with whom to share the information independent of their parents for the first time. Much of the adoption literature encourages families to allow the child to take the lead, both in deciding what they themselves want to know and with whom to share it. What remains unknown is how the children's friends will react. Once the information is shared, there is no turning back. Young, school-aged children cannot anticipate the ongoing curiosity of their friends or the direction in which their sharing of information may lead them. Further research into children's choices regarding public awareness of their adoptive status, and the reaction of friends would greatly enhance our understanding of how children experience this public/private dynamic.

These various approaches to communication show the development of a complex relationship between the initial importance of adoption in defining the family to the later integration of adoption into family life. Despite its increasing irrelevance day to day, respondents continue to contemplate adoption in relation to interactions with others, and develop an intricate system of evaluating its importance in encounters with friends, acquaintances, and social institutions.

*Race and Adoption*

The issue of race and adoption is multifaceted. For the purposes of this research, a discussion of race was tied to how the respondents perceived the importance of the appearance of racial similarities or differences within families, and the public's reaction to children who may look considerably different from their parents. In the first phase of the study, respondents uniformly indicated that race played a role in selecting the country from which they would adopt so as to keep the adoption free of the complication of racial issues. These White parents selected Romania in part because of the same-race identity of their children. Most were first-time parents, unsure of their skills, who felt transracial adoption was too personally risky. They commented, in particular, about the inability ever to put adoption aside publically if the children and parents looked significantly different from one another. This respondent is representative:

> I wouldn't have known how to handle that on top of everything else, so therefore, I purposely selected a child that I would not also have that to learn how to deal with, because I felt ... I wouldn't know what to do ... When I do see other adopted children whose parents are Caucasians, and they are anything but, I often think with sadness what extra burden they have ... I thought it would really be another layer of difficulties for parents. And I wasn't sure I would be very good at figuring out how to help the child with it ... of having to deal with nitwit adults – "Oh, where did you come from?"

By the second round of interviews, most respondents had changed their views considerably. For example:

> I think at the time I was adopting, I thought it was more important than I do now. I think at that time I couldn't imagine myself as the mother of a child from Korea, China or Latin America. That was because I wasn't very knowledgeable or experienced, but I

think now I could. And I see loving families can come from anywhere in the world, from different cultures and backgrounds, and I think my thought process ... about that has evolved and I've matured some.

Regardless of their level of comfort, race is still significant for these respondents. When questioned whether race was important to her family identity, this mother replied:

> In the [metropolitan] area, though, I don't think it's as much of an issue, just because there are so many mixed families, and so many adoptions from different countries. I mean, having a child from Romania, yes, it does tend to look more like you than if you have a child from Asia. I think if you asked me that question if I lived in the mid-west in a small town where I was growing up, I'd probably have said, yes, because you didn't come across that much diversity. It would have been much more unusual.

Another respondent considered the internal structure of her family when considering a second adoption:

> I may want to make sure that child will work in our family ... It would be easier if the child was from the same cultural background ... it's more culture than race. Then I might find that difficult. As good as I feel as a parent that I am, to add that might be a little burdensome.

Despite their increased comfort with their status as adoptive families, the respondents are keenly aware of what they describe as the public intrusion into a private realm that may result when transracial families go about their daily lives. Again, we see a situation faced by adoptive families where they must consider their private family identity in relation to the larger, public world. It is significant to note that respondents' increased comfort with the experience of adoption over time enabled them to lessen their concerns about being seen as an adoptive family in public.

*Ties to Romania*

Even though the children in these families share the same "race" as their parents, the culture from which they come is significantly different from that of the U.S. Finding ways to incorporate an understanding of Romanian heritage into the family is an additional task these families take on, and a further example of the important relationship between private family life and the public world of culture and politics.

Respondents acknowledge that Romania was not significant to them until they decided to adopt a child from there, and it was the unique intersection of the timing of their search for a child at the same time Romanian children became available.

> It wasn't that I wanted to adopt a child from Romania particularly, but as far as we've adopted these children, I've paid more attention to Romania because we've adopted children from there.

From the beginning, in part because of the international publicity about orphanage conditions, these respondents experienced the intrusion of public crises into their private lives.

> I think it makes her adoption unique. So many people were moved by the Romanian orphans ... that they attribute to us that it was a mission of mercy.

Yet this same respondent, some years after the adoption took place pointed out that:

> I do not see Romania playing much of a role in her life. She is an American now. Her only connection to Romania would be the fact that she was born there. Very little else is relevant.

Even though the immediacy of the political and economic conditions that led to these adoptions has past, families find themselves seeking ways to demonstrate the importance of Romania, in all its complexity, to their children. Parents want their children to appreciate the culture. As one respondent relates:

> They know a little bit about Romania ... They know where it is on the map. They know they're from there. They know a little bit about what some of the Romanian food tastes like. A little bit about the language ... If they'd show more interest, I'd certainly try and get more information for them. They sort of take it for granted because it's just part of their life ... They're more interested in other things at this point.

This is a fairly typical response in a variety of families that adopt internationally. Yet, the unique political conditions in Romania, the deprivation in the early lives of institutionalized children, and the intense media scrutiny, caused the respondents to feel a special sensitivity to the ramifications of their children's adoptions. They were especially concerned about how to represent Romania to their children and to diminish any stigma that may be attached to them. These two respondents explain:

> I see her as like most of the kids that came from Romania. I believe most of them were young and healthy, and I think because she wasn't in a horrible institution for a long time, she escaped some of the consequences. And in that way she is not like kids who spent years there ... She may at some point hear some negative comment about screwed up kids from Romania or something, but I think she is going to have that strong enough sense of self that it is not going to have a big impact on her or her family ...
>
> If I see something that's showing something positive. I'd like to try and balance ... adoption issues with some more positive cultural ... I'm sure there will be some questions about that though. People will always ask: "How well-adjusted are these children?"

This second respondent also remarked about her children's perceptions about Romania, and her comments are representative of most respondents:

> I don't think they're particularly interested. It's sort of just accepted along the same lines that I think in terms of my parents or my husband's parents ... It's sort of a given. I don't think they really question it a lot, or frankly, think about it that much. They certainly know they're adopted. They'll tell you they're adopted and if Romania comes up in the news or something, they'll point it out ... In th[is] area, they know so many children from different countries, to them it's sort of normal that everyone is born in a different country. I guess because it's more commonplace that they haven't, and because we have tried to approach this very matter-of-fact, that they haven't had as many questions or uncertainties about it.

Thus, Romania is central to how the families were formed, and persists today to factor into how each family defines itself, albeit, in more subtle ways than when the adoptions first took place. The social crises in Romania at the time of the adoptions have a long-term impact on how parents anticipate explaining the circumstances of their children's adoptions. Despite the fact that the circumstances surrounding the adoptions are mostly irrelevant day to day, they explain how and why these families were formed. Thus, the adoption experience is at the core of their identity and is the basis of adoption as a social construct. To the extent that families expose themselves to Romanian culture, they are drawing the public sphere into their private lives. When the children are old enough to make independent choices about involvement in their culture of origin, they will be exerting their own ideas about the relationship between the private and public realms. Ultimately, they will have to come to terms with the unique historical events, political and economic turmoil, and the poor treatment of institutionalized children that put them on the path to adoption.

*Birth Mothers*
Perhaps no issues in adoption are more intensely personal than those that involve the birth family. While other birth family members are important, especially birth fathers and siblings, it is the birth mother that receives the most attention in the adoption literature and from the respondents in this study. Popular literature has us believe that international adoption has increased in part because of the potential for birth mothers in domestic adoptions to attempt to reclaim their biological children. Several highly publicized cases of legal conflicts in domestic adoptions have certainly made adoptive parents nervous, and brought widespread, and often negative public attention to adoption issues that are not understood well outside of

*The Intersection of Private and Public Experience* 207

the legal arena and the families themselves. This issue alone has added to the social stigma associated with adoption.

Among the respondents in this study, there is considerable positive sentiment toward birth mothers, indeed, a desire for connection. When asked about birth mothers and the potential for meeting them in the future, respondents on the whole were both sympathetic to birth mothers and supportive of searches, though with some qualifications. Long after the children have settled into their families, respondents still had strong views about the birth mothers. One respondent expressed interest in contact:

> My big thing is like I wish that we had a way to contact her ... We don't have that option with her and you know we think about her and the wonderful blessing she has given us, and we really can't give anything in return.

Another respondent echoed these thoughts:

> ... part of me feels guilty that I have this beautiful child and she doesn't ... If it were a positive thing for her to know that [she] was fine and to have some contact, then it would make me feel less guilty. It would make me feel better. Also, it would make me feel like ... that connection was re-established such that if [our daughter] wants contact, it would [happen]. I worry about losing the trail.

Some respondents discussed birth mothers in relation to helping their children understand the conditions under which the adoption took place:

> I want her to understand that her birth mother made an incredible, difficult and loving plan for her and that it wasn't that she wasn't wanted by her biological family, but it was just the best choice they thought they could make for her, and how blessed we feel.

Respondents were generally supportive of their children's potential desire to search for birth mothers and other family members when they got older. They understood the search to be important to both their children and the birth relatives, particularly the mother. Still, there is some anxiety associated with the search. As one respondent reflects:

> I think of her only in terms of hoping that her mind would be put to rest ... The only other thing I think about is my fear that if he searches for her and actually finds her and she [is] still ... alive, that she would say something to save face for her own part; to say something like, "they stole you from me," or something. And the only time I think of her is imagining a situation down the road that would completely disassemble [his] whole life ... finding your birth mother and hearing the words, "They stole you from me. They ran away from me. I did not want to do this." So occasionally that runs through my mind.

Despite these reservations, this respondent was the only one who reported that she had written a letter to the birth mother, and has made the point that she would support a search despite her reservations. Perhaps her fears are a reflection of the public awareness of the black market trade in adoption that took place in Romania, the publicity of which influenced the move to curtail international adoptions there in the summer of 1991. Overall, the findings show that from the decision to adopt internationally to thoughts about searching, respondents are influenced by the connection between this most personal and emotional experience with the public world of politics and other social forces.

## DISCUSSION

By examining the ongoing process of the social construction of these families, the research has revealed a dynamic relationship between private family experience and the public world. The approximately 6 years between the time the adoptions took place and the second set of interviews can be marked by three distinct stages. As families moved through each successive stage, adoption became an increasingly private experience, yet the public world beckoned and families continually assessed ways to address the intersection of the two arenas.

The Initiation stage included the decision to adopt from Romania as influenced by the sudden availability of children, their obvious and well-publicized need for care, and the role of race in forming the family in the first place. This stage was characterized by numerous public affirmations of the adoption from the highly structured legal steps in the process, to travel to Romania, bringing the children home, and introducing them to family and friends. Respondents were comfortable with publically revealing their new family status.

Soon after the adoptions, a second, Stabilization stage emerged in which families persisted in publically and legally defining themselves by arranging for citizenship and re-adoption in the U.S. It was characterized by openness about how the families were created, and at the same time, overall stabilization of day-to-day life. Through the toddler and pre-school years, simple ideas about adoption were introduced to the children, as was the culture of Romania. Activities internal and external to the families helped cement private family units and bring them into conformity with the state-defined status of legitimacy. This stage represents the greatest equilibrium between the public and private spheres, lasting until the start of formal schooling and the children's emerging maturity.

The Stabilization stage was followed by a third stage, Integration, developing at the time of the second interviews, and presumably continuing for several years. At this stage, routine family life took precedence, while public acknowledgment of adoption faded into the background. Adoption remained central to family identity, however, as exhibited by respondents' discussions about communication with people outside their families, the importance of race, the ongoing connection to Romania, and feelings about birth mothers. Respondents developed a heightened sense of public perceptions about adoption in general and Romania in particular, and tried to find ways to incorporate that understanding into family life. In this stage, awareness of social stigma grew at the same time children became more cognizant of the meaning of adoption and they took their first independent steps into the public world of school. Thus, this stage marks the period of greatest privatization of the adoptive status of the family at just the moment when the child enters her/his first major public role. As this stage plays out, one could speculate that it presents the greatest opportunity for tension where the two spheres intersect, yet the private sphere dominates in the incorporation of the meaning of adoption in each family.

Examining specific areas explored in this stage, communication about adoption, race, ties to Romania, and birth mothers, we can see the relevance of the dynamic between public and private spheres. Communication about adoption occurs at increasingly sophisticated levels as children get older, and family members must negotiate what and how to communicate with each other and outsiders. They believe they must prepare their children for the potential of stigma should their adoptive status be publically revealed. At the same time, they try to convey normalcy in their unique status. As the research shows, race figured prominently in the decision to adopt. The fact that parents were aware of the significance of race in keeping adoption private now plays an important supporting role in maintaining their privacy as an adoptive family, and provides a context in which to address cultural issues. The findings regarding communication and race are particularly useful in observing perceived societal opinions about adoption through the lens of an adoptive family. Sensitivity about public reaction to their status shapes the ways in which the families present themselves to friends, schools, and the general public.

Parents appear to continue to remind their children of their Romanian heritage, but not in significant public or private ways. It is put aside for the most part. In regards to birth families, for now, privacy has remained central to respondents' approach to both understanding and potentially reaching out to birth families, particularly mothers. This privacy, however, has generated feelings of guilt and concern for the well-being of birth mothers. Respondents appear comfortable with the idea of searching for birth mothers once the children are older, which would then open this most private realm to public discourse.

It remains to be seen how long the third stage, Integration, will last, and what will replace it. Undoubtably, families will continue to address adoption as their children move toward adolescence and adulthood. For their part, the children will begin to make their own decisions regarding the importance of adoption as they continue to construct their identities. They will decide with whom to share the information and whether to seek more information on Romania and their birth families as they move forward to adulthood.

Future research should engage the children directly in order to understand their experiences of adoption. Exploring what children choose to share, and with whom, would greatly enhance our understanding of how children navigate the public arena while addressing their personal concerns about adoption. In addition, learning about children's experiences internal to their families regarding their perceptions of how information sharing is handled, the importance of Romanian culture to their identity, and their feelings about birth mothers would add an important dimension to this research.

# CONCLUSION

This study addressed the relationship between the private and public experiences of adoption and showed how a sociological understanding of adoption must include an exploration of how these two arenas dynamically intersect over time. In reading the words of the respondents themselves, we saw the complexity of how adoptive families develop their identities over time. We observed how families navigated their own internal family experiences, deeply influenced by the specific public events that took place in Romania and by their perception of society's understanding of adoption. The families in the study moved through progressive stages in which adoption became incorporated into family identity, while becoming less overtly important publically. While the daily life of the families were seemingly unaffected by their early experiences in the adoption process, over time those experiences and the social and political context of Romania continued to influence the social construction of these families. This study contributes to our understanding how the family develops as it interacts with public institutions, and how deeply connected these public and private contexts are as families are socially constructed.

## ACKNOWLEDGMENTS

Many thanks to Suzanne Hoelgaard for a critical reading of an earlier version of this paper, and to Katherine Brown Rosier for her encouragement and suggestions. Much gratitude is owed to the respondents who shared their thoughts and their time so willingly.

## REFERENCES

Bartholet, E. (1997). Adoption and stigma. In: A.S. Skolnick & J.H. Skolnick (Eds), *Family in transition* (9th ed., pp. 242–255). New York:Addison-Wesley Educational Pubs, Inc.

Bascom, B. B., & McKelvey, C. A. (1997). *The complete guide to foreign adoption.* New York: Pocket Books.

Daly, K. (1988). Reshaped parenthood identity: The transition to adoptive parenthood. *Journal of Contemporary Ethnography, 17*(1), 40–66.

Defense for children international and International social service (DCI/ISS). (1991). *The adoption of Romanian children by foreigners.* Geneva, Switzerland.

Feigelman, W., & Silverman, A. (1983). *Chosen children: New patterns of adoptive relationships.* New York: Praeger.

Goldberg, R. (1997). Adopting Romanian children: Making choices, taking risks. In: H. E. Gross & M. B. Sussman (Eds), *Families and adoption* (pp. 79–98). New York: The Haworth Press.

Goldberg, R. (2001). The social construction of adoptive families: A follow-up study on adopting Romanian children. *International Review of Sociology, 11*(1), 89–101.

Groza, V., Ileana, D., & Irwin, I. (1999). *A peacock or a crow: Stories, interviews, and commentaries on Romanian adoptions.* Euclid, OH: Williams Custom Publishing.

Harsanyi, D. P. (1994). Romania's women. *Journal of Women's History, 5*(3), 30–54.

Haugaard, J. L. (1997). Research digest. *Adoption Quarterly: Innovations in Community and Clinical Practice, Theory and Research, 1*(1), 75–79.

Kligman, G. (1998). *The politics of duplicity: Controlling reproduction in Ceausescu's Romania.* Berkeley, CA: University of California Press.

Marcovitch, S., Cesaroni, L., Roberts, W., & Swanson, K. (1995). Romanian adoption: Parents' dreams, nightmares, and realities. *Child Welfare, LXXIV*(5), 993–1017.

Melina, L. R. (1989). *Making sense of adoption: A parent's guide.* New York: Harper & Row, Publishers.

Miall, C. E. (1996). The social construction of adoption: Clinical and community perspectives. *Family Relations, 45*, 309–317.

National Adoption Information Clearinghouse. (2000). *Intercountry adoption.* Retrieved June 5, 2000 from http://www.calib.com/naic/adptsear/adoption/research/stats/intercountry.htm.

National Council for Adoption, Inc. (1993). *National adoption reports.* Washington, DC.

Nicolaescu, M. (1994). Post-communist transitions: Romanian women's responses to changes in the system of power. *Journal of Women's History, 5*(3), 117–128.

Serrill, M. S. (1991). Going abroad to find a baby. *Time, 138*(15), 86–88.

Smith, S. L., & Howard, J. A. (1999). *Promoting successful adoptions: Practice with troubled families*. Thousand Oaks, CA: Sage.
Taylor, P. (1992). March 1. Unwed white mothers seen much less likely now to offer babies for adoption. *The Washington Post.* P. A11.
Tizard, B. (1991). Intercountry adoption: A review of the evidence. *Journal of Child Psychology and Psychiatry, 32*(5), 743–756.
United States Department of State. (2003). *Immigrant visas issued to orphans coming to the U.S.* Retrieved January 3, 2003, http://travel.state.gov/orphan_numbers.html.
Verhulst, F. C., Althaus, M., & Versluis-Den Bieman, H. J. M. (1992). Damaging backgrounds: Later adjustment of international adoptees. *Journal of the American Academy of Child and Adolescent Psychiatry, 31*(3), 518–524.
Watkins, M., & Fisher, S. (1993). *Talking with young children about adoption*. New Haven: Yale University Press.
Wilkinson, H. S. (1995). Psycholegal process and issues in international adoption. *The American Journal of Family Therapy, 23*(2), 173–183.

# PART II:
# INNOVATIONS IN THEORY AND RESEARCH METHODS

# CHILDREN'S AGENCY AND CINEMA'S NEW FAIRY TALE[*]

Ingrid E. Castro

## INTRODUCTION

The pretty girl with raven hair sings as she works and dreams of wonderful days ahead. The girl's dream is deferred by the wickedly jealous stepmother who sends a trusted guard to commit murder. The man, overwhelmed by the girl's inherent goodness is unable to complete his deed, and warns her to run away and never return. She travels deep into the woods and is helped by friendly forest creatures with big eyes. They take her to a small cottage and she falls asleep, to be awakened by several small men who find it in their hearts to allow her to remain. The miniature men leave for work the next day, warning the girl of the stepmother and her trickery. The nasty woman disguises herself and easily convinces the girl to take a bite of the religiously symbolic apple, after which the girl is induced into a coma. The small men return, chase after the horrible stepmother and cause her to fall to her death, after which they do not bury the beauty-girl, but instead leave her ensconced in a glass tomb for all to see. The gallant prince finally arrives and kisses her,

---

[*] Thank you to Dean Silvers and Rod Hall Agency for their assistance in the copyright clearance process necessary for this chapter's publication. I extend my warmest thanks and highest regards to Lisa Krueger-Chandler (writer and director of Manny & Lo, 1996) and Naomi Wallace (writer of Lawn Dogs, 1997) for their sincere consideration, kind and insightful comments, and final approval for the use of dialogue from their truly inspirational films.

true love breaking the apple's spell and allowing the girl to ride away on the horse with the true hero, leaving behind the woodland creatures and small men forever. Sunlight beaming, girl beaming, small men and creatures beaming. All is right with the world.

Snow White. Truly, most twentieth century cinematic interpretations of classic fairy tales are the same. Change the title, replace one prince charming with the other, one evil stepmother with another, some woodland creatures with underwater ones, an apple with a rose or a bed, change the innocent from a brunette to a blond to a redhead. In the end, the moral is the same. Kids can't make it alone. They shouldn't even try. When they do, their innocence clouds their judgment, their fears take over, their lives are suspended until they are rescued by someone who knows better. Most of these young people are girls, becoming indentured women once the right guy comes along.

The history of the fairy tale is one filled with evidence of the influence sociopolitical reality can have over an established art form. Initially, fairy tales were fables intended for adult consumption, only to be transformed into writings for children during the early to mid-nineteenth century. In order to satisfy pressure applied by middle-class and aristocratic adults, such fairy tale raconteurs as Anderson and the Brothers Grimm added Christian and patriarchal messages (morals) meant for children (Zipes, 1994, 1997). What resulted is the sanitized and westernized version of the fairy tale, which instills children with doubts about the world that surrounds them, purportedly addressing internal conflicts associated with growing older (Zipes, 1994; Shokeid, 1982; Cashdan, 1999). Zipes (1994) states that this change in the fairy tale has resulted in concealing reality from kids, giving them a false impression of their adolescent and adult futures.

Tales of the "classic heroine" like Snow White, Cinderella, and Sleeping Beauty have also suffered from the revisioning/reversioning of the fairy tale. These, as well as other female protagonists, have lost much of the voice and action initially allotted to them and/or their storylines, becoming the suitable and agreeable females we know today. Typically,

> ...female protagonists are said to be relegated to passive roles, relying on others to provide guidance, motivation, and solutions to their problems. In many of the fairy tales, they are discouraged from speaking their minds or acting on their own initiatives. Their representation is stereotypical; they are...ultimately depict[ed] as inferior to the civilized and rationalized representations of patriarchal roles and values (Jones, 1995, p. 65).

A wealth of information is currently available on the feminist critique of the fairy tale, which goes beyond the scope of the present discussion.

Suffice it to say that young females within fairy tales are rarely allowed to be anything other than the ingénue whose innate foolishness has become fundamental.

Children's images in film have not fared much better through cinematic history. Typically children on the screen have been depicted as either the innocent or the hellion (Jackson, 1986). There was, however, one decade where children were consistently represented as capable. "This was the precocious imp, the savvy, know-it-all child who is frequently more competent then the adult he or she encounters." (Jackson, 1986, p. 154). The decade was the early 1970s to early 1980s, and Jackson (1986) attributes this cinematic shift, in part, to the tides of the times and the changing family structure that accompanied it, swiftly assuring parents that latchkey kids could care for themselves. Once again we are shown that film, as in fairy tale, is meant to satisfy the needs of the adult population, assuaging their own concerns and consciences; spurring children's imagination or self-actualization by such images was merely a side effect.

A short discussion of the history of the fairy tale film is paramount to ultimately recognizing the power adults hold over the images for and of children. The first fairy tale feature presented in animation was *Snow White and the Seven Dwarfs*. In 1937, this feat of modernity made in color and including music was a Disney triumph (Zipes, 1997). What this film did, ultimately, was give Walt Disney the power to present his versions of fairy tales to millions of children and adults the world over, adaptations which managed to make the previously edited tales even more sterile and sticky sweet. Ever since, Disney as a corporation has continued the tradition of presenting young women as actionless, their power lying only in their long tresses, budding adolescent bodies, and lilting voices. Recently, Disney has reacted to criticism of said representations (like Aladdin's Jasmine and The Little Mermaid's Ariel) with what they deem to be the powerful and gender-forward heroines Pocahontas and Mulan. The result has been less than stellar, their naïve femininities merely hiding slightly under the surface instead of the overt examples of the past.

Some new fables are being told in independent, live action film, stories of girls who do not cower from fighting the malevolence surrounding them, girls who make their futures instead of allowing others to dictate them. Two such films are *Manny & Lo* (Krueger, 1996) and *Lawn Dogs* (Duigan, 1997). Primarily, these films allow children a great amount of agency in their lives. They are decision makers, risk takers, and rule defiers. From the onset of these films, the girls are in charge, both in storyline and in story presentation. Through the films we gain insight into some of the very real ways cinema can influence our thinking about children, their capabilities and their influences in our world.

## A SHORT SYNOPSIS OF BOTH FILMS

### *Manny & Lo*

This film is narrated by the younger of two sisters, Manny (Amanda), who is 11 years old. Manny and her older sister Lo (Laurel, age 15) are parentless, their alcoholic mother having previously died and their father never being mentioned. They are "on the run," both having left their foster home placements, traveling in a station wagon that has seen better days. They sleep where they can, whether it be lawn, woods, or model home, stealing gas and food along the way from unsuspecting travelers and shopkeepers alike.

From the onset of the film, it is implied that Lo is pregnant and ignoring the telltale signs of tight-fitting jeans and fatigue, eventually admitting to her situation after awaking to find Manny with a close ear to her stomach. Lo attempts to get an abortion but the clinician refuses because she is too far along. Manny and Lo find themselves appropriating a winter cabin to wait until "this thing hits." Lo advises that they go into town and find a book on babies, where they come across middle-aged Elaine, a woman dressed as a nurse working in a baby store, who seemingly knows everything there is to know about birthing and young ones.

The sisters decide to kidnap Elaine, holding a hunting rifle to her back and telling her to write a note explaining she is going on vacation. Initially Elaine is an unwilling captive, going on a hunger strike, refusing to speak and trying to gain the combination to her foot shackles through painstaking trial and error. However, one day the sisters find Elaine attempting to send smoke signals from the front yard, and in the process of bodies scurrying Elaine sees Lo's stomach and understands her purpose. Elaine begins to eat, cooking nutritious meals for herself and her captors, advising Lo to cease smoking for the health of herself and her unborn.

As the days pass, the three grow closer, enjoying such wholesome familial activities as living room camaraderie and singing songs around a campfire. Eventually, the owner of the cabin returns for a weekend of respite, and Manny secretly observes Elaine hitting Mr. Humphreys over the head and dragging him out to the barn. Elaine then pushes his car out of sight, and neither Manny nor Elaine informs Lo of the "close call." Lo decides that she is going to give her baby to Elaine, telling her the reason is

Children's Agency and Cinema's New Fairy Tale                    219

simply because Elaine is "the real thing." Promptly, there is a ruckus as Mr. Humphreys escapes and Lo, very angry, forces them all in the car, abandoning Elaine on a bridge and driving on with Manny.

Lo, not surprisingly, goes into labor the next day, and Manny is forced to drive them back to the bridge and find Elaine, who assists in the birth. The four set off together, in the hopes of finding somewhere to settle.

## Lawn Dogs

Ten-year-old Devon narrates this film; an only child, Devon and her parents have recently moved to an upper middle-class gated community ironically dubbed "Camelot Gardens." Devon's parents are obsessed with appearances, her father a member of almost every board in the area, in an attempt to "have a real say." Her mother stays at home, gardening and hostessing parties for neighbors. The first day of the opening sequences shows Devon dressed in her Young Ranger outfit, baking thumbprint cookies to sell to certain neighbors in the area. Her parents send her off with a methodologically constructed list of where to go, warning her to look both ways, stating, "Whatever you do, don't go outside the gates." Devon has other plans, however, and promptly leaves the neighborhood to walk along a country road with her red wagon full of cookies. She comes upon a mailbox and enters a clearing in the forest, where she finds a trailer. Here she is discovered by Trent, a 21-year-old who does lawn work in her neighborhood.

Over time, Devon and Trent become friends. Devon lies to her parents continually, telling them she is spending time with girls her own age on the safe neighborhood streets, all the while going to Trent's where she is free to say, think, and do what she wants. Trent, meanwhile, is having an affair with an older teen from the development, as well as being harassed by several pseudo-macho neighborhood teens, one of whom is, ironically, having an affair with Devon's mother. This teen, Brett, attempts to molest Devon during a barbecue at her parent's home, after which Devon informs her parents of the misdeed. Her parents are incredulous, asking why she let him do so. Devon promptly changes her story, and tells her parents he was just tickling her.

Devon's mother observes Devon and Trent in their yard, how they interact, sees Trent giving Devon a turtle he had rescued along his mower's path. Devon's mother becomes suspicious, informing the community's security guard of the gift. The security guard tells Trent it is best if he keeps to himself while working. Trent does not heed the advice, instead bringing Devon to his childhood home, where he is visibly upset by his parent's health and poverty, as well as the fact that earlier that day the neighborhood teens had dumped sugar in his mower's gas tank, swiftly taking away his means of living. On the way home to Devon's development, the two share a very special moment where Devon, stating that Trent is her best friend, shows him her scar from open heart surgery. In return, Trent shows Devon his scars from being shot in his youth. Afterward the two see a neighborhood bully's dog, and Devon proposes they catch him. Trent has other ideas, however, and runs over the dog with his truck, eventually beating it to death with a two-by-four while Devon watches.

Devon runs to her parents, shaken by the malicious deed Trent has committed. Her parents probe her and ask over and over if Trent "touched" her, which she admits to. That is all they need to go on a witch-hunt, with the security guard, the dog owner, Devon's father, and Devon driving around to find Trent. Eventually, despite Devon's attempt to divert the small mob, they arrive at Trent's trailer, where Devon's father and the dog owner beat Trent within inches of his life. Devon takes her father's gun out of the glove compartment and shoots the dog owner, telling Trent to run far away, forcing her father to relinquish his wallet and contents for an easier escape.

Trent drives away and Devon's father is left a broken man, crying at the mercy of his armed daughter who has climbed a tree.

## ONCE UPON A TIME...

Fairy tale elements are unmistakable in both *Manny & Lo* and *Lawn Dogs*. In both we have a sense of dissatisfaction in life, the main characters simultaneously running away from something and running toward something else. There are evil parents and dead parents, both of which are prerequisites in fairy tale lore. Additionally, we have children, an obvious requirement. A close read of the opening scenes of both films will assist in establishing the fairy tale tone of the films as well as provide a basis of striking similarity between the two films.

*Manny & Lo* begins with unclear pictures of green foliage, hands in water, and a person with red hair wearing white clothing and sensible shoes. Ethereal music is playing in the background, and the voiceover comes in the form of narration by Manny, who asks: "Did you ever dream about someone, before you saw them in life? Sort of like you made them up but you didn't. They really happen, things like that. I swear they happen all the time."[1] Within the next few cinematic shots we see Manny, waking from sleep, looking at the blue sky. We are introduced to Lo soon after, who complains that she thought they were in a park (in actuality, they spent the night camping on a well-trimmed lawn). This lawn belongs to a typical upper – middle-class family, the patriarch screaming at them to move along while Manny and Lo take turns urinating on his property. They get in the station wagon, and Lo drives away facetiously apologizing, running over a child's toy in the process.

*Lawn Dogs* opens with an unclear picture of a girl in a white dress playing in a meadow surrounded by the blue sky. The audio comes in the form of narration by Devon, who states "Once upon a time, in a far off land, lived a girl with her mother and father. Their village was surrounded by a high wall. Outside the wall was a forest. Home to Baba Yaga[2]... inside the wall, the girl was safe." The picture changes suddenly to well-manicured lawns, each looking just as nice as the next. We see cookie-men lined up on a baking sheet, and then Trent, mowing a lawn. A neighborhood youngster dressed as a cowboy holds a toy gun to Trent's head. Flash to Devon, who is placing raisins on the cookies as bellybuttons. A fly lands on a cookie, and she squishes it in its proper place. Finally we see Trent, continuing with his mowing, who runs over the boy's cowboy hat in the process.

The parallels between the opening scenes are striking. We have two young girls, both dreaming: Manny literally and Devon figuratively. The narration is very similar, speaking of their lives as mythical stories, conducted by the youngest main characters of both films. *Lawn Dogs* takes the fairy tale beginning quite seriously, utilizing the classic "Once upon a time..." while *Manny & Lo* modernizes the beginning, making it more personal, and directing it toward the viewer.

The first clear pictures we get of anyone are of the respective narrators, both small blond girls. Each film also includes very direct and stark contrasts of stratification: *Manny & Lo* shows us poverty and wealth through the differences between the girls and the family who owns the lawn, while *Lawn Dogs* provides the same distinction through the differences between Trent and the families whose lawns he mows.

Finally, both sequences conclude with equally significant images. Manny and Lo urinating on the well-manicured lawn, Devon smashing a live fly into the cookies she is to circulate in the neighborhood. The introductions culminate in Lo running over the child's toy with her car, and Trent running over the child's toy with his lawnmower. The acts are swift and yet extremely symbolic, where the perceived definition of "perfection" for the child in the nuclear family is destroyed. Also, the various acts of defiance and demolition allow the viewer an understanding of the control all four of the characters have ... even though they are the "underdogs" they are not powerless in their actions ... they have committed small yet meaningful rebellious acts of will.

Both of these films begin with scenes that are placed out-of-doors, which is clearly purposeful. Children are consistently linked with the outer world. The realm of trees and bugs and the sky is always connected more to childhood than adulthood. This is the space where children can run free, the world where kids can be kids. In recent decades, with greater adult fear of the unknown and increasing child-oriented technology, the outside world has become a mystery for children, no longer emulating freedom but constraint. In fact, Devon states in *Lawn Dogs* that she does not like kids her age because they "smell like TV." These are the types of images we get of Manny & Lo, Devon & Trent; children and young adults who are seemingly trapped in their present lives, but who are in actuality not powerless to change the lifestyles they have been handed.

Researchers and laypeople have traditionally viewed children as non-actors. As such, established models of socialization and development define children as passive (Corsaro, 1997; Thorne, 1987; Lee, 1998; James, 1998). One does not have to reach too far back in history to evoke the language used in such paradigms: terms such as "tabula rasa" imply that children are merely vessels to be filled up through the process of teaching and learning, unable to act until such time as they have adequately matured. Such discourse has led to limiting ideological statements that children are "partially cultural" (therefore implying cultural deficiency), lacking in knowledge and insight, immature and incapacitated, all of which places them in the lowest and most marginal societal positions, beneath adults and adolescents (Wulff, 1995; Corsaro, 1997; Macklin, 1992). One possible reason for the characterization of children as submissive is the attempt to "keep them in check" children have been feared as threats to adult society and social order (Thorne, 1987; James, Jenks, & Prout, 1998; Corsaro, 1997). Certainly, more often than not, the "willful" child is believed to be the one who needs structure, guidance, limits, and more recently, rehabilitation and drug therapy.

The writers and directors of *Manny & Lo* and *Lawn Dogs* remarkably do not fall into the largely prejudicial trap of characterizing children as actionless. Just the opposite occurs: motivating the entire storyline in both films is the primary tenet that youth are actors in their own right. They make decisions, they accept the consequences of their choices, and they hold very strong opinions, all of which reflect the belief that children are capable and often very sophisticated beings.

## THE ROYAL COURT

In many classic fairy tales, the structure of the family is slightly off balance from the norm, where the damsel in distress is somehow being punished because her biological mother died in childbirth, her biological father died sometime later, and consequently her stepmother is a horrid human being who cannot find it in her heart to love her newly acquired children. The past century's interpretation of fairy tales amounts to an attack on anything other than a nuclear family: children who are parentless or without a biological tie to their birthing origins are doomed to endure shaken foundations and resulting tragedies.

The two films discussed here do not present biological families as the end all and be all of normalcy. Rather, *Manny & Lo* and *Lawn Dogs* present the nuclear/biological family as troubled and the alternative family as not only acceptable, but also potentially optimal. Manny and Lo are two girls who are making it "OK" on their own. There is no greatness here, merely survival. Elaine entering their lives is an unexpected positive change. Throughout the film, Manny is consistently bringing up their mother to Lo, wanting to talk about her, performing acts to remind herself of their mother, such as spraying "mom's" brand of deodorant on bed sheets. Lo's reactions to all of Manny's attempts are resoundingly negative, stating over and over that their mother was a drunkard who did not take care of them when she was alive.

Elaine, however, is someone who appears to be extremely maternal in nature, someone both of the girls can admire and respect, just as Lo states in her comment about Elaine being the "real thing." This is in direct contrast to Lo's opinions of their own mother, narrated by Manny:

> Lo used to say there were people who were born the family type and people who weren't and there was no use feeling bad about it if you weren't. She said that since our mother was never the mother type, that just meant me and her were the naturally independent type.

A later exchange between Manny and Elaine is also pertinent to the present discussion:

M: You don't have a family, do you, Elaine?
E: [Long pause] Some people have a gift, Amanda, but they're not able to use that gift at the usual time. Sometimes they're forced to wait until their body is no longer able to package that gift. Do you understand?
M: [Looks confused] No, not really.

E:  Well, when I was younger, when my physical side was ready to produce, it happened that my emotional side, how do you say it? Um [teary eyed], it was cluttered.
M:  Cluttered?
E:  I'm afraid I was not terribly unified as a younger person. But, um, I'm much, much better now.
M:  That's good.
E:  And there's all sorts of ways to give a gift. Not just one way. And not just the obvious way. Does that make sense?
M:  Yeah, it sort of does.
[E rises and M looks at her through her magnifying glass, where E closely resembles the woman in her blurry dream from the beginning scenes of the film].

This conversation is very important to the film's driving focus on the ebb and flow of familial capability. Just because someone appears to be "motherly" (as reflected in such acts as Elaine calling Manny and Lo by their full names, Amanda and Laurel) does not mean that she is in fact a mother. Additionally, the theme of alternative ways of giving and receiving are of primary concern, sending the message to viewers that different is not always negative in connotation. The group that drives away in the station wagon is not a typical family unit. There are two sisters, a newly born son, and an unrelated older woman who is now in their family, although not necessarily the mother or sole caretaker to all.

*Lawn Dogs* presents us with Devon, who exists in a not-so-perfect nuclear family. She is an only child, and therefore representative of the smaller familial unit that makes up the modernly wealthy. Her family is not ideal by any means, however. Her father is concerned with his appearance to the community at large, her mother with the next adulterous tryst she can sneak with the boy next door. Devon is subjected to all of the aches and pains associated with parents telling their children exactly what to do with their days; her summer supposedly being filled with selling cookies to all of the neighbors who are deemed worthy by her parents.

Throughout the film Devon's father makes statements to her about how she does not have to tell anyone about her past (including her operation). He tells her she must make new friends and become very popular, because popular people are "never boring." He states that she is to change herself into a "New Devon," the person she (read he) wants. The requisite "I Love You, Sweetheart," a meaningless afterthought, follows all of his not-so-subtle critiques of his daughter. In addition to the direct remarks, Devon, as the oft forgotten child, overhears numerous conversations pertaining to her that take place between her parents. Ultimately, Devon's father believes that Devon is not adequately fulfilling her role as a good child, as reflected in the following statement made to his wife: "She could at least pretend to be happy. When I was a kid, that's what you did for your parents."

Devon protests, committing small acts of dissent against her mother and father, including giving her cookies away, mooning her father from a distance, urinating on her father's car, and taking off her bedclothes while standing on the eave of her house, howling at the moon. Devon's largest, most obvious protest is the meaningful friendship she forms with Trent, the poor semi-servant yokel who everyone says is "trash." Devon's true family is Trent, the boy she steals chickens with, dances on top of cars with, laughs with, and shares her literal and figurative wounds with. The scene where Devon makes the decision to show Trent her heart surgery scar is pivotal since this is her most private secret. She bares her severed chest to Trent, an act that is extremely important considering that children's bodies are both "products of and resources for agency, action and interaction" (Prout, 2000). This is her body and she will do with it what she pleases, and in effect she utilizes it through action, for interaction, and because of an agentic choice.

Devon's last acts are her most startling, shooting a neighbor and robbing her father at gunpoint, which display her dissatisfaction with everyone who has ever told her who to be and how to be and what to be as a "child" in a world demarcated by two groups: the haves and have nots. Devon is an example of why upper-class nuclear life is often times less than perfect. The gates do not keep the bad seeds out; instead, the people sheltered inside such communities create their own tangled vines of negativity. In the end, Devon is left alone in a tree telling the story of "Once up on a time…" however the story is now of her relationship with Trent, and how they found and helped one another on their journeys to another reality.

The stories of Manny and Devon include stark examples of agentic actions youth can take when given, or not given, the opportunity to do so. What exactly is agency? There are different forms of agency, which can be defined in a variety of ways according to agency's relationship to desire, identity, environment, habitat, and culture (Thorne, 1987; Tsushima & Burke, 1999; Wulff, 1995). Agency is closely related to one's sense of self; it is a "property of persons" culturally and temporally located (McCarthy & Crichlow, 1993; Nucci, Killen, & Smetana, 1996; Nucci, 1997; Lee, 1998). As a whole, agency concerns action initiated by choice (James, et al, 1998). Agency relates to children's ability to operate independently from adults, whereby kids are often required to consciously alternate between different agentic styles in order to be effective social actors (Nucci et al., 1996; James & Prout, 1995). Agency, when considering "the child," requires a consideration of power, status, and context (Turiel, 1997). For children, the simple fact of their young age dictates specific types of restrictions be placed upon their time, access, and control, and yet kids learn to navigate the small controlled spaces to which they are relegated, persistently exercising agency (James et al., 1998; Gordon et al., 1999). Agency in motion is probably the most obvious in children, as opposed to other segments of the population, since kids are so regularly and categorically marginalized and infantilized.

Both *Manny & Lo* and *Lawn Dogs* take idealized notions of the family and twist them into alternative visions, ones which center on friendship rather than blood, and in so doing, the twentieth century fairy tale is turned on its head. No longer does the girl need the prince to find everlasting happiness, or salvation for that matter. All a child really needs is someone to truly take notice and participate in conversations about the small and large worlds they come across in their everyday lives. When this is not provided, the child will take the necessary course of action to fill the void, utilizing agency in its truest form to protect his or her own interests, mental health, and well-being.

## SEARCHING FOR THE ORACLE

Typically, current representations of fairy tales do not allow for the youth to become adults in pages or on screen. Someone older and wiser rescues the troubled from their destitute existences, whisking them off to once again be taken care of by someone with more power, more money, and more common sense. One assumption our society continues to make is that the adult "knows best." The situation is quite different in *Manny & Lo* and *Lawn Dogs*; here, the youngest of the characters is the wisest, holding the clearest understanding of the situation and perception of truth. The stories these films tell project Manny and Devon as more often than not the most insightful of all characters. Both are girls with definite opinions on the people in their lives, the worlds they occupy, and the errant ideologies they are subjected to by important relational others.

In all of her relationships, Manny is the girl who is most adept in navigating individual personality traits. She is able to recognize that Lo can "keep from noticing something longer than anybody" and as such, she does not push the issue of her sister's pregnancy, nor question the fact that Lo needs to believe Elaine would escape at any moment, given the opportunity. In her relationship with her sister, Manny suggests things subtly, while Lo is completely opposite, a brash young woman who orders Manny around. Manny is continually cleaning up after Lo's messes and mistakes, keeping secrets that need to be kept and voicing what needs to be said when necessary.

The value of Elaine is initially recognized by Manny in the film. Lo may be the one who orchestrates the kidnapping, but it is in fact Manny who initially draws Lo's attention to the woman in the baby store. In her relationship with Elaine, Manny offers small tokens of apology for the kidnapping, such as music for Elaine's room, food for her to eat, waving flashlights in the dark to entertain her, and a small lizard she hypnotizes while playing in the woods. When the sisters abandon Elaine at the bridge toward the end of the film, it is Manny who gathers a blanket, food, music, and other items to sustain Elaine. Finally, when Elaine tells Manny she would like her to write a 500 or more word essay on "certain lessons" learned about "taking hostages," and that she fully intends to write one herself (in reference to taking Mr. Humphreys captive), Manny responds: "Well, if it would make you feel better, Elaine." All of these examples display Manny's understanding of what she should do in certain situations to care for the feelings and comfort of those around her.

Devon also holds insightful knowledge about certain truths in her world that others around her do not have the ability to recognize. Throughout the film, Devon is the one who is most critical of the stratification that divides herself and Trent. Instead of avoiding such topics, Devon confronts them, asking questions and having lengthy discussions with Trent on such issues driven by money and position. Devon's disapproval of the schism between poor and rich, and of her father's classist ideals, is evident in the following exchange:

D: People say you're trash.
T: Yeah, I guess they do.
D: I wouldn't like that.
T: You get used to it.
 [Trent intently oiling his chainsaw]
D: My father says if everyone worked hard, there wouldn't be any poor people. You're a poor person, aren't you? He says that anyone who works hard can be rich just like them.
T: Sounds like you got a smart daddy.

D:         [Shrugging in protest]. Trash is something you put a lid on 'cause it stinks. You don't smell that bad.
T:         [Laughing] That makes my day. [Pause, head down] The way I see it, you got people who own lawns and people who mow 'em, and they're never the same people.

A few scenes later:

T:         We can be friends if you can keep it a secret.
D:         What's wrong with you and me being friends?
T:         Well, for one thing, I'm a country bumpkin... I'm piss poor...
D:         Do you want me to feel sorry for you?
T:         Oh, I don't know.
D:         Well, you can forget it.

A prerequisite for a modern representation of the fairy tale dictates that the fable must address social issues including class differences and power so that the tale will be appealing to adults, while at the same time "must reinforce a notion of power within the children of the upper classes and suggest ways for them to maintain power" (Zipes, 1994, p. 33). What is interesting about the narrative of *Lawn Dogs* and Devon in particular is that socioeconomic status, wealth, and power differentials are not held as a ubiquitous standard, instead such classifications are addressed and critiqued. Therefore, the required inclusion of power and class within fairy tale structure remains intact, although the route through which *Lawn Dogs* discusses such issues allows the story to become something altogether less compliant. Devon, at the age of 10, is able to explain to her much older best friend what friendship really is, finding commonality through shared experience, and sometimes finding commonality through distinct difference.

There are a few places in the film where Devon witnesses inequality between groups. Two such scenes of contrast are Devon's mother's reaction to Trent and Devon's visit to Trent's family's home. In the first comparative scene, Devon asks her mother if she can take a drink to Trent who is mowing their lawn, and her mother takes the "good" glass out of her hands and gives her a plastic cup from underneath the sink to use instead. Later, when Devon is at Trent's family home she is told by Trent's mother to get the "good" glasses, plastic novelty cups similar to the one her mother gave Trent. The saying "One man's trash is another man's treasure" is applicable here, where the two families are living in extremely different socioeconomic worlds, reflected by something as simple as what type of vessel contains a drink. Gaskins, Miller, & Corsaro (1992) discuss children learning culture, where a set of practices, beliefs, and interpretive frameworks are imbued to become a "member of a culture," membership which is limiting and enabling to children (p. 6). Similarly, Nucci et al. (1996) have found that interactions between class and culture can potentially both constrain and broaden autonomy in children. In the film, Devon has visual reactions within these two scenes, slight pauses and disapproving/questioning looks displayed on her face. Therefore, Devon's critical interpretation of her family's and Trent's family's cultures (and inequalities), and, following, her social position compared with Trent's, can only happen once she has become a member of her own status, a position which is limiting while at the same time enabling.

Throughout the film, Devon is more adult than those physically larger than her. She recognizes when to talk and when to stay quiet with her parents, she consistently picks her battles in life, and she knows that her parents are using her for their own gain. In fact, Devon narrates her life in the following way:

> At the edge of a big dark forest lived a girl and her mother and father. One day, her mother said "I shall make you a batch of cookies and you must go and sell them in the forest." Now, the girl was not stupid. She knew they were trying to get rid of her but her father said "Don't argue," so she went. The girl walked on 'til she came to a clearing in the forest.

In the end Devon is the strong one, the person not physically or emotionally broken from the altercation between her father, the dog owner, the guard, and Trent. "Home is in my hands" are her parting words to Trent. She knows she is the touchstone for Trent in this crazy world where people are valued for what they have instead of who they are.

The interrelated concepts of language and voice are a key route through which the agency of children is enacted. Through their growing ability for verbal expression children create conversations necessary for them to establish action. Children are born into webs of power and kids have the ability to access their own power through discourse (Gittens, 1998; Caputo, 1995). Reflective of this fact, both Manny and Devon express their ideas, concerns, and insights verbally to other characters in the films as well as the viewer in order to establish their roles as meaningful actors.

Typically, the lines drawn between adults and children are centrally defined by age. Manny and Devon enable us to understand that sophistication is not always related to developmental age; instead, insight and authority can come from life lived and experiences had at any given moment in time. In both of these stories the teller holds the power and, to paraphrase Devon, it is in their hands, nowhere else.

## OVER THE RIVER AND THROUGH THE WOODS

As mentioned previously, the outside world of the growing earth exemplifies the wonder of youth. We think of the lucky child as she/he who may discover a nest aloft filled with eggs or who spends a dusky night catching fireflies in a jar. In fact, a toddler I know has recently begun to talk, and one of her first attempted words was "flower." She is evidence that nature continues to capture the imagination of children, and it offers them an inspiration of possibility perhaps matched only by the adventure and amazement found in books.

Enter the fairy tale. When we are children and hear that certain story for the first, or perhaps thousandth, time the girl's initial step into the woods fills us with trepidation and expectation. The forest is the turning point, the gateway to the place where all action is unpredictable. The enchanted forest symbolizes the unknown, containing unimaginable dangers while simultaneously offering protection (Cashdan, 1999). Therefore, children find simple pleasures and new excitement through a link between the welcome cover of trees and trepidation of darkness. This duality is reflected in the construction of the fairy tale itself, which separates us from the world of our familiar and introduces us to something/somewhere else, suggesting a feeling that is both "frightening and comforting" (Zipes, 1983). In his classic treatise on fairy tales, *The Uses of Enchantment*, Bettelheim (1976) states that "The forest...symbolizes the place in which inner darkness is confronted and worked through; where uncertainty is resolved about who one is, and where one begins to understand who one wants to be" (p. 93). Just as, for better or worse, Snow White enters the forest and ultimately emerges an older, if not wiser, young woman, Devon and Manny do so as well, a move that allows them to develop inwardly and interpersonally.

Much of the storyline of both *Manny & Lo* and *Lawn Dogs* takes place in the woods. The sisters find the cabin in the woods; Devon finds the trailer in the woods. Both places are an escape from these girls' everyday realities, allowing them to consider what to do next. In both films, the woods offer protection from the outer world that has, until this point, shown them nothing but ill-attention. The woods additionally give the girls respite and solace; there is a visible relaxation in the characters' demeanors when they are in these places as compared to others more suburban in construction.

While in the forest, Manny is able to discover happiness and relational well-being. She finds herself to be a magician with hypnotic powers, enabling her to give the amphibian gift to Elaine. This is also the place where she is the fortuneteller, realizing that Elaine is the woman in her dream from the onset of the film. Most importantly, this is the place she finds herself to be an ordinary girl. One day Manny is exploring the area and comes upon a boy playing alone. She spies on him for a while, cautious to approach. They eventually meet and interact a few times through the film. Manny is by all accounts a loner before Elaine and Chuck; she is often left to occupy herself through her own devices, and it is the forest that brings other people into her life besides her sister Lo.

Throughout the film Manny has a particular obsession with collecting photos. Everywhere she goes she swipes pictures of people she does not know like the prerequisite false family photo that comes with the frame on display in the model home and a shot of the family who owns the cabin in the woods. She obviously craves proof of the happy times and smiling faces that accompany illusively perfect families. The woods set the stage for the acquisition of photos not of the unknown, but of her new friend and family member. Elaine allows Manny to have a photo taken while she worked at her father's convalescent home; Chuck offers her a school photo. For the first time she has obtained the shots because they were given to her, not because she stole them. Ultimately, the forest allows Manny to discover that she is a great deal more than just Lo's sister, she is a person who is interesting and worth knowing on her own accord.

Devon also is able to discover herself in the wood. As previously stated, Trent's trailer and surrounding topography provide her solace from Camelot Gardens and all that lies within. When Devon initially discovers Trent's trailer, she removes one of her white and red Young Ranger socks and hangs it on the mailbox, identifying this place as important and worth revisiting. This marker also serves for what Corsaro (1985) labels "protection of interactive space" (p. 122); the sock a type of foreshadowing for the significance of the space where Devon and Trent will ultimately have some of their most important and socially meaningful interactions. Finally, the sock represents a typical fairy tale component, where the character will leave something personal along the path to insure the way will not be lost. Certainly more permanent than a breadcrumb, this flag will remain for her to recognize in the future.

The tree Devon climbs at the end of the film is also extremely symbolic of her growth in relation with the forest. The tree standing outside of Trent's trailer is an ominously protective giant that Devon and Trent decorate with red ribbons. Devon has obvious affinity with this tree, the very same she climbs after shooting her neighbor, robbing her father, and assisting Trent to escape into the world beyond. The act of climbing the tree enables her to be physically taller than all of the adults who are in various states of disarray below her, representing her ability to remove herself, once again, from all of those people who dictate the world to her instead of allowing her to experience it for herself. Many people talk of the world to Devon, saying things like "The world is at your feet" and "There's a girl who's out to conquer the world."[3] Only because of her journey into the woods does Devon find her place in this world; the forest gives her Trent, and the tree that lies within its borders provides her the height to rise above the rest.

*Manny & Lo* and *Lawn Dogs* utilize the forest as a protective structure. In both films, the newly formed kin networks between Manny, Lo, and Elaine, and Devon and Trent are permitted to flourish within the wild. These relationships are allowed to form and burgeon because of their location in an outer rim of society. No longer in the center (suburbia), Manny and Devon are welcomed by the outdoors, that place where children may once again realize that, after all, the world is large and at times still filled with possibility.

## AND THEY LIVED HAPPILY EVER AFTER...

The conclusions of both films do have some elements of a modern fairy tale. A feeling of relief is felt: Manny and Lo found Elaine, and vice versa; Devon and Trent found each other and, more importantly, Devon has found herself. However, there is no white horse, no knight providing safety, no riches or large palace waiting. Ultimately, the sun is shining and the dreams have been realized, and that is enough.

But is it really enough? While looking at the covers of both videotapes for the exact year of release, I discovered the ratings of both films. In big bold lettering "R" stared back at me. Was it the language? The guns? The nudity and the sex? Certainly. However, earlier I mentioned that theorists such as Thorne (1987) and Corsaro (1997) have stated that adults fear the power children could gain, infantilizing them to sustain social hierarchy. A partial alternate explanation for these ratings is the fact that adults are handing out the letters. All fairy tales must pass the censorship of adults to insure mass circulation (Zipes, 1994). I suspect that the overarching theme of children displaying agency, utilizing their power and refusing to commit "crimes of obedience" (Laupa, Turiel & Cowan, 1995) was, and still is, threatening to adults. Although various populations could benefit from the tales told through Manny and Devon, it is youth who could actually gain an amount of self-actualization from these characters, and it is these very same people who are not permitted to view these on-screen visions.

Adults do not exactly prefer to see visions of children as agentic or knowledgeable on screen or in life. In fact, Cross (2004) has recently argued that American adults in particular have a "love affair" with images of children's "wondrous innocence". He goes on to explain that

> The look and appeal of wondrous innocence survive along with its paired opposite, sheltered innocence. And given the way that modern parents imagine the child and use these images for their own purposes, it may be inevitable that disappointment and frustration with the results will continue (p. 202).

Therefore, expecting children to be inherently innocent or treating children as such in life or on screen or on page within modern tales and modern times is ultimately going to lead to disappointment because of unrealistic expectations. The alternate representations of Devon and Manny are by some measure more satisfying to adult viewers than say, for example, Sleeping Beauty or Snow White. As proof, these two films as well as a few others that portray child and adolescent agency are always the most popular in my Sociology of Film course because the fairy tale elements do not overshadow the central theme of kids who make decisions, take action, and come in contact with real life and accompanying real problems.

Fairy tales are not written in stone, that much is for certain. What we assume are the classics of the Brothers Grimm, Hans Christian Anderson, and Mother Goose have been adapted from oral legend in existence years before these interpreters ever picked up a pen. Fairy tales are not ageless or universal: they continue to be modernized; their cultural features being replaced and societal influence being reflected in page and on screen (Zipes, 1983; Rohrich, 1986). Take, for example, *Manny & Lo* and *Lawn Dogs*. There are very strong reinterpretations of two classic fairy tales in these films. *Manny & Lo* is in many ways a modern version of *Goldilocks and the Three Bears*. Two blonds leave home ultimately to find a cabin in the woods where they can rest, sleeping in another family's beds, eating another family's food, and are unfortunately discovered by the owner of the cabin. Lawn Dogs is strewn with similarities between Devon and *Little Red Riding Hood*. A young girl ventures away from home with food to come upon a house in the woods occupied by a stranger. Also, the color red is continually affiliated with Devon throughout the film: her wagon full of cookies, her Young Ranger socks and beret, the ribbons tied on the tree, a towel and a comb she gives to Trent at the end of the film.

From these two films we see there is room for new versions of fairy tales that take into account the various ways children are not just victims to social problems in their everyday lives, but actually interpret and navigate such realities as well. Children are able to recognize and be critical of power differentials, be sensible and realistic in their behavior, and have a very strong sense of order and disorder in society (Cullingford, 1992). The stories of Manny and Devon demonstrate that kids may have power from the onset, and in their case this power allows them to find the missing kin link through agency and autonomous decision-making. There is such a thing as the "liberating fairy tale," one that reflects "a process of struggle against all types of suppression and authoritarianism" (Zipes, 1983). There have always been writers who present alternative visions that permit us to question the world placed upon us, and in their stories the reality dictated by adults may just be an illusion, and the "subversive power of their art" continues to thrive (Zipes, 1983, 1997). Ultimately, the point of the fairy tale is to enable us to believe in "human triumph against an impossible world" (Shokeid, 1982), to give us a different pair of eyes, ones that can see through the cloud that often surrounds us, regardless of age.

Manny and Devon are both very good representative indications of what Corsaro (1997) has deemed interpretive reproduction. Their "creative appropriation of information and knowledge from the adult world" is apparent throughout both films (Corsaro, 1997, p. 41; Johnson, 2001, p. 80). Ideas about inequality in reference to socioeconomics, work, family, friendship, and age are woven somewhat discretely within the storylines that are couched in a basic tenet of a fairly loose definition of kinship. The unique situation of these two girls being relatively autonomous allows the characters to display enormous amounts of agency. This is somewhat in contrast to a more realistic reality that children are constrained in society and subordinated by general social structure (Johnson, 2001). Manny, a runaway orphan whose only social contact is a slightly older irresponsible sister, realizes long before Lo that "no one" is looking for them (or looking over them), therefore giving her almost free rein of her social space. Devon's family is constraining in what views they wish their daughter to adopt and in what ways they wish their daughter to appear to others: they are all content, no quality. In every other way Devon is free of her parents since they do not take the time to investigate the truths of Devon's day-to-day activities, let alone actually see her: Devon's parents merely hold the image they have created of her. Therefore, Devon is also relatively free to navigate her social space since her parents choose to see what they want to see, and that actually is not much. Manny and Devon are new versions of childhood, one where children can be active in their creation of family, friends, ideologies, and selves.

The fact that *Manny & Lo* and *Lawn Dogs* are rooted in fairy tale structure makes sense. For most adults, agency in children continues to be a myth, something hard to prove and equally hard to swallow. Fairy tales are the place where dreams of a future are possible, and the stories of Manny and Devon are the archetype from where possibility grows.

## NOTES

1. *Strange Things Sometimes Still Happen*, the title of Carter's (1993) book on fairy tales, is strikingly similar to Manny's opening speech.
2. Throughout the film's narration, Devon often speaks of Baba Yaga, a witch present in Slavic/Russian folklore. Baba Yaga has a bone leg and eats human beings (especially children) as if they were chickens. This sorcerer often assists a male hero with a goal, giving him items to show him the way. Baba Yaga is always ambivalent, both a helper and opponent of the protagonist who lives in the wood (Tatar, 1992; Cashdan, 1999; Zipes, 2000). See "The Enchanted Forest" section for more on the duality of the wood.
3. An added significance to Devon's relationship with the tree is a parallel to Buryat Mongols, whose lands lie on the border of Russia (similar to the Baba Yaga folklore origins). The Buryat tie ribbons around large or unusual trees that are believed to house spirits. A decorated tree symbolizes the center of the world, where "heaven and earth touch, where all times and places converge." http://www.buryatmongol.com/modon.html.

## REFERENCES

Bettelheim, B. (1976). *The uses of enchantment: The meaning and importance of fairy tales*. New York: Alfred A. Knopf.
Caputo, V. (1995). Anthropology's silent 'Others': A consideration of some conceptual and methodological issues for the study of youth and children's cultures. In: V. Amit-Talai & H. Wulff (Eds), *Youth cultures: A cross-cultural perspective* (pp. 19–42). London: Routledge.
Carter, A. (Ed.) (1993). *Strange things sometimes still happen: Fairy tales from around the world*. Boston: Faber and Faber.
Cashdan, S. (1999). *The witch must die: How fairy tales shape our lives*. New York: Basic Books.
Corsaro, W. A. (1985). *Friendship and peer culture in the early years*. Norwood: Ablex.
Corsaro, W. A. (1997). *The sociology of childhood*. Thousand Oaks: Pine Forge Press.
Cross, G. S. (2004). *The cute and the cool: Wondrous innocence and modern American children's culture*. Oxford: Oxford University Press.
Cullingford, C. (1992). *Children and society: Children's attitudes to politics and power*. London: Cassell.
Duigan, J. (Dir.), (1997). *Lawn Dogs* (Mischa Barton & Sam Rockwell). Strand Releasing.

Gaskins, S., Miller, P. J., & Corsaro, W. A. (1992). Theoretical and methodological perspectives in the interpretive study of children. In: W. A. Corsaro & P. J. Miller (Eds), *Interpretive approaches to children's socialization* (pp. 5–24). Jossey-Bass: San Francisco.

Gittens, D. (1998). *The child in question.* New York: St. Martin's Press.

Gordon, T., Lahelma, E., Hynninen, P., Metso, T., Pulmu, T., & Tolonen, T. (1999). Learning the routines: "Professionalization" of newcomers in secondary school. *Qualitative Studies in Education, 12*(6), 689–705.

Jackson, K. M. (1986). *Images of children in American film: A sociocultural analysis.* Metuchen: The Scarecrow Press.

James, A. (1998). From the child's point of view: Issues in the social construction of childhood. In: C. Panter-Brick (Ed.), *Biosocial perspectives on children* (pp. 45–65). Cambridge: Cambridge University Press.

James, A., Jenks, C., & Prout, A. (1998). *Theorizing childhood.* New York: Teachers College Press.

James, A., & Prout, A. (1995). Hierarchy, boundary, and agency: Toward a theoretical perspective on childhood. *Sociological Studies of Children, 7,* 77–99.

Johnson, H. B. (2001). From the Chicago school to the new sociology of children: The sociology of children and childhood in the United States, 1900–1999. In: S. L. Hofferth & T. J. Owens (Eds), *Children at the millennium: Where have we come from, where are we going?* (pp. 53–96). Amsterdam: JAI.

Jones, S. S. (1995). *The fairy tale: The magic mirror of imagination.* New York: Twayne Publishers.

Krueger, L. (Dir.) (1996). *Manny & Lo* (Mary Kay Place, Scarlett Johansson, & Aleksa Palladino). Sony Pictures Classics.

Laupa, M., Turiel, E., & Cowan, J. P. (1995). Obedience to authority in children and adults. In: M. Killen & D. Hart (Eds), *Morality in everyday life: Developmental perspectives* (pp. 131–165). Cambridge: Cambridge University Press.

Lee, N. (1998). Towards an immature sociology. *Sociological Review, 46*(3), 458–482.

Macklin, R. (1992). Autonomy, beneficence, and child development: An ethnical analysis. In: B. Stanley & J. E. Sieber (Eds), *Social research on children and adolescents: Ethical issues* (pp. 88–105). Newbury Park: Sage.

McCarthy, C., & Crichlow, W. (1993). *Race, identity, and representation in education.* New york: Routledge.

Nucci, L. P. (1997). Culture, universals, and the personal. In: H. D. Saltzstein (Ed.), *Culture as a context for moral development: New perspectives on the particular and the universal* (pp. 5–22). San Francisco: Jossey-Bass.

Nucci, L. P., Killen, M., & Smetana, J. G. (1996). Autonomy and the personal: Negotiation and social reciprocity in adult-child social exchanges. In: M. Killen (Ed.), *Children's autonomy, social competence, and interactions with adults and other children: Exploring connections and consequences* (pp. 7–24). San Francisco: Jossey-Bass.

Prout, A. (2000). Childhood bodies: Construction, agency, and hybridity. In: A. Prout (Ed.), *The body, childhood and society* (pp. 1–18). Houndmills: Macmillan Press.

Rohrich, L. (1986). Introduction. In: R. B. Bottigheimer (Ed.), *Fairy tales and society: Illusion, allusion, and paradigm* (pp. 1–12). Philadelphia: University of Pennsylvania Press.

Shokeid, M. (1982). Toward and anthropological perspective of fairy tales. *Sociological Review, 30*(2), 223–233.

Tatar, M. (1992). *Off with their heads! Fairytales and the culture of childhood*. Princeton: Princeton University Press.
Thorne, B. (1987). Re-visioning women and social change: Where are the children? *Gender & Society, 1*(1), 85–109.
Tsushima, T., & Burke, P. J. (1999). Levels, agency, and control in the parent identity. *Social Psychology Quarterly, 62*, 173–189.
Turiel, E. (1997). Beyond particular and universal ways: Contexts for morality. In: H. D. Saltzstein (Ed.), *Culture as a context for moral development: New perspectives on the particular and the universal* (pp. 87–105). San Francisco: Jossey-Bass.
Wulff, H. (1995). Introduction: Introducing youth culture in its own right: The state of the art and new possibilities. In: V. Amit-Talai & H. Wulff (Eds), *Youth cultures: A cross-cultural perspective* (pp. 1–18). London: Routledge.
Zipes, J. (1983). *Fairy tales and the art of subversion: The classical genre for children and the process of civilization*. New York: Wildman Press.
Zipes, J. (1994). *Fairy tale as myth: Myth as fairy tale*. Lexington: The University Press of Kentucky.
Zipes, J. (1997). *Happily ever after: Fairy tales, children, and the culture industry*. New York: Routledge.
Zipes, J. (Ed.) (2000). *The Oxford companion to fairy tales*. Oxford: Oxford University Press.

# CHILDREN AS SOCIAL MOVEMENT PARTICIPANTS

Diane M. Rodgers

## INTRODUCTION

Although the popular image of social movement protest is tied to youth, this image is not generally extended to younger children. Children throughout history have participated in social movements, and yet the social construction of children as wholly innocent acts as a barrier to their perceived involvement. Childhood itself is viewed as a protected and universalized space, thereby denying its multiple social locations. Indeed, if children were viewed as inhabiting a socio-political location this might actually be seen to warrant their movement participation. As it stands, however, the reality of children clashes with the preferred image and therefore children appear to be the most understudied of all social movement participants.

The new paradigm in recent childhood studies places emphasis on children as social actors (Aries, 1962; Boyden, 1997; Corsaro, 1997; Prout & James, 1990; Jenks, 1996). Many researchers in the field of children's culture have called for the acceptance of children as socially located (Adler & Adler, 1998; Connolly, 1997; Rose, 1998). And some have noted in particular the ability of children to be socio-political agents, who negotiate with others within their structured environment (Jenkins, 1998; Spaulding, 1997; Mayall, 1994, 2002; Waksler, 1991). Overall, this work views the child as having agency, which would point to the ability of children to be social movement participants.

Yet, thus far, the major emphasis in the social movement and social problems literature has concerned the child as object or symbol; this can be exemplified in Best's notion of "claims-making" of social movements that use the image of child as victim. In his work on missing children, for instance, the construction of children as social problem is explored and challenged, especially concerning the use of contentious statistics to exaggerate claims (Best, 1987). This has been a very important work documenting the use of childhood as symbol in the rhetoric of social movements. However, its primary aim has been, as his edited book volume title suggests, "Images of Issues" (Best, 1989), and is not meant to be an analysis of the direct participation of children in social movements.

The children's rights movement led by adults has also been largely concerned with children as social problems and not as social movement participants (see Oakley, 1994; Strandell, 2002). These children's rights organizations have been "for the benefit of" children and use the image of a protected childhood as a symbol. The literature on this social movement focuses on the protection of children, generally within the legal realm. Some critique has arisen as to the absence of actual children in the children's rights movement, which denies them agency in matters that are allegedly in their best interest (Alderson, 1994; Lansdown, 1994; Melton, 1982).

An area of research that does go beyond children in the abstract or as social problem is that of gauging children's political awareness. Children are asked to share their attitudes and awareness of political or social issues including voting and political candidates to a variety of other civic responsibilities (Andrain, 1971; Coles, 1986; Cullingford, 1992; Oppenheim & Torney, 1974). This research is meant to be a measure of attitude, not action by children.

In a more ambiguous case of analyzing civic awareness, King (1994a, b) explores the new liberal environmental "movement." Children are drawn into this movement with a sense of civic/consumer responsibility largely promoted through the media and schools. On the one hand, King notes that children derive a sense of agency from their attitudes toward "saving the planet," but she also points out that this agency is greatly circumscribed by the de-politicized nature of the discourse.

Overall, the existing research has been either to present how the image of childhood has been used in social movements or to try and ascertain children's awareness and citizenship through their attitudes. Neither of these avenues of research can fully explain the child as socio-political agent as much as studying their actual participation can. To discuss children's actual participation in social movements not only uncovers questions about childhood, innocence and socio-political location, it alters the discussion of inequalities and oppression that effect children and includes the possibility of children having a voice in their own lives and even taking action.

What is needed now is a way to theorize about the actual participation of children in social movements rather than simply their representation in movements. I would like to provide a broad typology for the ways that children are involved in social movements as actual participants. This typology will be derived from the descriptive accounts of children participating in social movements and is meant to encourage more research into this phenomenon. The first type of participation is what I refer to as strategic participants. This category goes beyond slogans such as "it's a child not a choice." In this strategic action carried out by adults in social movements, the idea of children's innocence actually becomes embodied in child participants. In the second type of participation there are children who are involved in social movements only through the involvement of their parents or other adults. They may be present at meetings, protests, etc. because they are brought along or the gatherings are in their home. This inclusion may or may not be meant as political socialization by parents. These children are what I will refer to as participants "by default." Perhaps the most difficult to discuss is the final category, that of children who play active roles in social movements. Examples are child strikers, marchers, resisters, etc. These are simply termed active participants.

These three ideal types sometimes overlap in real life, as I will illustrate with later examples, however, this typology gives some sense of the varied participation of children in social movements. None of the participation described in these categories has been broadly discussed in social movement literature or placed into any theoretical framework. The children's culture literature does acknowledge agency and children as socio-political actors, pointing to the capability of children as social movement participants.

## STRATEGIC PARTICIPANTS

Social movement leaders, aware of the general cultural notions of childhood and potentially sharing in these to some extent, may use these notions as a strategy to gain sympathy for and draw attention to their cause. They move beyond using childhood as a symbol in rhetoric or visual representations and actually include children as physical participants in marches, protests and rallies. What is important about this shift from symbol or rhetoric to actual participant is that children as social actors can then begin to take part in a social movement. This opens the door for them to interpret, negotiate and even potentially move on to more active involvement. The risks involved in having children participate in strategic acts may seem reasonable to adults when they believe that children are being harmed by oppressive forces or social injustices as it stands. For this category, I would like to use several historical cases where children's strategic participation has been well documented; I will also provide a more recent case.

In 1912 during the textile worker's strike in Lawrence, Massachusetts, the Industrial Workers of the World (IWW) implemented a strategy borrowed from Europe. Though relief of the strikers was organized as effectively as possible, adequately feeding all the workers was difficult. Children were sent away to sympathetic families in other cities for strike relief, which was also used to garner public support for the cause (Kornbluh, 1964). Public sympathies were hoped for as the plight of the workers was conveyed in the papers. Even as the IWW was aware of the power of this tactic to raise awareness, so were the mill owners and the city leaders who decided to not allow the children to leave.

> ... the children, arranged in a long line, two by two, in orderly procession, with their parents near at hand, were about to make their way to the train when the police, who had by that time stationed themselves along both sides of the door, closed in on us with their clubs, beating right and left, with no thought of the children, who were in the most desperate danger of being trampled to death. The mothers and children were hurled in a mass and bodily dragged to a military truck and even then clubbed, irrespective of the cries of the panic-stricken women and children (Renshaw, 1967, p. 218).

This event turned out to be a very successful tactic. The public was shocked at the condition of the children and newspapers began supporting the strike. In the brutal arrests, public protests increased dramatically and helped the strikers finally win their demands.

The second historical case comes from the Civil Rights movement. In 1963, the Southern Christian Leadership Conference (SCLC) came up with a strategy for integration of Birmingham, Alabama's downtown, which they called Project C for "confrontation" (Williams, 1987). Marches on the downtown were part of confronting discriminatory downtown businesses. However, as many demonstrators were being jailed, including King himself, the demonstrations were losing support. When King and Abernathy were released on bond, they and others began to plan the next phase of Project C, which ended up including children as strategic participants.

James Bevel, a veteran of the student sit-ins in Nashville, had devised a strategy. He wanted to use Birmingham's black children as demonstrators. Bevel argued that while many adults might be reluctant to march-afraid of going to jail at the cost of their jobs – children would be less fearful. Also, he told King, the sight of young children being hauled off to jail would dramatically stir the Nation's conscience (Williams, 1987, pp. 188–189).

And indeed this strategy was successful:

Across the nation people watched television pictures of children being blasted with water hoses and chased by police dogs. Newspapers and magazines at home and abroad were filled with reports and photographs. The news coverage shocked the American public (Williams, 1987, p. 191).

Not only did this bring outside support to the movement and pressure on the federal government to offer assistance, it garnered support from local blacks who were "unsure" of the demonstrations, even the ones populated by adults.

A more current use of this strategy can be seen through some of the organizing to abolish child labor internationally. The child worker as exploited victim has been highlighted through the efforts of adult organizations. As an act of protest against the continued use of child labor, adult organizers created a "Global March Against Child Labour." The Global March was a worldwide march, which began in January 1998 and continued for 6 months until the International Labor Organization (ILO) convention. Marchers then attended the ILO convention in Geneva, where they campaigned for an end to the worst types of labor for children. Throughout the march, the organizers utilized former and current child workers as part of their "core marchers" (those who marched in several countries) to provide the visual impact of children advocating for the end of child labor. It is clear, however, that these children were largely strategic participants, as the march was organized by adults – "for the benefit of children."

At the launch of the campaign in India, the Global March organizers assembled 3,000 children from 22 schools for a press event. After some speeches by children, Kailash Satyarthi, adult organizer and chairperson of the Global March, spoke and then "led the children in their March ... which was indeed a symbolic representation of the [larger] March" (Global March, 1997, p. 4). *Footprints*, a newsletter originating from the Global March International Secretariat, reports the event as "a colorful sight with thousands of children carrying banners and shouting slogans ... " (Global March, 1997, p. 4). The combined use of children and other childhood symbols of innocence at this event attracted favorable attention: "The launch concluded with the children releasing balloons. Soon, the clear blue

Delhi sky was split into an array of colours indicating freedom and happiness. The response to this event was very encouraging and it was covered worldwide by both the print and electronic media" (Global March, 1997, p. 4). Other countries involved in the March also used the strategy of child participants and balloons.

Including children as actual participants, given the symbol they represent, seems to be a powerful movement tactic that the public responds to. This strategy that plays into the cultural ideas about children downplays much active awareness or involvement of children, especially in its image to the public. This is one reason the strategy works; the child as victim highlights the extremes of injustice. It is important to acknowledge, however, that children are actually participating and may become politicized through this process despite the image they are portraying in public. This is where overlap with children as active participants can occur.

## PARTICIPANTS BY DEFAULT

Some young children end up at demonstrations and political meetings "by default;" this occurs through the involvement of their parents or another adult. These children may be exposed to political jargon, strategies and goals of the movement simply by proximity. Current research is fairly inconclusive as to the degree that this politicizes children. The extent that parents are conscious of their child being a participant simply by virtue of being brought along will coincide with how aware they are of their child being a capable social actor. Some parents may just be bringing the children as a matter of convenience, unaware of the potential for agency. Other parents may count on children's understanding and agency as they hope for political socialization through exposure. An example of the latter can be found in the following self-described anarchist mother's account:

> Anarchist parenting means getting your children involved in political activities at a young age. Children have a keen sense of justice (and injustice). My daughter is able to understand the reasons for all the demos, marches and boycotts we participate in. Going to events and meetings with both her parents has taught her that political work is part of everyday life and that when you see an injustice, you have to act (Baker-Cristales, 2001, p. 10).

DeMartini (1990) views this kind of exposure of children by their parents as a case for the normalization of social movement participation. As "normal political action," social movement participation is sustained over time and becomes intergenerational due to political socialization, according to

Children as Social Movement Participants 245

DeMartini. However, it is not always the case that this political socialization will result in intergenerational political involvement.

Blee's (2002) study of the Hate movement documents extensive socialization of young children into the values of the movement:

> The children are ushered into a world of racial and religious hatred at a very early age. Homes are strewn with drawings, photos, flyers, videos, and pamphlets filled with vicious lies and threats against racial and religious enemies .... A particularly pernicious means of targeting the very young is the racist comic book, like the New World Order Comix published by the National Alliance and distributed by skinhead groups (pp. 126–127).

Despite this intense socialization, Blee (2002, p. 128) notes that: "The extent to which parents succeed in transmitting racial hatred and racial activism across generations is unclear." Some of the adult accounts of learning racism from their family actually turned out to be false, and the stories that they had created were attributed by Blee to be a fabrication to bolster their racist identity. Nevertheless, some Klan parents do include their children in activities in hopes that they will adopt movement goals and practices:

> From birth, some Klan children are installed in a 'Kid Klan Korp,' preparing them for a life of racial activism. Garbed in miniature Klan robes and flaunting imitation torches and guns, they are introduced to racist activism as fun and frolic. One woman told me, 'At night, the lighting of the crosses, that is a big to-do. The men, of course, were in the front lines, the women were there, and there were lots of children too, lots of children running around and they were just so happy' (2002, pp. 126–127).

Some of participants by default may not have any consciousness as to the meanings of the events that they are taken to; their "happiness" may not be a result of embracing the ideologies of the movement. As one adult and former child participant recalls:

> I remember going to a situation that they call a rally. Now I know what it is. When I was little, going where I remember all these men talking and I remember my Dad saying, 'Be well behaved' and so forth. And I remember other kids. I got to play with other kids. It took many years before I realized that my uncle took me to a Ku Klux Klan meeting. I didn't even know what it was. It was a giant picnic, is what I thought. But when the men talked, I remember that you had to be hush-hush and you can go out and play with the other kids but don't disturb the meeting (2002, p. 128).

Children are also incorporated into adult social movement activities through "helper" activities. As Blee (2002, p. 127) describes: "Some children are assigned minor tasks in racists groups; thus, in one Klan chapter 'the kids fold the pamphlets and put them in plastic bags and then take them out at night and throw them on lawns.'" Although Blee is skeptical of any evidence of active participation on the part of these children, she is sure of the conscious socialization attempts and influence experienced by children in the hate movement as participants by default.

The Right to Life movement also consciously involves children in their meetings, campaigns and marches in the hopes of intergenerational movement participation. Through the many photos and captions of younger children found in the National Right to Life News (NRLN) (1998), children as participants by default become obvious. A picture of a very young child with a "Save the Baby Humans" button on his clothing and a "March for Life" button in his hands is given the caption: "John Clear of Lebanon, Ohio, attends his first March for Life in Washington Jan. 22 on his first birthday" (NRLN, 1998, vol. 25(3), p. 1). Presumably, Clear is there at the March with parents or relatives and not attending alone! Pictures from the 29th Annual National Right to Life Convention show pictures of children with their parents at the convention with one picture's caption describing the young child as "The Next Generation" (NRLN, 2001, vol. 28(7), pp. 18–19). The convention is billed as a family event with the registration form claiming to offer "family fun and fellowship" and includes "children and spouses" in the list of groups that the convention has something to offer. Childcare is provided (NRLN, 2001, vol. 28(2), p. 19).

Working on projects for the movement is seen as a way to include and socialize children as one photo's caption reads, "When entire families pitch in to work on behalf of the babies, it not only helps the cause, but also teaches a new generation of pro-lifers" (NRLN, 2001, vol. 28(11), p. 21). Children are participants by default as they attend rallies with their parents or relatives. A photo caption of young children carrying "Stop Abortion Now" signs (one held upside down) states: "These children sounded the message of the day at a pro-life rally in Salem, Oregon" (NRLN, 2001, vol. 28(2), p. 10). Another rally photo caption emphasizes that children are "small but plenty big enough to carry an important message" (NRLN, 1998, vol. 25(3), pp. 18–19).

An article in the newsletter, written by a young college pro-life activist, provides a description of being "taken along" as a child to his grandmother's activities:

> When I was growing up, my life was full of meetings. With my mother working nights my entire life, my grandmother, who had retired before I went to kindergarten, was my babysitter and first teacher. What an example she set for me! My grandmother was constantly heading off to the Right to Life Center for a meeting or envelope stuffing or to the State Fair booth. In second grade, I joined grandma as a volunteer for a local congressional campaign stuffing envelopes and going door to door doing lit drops (Jones, 2002, p. 30).

Although children are included in activities, this may be seen as a transition and not always an acknowledgment of their full understanding of movement goals. In fact, the transmission of goals and ideology to children seems to be a potentially ambiguous issue for parents as reflected in the rare article addressing children's involvement in the movement. (This can certainly be contrasted to the overt recruitment and movement education directed at teens.) In an article entitled "Explaining Abortion to Children," Amy Welborn urges parents to overcome their ambiguity and be explicit about ideology to children (in her terms this requires explaining abortion as "killing") (Welborn, 1998). Despite lack of full knowledge about the movement's ideology, an assumption is made that children share the views of their parents, as captions of photos not only depict children as the next generation but also as "pro-lifers" currently.

Children's photos are depicted in every issue of the NRLN. This could be seen as simply using children as a visual symbol, yet the photos also document the physical participation of children at movement activities as they are brought along by their parents or relatives. Therefore, these children are not just symbolic in representation but are actually participating by default and being exposed to movement activities and goals.

Some movements such as the Hate movement and the Right to Life movement include their children with the hopes of consciously socializing their children. Other movements may have a varied approach to inclusion of their children in movement activities. The Communist Party of the 1930s and 1940s also involved children as participants, yet some parents attempted to shield their children from their movement activities. As first hand accounts from adults who were children of communist party parents (known as "red diaper babies") have begun to emerge, more is known about the range of children's participation within this movement (Fried, 1993; Kaplan & Shapiro, 1998; Mishler, 1999). These adult accounts offer not only patterns of participation and socialization, but also the opportunity to see that not all children exposed to the movement adopted those beliefs later in life.[1] Some resented their involuntary participation by default or the confusion they had concerning their parents' activities. Also not all parents wished for their children to be too aware of, or involved in Communist Party activities, and yet, children had some level of exposure just the same. As Kaplan and Shapiro explain:

> Among the parents who avoided overt instruction were those who did so, with varying degrees of self-awareness, to allow children freedom to assimilate and integrate rather than merely imitate adult political beliefs. Some parents, motivated by fear, wanted to protect their children by not burdening them with potentially harmful knowledge. Some

may have worried that if they pushed too hard in one political direction their children might turn against them and what they stood for. Often, parents held back information by a process that itself was laden with fear, confusion and secrecy. Picking up on the emotion without the content, their children felt anything but protected (Kaplan & Shapiro, 1998, pp. 7–8).

There is a continuum for the comprehension of movement goals and ideology by participants by default. Even when children do understand the ideology and goals of a movement through their exposure as participants by default, at what point (if ever) do participants "by default" find themselves on the path to being a more active participant? Baker-Cristales describes her daughter as understanding the meaning of the "demos, marches and boycotts they participate in," and yet does this make her daughter an active participant or simply a child aware of her parent's political involvement?

One "red diaper baby" entered into her parent's political world "by default," and yet, at the same time she describes how she consciously embraced ideologies and actions as a young child activist:

> I acquired my political consciousness, my political identity, and my dreams by direct observation, participation, and osmosis. With fierce devotion, my parents lived their beliefs, shared them with me, and included me in their political activities.
>
> I grew up going to meetings and demonstrations, learning how to make stencils, running mimeograph machines, collating, stapling, stuffing and sealing envelopes. What I liked best-but never learned completely was the switchboard. Most of the time I enjoyed participating, feeling a part of some great invincible yet clandestine force (Patterson, 1998, p. 111).

This participant by default ends up transforming her parent's political world into her own unique experience. This becomes even more apparent as she recounts the mixture of her parent's influence and her own beliefs:

> We always marched in May Day and Labor Day parades. I'd avoid looking at the faces of angry bystanders for compassion or reason while trying to dodge the rotten eggs and tomatoes and epithets. My parents must have inspired me in a certain confidence with their own courageous posture as their hands tightly gripped mine; I always wanted to carry the banners or placards and always shouted the slogans. Perhaps I was seduced by the sense of danger and their bravery.
>
> Both parents, but especially my father, were acutely aware of the need to talk with me to counter the daily barrage of anticommunist propaganda in the media. I was about eight or nine the first time my father was jailed. From prison he wrote me long, wonderful letters, urging me to believe in ' a world without hungry children' where 'strawberries and cream for breakfast for everyone' was possible. I believed that the men who ran our country, allowing lynching, segregation, hunger, joblessness, ghettos, and hopelessness alongside an idle rich class, should and could be overthrown (Patterson, 1998, p. 113).

Child participants by default may come in contact with other children of movement activists. This can then serve as an even wider source of influence that reinforces movement ideology and goals:

> Our closest family friends were other Black communists and their families. My best friends were their children. Many of us lived near each other in Brooklyn. For several summers I was sent to a Left children's camp called Higley Hill, a truly magical place in the woods of western Vermont. For the children of persecuted leftists, it was a breath of fresh air, a place where we could be ourselves and express our real beliefs unencumbered, where we reinforced those beliefs and that identity by trying to briefly live a happy communal lifestyle (Patterson, 1998, p. 113).

Children are often exposed to social movements through parents or other relatives. They are participants by default at meetings, rallies and protests. They may double as symbols, as is the case for the Right to Life movement's use of photos of children at events, or they may evolve into active participants as the recollections of "red diaper babies" sometimes suggest. Children may have little awareness of the events that they are a part of or they may reject the politics they were exposed to by default.[2] Yet, the idea behind a participant "by default" category is to note participation as it exists, not as it may be construed or manipulated or what it may become in the future. As Cook (2002, p. 5) notes, researchers under the new paradigm of childhood studies "insist on capturing the lived situatedness of children and their understandings. The point of the new childhood studies is to dismantle the epistemological hegemony that has regarded children as being merely in transition, as nothings and nobodies in the here and now."

## ACTIVE PARTICIPANTS

Children have been subject to oppressive conditions that are even difficult for adults to withstand. Despite our image of childhood as a protected safe space, for many children this space is full of dangers and hardships. Children have never been excluded from any of the conditions that might lead to resistance or participation in a social movement. They are involved in such situations as war, slavery, abuse, homelessness, poverty, racism and sexism. Even if a child does not experience severe oppression first hand, she/he may otherwise develop a social consciousness. What distinguishes a child as an active participant? Beyond the exposure to certain oppressive conditions themselves and resulting awareness of social injustice or social movement goals, the child must then decide to voluntarily participate in a social movement.

Although not all participants by default end up becoming active participants based on their exposure to their parent's political involvement, some do end up becoming active even as children. Some adult "red diaper babies" accounts convey a conscious decision to become more active. Tom Berry expresses this transition vividly:

> I came of age politically on a sunny Saturday morning in April when I was ten. Making up some excuse to give my parents, I left our lower Manhattan apartment after breakfast. Feeling a sense of adventure, I self-consciously strode through our housing project to the Woolworth's store on 14th Street. As I passed the playgrounds already full of kids, I was mindful of a purpose that set me apart, a different reason for being out early on such a morning.
>
> There was already a picket line when I got to Woolworth's, a sparse circle of protestors in front of the store. Most were carrying placards supporting the struggle to integrate Woolworth's lunch counters in the South. I remember mostly white people, one or two Black people, no other kids. I think I was disappointed the line wasn't longer, my sense of being part of a larger cause somewhat deflated. On the other hand, the small size of the group meant that my arrival made a difference–and also made it harder for me to leave. Once there, I was immediately either "in" or "out." There was no buffer zone of public space from which I could anonymously observe the scene before deciding to join in. I was welcomed into the circle by a middle-aged Black woman, who seemed to be in charge. I was handed a placard, and suddenly I wasn't outside anymore ... .
>
> I left Woolworth's that day feeling both relief and exaltation. When I returned home for lunch, my parents were supportive but puzzled as to why I hadn't told them beforehand. The reason was clear to me: to do so would have been like asking permission, and picketing Woolworth's would have been that much less my own (Berry, 1998, pp. 286–287).

Red diaper babies were not only exposed to the movement directly through their parent's activities. Some children were involved in separate schools, camps and children's organizations. One organization was the Young Pioneers, which were formed as a children's political organization within the Communist Party. This group was linked to the Young Communist League (YCL) for those 16 and older. Beside their own agenda, the YCL helped organize the Young Pioneers. The point of both these organizations was to encourage the active participation and political autonomy of children. The Young Pioneers were not only involved in actions themselves but they organized other children as well. This was especially true of their organizing of the children of strikers. "The Young Pioneers organized children's organizations among strikers children-a means of building support for the strikes among the worker's families as well as spreading the political message of the Young Pioneers among the children" (Mishler, 1999, p. 51). Children's exposure to social movement ideology and practices can not only lead to active participation, but also potentially creates the ability to recruit other children into the movement.

The earlier case of the Civil Rights march in Birmingham is an example of the overlap that can happen between children used as strategic participants and children as active participants. Children, some as young as 6 years old, had volunteered to participate in the "children's" march. They were then asked to view a film on the student sit-in movement before they took part in the demonstrations and Dr. King addressed the children before they began their march. The child demonstrators went on to march for 4 hours, and at the end of that day 959 children had been arrested and put in Birmingham jails. The marches continued because the next day more than 1,000 children chose to stay out of school to march; fire hoses and police dogs were used against the child marchers. The force of the water from the fire hoses knocked children down, and they were "slammed into curbs and over parked cars" (Williams, 1987, p. 190). Although it was the image of the children as victims that brought the nation's attention to Birmingham, it was volunteering to march and the rather conscious preparedness that took place beforehand, which turned these strategic participants into active participants.

More recently in transnational movements for human rights, labor and peace, children are taking an active part. This is true of many of the social movements in Latin America, including that of the Zapitistas (Liebel, 1996; Navarro, 1999). In Colombia, a Children's Movement began in 1995 in the town of Aguachica when children asked the mayor of the town to be allowed to be involved in a municipal vote to decide whether the residents wanted peace in the war-torn town. They went "campaigning" for peace, singing songs in the streets and urging children to choose peace. Although children did vote in the adult election, their votes were not counted. The children then wanted a special election that would allow children to vote on their rights. Various adult organizations helped this new Children's Movement create an election known as the Children's Mandate for Peace and Rights. Children actively participated in this campaign for peace and rights by designing materials in other languages, creating games about rights and teaching them in schools and at meetings, and by speaking out at press conferences and town meetings about peace and their rights.

The election was held on October 25, 1996. More than 2.7 million children voted for rights to peace, justice, education and a safe environment (Cameron, 2000, p. 42). This Children's Movement continues to work on peace issue with adult organizations, expanding adult's conceptions of what constitutes peace activities.

> The Children's Movement sees that making peace in homes and on the streets is just as important as making peace in the war...[are] suggesting, in effect, that virtually anything that helps to improve the quality of life in a community affected by violence counts as peacemaking. By extension, any child who is involved in such activities in Colombia is considered a de facto member of the Children's Movement for Peace (Cameron, 2000, p. 44).

A Working Children's movement has been building in Latin America, Asia and Africa. These active participants do not agree with the direction that adult organizations have taken in their campaigns to end child labor. They have criticized some of the ILOs decisions that did not take into account working children's viewpoints and they issued a boycott of the Global March against Child Labor.[3] These children are forming independent unions "of and by working children" (Swift, 2001, p. 191). One of the largest of these organizations is Bhima Sangha in India whose president, Uchengamma, is a 13-year-old girl. Bhima Sangha reaches out to at least 13,000 children in urban and rural areas, some of whom are workers as young as 6 years old (Swift, 2001, p. 194). This children's union organized the First International Meeting of Working Children held in Kundapur in 1996. At this international meeting representatives created the Kundapur Declaration which states:

1. We want recognition of our problems, our initiatives, proposals and our process of organisation.
2. We are against the boycott of products made by children.
3. We want respect and security for ourselves and the work we do.
4. We want an education system whose methodology and content are adapted to our reality.
5. We want professional training adapted to our reality and capabilities.
6. We want access to good health care for working children.
7. We want to be consulted in all decisions concerning us, at local, national or international level.
8. We want the root causes of our situation, primarily poverty, to be addressed and tackled.
9. We want more activities in rural areas and decentralisation in decision making, so that children will no longer be forced to migrate.
10. We are against exploitation at work but we are for work with dignity with hours adapted so that we have time for education and leisure (Liebel, Overwien, & Recknagel, 2001, p. 351).

Children actively organizing by forming unions and striking for better working conditions are not actually a new phenomenon, some were formed previously in the early 1900s (Nichols, 1903; Walling, 1904). The Communist Party of the 1930s and 1940s encouraged and reported the existence of children's unions and strikes which paralleled their sense that children should form a separate oppositional culture from mainstream culture and even sometimes from adults (See Mishler, 1999 for a complete account of the evolving ideology concerning children's active participation in the Communist Party within the United States.).

However, the participation of these children currently is seen as something new and is termed "protaganism" to illustrate their role as active participants in their own struggle (See Cussiánovich in Liebel et al., 2001 concerning the choice of this term.). They are organizing to help each other with improving working conditions and overcoming discrimination. They demonstrate and negotiate as a collective group concerned with issues of work, education and healthcare for themselves and their community.

These children's unions are generally comprised of children and adolescents and some of their networks are international, although some prefer to remain local in focus. The fact that these children interact with their adult allies does not take away from their active participation in a social movement for their own cause. In fact, this relationship seems more similar to the interconnections made in many social movements as alliances are created to assist each other in achieving goals through sharing resources (Flynn, 1973, p. 279; Swift, 2001, p. 191). The adults that are allies to the working children's movement understand that their involvement is not one of paternalistic protectors and that this new and dynamic relationship will necessitate a change in old hierarchies.[4] As the adult organizers of The Concerned for Working Children phrase it:

> Children have asserted their right to intervene in their environment and change it for the better. As a result many of us have realised that the active and equal participation of children in all matters concerning them is both realistic and beneficial. However in order to enable this we adults and adult led organizations have to examine ourselves critically and redefine our roles, sometimes to the extent of unlearning what we thought to be "right" and reconstructing ourselves closer to the children's paradigm (Reddy & Ratna, 2002, *The Context*, para. 5).

Both children and adults recognize that currently children's organizations are limited in some respects toward full citizenship and self-advocacy. The organizations lack many legal rights and recourses that are available to adult organizations. Adult organizations may assist at the direction of child protagonists while both work toward expanding the legal rights and social recognition of working children's organizations (Liebel et al., 2001).

Children as active participants in social movements may change definitions of goals, strategies and memberships in movements according to their own perspectives. Children may also be active participants in movements that directly affect them and enlist adult allies as needed. There are many conditions that can lead to a child becoming an active participant, including having been a strategic participant or a participant by default.

## CONCLUSION

A typology of children's participation in social movements provides a framework to study children's agency rather than simply their representation. Children are socio-political actors who negotiate with their environment; to acknowledge children as actual participants in social movements underscores this ability for interpretation and action. Children participate in social movements on many levels: as strategic participants, as participants by default and as active participants. Precisely because children have agency, these categories cannot be seen as permanently fixed or static nor do they imply any particular "stages" for participation. For instance, as shown throughout this paper, strategic participant's direct involvement with social movements may push them into more active participation; participants by default may not end up being politically socialized by the contact they have with their parent's activities; and active participants may be partly constrained by adult attitudes, lack of political rights and recognition. The main point is, children do participate, and taking this seriously means acknowledging that their participation not only exists, but also requires an attempt to understand the meanings of this participation – for children themselves, and for social movements.

The social movement and social problems literature has created an awareness of the symbolic power of childhood as rhetoric in movements, yet this work has not addressed children's direct involvement with social movements. And while the research on children's attitudes comes closer to a subject-oriented approach to children in the political realm, it also leaves gaps in our knowledge of children's political action. Viewing children as social movement participants and understanding that children do have a socio-political location is essential for a fuller accounting of social movements and children's agency. The goals of social movement research are to explore not only the rhetoric of movements, but the actors as well. Thus far, only the rhetoric of children in social movements has been addressed and children as social movement actors have been largely ignored.

Social movement theory would be enriched by treating the child as a socio-political actor, as advanced by the literature on children's culture. This growing body of literature has provided an analysis that not only uncovers the social construction of childhood, but also, as a result of breaking out of a strictly developmental model, views children as competent social actors. This encompasses children's negotiations of meanings, resistance and active involvement in the social world, which are certainly prerequisites for social movement involvement. Therefore, a typology of children as social movement participants also contributes to the growing body of work in children's culture by continuing to challenge ideal notions of childhood and by emphasizing the social location and agency of children.

# NOTES

1. As Cahill (1994) suggests, "Despite the often distorting creativity of human memory, there are also lessons for students of social life in adults' reflection upon and reconstruction of their own childhood. Although our equally treacherous prophesying may seem more impressive, we would be remiss to ignore folk wisdom about the benefits of hindsight. Examining where even remembered childhoods have led can balance and benefit our more common practice of predicting were lives might lead. Such examinations may instruct us in the course lives tend to take under different social conditions and about the residues of past biography that can settle into later lives" (p. 3).

2. This paper does not fully explore political socialization issues but rather exposure through participation by default. The intent of some parents or movements in general may be to socialize children into the movement, however, this is not always the case as some parents simply expose children indirectly as they are attending or holding meetings, going to rallies, etc. Some parents also work to shield their children from political activities. The evidence on how well socialization works seems inconclusive. What I am concerned with is that there are children at meetings; rallies etc. and that in essence they are participants of sorts. Their actual numbers, their impressions, their awareness at that point has been understudied and would be important to understand as something other than a transition phenomenon.

3. Within the organization of the ILO exists IPEC, the International Programme on the Elimination of Child Labour. IPEC consists of adults that work "for the benefit" of children and whose goal is to end child labor. IPEC lists its partners as: governments, employers, NGOs, teachers and workers. The partnership with workers consists of adult trade unions who will work for the benefit of children in ending child labor. The only involvement of children outside of symbolic visual representation can be found in the program SCREAM, which stands for Supporting Children's Rights through Education, the Arts and the Media. According to the pamphlet for SCREAM, its adult organizers recognize the "important role" that young people have to play and they understand what they "bring to the campaign." Their education package reveals that the young people they are referring to are not

child workers themselves but adolescents who will be made aware of the problem of child labor by an adult educator and then instructed on how to use the arts and media to stop child labor (http://www.ilo.org).

4. The influence of children as active participants in child labor issues has been felt in the change within the adult discourse. In a recent Footprints, Global March organizers are attempting to address their change in attitude (and coincidently attempt to defend themselves from the charge of using children only as strategic participants). It is clear that some of these children may have become politicized and are now active participants. This was not necessarily the intention in 1998. Rigoberto Morales, 16-year-old Core Marcher and former child worker from Guatemala writes: "In the past, children have been invited to many events and conferences to 'express' themselves. We should not confuse the term 'express' and 'participate.' Many times what we erroneously call child participation is the use of children to attract attention of the media and encourage publicity ... Our challenge is to start the process of appropriately preparing children so they can participate more actively. This includes involving them in planning, decision-making processes and follow up activities ... . Let's begin now by including the issue of participation in the agendas of our organizations. Programs focused on the conditions of children should have input from those that will be the direct beneficiaries. It is important that we facilitate forums where children can select their own representatives and leaders" (Global March, 2003, p. 1).

# ACKNOWLEDGMENTS

I would like to thank Matt Lammers and Althea Harris for reading earlier drafts of this chapter. I also greatly appreciate the invaluable comments and suggestions from Katherine Brown Rosier, her assistant Michelle Wilson, and an anonymous reviewer.

# REFERENCES

Adler, P. A., & Adler, P. (1998). *Peer power: Preadolescent culture and identity*. New Brunswick, NJ: Rutgers University Press.
Alderson, P. (1994). Researching children's rights to integrity. In: B. Mayall (Ed.), *Children'childhoods: Observed and experienced* (pp. 45–62). London: The Falmer Press.
Andrain, C. F. (1971). *Children and civic awareness: A study in political education*. Columbus, OH: Merrill.
Aries, P. (1962). *Centuries of childhood: A social history of family life* (Trans. R. Baldick). New York: Knopf.
Baker-Cristales, B. (2001). Anarchist child rearing in a capitalist society. *Onward, 2*(2), 10.
Best, J. (1987). Rhetoric in claims-making. *Social Problems, 34*, 101–121.
Best, J. (Ed.) (1989). *Images of issues*. New York, NY: Aldine de Gruyter.

Berry, T. (1998). From Woolworth's to Managua. In: J. Kaplan & L. Shapiro (Eds), *Red diaper: Growing up in the Communist left* (pp. 186–189). Chicago: University of Illinois Press.

Blee, K. (2002). *Inside organized racism: Women in the hate movement.* Berkeley: University of California Press.

Boyden, J. (1997). Childhood and the policy makers: A comparative perspective on the globalization of childhood. In: A. James & A. Prout (Eds), *Constructing and reconstructing childhood: Contemporary issues in the sociological study of childhood* (pp. 190–216). London: The Falmer Press.

Cahill, S. (Ed.) (1994). Introduction. *Sociological studies of child development* (Vol. 4, pp. 1–7). Greenwich, CT: JAI Press.

Cameron, S. (2000). The role of children as peace-makers in Colombia. *Development, 43*(1), 40–45.

Coles, R. (1986). *The political life of children.* Boston: Atlanta Monthly Press.

Connolly, P. (1997). In search of authenticity: Researching young children's perspectives. In: A. Pollard, D. Thiessen & A. Filer (Eds), *Children and their curriculum: The perspectives of primary and elementary school children* (pp. 162–183). London: The Falmer Press.

Cook, D. T. (Ed.) (2002). *Symbolic childhood.* New York: Peter Lang.

Corsaro, W. (1997). *The sociology of childhood.* Thousand Oaks, California: Pine Forge Press.

Cullingford, C. (1992). *Children and society: Children's attitudes to politics and power.* New York, NY: Cassell.

DeMartini, J. R. (1990). Social movement participation as normal politics. Paper presented at the annual meetings of the International Sociological Association.

Flynn, E. G. (1973). *Rebel girl: An autobiography, my first life (1906–1926).* New York: International Publishers.

Fried, M. (1993). For generations that follow: The impact of the McCarthy era on 'red diaper babies'. Paper presented at the annual meetings of the Society for the Study of Social Problems.

Global March. (1997). *Footprints, 1*(1), 4.

Global March. (2003). *Footprints, 5*(1), 1.

Jenks, C. (1996). *Childhood.* London: Routledge.

Jenkins, H. (1998). Introduction: Childhood innocence and other modern myths. In: H. Jenkins (Ed.), *The children's culture reader* (pp. 1–40). New York: New York University Press.

Jones, D. (2002). Reflections of a college kid: Meetings, mentoring, and grooming the next generation of pro-life leaders. *National right to life news, 29*(1), 30.

Kaplan, J., & Shapiro, L. (Eds) (1998). *Red diaper: Growing up in the communist left.* Chicago: University of Illinois Press.

King, D. L. (1994a). Captain planet and the planeteers: Kids, environmental crisis, and the competing narratives of the new world order. *Sociological Quarterly, 35,* 103–120.

King, D. L. (1994b). If we don't do anything now, there won't be anything left: Categories of concern in children's drawings of environmental crisis. In: J. Best (Ed.), *Troubling children: Studies of children and social problems* (pp. 221–246). New York, NY: Aldine de Gruyter.

Kornbluh, J. (1964). *Rebel voice: An IWW anthology.* Ann Arbor, MI: University of Michigan Press.

Lansdown, G. (1994). Children's rights. In: B. Mayall (Ed.), *Children's childhoods: Observed and experienced* (pp. 33–44). London: The Falmer Press.

Liebel, M. (1996). Children's social movements in Latin America. *Forschungsjournal Neue Soziale Bewegungen, 9*(1), 96–101.
Liebel, M., Overwien, B., & Recknagel, A. (Eds) (2001). *Working children's protagonism.* Frankfurt am Main: IKO – Verlag für Interkulterelle Kommunikation.
Mayall, B. (Ed.) (1994). *Children's childhoods: Observed and experienced.* London: The Falmer Press.
Mayall, B. (2002). *Towards a sociology for childhood: Thinking from children's lives.* Buckingham: Open University Press.
Melton, G. B. (1982). Children's rights: Where are the children? *American Journal of Orthopsychiatry, 52*(3), 530–538.
Mishler, P. C. (1999). *Raising reds: The young pioneers, radical summer camps, and communist political culture in the United States.* New York: Columbia University Press.
National Right to Life News (NRLN). (1998). *National Right to Life News.* Washington: National Right to Life Committee, Inc.
National Right to Life News (NRLN). (2001). *National Right to Life News.* Washington: National Right to Life Committee, Inc.
Navarro, F. (1999). A new way of thinking in action: The Zapatistas in Mexico – a postmodern guerilla movement? *Rethinking Marxism, 10*(4), 155–165.
Nichols, F. H. (1903). *Child unions in the silk mills. The public 5 March 14.* Chicago: Public Publishing Co.
Oakley, A. (1994). Women and children first and last: Parallels and differences between children and women's studies. In: B. Mayall (Ed.), *Children's childhoods: Observed and experienced* (pp. 13–32). London: The Falmer Press.
Oppenheim, A. N., & Torney, J. (1974). *The measurement of children's civic attitudes in different nations.* New York: Wiley.
Patterson, M. L. (1998). Black and red all over. In: J. Kaplan & L. Shapiro (Eds), *Red diaper: Growing up in the communist left* (pp. 110–115). Chicago: University of Illinois Press.
Prout, A., & James, A. (1990). A new paradigm for the sociology of childhood? Provenance, promise and problems. In: A. James & A. Prout (Eds), *Constructing and reconstructing childhood: Contemporary issues in the sociological study of childhood* (pp. 7–34). London: The Falmer Press.
Reddy, N., & Ratna, K. (2002). A journey in children's participation. Compiled and edited for The Concerned for Working Children. Retrieved July 17, 2003, from http://workingchild.org/protagonism/childsparticipation.html.
Renshaw, P. (1967). *The Wobblies.* New York: Doubleday and Company.
Rose, J. S. (1998). The case of Peter Pan: The impossibility of children's fiction. In: H. Jenkins (Ed.), *The children's culture reader* (pp. 58–66). New York: New York University Press.
Spaulding, A. (1997). The politics of primaries: The micropolitical perspectives of 7-year-olds. In: A. Pollard, D. Thiessen & A. Filer (Eds), *Children and their curriculum: The perspectives of primary and elementary school children* (pp. 101–121). London: The Falmer Press.
Strandell, H. (2002). On questions of representation in childhood ethnography. In: D. T. Cook (Ed.), *Symbolic childhood* (pp. 17–35). New York: Peter Lang.
Swift, A. (2001). India – tale of two working children's unions. In: M. Liebel, B. Overwien & A. Recknagel (Eds), *Working children's protagonism* (pp. 181–195). Frankfurt am Main: IKO – Verlag für Interkulterelle Kommunikation.

Waksler, F. C. (1991). Studying children: Phenomenological insights. In: F. C. Waksler (Ed.), *Studying the social worlds of children: Sociological readings* (pp. 60–69). London: The Falmer Press.
Walling, W. E. (1904). *A children's strike on the East Side. Charities 13 Dec. 24*. New York: The Society.
Welborn, A. (1998). Explaining abortion to children. *National right to life news*, 25(8), 9.
Williams, J. (1987). *Eyes on the prize: America's civil rights years 1954–1965*. New York: Penguin Books.

# 'YEAH, ME TOO!': ADOLESCENT TALK BUILDING IN GROUP INTERVIEWS

Laura Fingerson

## INTRODUCTION

How do researchers capture children's and adolescents' cultures and peer interactions? Ethnography, as argued by several sociologists including Corsaro (1996), is indeed a valuable method for understanding everyday life. However, what about issues that are sensitive? What about issues that are salient in the lives of children and adolescents, yet are not talked about in settings generally accessible to researchers such as schools, youth groups, community centers, and extracurricular programs? Family issues such as divorce, for example, might be highly salient in a child's life, yet not talked about during school lunch in front of an adult researcher. Children talk with their friends and peers about divorce, share stories and experiences with divorce, and interpret the meanings of divorce in groups.

Group interviewing is an effective and efficient method of accessing children's cultures, particularly around sensitive issues. In my research, high school age girls and boys discussed the body and menstruation. The teens had much to say about these issues, yet ethnographic evidence does not show this. In this paper, I use group interview discussions on menstruation to illustrate three methodological points. First, group interviews are a good way to observe adolescent talk: how adolescents collectively learn and socially construct issues relevant to their lives. Second, group interviewing provides access to the story-telling culture in peer groups. Third, group interviews can be analyzed sociolinguistically to explore not only the "what" (the content) of their talk but also the "how" (the structure) of their talk.

## SYMBOLIC INTERACTIONISM

Before delving into the details of group interviewing, we must consider the theoretical framework in which group interviewing can be effectively based. In symbolic interactionism (SI), reality is comprised of symbols and meanings that are created and interpreted through social interaction (Mead, 1934). Thus, an event itself cannot determine how people will understand the event. Instead, there are multiple potential meanings of that event and people assign significance to select meanings through social interaction and social experience.

Although there are many different approaches in SI, Charon (1998) outlines several key ideas. First, social interaction is the unit of study. In order to understand humans, we must examine what humans do and how humans interact with one another. Social interaction is based on language and the collective interpretation of symbols. Second, we act according to our definitions of the situation and we in turn create and negotiate these constantly shifting definitions through social interaction. It is through interaction that we determine the definition of the situation, what is salient in our world, and how we construct our meanings of events. Finally, we are active and dynamic agents in our social worlds and we have an active relationship with our environments. We do not simply respond to stimuli, but we consciously act in and on our realities.

Children and adolescents collectively form their understandings and constructions of their lives, particularly of salient and sensitive issues, through social interaction. They acquire social knowledge through interaction with others as meanings are constructed through a shared process. Various issues such as sensitive topics are learned about and are rendered salient through adolescents' social interaction and their talk. Over time, this social interaction among groups leads to a shared view of reality. The teens collectively construct their definitions of the situations and then act upon the world according to those definitions.

## CONCEPTUAL AUTONOMY AND INTERPRETIVE REPRODUCTION

Group interviewing captures the here and now – children's own current interpretations of their world. Research often explores adult reflections on their lives as children, but it is equally important to see what is important in the lives of children and adolescents *now* and to hear the stories and thoughts from children themselves (see e.g., Christensen & James, 2000; Corsaro, 1997; Thorne, 1987).

The main premise of the "new sociology of childhood" is that there is a conceptual autonomy of children and children's issues. Children are the center of analysis in terms of who they are now, rather than thinking about who they might become. The notion of "conceptual autonomy," articulated by Thorne (1987), means that we should observe children directly and that they should be the center of research efforts rather than being relegated to the periphery or seen only in terms of their dependence on adults. Children are actors continually creating and recreating their own cultures and social organizations.

Qvortrup (1991, 1994) defines what he calls a "new paradigm" for the study of childhood and children. He argues that childhood should be seen as a "structural form," a separate social structure. This means that childhood is autonomous from other social structures defined by sociologists, such as the family, government, or education, although it continually interacts with these other structural forms. Childhood is a permanent structure in society with its own activities, time and space, even as its members are being continually replaced through aging and new generations. We need to deal with children as "human beings," instead of "human becomings" (Qvortrup, 1994).

At the same time, children are a "minority" group as adults have structural power over children in our culture. Children are learning how to be adults, learning adult roles, and as apprentices, they are less powerful than their adult teachers. Just as gender relations are vital in understanding women's experiences, generational relations are vital in understanding children's experiences (Mayall, 2000; Thorne, 1987). Thorne contends that we need to give voice to children and children's experience, just as feminism has given voice to women and women's experience. In doing this, we recognize children's subordination to adults and their place within the hierarchy of our social structures and we can then work to empower children. It is a fallacy, Qvortrup argues, to assume that children do not deserve equal treatment in our society simply because of their age. Children are active agents and co-constructors of their own cultures, and should not be relegated to secondary status.

Qvortrup and Thorne develop these ideas in response to an overdependence on socialization and developmental models of childhood that derive from dominant psychological traditions. Traditional research on children relies heavily on the socialization model, which asserts that children's primary role is to learn how to be functioning adults in society (Alanen, 1990). Critics argue that this model is too heavily based in notions of individual development, rather than social interaction (Frønes, 1994), cannot account for change if roles are simply passed from one generation to the next (Lees, 1993), and views children and childhood from adult and social institutional perspectives, not in terms of children's own worlds (Alanen, 1990). In socialization models, childhood is "negatively defined," which means that children are not defined by what they currently *are*, but what they will *be*. Finally, these models place children as passive recipients of adult culture rather than engaged actors within their own cultures.

In contrast, Corsaro (1997) and Thorne (1987) argue that children develop their own cultures and social organizations. Children's culture is not simply based on adult society as the socialization model implies. Rather, children's culture has aspects unique only to them. Mishler (1979), for example, uncovers an elaborate system of trading and bargaining of food among 6-year-olds that is based on ritualized talk and an emerging social structure. This type of trading is not found in adult culture, but is created and maintained solely by the children involved. Similarly, Shade-Poulsen (1995) finds a separate and unique youth culture that uses models appropriated, yet altered significantly, from adult culture. In Algeria, a youth-based music genre called raï was developed, popularized and spread entirely by youth, outside of the official adult-run music industry.

In response to socialization theory, Corsaro (1997) developed the "interpretive reproduction" theoretical approach, which stresses children's unique cultures as they are intersected by the larger social structures of education, family, community, economics, religion, culture, politics, and work. Central to this approach is the importance of collective, collaborative and communal activities in which children negotiate, create, and share cultures with each other and with adults. The theory is interpretive, in that children actively interpret their worlds and adult information in creative and innovative ways. It is reproductive as children are not simply passive recipients of adult socialization and culture, but actively contribute to cultural production and change through their negotiations with adults and in their own peer cultures. In contrast to previous theories of children that focus on individual development and socialization, Corsaro develops a theory emphasizing children's autonomy, agency, collective nature, experiences, play, and the notion of childhood as a social structure.

Group interviewing is ideally suited to follow notions of conceptual autonomy and interpretive reproduction where children occupy their own space and actively create their own cultures and constructions of their worlds. For example, in my research, rather than depending on adult memories and recollections of menstruation that most research has relied on, I explore adolescents' talk surrounding menstruation, their individual and collective interpretations of menstruation, and how menstruation is used in their social interactions as a resource of power, resistance, and agency (Fingerson, 2001). Adolescents construct and interpret menstruation and the body together through peer social interaction and intersecting the larger social structures of family, school, and culture. Although they learn about menstruation from the larger adult world along with their peer interactions, the teens still develop and act within their own unique cultures.

## COLLABORATIVE TALK AND SOCIOLINGUISTICS

Group interviewing provides access to how children and adolescents build their talk together (Eder & Fingerson, 2002). Because group interviews are audio-recorded and often video-recorded, researchers can conduct detailed sociolinguistics analyses of group talk. Teens, for example, not only engage in collective talk, where two or more individuals participate in a conversation, but also in collaborative talk. Collaborative talk is a "cultural routine" in which participants build upon each other's utterances through support or ratification of previous utterances (Corsaro, 1997). It reinforces the group's cohesion and solidarity through the sharing and receiving of views, opinions, and knowledge and through the attempt to reach a shared understanding of a phenomenon (Corsaro, 1997; Eder, 1988; Fingerson, 1999). Collaborative talk builds upon and further strengthens individual and collective interpretations through affirmation and support of a speaker's ideas. In order to have successful collaborative talk, individuals must have shared experiences.

The rich textual data in group interviews are also amenable to sociolinguistic analysis, which can explore the structure of the collaborative talk (Eder & Fingerson, 2002). Older children have been neglected in the study of sociolinguistics (for exception, see Hoyle & Adger, 1998). The focus has traditionally been on infants and young children and their language acquisition and early use (Finegan, 1998).

Sociolinguistics, as Briggs (1986) notes, is the study of language structure and use in society. In particular, sociolinguistics explores language within its social and cultural context and as embedded in larger discourse (Finegan, 1998). It views language as a social resource and examines language in its larger social context (Grimshaw, 2000). Also, sociolinguistics is interested in how social-cultural competence and evaluative orientations are achieved through talk (Grimshaw, 2000). Sociolinguistic analyses are deeply rooted in symbolic interactionism, as language is a symbol to be interpreted through social interaction. Sociolinguistics seeks to uncover the structure of these interpretations. Through sociolinguistic analysis, we can explore what adolescent talk represents, such as how it might fit into power relations, structures of resistance, and concepts of agency.

## MENSTRUAL TALK AS A CASE STUDY

In this paper, I use examples from group interviews conducted on adolescents' attitudes toward and talk surrounding the body and menstruation. For the girls and boys interviewed, menstruation is not simply a personal bodily event. Rather, menstruation is used as a resource in social interaction, for telling stories, and for making connections with others through shared experience. Christensen (2000) finds that children experience their bodies in terms of the social. In describing their bodily functions, children emphasize their own actions and their social interactions with others, rather than simply talking about their bodies as isolated entities. Children think of illness not simply as a bodily phenomena, but rather as a disruption to their everyday activities and routines; a change in their social interactions. Recovery and feeling better are also expressed in terms of the social. For example, one of Christensen's participants, a 7-year-old, said that recovering meant a resumption of her daily activities: "to do as I usually do." She frames her recovery in terms of social interaction, not how her individual body is feeling.

Similar to Christensen's findings among young children, the teens in my research do not focus on the physical bodily functions of menstruation, but rather, the social and personal experiences and consequences of menstruation. For example, girls help each other when they need pads, boys can be sensitive to menstrual symptoms, and, most importantly, both girls and boys share their menstrual experiences and menstrual knowledge with each other in social talk.

The teens are comfortable sharing their menstrual experiences in the group interviews. For example, one girl shares her frustrations with being splashed and getting wet at the pool while on her period. Another talks about how she had cramps during sports practice and the difficulty she had explaining it to her male coach. Girls also share their physical menstrual experiences, such as how heavy or light their flows are. Several girls shared their menarche stories, which often involved feelings of embarrassment. These narratives are often laughed about now in peer interactions, in remembrance and reflection of a time when they were all more inexperienced and unsure. In the group interviews, the girls are very comfortable with even this very intimate level of menstrual talk. Boys often laugh and joke about their female friends' experiences and about their own experiences dealing with their female friends' mood swings. Although the boys are not as comfortable talking about the details of menstruation (in part because they lack knowledge about it), they share their social experiences related to menstruation with each other in the interviews.

The social aspect of menstruation is important for the girls and they enjoy participating in a special, shared menstrual discourse. One of the girls noted in her individual interview how excited she was to get her period because then she could "talk" and "complain" along with the older eighth graders at lunch. Another girl said that she would be happy if she never had to menstruate again, but also thinks that she would "lose something." She enjoys teasing her guy friends about menstruation and she enjoys the funny social interaction that accompanies the experience.

## THE INTERVIEW DESIGN

In designing the interviews, I was interested in the social interaction, the process of shaping and participating in menstrual talk, the conversations and opinions adolescents have about menstruation, and the ways menstruation enters into their social lives. In the data collection, individual interviews were also conducted to explore each teen's individual understanding of menstruation and their individual experiences with menstruation. In order to better interpret the collective and collaborative discussions in which the adolescents are engaging with their peer groups, I also needed to understand their individual histories, family setting, and social context

(Fingerson, 1999). I also wanted to make a personal connection with each participant.

A male research assistant, Paul Namaste Ruggerio, conducted the individual and group interviews with male participants. Paul's help was invaluable as he was able to connect with the boys on the issues of body and menstruation which I, as a female, never could. Other female researchers have interviewed both boys and girls on issues of body, sexuality, and puberty (Martin, 1996), but I believe that the narratives the boys' engaged in with Paul were much more reflective of their "natural" talk than if I had been the one conducting the interview. Just as I was able to bond with the girls, Paul was able to bond with the boys and draw on his own experiences as a male in his interactions with them.

In this research setting, we used only single-gender groups. There is certainly an interconnectedness between boys' and girls' talk, opinions and beliefs about menstruation and body issues. However, boys and girls do not talk about these issues comfortably and honestly in mixed-gender groups in natural settings. Also, boys' discourses are structurally more powerful in mixed-gender interaction and girls may be silenced by their attitudes and talk in a mixed-gender discussion. Finally, boys and girls have different communication styles that may conflict and result in frustrations and misunderstandings (Scott, 2000). In future research, it would be interesting to conduct mixed-gender groups as a point of comparison to the findings in single-gender groups.

After conducting pilot groups to test the questions and format of the interviews, Paul and I interviewed adolescents drawn from on-going community groups in central and southern Indiana ages 14 through 19. Twenty-six girls participated in seven group interviews and 23 individual interviews. Eleven boys participated in two group interviews and 11 individual interviews. The size of the group interviews ranged from two to nine participants. Most of the teens are white while two are biracial and one is a Korean immigrant. All of them have working or middle-class backgrounds. In the individual and group interviews we first asked questions about how teens feel about their bodies, weight, strength, and athleticism; and then we explored how they feel about menstruation, what they know about menstruation, and their experiences with menstruation. Overall, the teens seemed to enjoy participating in the research and enjoyed telling us their stories, both collectively in the group interviews and individually in the individual interviews.

By drawing from existing on-going groups (including community groups, girls' clubs, boys' clubs, and teen councils), the interview groups were composed of teens who knew each other and had a shared history of experiences. The kids come together on a regular basis and have developed relationships with each other in the group over time. These relationships are invaluable in the group interviews as there is an existing shared community of talk. The participants often refer to past shared moments giving evidence of their collective history. Because these groups are on-going, they are as "natural" a setting as can be found for group interviews (Eder & Fingerson, 2002). In group interviews where participants are taken from an existing group of friends or peers, the conversations in the focus group are more indicative of those occurring in a natural setting (Albrecht, Johnson, & Walther, 1993). Also, the interaction in group interviews can elicit more accurate accounts as participants must defend their statements to their peers with whom they interact on a daily basis.

However, even by using on-going groups, the group interview setting is not "natural" as we might find in an ethnographic setting. At the end of the group interviews with the teens, we asked them what they thought about the research interviews and if they would have conversations like this in their real lives. I wanted to assess their comfort level with the interaction and if they thought it was in any way reflective of real life. Often, the girls would first say "no," they would not have conversations like the interview. But then, most would think back and say "yes," and remember specific instances when they had discussed these very same issues with friends. The boys acknowledged that talking about menstruation among other boys is often "taboo. It's like Area 51." ("Area 51" is a highly classified military base in Nevada, subject of many rumors and conspiracy theories.) Yet, they say that they are curious about it and that they would talk about it among close male and female friends and their mothers. They would also joke about it in public. The boys' groups also agreed that they would not bring it up in public themselves, but would certainly talk about it if it came up from an external source, such as a boy with girlfriend problems because "she's PMS-y."

The interview data, both audio- and video-recorded, were transcribed in full. Each utterance in the interviews was transcribed, including fillers such as "uh," "like," "you know," and "mm." Following DeVault (1999), it is important to include the "inelegant" features in these adolescents' talk rather than editing out seemingly extraneous words. Rather than being unnecessary as some researchers have argued (Martin, 1996), these words highlight the structure and distinctiveness of adolescent talk about the body and menstruation. In addition, such fillers can indicate uncertainty and/or discomfort with a particular topic.

## REFLEXIVITY: THE RESEARCHER'S PLACE IN THE INTERVIEW

In an interview, just as with any other social interaction, the participants involved negotiate and construct interpretations and meanings of that interaction. Researchers must be committed to reflexively examining their role in the creation of the data and the interpretations (DeVault, 1999). Thus, it is important to examine the *interviewer's* place in the research context as the researcher affects any data generated, particularly with issues of the body and bodily experience (Zola, 1991). My approach to the research is reflexive, which means that not only do I acknowledge my own academic preconceptions and prejudices, but I also recognize that Paul's and my personal background and history influence the research and my interpretations of that research.

I conducted the individual and group interviews with the girls. I am a tall, white woman. At the time I was 25 years old, normal weight, and not particularly athletic although I lettered in varsity sports in high school and played intramural flag football in graduate school. During the months of interviewing, I began a fitness program of healthy eating and exercise. This made me acutely aware and sensitive of not only my own body, but also the girls' bodies and body views in our discussions of the body, weight, and athleticism. I was born and raised with professional parents in the Minneapolis-St. Paul, Minnesota area. I am straight, married, and my wedding rings were quite visible on my hands. The participants knew I was in graduate school in Sociology and that this project was for my Ph.D. dissertation. They knew the data collected would turn into a book that someday they could read. I also felt I connected well with the girls as I was able to relate to them on several levels, not just as a fellow menstruating woman who has issues with her body. For example, some of the girls were making college plans and I was able to chat with them about colleges, military academies, and experiences at the local university to which many hoped to apply.

Paul conducted all of the individual and group interviews with boys. At the time, he was a second-year graduate student whom I selected as my research assistant because of his extensive experience with youth, his rapport with teens, his interest in education, and his enthusiasm for my particular project and life in general. He was also involved in research on women's infertility so I knew he was familiar with issues of the body. Paul is also very "cool." He was young (age 31 at the time of the interviews), slightly balding and has a goatee. He is self-described as heterosexual, of average male

'Yeah, Me Too!': Adolescent Talk Building in Group Interviews 271

height (slightly shorter than I, in fact), and has an athletic build with a bit extra around the middle. He is from the Boston area and participated in varsity sports both in high school and college. Also, he is very comfortable with and in his body – much more so than I was at the time. Paul was able to connect with the boys on many different levels, which significantly increased his rapport with them. For example, the boys would mention their hobbies or outside interests, such as the Boy Scouts, drama, fencing, baseball, and Paul was able to share some of his own experiences in those areas.

Both Paul and I dressed in casual clothes (e.g., jeans and a t-shirt) similar to what the teens might be wearing themselves. We were conscious in our dress and appearance to make sure that we did not appear as adult authority figures (e.g., we did not carry briefcases!). We attempted to connect with the teens on their own level. During the group interviews, we participated as little as possible to let the teens discuss the issues on their own. However, we did offer our own laughter and occasional comments so the teens would feel comfortable with us as semi-participants, rather than as strict observers. After the "official" part of the interviews were over, we participated with the teens in their talk just as much as any other teen would (such as in Example 3, below). We wanted to "hang out" with the teens as much as possible before and after the interviews to emphasize our status as non-authority figures.

It is important to understand not only our interviewing style, but also our physical characteristics and appearance in order to reflect on how the adolescents may have perceived us. Had we been significantly older, non-white, non-straight, or not particularly "cool," the teens may have responded to us and in the interviews in different ways. The quality of the data we generated with the research participants speaks for the particular type of rapport Paul and I developed with the teens. Their individual and group discussions are extended, lively, and we and the participants had a lot of fun.

The teens shared many personal thoughts and feelings about their bodies with us in the individual and group interviews. I think it was easier for the teens to be honest about their weights, athleticism, and body views with Paul and I because we were young adults. They are adolescents and thus are in an entirely different place in the power structure so in describing and discussing their own bodies, they would not be comparing themselves to us. Rather, they would compare themselves to others in and closer to their own age group. For example, the girls could feel comfortable saying that they think their thighs are too big to me without worrying about my feelings or comparing themselves to me. At the same time, Paul and I are adults and we are the ones with the tape recorders and asking the questions. Although we attempted to minimize power differences as much as possible in the group and individual interviews, we still have to recognize that we are not "one of the gang."

## GROUP INTERVIEWING WITH ADOLESCENTS

In group interviewing, researchers can access how children and adolescents develop and sustain their interpretations of the world. The following sections explore how through group interviewing we can see how girls and boys develop a shared worldview, how they accomplish group talk, and how the girls engage in supportive storytelling.

*Development of a Shared Worldview*

In group talk, the girls and boys share their interpretations of menstruation with each other and develop a shared understanding of menstruation. In her response to the question, what if men could menstruate, Erica shows in her group interview who she feels has the power in society: "If guys could get pregnant, there wouldn't be anything, like, about abortion, like no one would protest or anything, because they'd wa- they would, like, understand why you should be able to have that choice, you know." This line of thinking is continued by the others in the discussion:[1]

**Example 1.** Group Interview (Leslie age 16, Kassie age 16, Lacey age 16, Korrine age 15, Krissy age 16, Erica age 15, Linda age 16)

| | |
|---|---|
| Laura: | Do you think there would be any differences, if guys could menstruate and women couldn't? |
| Leslie: | Yeah. |
| Kassie: | Yeah. |
| Lacey: | It wouldn't be as- |
| Korrine: | Like, there'd be a lot more male products. |
| Kassie: | What? |
| Krissy: | I think you'd get days off work for menstruating? |
| Leslie: | Yeah. |
| Kassie: | Yeah. |

'Yeah, Me Too!': Adolescent Talk Building in Group Interviews 273

Erica: Me, too, yeah, definitely.
Linda: It'd be national take-a-day off for your period law.

These girls recognize the gendered power structure in our society and that it affects their own lives on an everyday level in dealing with menstruation. They analyze their situation and hypothesize that if women were in power, they might even get a day off from work while on their periods. In this section of the discussion, the girls offer several agreements and supportive statements. Lacey attempts to start brainstorming what might be different, but Korrine interrupts her and provides the first idea. Krissy adds her idea and, after more agreements, Linda follows up with an even grander idea.

Later in the discussion, the girls generate a similar mode of brainstorming and supportive agreements as they develop a shared worldview. The girls talk about how they do not like society's secretive and dirty attitudes toward menstruation:

**Example 2.** Group Interview (Kassie age 16, Leslie age 16)

Kassie: I wish we weren't so hush-hush about it.
Leslie: Or about- or like it's dirty.
Kassie: Yeah, like it's some dirty thing. Like, what's that book? What is it? Carrie? Carrie.

Kassie refers to the popular Stephen King novel and film, *Carrie*, which describes Carrie's menarche and how Carrie's mother defines it as dirty, gross, and sexual. The girls do not see menstruation as dirty or unclean and wish society, including the mass media, felt differently about menstruation. Through group talk, the girls develop their *own* views on menstruation. They reject the dominant culture's definition of menstruation as dirty and together, the girls develop a different worldview.

Through group talk, the boys learn from one another about menstruation, something they can only experience through social interaction. In the following group interview, the boys learn about menstruation from each other. Paul asked at the end of the group interview if the boys had any questions about menstruation or any of the topics they have talked about during the discussion. In this group, Jim asks the first question:

**Example 3.** Group Interview (Jim age 18, Matt age 17, Derek age 19, Dave age 15)

Jim: What's with the chocolate thing? That's always... Is it a craving?
Paul: That's actually its actually, I think it's mainly the sugar.
Jim: It's the sugar need? So you can give skittles and they'll be fine? He he.
Paul: Probably yeh.
Matt: Here's some skittles, I hope you're fine in a couple of hours, he he.
Paul: You never know, maybe there's just something special about chocolate.
Jim: I don't know. It s just =
Paul: = I know what you mean.
Jim: I've been around like my aunts and girlfriend and friends of hers and people I know saying I need some chocolate and I'm like 'No, no. Go away. I don't want to talk to you now because you're going to bring up something about something that happened.'
Paul: Oh, so you're assume if they're asking for chocolate.
Jim: Well, not necessarily. I'm just saying, I can just hearing it coming before it even starts out. And some of them will be like 'Man I need some chocolate, I have that craving because its that time.' I'm like okay here's my candy bar, leave.
Matt: Here's your candy bar, get away from me.

Together, the boys in this group try to further develop their limited information about menstruation and understand why girls respond to menstruation and symptoms in the way that they do. Paul participates with the boys in this talk sequence as they all construct a shared view on menstruation. This example shows boys talking more positively about menstruation. However, many boys learn from each other about how menstruation can be annoying and to try to avoid girls who are menstruating. Many boys often report that girls complain about getting their periods and if they are experiencing menstrual symptoms, they often take out this frustration on the boys and get "pissy." When Paul asked what the first word or phrase the boys thought of when he says the word "menstruation," the boys in one group interview said "Girls getting pissy" and "PMS." In talking with other boys, the male respondents offer advice and strategies to them on how to deal with the negative interactions with menstruating girls.

## Accomplishing Group Talk: Supportive Talk

Group interviewing can capture how adolescents accomplish their talk in groups. It is important to note that the boys' group talk was not as developed as the girls' group talk. This is because for boys, menstruation is a delicate issue because of their discomfort and uncertainty. The girls are more comfortable with the topic and can develop elaborate talk in their group interviews. However, even in the talk about the body (before we discussed menstruation), the boys' talk was not as collaborative or based on storytelling as the girls' was. Given the data I collected on the body and menstruation, there is no way to compare the boys' and girls' talk on this level. Future research might explore an issue specific to boys' experiences or an issue that is less gendered to compare the structure of this type of talk among girls and boys.

Girls rely largely on supportive forms of talk. This is discussed further below in terms of supportive stories, but briefly, the following example highlights a particularly strong moment of supportive talk. In their peer interactions, most of the girls share experiences they have with menstruation. They talk about their own experiences and learn of their peers' experiences. This sharing helps the girls understand menstruation and be reassured that their experiences are "normal" and shared by others their age. In one of the group interviews, the girls share their symptoms with each other during their discussion about menstruation. Each girl describes her symptoms to the group. This is a particularly salient moment of talk as this sequence of talk was not in response to any of my questions, rather, it emerged out of their own discussion.

**Example 4.** Group Interview (Korrine age 15, Greta age 15, Kassie age 16, Krissy age 16, Lacey age 16, Leslie age 16)

| | |
|---|---|
| Korrine: | No one knows when I'm on my period. It doesn't affect me at all. |
| Greta: | No one knows unless I tell them. |
| Kassie: | I'm just not comfortable while I am. |
| Korrine: | Yeah. |
| Krissy: | I get hungry. |

| | |
|---|---|
| Kassie: | So, the only thing tha- |
| Lacey: | I don't eat during my period. |
| Greta: | Neither do I. I'm not hungry at all. |
| Korrine: | I lay on the floor and cry when I have mine. |
| Lacey: | I get sore. |
| Leslie: | I've got some cramps badly. |

In group talk about menstruation, these girls tell each other their experiences and learn about the variety of ways menstruation, a physiological phenomenon they share, is experienced differentially by the girls. They also reconfirm that their own experiences are "normal" as others in the group share them. The girls socially construct menstruation as something that has symptoms, which are normal and experienced by others. They build their talk around their shared experiences and by doing so, construct themselves as part of the group of menstruating women. They implicitly affirm an experience that boys do not share.

In this discourse, the girls share a supportive style of talk as evidenced by the repetitions, agreements, and expanded remarks. Throughout the interviews in this research, much of the menstrual talk shared by girls is based in such supportive talk. Through repetition, Greta affirms Korrine's statement that "no one knows" when they are on their periods. Korrine and Greta both show agreement through Korrine's "Yeah" and Greta's "Neither do I" statements. Finally, Lacey and Leslie both expand on Korrine's statement of her painful symptoms in the last three lines with "I get sore" and "I've got some cramps badly." The girls, in this sequence in particular, use their talk to support each other and create a shared community of experience surrounding menstruation.

Also, as the talk in this example progresses, the symptoms the girls report feeling escalate in severity, as if the girls are engaging in "one-upmanship" in cataloguing their list of symptoms. Interestingly, Korrine initially says that her period "doesn't affect me at all" but then, in order to take part in this "one-upmanship," she says that she lays on the floor in tears when she menstruates. This is supportive of the other girls' talk, but also brings in the competitive element where each girl tries to report the most severe symptoms. This parallels an experience that Katie, a girl in another group, shares in her individual interview where she says she and her friends tell the equivalent of fishing stories, vying for who has the worst symptoms. As the girls continue their talk beyond the transcript reported here, they discuss how long their periods are and talk about who has had the longest period.

## Girls' Supportive Stories

The girls interviewed told stories about talking about menstruation with friends, sharing their symptoms and their strategies for managing menstruation, talking about their cycles and how they feel during their periods, sharing stories about going to the gynecologist, talking about which products they use, and sharing stories about humorous menstrual experiences. As Thompson (1995) found in her interviews with girls about romance, sexuality, and relationships, the narratives they told sounded almost rehearsed. This is because they are rehearsed, in a sense, as they are told over and over again with their friends.

Group interviews are excellent ways of capturing these stories. In the girls' group interviews, their talk about menstruation is comfortable and it is clear that this talk is not unique to the group interview setting, but that they share these same stories within their peer cultures. The girls also often share others' stories in the group interviews, which shows that they talk about body and menstruation in everyday conversations. Otherwise, they would not know others' stories. By engaging in storytelling, the girls in the following examples celebrate empowerment, commiserate with one another in embarrassing moments, and learn from each other how to manage menstruation.

*Empowerment Stories*
In the following transcript, the girls talk about how their male teachers are "scared of" menstruation. Kassie, recognizing male teachers' discomfort, says that menstruation is "your defense toward any male teacher." This example shows not only how these men negatively respond to menstruating girls, but also how the girls use that power as a "defense" against this construction. This points to the complexity of power in menstrual discourse and the agency girls can develop because of menstruation.

**Example 5.** Group Interview (Lacey age 16, Linda age 16, Leslie age 16, Kassie age 16, Korrine age 15, Greta age 15)

| | |
|---|---|
| Lacey: | 'Yeah.' If I ever get to class, like, you know, late, and my teacher's, like, 'Where were you?' He doesn't li- he hates my guts, mostly. |
| Linda: | Who? |
| Lacey: | Mr. Pease. I was like, 'I was at the nurse.' He was, like, 'Where's your purs- your pass?' I was like, 'I had to get something.' 'Oh, okay.' |

Leslie: They're scared of it. It's so funny.
Kassie: Oh, I know. It's like your defense toward any male teacher.
Leslie: If they're like, 'Why did you skip class?' 'I lost the string.' [group laughs]
Kassie: Yeah. No, seriously, that's what Mr. Brinstein, I came in, like, twenty minutes late one day, and he was like, 'Where have you been?' And he hated me, and I was just, like, 'I had a female problem.' He said, 'Okay.' [group laughs]
Leslie: But one day, he was like, I was like, 'Can I go to the bathroom?' He was like, 'Why do you have to go to the bathroom?' I was like, 'Because I have to go to the bathroom.' He was like, 'Oh my gosh, okay,' and he, like, throws the pass at me, and he's like, 'Go, go.' [insistently]
Kassie: When they know you're on your period, they're, like, afraid to make eye contact with you, like they're going to catch it or something.
Korrine: It's contagious.
Greta: Contagious PMS.
Lacey: This girl that sits behind me in journalism, she said that one of her teachers wouldn't let her go. She was like, 'If you don't let me go, I'll bleed all over your classroom.' [group laughs]

In this example, Lacey starts with her story in Mr. Pease's class. Leslie offers support for Lacey's story by adding that male teachers are "scared of menstruation" and affirming Lacey's contribution by saying the topic is "so funny." Kassie then agrees with Leslie and provides new information that the girls can use menstruation as a source of power in their interactions. After Leslie's agreement, Kassie adds her own story about Mr. Brinstein's class. Leslie then adds yet another story, also in this same class. Kassie, Korrine, and Greta all provide support and add a new word ("contagious") to the discussion. Lacey continues and adds yet another story from another class. Through this collaborative talk, we can see how the girls use their group talk as a "supportive-stories" session as each adds another story in support of the topic, in this case how male teachers are "scared" of menstruation. The girls analyze their experiences and share ideas on why the teachers respond the way they do. The girls collectively try to understand and interpret their worlds.

### Embarrassing Moments

Sharing embarrassing moments in group talk helps form a community of women and shared experience for the girls to belong to. Many girls enjoy sharing stories about moments that at the time were very embarrassing, but now they can laugh about their experiences as they are wiser and more experienced with menstruation and their bodies. They laugh at their experiences from when they were younger and were less sure of the process of menstruation and how to manage menstruation.

During school hours, girls must manage their menstrual products and many girls tell narratives about handling this responsibility. In one group interview, the girls collaboratively share an embarrassing story about unsuccessfully concealing their menstrual products:

**Example 6.** Group Interview (Greta age 15, Leslie age 16, Lacey age 16, Kassie age 16)

| | |
|---|---|
| Greta: | Wasn't like Sue Heinz or Allison or somebody that was in eighth grade algebra, and- |
| Leslie: | That would be me. |
| Lacey: | And, in her folder- |
| Leslie: | Tell it. |
| Lacey: | I almost forgot about that. |
| Greta: | Who was I talking to- |
| Lacey: | I don't know, but it was. |
| Greta: | Sue was, like, 'Can I have the English notes?' or something. I was like, 'Sure.' So, I rip out my folder, and my pad had somehow, it was just loose in the bag, it had gotten stuck in the folder. So, I was li- I think there was somebody between me and Sue. I think it was a guy, too, and I was like, 'Can you pass this to Sue?' And it, like, falls out. It hit her in the head, too, it, like, it just flew to her forehead. |
| Lacey: | I was looking ( ). And I was like, 'Well, here it is,' pull out my pad, and it flies across, 'That's mine.' I had to, like, go over, like, pick it up. It was so embarrassing. |
| Kassie: | You know what they did to ( ) Freshman year. She was sending one to me, so I was like, 'That's it.' So, I reached in my bag, and it was in Mr. Berry's room. And, like, someone, I don't know, we were sitting there doing class work or something, and I pulled it out, and I threw a pad across the room, and it landed on her desk. She was like [ ], but, like, no one else around her |

|  |  |
|---|---|
| | noticed. And, then, remember that when I pulled that pad out, and I was just like, 'Pa-ching.' |
| Leslie: | You got me. |
| Kassie: | Oh, did it hit you? |
| Leslie: | No, it hit my desk or- and I was like, 'Here.' |
| Kassie: | Yeah, and then everyone was like, 'What the-?' It was funny. |

This sequence is a storytelling session where one story builds upon another, all in the mode of supportive talk. First, Greta brings up a story that Leslie and Lacey immediately recognize. Greta and Lacey collaboratively tell the story and share their experiences in this embarrassing moment. This story reminds Kassie of a similar story that she shares. The first story is particularly embarrassing as it shows instances when pads or tampons end up where they are not supposed to be: in public space. However in the second story, Kassie challenges the non-public nature of menstrual products and tosses a pad to a friend during class. She laughs at the incident precisely because she broke the norms of handling menstrual products. In both of these stories, the girls negotiate if pads in public spaces is embarrassing (as Lacey evaluates the first story) or funny (as Kassie evaluates the second story). In contrast to Lacey's feelings, Kassie thinks that having pads out in public should not be embarrassing and actively resists this embarrassment. This parallels the theme of Examples 1 and 2 where the girls develop and negotiate their own unique worldviews that are sometimes in opposition to dominant culture. Also, in each of the stories, it is this evaluation of the story as embarrassing or funny that marks the end of one story and signals that another line of talk may begin.

*Sharing Personal Strategies*
Many girls also share strategies for handling menstruation with their peers. Through their storytelling, the girls learn from each other about ways of dealing with and managing menstruation. In this next example, we can see how girls share several stories and explain their stories to each other in group interviews. Rather than one girl explaining a story to one interviewer, the girl is held accountable to her story by others in the group. Additionally, through the stories told in this group interview, the girls learn about how to use tampons. This example in particular replicates a natural mode of talk where girls share and compare information on topics of interest to them. In this group, the girls collaboratively talk about tampons, problems they have had, and what girls should and should not do when using tampons.

**Example 7.** Group Interview (Kassie age 16, Erica age 15, Leslie age 16, Lacey age 16, Greta age 15, Linda age 16)

Kassie: I remember the first time I actually got one [a tampon] in right, and, like, I fol- it was a really painful experience. I was like, 'Ah.' [noise like in pain] It really hurt a lot.

Erica: One of my mom's friends, when she was younger [interruption from mother] Anyway, one of my mom's friends was, like, after she hadn't been on her period, like, very long, she put in a tampon, she was like twelve, she put in a tampon and forgot it was in there, and then later, she put in [another one.

Leslie: [another one.
Erica: Yeah.
Lacey: I've heard about that.
Laura: Who?
Erica: And, like, she was, one of my mom's friends, and she, like, forgot about it, and then, like, after a couple days, like after two or three days, it really started to hurt, and she went to the doctor to see what was wrong =

Leslie: How could you forget?
Erica: = and they had to, like, surgically remove it.
Kassie: Oh.
Greta: She had two tampons in there, and she forgot about both of them?
Erica: No, one. She put one in, forgot it was there =
Lacey: Put the other one in
Erica: = and put the other one in, another one over it.
Linda: Well, people on my soccer team last year used to put two in at the same time, just because
Kassie: Just because it would work.
Lacey: Oh my God. Really?
Erica: Oh my God, are you kidding me.
Leslie: Oh my gosh.
Laura: What happened, what?
Linda: People, like, on my soccer team used to put two in at the same time, just because.
Laura: Ow.

| | |
|---|---|
| Kassie: | Because when you're running around = |
| Linda: | Right. |
| Kassie: | = it can- it starts to come out. |
| Linda: | When you play soccer and, like- |
| Laura: | The tampon starts to come out? |
| Kassie: | Yeah, it's weird, it's gross. And you're just like, 'Shit.' Yeah, I know a lot of people that did that. |
| Greta: | Two in, that's bad. |
| Laura: | No, I don't even- |
| Kassie: | Yeah, because you can't use the big ones when you play soccer, it's just uncomfortable. You have to use the little ones. |
| Greta: | There's, uh, uncomfortable normal. |
| Kassie: | I don't think I have that much room up there. |

In this sequence, the girls share their experiences with tampons and learn from each others stories. Responses such as Lacey's "oh my God, really?" and Leslie's "How could you forget?" indicate that the story being told is something new that the girls learn about and actively respond to. Also, the girls share several narratives in this sequence, with one story reminding another girl of a story and so forth.

First, Kassie talks about how putting in her first tampon was painful. Erica is then reminded of a story she heard from her mom about a painful tampon experience and in relating this story, the other girls learn about how not to use tampons. When Greta asks a question about the story, Lacey is able to collaboratively respond along with Erica. This story about how tampons can be dangerous prompts Linda to talk about girls on her soccer team who put in two tampons at one time. Kassie completes Linda's sentence with "just because it would work." In this story, this use of tampons is common and "normal" for the soccer players. The first stories about tampons as problems promote talk about tampon-use strategies. In the sequence, Kassie offers a second sentence completion to Linda's "because" when she says "because when you're running around." Linda and Kassie both explain why this strategy of managing menstruation is used by the girls on the soccer team. Kassie expands on the menstrual strategy by saying the soccer players use two small tampons, not two large ones. Later in the sequence, both Greta and I show through talk how we learn about the possibilities of using more than one tampon at once from the story. Kassie concludes the narration by agreeing with our learning saying, "I don't think I have that much room up there."

The girls in this sequence tell stories that in terms of content, are used to share strategies for managing menstruation, and in terms of structure, are formed as supportive collaborative talk. The collaborative stories give both practical information on tampon use and emotional support for issues with menstruation. Together through their talk, the girls construct their views on tampons and what happens when girls use tampons. They negotiate what works and what does not work when wearing tampons. In their talk, they show the process of their learning and construction of tampon use. In addition, they establish what is "normal" by starting the talk with a scary story and ending it with the wearing of two tampons at once, which is "normal." Tampon use is a highly salient issue for many adolescent girls as it deals with the inside of their body and their vaginas, areas they are uncomfortable with and know very little about. However, talking about menstruation and tampons is one of the few spaces where women feel free to talk about their reproductive anatomy in very intimate ways.

*Stories and Supportive Talk*

Plummer (1995) develops a "sociology of stories" in which he investigates the structures and formats of telling stories. He argues that stories are not simply texts, rather, they are "social actions embedded in social worlds" (p. 17). We use stories to construct our meanings and understandings of our lives. When examining stories, Plummer asks why people tell the stories, why they do not tell them, how they select their language to articulate their experiences, how they find and assert their voices, and how the listener hears and interprets the story. He is concerned not with just what the teller is saying, but also the social processes involved in the telling. Stories are socially produced in distinct social contexts by the teller who is an embodied person experiencing his or her everyday life. For Plummer, stories are both symbolic interactions and political processes as they show the power and agency in the tellers' lives. The listeners are the interpretive community for the story and they collectively construct their understandings of the story with the teller.

In their interviews, girls share elaborate stories with each other and with me, both individually and collaboratively. These stories the girls share address two of Plummer's questions derived from his sociology of stories. First, what are the social processes of producing and consuming stories, how do people construct their stories, why do people tell the stories, and how are the listeners interpreting those stories? Second, what are the social roles that stories play, how do the stories affect the lives of people, and how do they both conserve and resist structures in society? In the interviews, girls share with each other their stories of empowerment, menarche, embarrassing moments, and strategies for managing menstruation. These stories are shared in collective and often collaborative talk and are interpreted by the listeners as supportive and affirming of their own experiences. The girls in the examples shown above tell their stories in a supportive manner to offer emotional support and practical strategies for menstruation.

Through telling these stories the girls construct their understandings and interpretations of menstruation both in the telling of the story and the reactions of others to the story. The girls construct a community of shared experience through sharing their narratives. Plummer (1995, p. 174) contends that "stories need communities to be heard, but communities themselves are also built through story telling. *Stories gather people around them*: they have to attract audiences, and these audiences may then start to build a common perception, a common language, a commonality" [italics original]. O'Grady and Wansbrough (1997, p. 61) agree and find this holds true particularly for women's experience with menstruation saying that, "*Together* – telling our stories, listening and learning – this is how we women come to understand the secrets of our bodies" [italics original]. In this research, the girls in the interviews form supportive communities by talking about their menstrual experiences and through group interviewing, researchers can capture such storytelling sequences.

## CONCLUSION

In their talk during the group interviews, the girls and boys show how they differentially experience and construct menstruation in their social interactions. The teens interpret menstruation based on their own experiences and use these interpretations in their group talk and thereby reproduce them in their teen cultures. These menstrual constructions are affected by the wider world such as from discussions with adults, other family members, and talk in school, but they are created and negotiated by the teens themselves within their peer cultures and group talk.

As they share their menstrual stories and strategies using a supportive talk structure, the girls form a community of mutual understanding and experience. When girls tell menstrual stories, they constitute themselves as girls, as women, and as female. Their gender identities are reaffirmed as they discuss a set of experiences they share because they are women. For girls in particular, the way the story is told and received connects them to their identities. Boys also create their sense of self and identity through sharing menstrual experiences. They affirm their gendered identities as men, as non-menstruants, as those who must respond to and interact with women who undergo a physical process that is not entirely clear to them.

These examples highlight how group interviewing can be used to capture how children and adolescents develop a shared worldview, accomplish their group talk, and develop supportive stories. These are aspects of talk that teens might also use in other contexts, such as divorce, family problems, or issues of sexuality. Teens benefit from sharing these experiences with their peers to gain understanding of their own lives and their peers' lives. Any aspect of teens' lives that are sensitive and salient might not easily be accessed through ethnography, but are often talked about in peer group settings.

Thus, as shown in these examples of teens talking about menstruation, group interviewing is an effective method for: understanding how teens develop a shared understanding of salient issues in their worlds; accessing more sensitive issues that would not necessarily come up in ethnography (such as in a school or youth group); and performing sociolinguistics analysis so we can understand not just *what* teens are saying, but *how* they accomplish their talk.

## ACKNOWLEDGMENTS

I thank Katherine Brown Rosier and the anonymous reviewer for their helpful comments on earlier drafts of this manuscript. This paper benefited from conversations and collaborations with Donna Eder, Bill Corsaro, and Brian Powell. A version of this paper was presented at the 2002 annual meetings of the Midwest Sociological Association.

## NOTES

1. Transcribing conventions:... omitted text; - word that was cut off by next speaker; [ overlapping speech; = continued speech/latching; [word] explanatory information for reader; (...) inaudible speech; (word) barely audible speech with guessed word; ((pause)) a noticeable pause in the speaker's speech.

# REFERENCES

Alanen, L. (1990). Rethinking socialization, the family and childhood. *Sociological Studies of Child Development, 3*, 13–28.
Albrecht, T. L., Johnson, G. M., & Walther, J. B. (1993). Understanding communication processes in focus groups. In: D. L. Morgan (Ed.), *Successful focus groups: Advancing the state of the art* (pp. 51–64). Newbury Park, CA: Sage.
Briggs, C. L. (1986). *Learning how to ask: A sociolinguistic appraisal of the role of the interview in social science research.* New York: Cambridge University Press.
Charon, J. M. (1998). *Symbolic interactionism: An introduction, an interpretation, an integration.* Upper Saddle River, NJ: Prentice-Hall.
Christensen, P. H. (2000). Childhood and the cultural constitution of vulnerable bodies. In: A. Prout (Ed.), *The body, childhood and society* (pp. 38–59). Houndmills, Great Britain: MacMillan Press.
Christensen, P. H., & James, A. (2000). Childhood diversity and commonality: Some methodological insights. In: P. H. Christensen & A. James (Eds), *Research with children: Perspectives and practices.* London: Falmer Press.
Corsaro, W. A. (1996). Transitions in early childhood: The promise of comparative, longitudinal ethnography. In: R. Jessor, A. Colby & R. Schweder (Eds), *Ethnography and human development* (pp. 419–457). Chicago: University of Chicago Press.
Corsaro, W. A. (1997). *The sociology of childhood.* Thousand Oaks, CA: Pine Forge Press.
DeVault, M. L. (1999). *Liberating method: Feminism and social research.* Philadelphia: Temple University Press.
Eder, D. (1988). Building cohesion through collaborative narration. *Social Psychology Quarterly, 51*, 225–235.
Eder, D., & Fingerson, L. (2002). Interviewing children and adolescents. In: J. F. Gubrium & J. A. Holstein (Eds), *Handbook of interview research.* Thousand Oaks, CA: Sage.
Finegan, E. (1998). Series forward. In: S. M. Hoyle & C. T. Adger (Eds), *Kids talk: Strategic language use in later childhood* (pp. vii–viii). New York: Oxford University Press.
Fingerson, L. (1999). Active viewing: Girls' interpretations of family television programs. *Journal of Contemporary Ethnography, 28*, 389–418.
Fingerson, L. (2001). *Social construction, power, and agency in adolescent menstrual talk.* Unpublished doctoral dissertation, Indiana University, Bloomington.
Frønes, I. (1994). Dimensions of childhood. In: J. Qvortrup, M. Bardy, G. Sgritta & H. Wintersberger (Eds), *Childhood matters: Social theory, practice and politics* (pp. 1–24). Aldershot, UK: Avebury.
Grimshaw, A. D. (2000). Sociolinguistics. In: E. F. Borgatta & R. J. V. Montgomery (Eds), *Encyclopedia of sociology* (pp. 2894–2912). New York: Macmillan Reference.
Hoyle, S. M., & Adger, C. T. (1998). *Kids talk: Strategic language use in later childhood.* New York: Oxford University Press.
Lees, S. (1993). *Sugar and spice: Sexuality and adolescent girls.* London: Penguin Books.
Martin, K. (1996). *Puberty, sexuality, and the self: Girls and boys at adolescence.* New York: Routledge.
Mayall, B. (2000). Conversations with children: Working with generational issues. In: P. Christensen & A. James (Eds), *Research with children: Perspectives and practices* (pp. 120–135). London: Falmer Press.
Mead, G. H. (1934). *Mind, self and society.* Chicago: University of Chicago Press.

Mishler, E. (1979). "Won't you trade cookies with the popcorn?": The talk of trades among six year olds. In: O. Garnica & M. King (Eds), *Language, children, and society: The effects of social factors on children's learning to communicate* (pp. 21–36). Elmsford, NY: Pergamon.
O'Grady, K., & Wansbrough, P. (1997). *Sweet secrets: Stories of menstruation.* Toronto: Second Story Press.
Plummer, K. (1995). *Telling sexual stories: Power, change and social worlds.* London: Routledge.
Qvortrup, J. (1991). *Childhood as a social phenomenon.* Vienna, Austria: European Centre for Social Welfare Policy and Research.
Qvortrup, J. (1994). Childhood matters: An introduction. In: J. Qvortrup, M. Bardy, G. Sgritta & H. Wintersberger (Eds), *Childhood matters: Social theory, practice and politics* (pp. 1–24). Aldershot, UK: Avebury.
Scott, J. (2000). Children as respondents: The challenge for quantitative methods. In: P. Christensen & A. James (Eds), *Research with children: Perspectives and practices* (pp. 98–119). London: Falmer Press.
Shade-Poulsen, M. (1995). The power of love: Raï music and youth in Algeria. In: V. Amit-Talai & H. Wulff (Eds), *Youth cultures: A cross-cultural perspective.* London: Routledge.
Thompson, S. (1995). *Going all the way: Teenage girls' tales of sex, romance, and pregnancy.* New York: Hill and Wang.
Thorne, B. (1987). Re-visioning women and social change: Where are the children? *Gender & Society, 1,* 85–109.
Zola, I. K. (1991). Bringing our bodies and ourselves back in: Reflections on a past, present, and future "medical sociology". *Journal of Health and Social Behavior, 32,* 1–16.

# ABOUT THE AUTHORS

**Julie E. Artis**, Associate Professor of Sociology at DePaul University, received her Ph.D. in Sociology from Indiana University in 1999. Her research interests include family, law, and child well-being. Her recent work has appeared in *Journal of Marriage and Family, Law and Society Review*, and *Violence Against Women*. She is currently investigating how family structure and parental resources influence child cognitive and psycho-social outcomes.

**Eric P. Baumer** received his Ph.D. in Sociology from the University at Albany, State University of New York in 1999 and is currently an Associate Professor in the Department of Criminology and Criminal Justice at the University of Missouri, St. Louis. His research is concerned primarily with how social structural and cultural features of communities affect individual behavior. He has examined this issue empirically in multilevel studies of the influence of neighborhood characteristics on individual-level outcomes, in macrolevel studies of urban crime levels and trends, and in case studies of crime and social control in Iceland and Malta.

**Ingrid E. Castro** received her Ph.D. in Sociology from Northeastern University and is an Assistant Professor at SUNY Potsdam where she teaches such courses as Sociology of Education, Social Problems, Sociology of the Family, and Sociology of Film. During her graduate years in the Sociology Department at Northeastern University she completed Graduate Certificates in Gender Studies and Cinema Studies. She has been the recipient of numerous research fellowships, including the American Sociological Association's Minority Fellowship in both Mental Health and General Sociology.

**Janet Enke** received her Ph.D. in Sociology from Indiana University, Bloomington. She is currently Chair of the Social Science Department at Metropolitan State University in St. Paul, Minnesota. Her earlier work focused on social relations and the peer culture of adolescent girls. She is exploring new directions for research.

**Laura Fingerson** is an Assistant Professor of Sociology at the University of Wisconsin-Milwaukee, where she started after earning her Ph.D. from

Indiana University. Her substantive work focuses on how adolescents use the body in their peer-based, gendered social interactions and she explores both qualitative and quantitative methodologies. She has forthcoming publications (in *Childhood* and an edited volume) and a book manuscript (under review) on how teens use the body, specifically menstruation, in their social lives. Other adolescence-related publications are in the *Journal of Family Issues, Journal of Contemporary Ethnography*, and the *Handbook of Interview Research* (Sage) and the *Handbook of Social Psychology* (Kluwer-Plenum). Her upcoming work will explore how teens make their food and physical activity decisions in their peer groups. She also is interested in how incoming college freshmen navigate the transition to adulthood.

**Roberta Goldberg** is a Professor of Sociology at Trinity University in Washington, DC. She earned her Ph.D. from American University. Her recent research focuses on international adoption, and she has published several articles on families adopting children from Romania. Currently, she is conducting research on families adopting school-age children from Russia. She is in the process of analyzing data from a recent survey on this experience. Her earlier research includes her book, *Organizing Women Office Workers: Dissatisfaction, Consciousness, and Action*. Goldberg teaches courses on sociology of the family, inequality and theory.

**David A. Kinney** received his Ph.D. in Sociology from Indiana University-Bloomington and did post-doctoral work at the University of Chicago. He is currently Professor of Sociology and Faculty Advisor for the Youth Studies Minor at Central Michigan University where he received the Provost's Award for Outstanding Research and Creative Activity. His publications have appeared in *Sociology of Education, New Directions for Child and Adolescent Development* (Jossey-Bass), *American Behavioral Scientist*, and the *Handbook of Symbolic Interactionism* (Rowman-Littlefield) among others. He currently serves on the Council of the Sociology of Education Section of the American Sociological Association and most recently collaborated with university students and youth attending an alternative high school on a community–university partnership designed to increase the numbers of first-generation college students.

**Amy Lutz** received her Ph.D. in Sociology from the University at Albany, State University of New York in 2002 and is currently Assistant Professor of Sociology at Syracuse University. She recently served as a Spencer Post-doctoral Fellow at the Center for Social Organization of Schools at Johns

Hopkins University. Her research examines the ways in which social, demographic, and geographic contexts affect educational achievement and attainment, as well as immigrant integration into host societies.

**Janice McCabe** is a doctoral student in the Department of Sociology at Indiana University. With the support of the National Science Foundation and the Association for the Study of Higher Education/Lumina Foundation, her dissertation uses in-depth individual interviews, focus groups, and egocentric network data on friendship to examine how students navigate the academic–social divide in college life at a large, predominantly white university. She is particularly interested in the relationship between academic and social life and ethnicity, gender, and student organizations. She recently has published a chapter with Donna Eder on the role of friends and peers in school in *Educating Adolescents: Challenges and Strategies*, edited by Tim Urdan and Frank Pajares, and an article on feminist self-identification among U.S. women and men in *Gender & Society*, among others. She also is part of a Kinsey Institute research team that is updating and extending the original Kinsey studies on sexuality.

**Diane M. Rodgers** is a doctoral candidate in the Department of Sociology at the University of Missouri-Columbia. Her research interests are social movements, theory, organizations, and historical sociology. Her other publications on social movements have appeared in *The Sociological Quarterly*, *Teaching Sociology* and the *Encyclopedia of Leadership*.

**Katherine Brown Rosier** is an Associate Professor of Sociology at Central Michigan University, where she has recently been awarded both the University's Excellence in Teaching Award, and the Provost's Award for Outstanding Research and Creative Activity. In addition to her recent work on earlier volumes of *Sociological Studies of Children and Youth*, she published a monograph entitled *Mothering Inner-city Children: The Early School Years* with Rutgers University Press in 2000, and other publications have appeared in *The Journal of Contemporary Ethnography*, *Human Development*, *The Journal of Comparative Family Studies*, *Review of Religious Research*, and several other journals and edited volumes. While maintaining her longstanding interest in the experiences of low-income African American children and families, she is also developing her interest in family policy, the Marriage Movement, and the American Religious Right. With colleague Scott L. Feld, she has written several articles on Louisiana's Covenant Marriage innovation.

## ABOUT THE AUTHORS

**Greg Scott**, Assistant Professor of Sociology at DePaul University in Chicago, Illinois, received his doctorate in Sociology in 1998 from the University of California at Santa Barbara. From 1995 to 2000, he served as Director of Research and Associate Director of the Illinois Attorney General's Gang Crime Prevention Center. There he conducted and supervised primary and evaluative research on prevention and intervention programs designed to further enhance local community capacity for responding to crime, delinquency, gang activity, and a host of associated issues. Since arriving at DePaul University in 2000, he has conducted quantitative, qualitative, and ethnographic research on injection drug use (hepatitis B vaccination clinical trials, HIV/AIDS transmission, opiate overdose, and sterile syringe exchange efforts), the relationship between street gangs and the reintegration of ex-offenders, and on community-based efforts to mobilize adolescent involvement in promoting social tolerance and combating bigotry and prejudice. Currently, he spends his time in the field working on an ethnographic study that documents the confluence of public health, culture, social organization, and law in "The Yard," a long-standing encampment of homeless injection drug users on Chicago's west side.

**Scott J. South** is a Professor of Sociology at the University at Albany, State University of New York. He received his Ph.D. from the University of Texas at Austin in 1982. His recent research focuses on the impact of migration and neighborhood context on adolescent behavior, racial and ethnic differences in geographic mobility and neighborhood attainment, and changing patterns of marriage and divorce. His recent publications have appeared in *the American Sociological Review, the American Journal of Sociology, Social Forces, Demography*, and the *Journal of Marriage and Family*.

**Linda M. Waldron** is an Assistant Professor in the Sociology Department at Christopher Newport University in Virginia. Prior to that, she worked as a TV News Producer in Atlanta. She completed her Ph.D. at Syracuse University with the support of an American Fellowship from the American Association of University Women, and a Mass Media Fellowship from the American Association for the Advancement of Science. Her dissertation is titled, "In the Wake of Columbine: How Youth Make Meaning of Violence, Schooling and the Media" (2002). She also holds an M.A. in Television/Radio/Film from the Newhouse School of Communications. She is a qualitative researcher, specializing in studies about children and youth, education, race–class–gender inequalities and the media.

# SET UP A CONTINUATION ORDER TODAY!

Did you know that you can set up a continuation order on all Elsevier-JAI series and have each new volume sent directly to you upon publication? For details on how to set up a **continuation order**, contact your nearest regional sales office listed below.

To view related series in Sociology, please visit:

## www.elsevier.com/sociology

**The Americas**
Customer Service Department
11830 Westline Industrial Drive
St. Louis, MO 63146
USA
**US customers:**
Tel: +1 800 545 2522 (Toll-free number)
Fax: +1 800 535 9935
**For Customers outside US**:
Tel: +1 800 460 3110 (Toll-free number).
Fax: +1 314 453 7095
usbkinfo@elsevier.com

**Europe, Middle East & Africa**
Customer Service Department
Linacre House
Jordan Hill
Oxford OX2 8DP
UK
Tel: +44 (0) 1865 474140
Fax: +44 (0) 1865 474141
eurobkinfo@elsevier.com

**Japan**
Customer Service Department
2F Higashi Azabu, 1 Chome Bldg
1-9-15 Higashi Azabu, Minato-ku
Tokyo 106-0044
Japan
Tel: +81 3 3589 6370
Fax: +81 3 3589 6371
books@elsevierjapan.com

**APAC**
Customer Service Department
3 Killiney Road #08-01
Winsland House I
Singapore 239519
Tel: +65 6349 0222
Fax: +65 6733 1510
asiainfo@elsevier.com

**Australia & New Zealand**
Customer Service Department
30-52 Smidmore Street
Marrickville, New South Wales 2204
Australia
Tel: +61 (02) 9517 8999
Fax: +61 (02) 9517 2249
service@elsevier.com.au

## 30% Discount for Authors on All Books!

A 30% discount is available to Elsevier book and journal contributors on all books *(except multi-volume reference works)*.

To claim your discount, full payment is required with your order, which must be sent directly to the publisher at the nearest regional sales office above.